SIXTH EDITION

Robert I. Landau
and Romano I. Peluso

Copyright © 1961, 1974 New York University Press
Copyright © 1985, 1992, 1998 Columbia University Press
Copyright © 2008 by Robert I. Landau & Romano I. Peluso

All rights reserved. No part of this book shall be reproduced or transmitted in any form or by any means, electronic, mechanical, magnetic, photographic including photocopying, recording or by any information storage and retrieval system, without prior written permission of the publisher. No patent liability is assumed with respect to the use of the information contained herein. Although every precaution has been taken in the preparation of this book, the publisher and author assume no responsibility for errors or omissions. Neither is any liability assumed for damages resulting from the use of the information contained herein.

Library of Congress Cataloging-in-Publication Data
Landau, Robert I.
    Corporate trust administration and management /
Robert I. Landau and Romano I. Peluso – 6th ed.
        p.   cm.
Includes bibliographical references and index.

ISBN 0-7414-4636-7

1. Trust indentures--United States   I. Peluso, Romano I.
    II. Title

Published by:

1094 New DeHaven Street, Suite 100
West Conshohocken, PA 19428-2713
Info@buybooksontheweb.com
www.buybooksontheweb.com
Toll-free (877) BUY BOOK
Local Phone (610) 941-9999
Fax (610) 941-9959

Printed in the United States of America

Printed on Recycled Paper

Published June 2008

CONTENTS

Preface   5

Part I: Administration

Introduction   10

1. Some General Principles of Corporate and Municipal Finance   11
2. The Trust Indenture   35
3. The Corporate Trustee   61
4. Municipal Trusts   102
5. Preparation, Execution, and Recording of Indenture   113
6. Issuance of Indenture Securities   131
7. Sinking Fund and Maintenance Provisions   150
8. Release and Substitution of Property   164
9. Indenture Covenants   183
10. Payment and Redemption of Bonds   210
11. Satisfaction and Defeasance   231
12. Default and Remedial Provisions   245
13. Rights of Security Holders   272
14. Bankruptcy and Reorganization   299
15. Specialized Trusts and Agency Appointments   327
16. International Financings   351

17. Servicing Debt Securities - Agency Functions — 362

18. Legislation, Regulation and Risk Management — 405

Part II: Management

Introduction — 434
19. Strategic and Tactical Planning — 437
20. Organization and Structure — 449
21. Training and Development — 460
22. Performance Planning, Evaluation And Career Development — 473
23. Acquisitions and Divestitures — 482

Part III: Reference Material

The Trust Indenture Act of 1939, as Amended — 493

Glossary — 546

Index — 594

PREFACE

Thirty five years ago, I began the first revision to the then definitive work on corporate trust administration. Throughout each of the revisions which appeared in 1974, 1985, 1992, and 1998, I have tried to maintain the original concept of a teaching vehicle. The objective was always to provide each new generation of account managers, administrators, and operations specialists with a systematic approach for learning the fundamentals of indenture trustee administration.

My colleagues will note that Romano I. Peluso joins me as co-author of the current Sixth Edition. Romano and I started our corporate trust careers at Bankers Trust Company (now Deutsche Bank) and we have worked together for more than 25 years. I say with pride that I was Romano's mentor for most of those years. We also both served on the Certified Corporate Trust Specialist (CCTS) Advisory Board of the Institute of Certified Bankers and on the ABA's Corporate Trust Committee. Romano has written extensively on current corporate trust industry issues for the American Bankers Association for the last 25 years. He currently is on the Editorial Board of *ABA Trust & Investments* magazine. He is an outstanding teacher, manager and a consummate professional with a wide breath of securities industry knowledge and experience.

In the current edition we have followed the pattern used in earlier editions, but with extensive changes in content and emphasis. We have greatly expanded the four chapters dealing with default and remedial provisions, the rights of security holders, bankruptcy and reorganization, and legislation, regulation and risk management. All the federal securities statutes are now described including the new statutes enacted since the last edition was published. A new section dealing with the "Chinese Wall." has been added. There is a new chapter on international financings with a section covering the differences of the trustee's role in the United States and the United Kingdom. We have increased the coverage of asset backed financings and Regulation AB, Regulation R, the commentary on the sale of securities pursuant to Regulation S/ Rule 144A, and secondary market disclosure for municipal securities. In addition, we have extensively revised and updated the Glossary, and have eliminated the exhibits which consisted of bank internal checklists.

During the last ten years, major shifts and realignments have occurred in the corporate trust business, with continued consolidations. Now there are only a handful of major corporate trust providers. There are still many, though smaller, providers and those that have undertaken to specialize in specific products or markets. We have witnessed the emergence and continuation of the so-called "middle office" which combines many of the functions and activities of relationship managers, administrators and operations specialists. In addition, there is a growing trend to broaden the involvement of individual corporate trust departments in products and markets that are outside of the traditional role of trust indenture administration.

It is very evident that client service, both real and perceived, will continue to be a major factor in the decision to use a particular trustee. Client service coupled with the increased use of computer applications, interfaces, and electronic movement of processed information by administrators, will be the really significant differentiating factor among trustees competing for new business. On the management side, the increased sensitivity to risk exposure and potential liability has greatly increased the need for a professionally competent and thoroughly trained staff.

The changes that have occurred during the past sixteen years, and the evolution of both the corporate trust business and the entire securities industry must be carefully considered and understood by every participant in this business. The players are not limited to indenture account managers, administrators, and operations specialists, but include all those persons engaged in the drafting of debt financing instruments and documents and the marketing of bond issues. Included also are those accountable for the enactment and implementation of statutes, rules, regulations, and other standards of performance applicable to the corporate trust industry.

It is evident that as we proceed into the 21st century, the participants in the industry will have to function in an environment which is significantly and dramatically influenced by events, transactions, and general economic conditions occurring in all the capital markets, both domestic and international. The future demands not only an acute sense of alertness to a changing and volatile financial environment, but also the flexibility to meet the requirements of changing patterns of both debt financing and information processing. To become a successful corporate trust professional, however, still requires a sound understanding of the basic concepts and principles, together with a great deal of imagination, plain old savvy, and a deep commitment to acceptance of responsibility and initiative.

Both Romano and I wish to acknowledge, with our deep appreciation and thanks, the very important and meaningful contributions that Nancy Kuenstner, Tom Foley, Frank Grippo, Harold Kaplan, Daniel Northrop, Stephen Norton, and Jack Stevenson made to this edition. Any errors, minor or major, are ours alone.

Robert I. Landau

May 2008

I

ADMINISTRATION

A trustee is held to something stricter than the morals of the marketplace. Not honesty alone, but the punctilio of an honor the most sensitive, is then the standard of behavior.

> Justice Benjamin N. Cardozo
> *Meinhard v. Salmon*
> 249 N.Y. 458, 464 (1928)

An indenture trustee is not subject to the ordinary trustee's duty of undivided loyalty. Unlike the ordinary trustee, who has historic common-law duties imposed beyond those in the trust agreement, an indenture trustee is more like a stakeholder whose duties and obligations are exclusively defined by the terms of the indenture agreement.

> Judge Richard J. Cardamone
> *Meckel v. Continental Resources*
> 758 F.2d 811 (2d Cir. 1985)

INTRODUCTION

The study of corporate trust and the administration of the provisions of indenture contracts, including the servicing of debt obligations issued under indentures, bond resolutions, or other agreements are difficult, time consuming, and complex. They require a basic understanding of the principles of corporate finance and fiduciary law, as well as detailed knowledge of relevant federal legislation and regulation governing the rights, duties, and liabilities of the debt issuer, the corporate trustee, and the security holders.

The chapters in Part I are designed to thoroughly familiarize corporate trust administrators, account officers, operations supervisors, and managers with legislation and regulations and with relevant principles, policies, and procedures that together constitute the fundamentals of "doing the work." Explanatory and supplementary footnotes have been included to provide additional clarity and references to appropriate books, articles, statutes, regulations, and judicial decisions.

The whole spectrum of activities and responsibilities involved in administering the trust indenture contract and its related agency services has been undergoing an evolutionary process for the more than one hundred years. Many of the statutory and regulatory changes have, however, been most evident during the past twenty five years. Given the rapidly changing and volatile nature of the securities market as it has evolved from a domestic to a global market and the technology changes in processing information and delivering transactions, there is every reason to believe that this evolutionary process will continue at an accelerated rate. Nevertheless, a sound understanding of the "basics"' continues to be essential to provide the corporate trust practitioner with the knowledge competencies to properly discharge his or her duties as a corporate trust professional.

ONE

SOME GENERAL PRINCIPLES OF CORPORATE AND MUNICIPAL FINANCE

The corporate trust indenture is undoubtedly one of the most involved financial documents ever devised. Even though development of a simplified or plain language form of indenture for issuing corporate securities has made the indenture provisions more widely and easily understood, administering an indenture still requires highly skilled and experienced personnel.[1]

Although a full discussion of the problems of corporate organization and finance is beyond the scope of this book, a basic knowledge and understanding of their main features are important even to the beginner in the field. As a preliminary, therefore, this chapter considers some of the essential concepts involved in the corporate form of business enterprise and its financing.

THE CORPORATE FORM OF BUSINESS ENTERPRISE

The most common form of business enterprise is the individual proprietorship, in which only the individual's own capital is invested. The owner operates the business alone or with one or more employees and is entitled to all the profits realized or, conversely, suffers all the losses. If the business should fail, not only the assets of the business but also all the personal assets of the proprietor are used to pay the business creditors. The partnership is similar in nature and, in effect, is simply the association of two or more individual proprietors in a common business undertaking. The main features of both these forms are the direct participation of the owners in the operation of the business and their unlimited liability for the business's debts.[2]

The corporate form of business enterprise, however, is different. A creature of the Industrial Revolution, the corporation has been vital, from the time of the British mercantile companies organized for colonial development, to the growth and development of the industrialized economies with which we are familiar.

A corporation is a creature of the state and exists only by reason of a charter granted by the state. In the early days of the United States, a corporation could be created only by special legislative enactment. This special charter was granted after careful consideration and usually was for a very special and limited purpose. Some corporations still exist with charters so granted. Today, however, all states have general incorporation laws, and the creation of a corporation is relatively simple.

Because a corporation is a creature of the state, it can exercise only those powers specifically granted to it by the state. These powers are enumerated in the corporate charter that is a basic document of every corporation. Incorporators may include in a proposed charter any power not prohibited by law or contrary to public policy. It is therefore the general practice for every charter to include a very broad grant of powers. From the viewpoint of corporate indenture financing, the essential powers are the right to borrow money and the right to mortgage and pledge the corporation's assets as security for this borrowed money. If a corporation performs or purports to perform an act for which it does not have authority, such an act is said to be *ultra vires*, and as such, may constitute a defense in a suit against the corporation arising from the act so performed.

A corporation is subject not only to the limitations contained in its charter but also to all laws and regulations promulgated by the legislature or a regulatory authority of the state of incorporation in addition to those of any federal agency having jurisdiction over the corporation or its business activities.

Another important corporate document is the corporate bylaws. Bylaws are the rules of procedure adopted by the stockholders and they can be amended at any time by a vote of the stockholders. They spell out such things as the form of the certificates of stock; the frequency, locations, and dates of stockholder meetings; the procedures for calling special meetings; the scope and functions of the board of directors and the various committees; the powers and duties of the principal officers; and other basic rules as may be necessary for or pertinent to the corporation's continued functioning.

The stockholders are the owners of the business and as such are entitled to a vote in the management of its affairs in proportion to their ownership of the outstanding stock. They are also entitled to share in the corporation's profits--but only through such dividends as may be declared from time to time by the corporate directors. These rights of ownership, however, differ markedly from those involved in other forms of business enterprises. For instance, the stockholders do not participate directly in managing the corporate business, and they are also protected by the limited liability in the corporate form of business. If a venture fails, the stockholders' investment in the business is likely to be lost, but their personal assets are not liable for the payment of the corporation's debts.

The purchase of stock in a particular corporation usually results from a desire to make a profitable investment of savings or excess funds rather than from a desire to participate in a particular type of business venture. Generally, such investments are for the purpose of receiving income through receipt of dividend payments or profits from the eventual sale of the stock at a higher price, or both. The concept of the pooling of funds of many individuals to make possible the conduct of business on the vast scale we know today was the great contribution of the corporate form of business enterprise.

The management of a corporation is vested in a board of directors elected by the stockholders. In some cases this board is made up entirely of people who are active officers of the corporation, but in publicly held corporations, it is more common for some of the directors to be drawn from prominent members of the community who are engaged primarily in other professions. The diversity of interests and viewpoints thus brought together is often helpful to the enterprise. Regardless of the composition of the board, the directors are primarily responsible for the affairs of the corporation and may become individually liable and accountable in other ways for unwarranted acts of the corporation.

The active management of corporate affairs is delegated to a corporate staff whose members work full time for the enterprise. These officers are appointed by the board and their functions are described in the bylaws or are prescribed by resolutions of the board. An officer has only such authority as is specifically granted or necessarily implied, and anyone dealing with a corporation should be certain of the authority of the officials with whom he or she deals and what constitutes proper authorization of any contract or undertaking.

CORPORATE FINANCIAL STATEMENTS

A corporation's activities are summarized in the records that the corporate officers are required to maintain. These records show the results of operations for designated periods and are forwarded periodically to stockholders, creditors, and others. It is customary to have these records audited at least annually by a firm of independent public accountants which furnishes a certificate of examination. Whenever a corporation issues securities publicly it must file certified financial statements with the Securities and Exchange Commission (SEC) and with each corporate trustee of its public debt securities.

Regulated industries, such as railroads, public utilities, banks, and similar corporations, are required to maintain their records in a uniform manner as prescribed by the particular regulatory authority having jurisdiction over them. Other corporations are not so restricted, so there may be some differences in the details required from various types of companies. In general, however, the development of modern accounting techniques and procedures and the requirements of federal tax regulations ensure substantial uniformity in the form and content of financial statements.

The corporate trust practitioner must be familiar with financial statements, and the more commonly used financial ratios. Secured corporate financings will typically require financial statement review and analysis skills. A discussion of the basic financial statements follows.

The Balance Sheet

The *balance sheet* presents a corporation's condition at a particular moment in its history. It also may be said to reflect the cumulative results of the company's operations from its inception to the date when the statement is rendered.

Assets are the property/items that the corporation owns or is owed, together with the investment or other use of funds that have come into its hands. Assets are customarily classified as "current" or "fixed." *Current assets* include cash and such items as will be converted into cash in the business's normal operations. Among such items are temporary investments, receivables (amounts owed by the company's customers), and inventories (either raw materials waiting processing or finished goods available for sale). *Fixed assets* include whatever buildings and real property that the company owns and uses in the conduct of its business; permanent investments that the company may have in other companies; and other types of property that may be necessary or incidental to its operations, but that are normally not held for resale. Such things as goodwill, patents, trademarks, and franchise rights are intangibles and may be included as assets if they have a real value. Another term frequently employed is *tangible assets*, which include all assets other than goodwill, patents, and other such intangibles which would have little, if any, value upon the liquidation of the business.

Assets are "balanced" against an equal amount of liabilities plus capital, which represent the source of funds by which the corporate assets were acquired. *Current liabilities* are the amounts due and payable within a specified period of time--usually a year--and incurred primarily in connection with normal business operations. The current asset and current liability accounts are considered the company's working capital accounts, and the excess of current assets over current liabilities is usually referred to as *working capital* or *net current assets*. Money borrowed for a period longer than one year is usually referred to as *funded debt* and is shown on the balance sheet as a *noncurrent liability*, although any portion of funded debt due within one year, either by reason of maturity or of a sinking fund obligation, is customarily included as a current liability.

Among the various forms of borrowing, the ordinary bank loan, generally used to provide additional working capital, matures within a relatively short time, although in recent years, such loans have been for longer than the traditional one to three years. Since many businesses operate on a cyclical basis during the year, there may be periods of heavy inventory accumulation, such as for the purchase of raw materials for fabrication or processing. These periods often require heavy bank borrowing to provide funds to purchase these raw materials. During the ensuing period of heavy sales, the finished goods are disposed of, inventory decreases, and the resulting surplus of cash is used to pay off the bank loans. It is much less expensive to meet temporary heavy cash requirements by means of bank credit than to provide permanent capital sufficient to meet the company's peak cash demands. All these transactions, as they occur, are reflected in the company's *working capital accounts*. Funds needed for capital or fixed property purposes are borrowed for longer periods of time and it is this type of borrowing with which we will be concerned in our consideration of the trust indenture.

Another type of permanent capital is that supplied by the owners of the business, that is, the stockholders. The net amount invested by the owners--the amounts paid in for purchase of stock plus undistributed earnings that have been reinvested in the business--accounts for the rest of the liability side of the balance sheet.

Income and Retained Earnings Statements

The principal source of the company's income is the sale of its products, and the first item on the income statement is the amount of the net sales for the year, together with other earned income. This may include interest on temporary investments, income from investments in other companies, the excess of proceeds over book value realized from the sale of fixed assets no longer required in the business, and other similar items.

From this item is deducted the cost of the goods sold, including the cost of the raw materials and the costs directly chargeable to manufacturing operations. These costs will tend to vary in almost direct proportion to the volume of goods produced. Costs that are more or less "fixed" without regard to fluctuations in the volume of business are the expenses of the sales force, advertising, general office, and other similar charges. These are usually shown separately on the income statement and in such detail as may be appropriate for proper presentation and understanding. To calculate the net income resulting from the year's operations, the manufacturing and general expenses from net sales are deducted.

The charge for *depreciation* is a noncash expense. While certain assets represent permanent investments, they will in time become worn out as they are used in the manufacturing process and have to be replaced. It is therefore necessary to charge against each year's income an appropriate amount to represent the deterioration or decrease in value of such fixed assets. This is the *depreciation charge*. There are a number of ways in which depreciation may be computed, but in general, the charge theoretically represents the portion of the total value of the fixed assets that were used up in the year's operations.

Other expense items that might be included would be losses on sales of investments or fixed assets, amortization of discounts on funded debt obligations sold below par, and so on. The final deduction is the amount of income taxes incurred for the year, and the resulting balance is the corporation's net income from all activities during the period.

Retained earnings are the earnings of the company that have been reinvested in the business rather than distributed to the stockholders.

Changes in the Financial Position Statement

The final example of a common type of financial statement is a Statement of Changes in Financial Position, also sometimes called a Sources and Uses of Funds statement. This type of statement is helpful in considering the financial transactions of a corporation. All corporate transactions are expressed in terms of dollars, but many transactions take place each day without a concurrent transfer of dollars. Goods are bought to be paid for at a later date; wages, taxes, and other items of expense accrue that require cash outlays in the future; and similarly, sales are made on credit or services are performed to be paid for over a period of time.

Financial officers must plan to provide the cash, when required, to meet the payments called for by the corporate operations. Similarly, the primary concern of anyone extending credit to the company is that funds will be available to meet the service payments on the debt as they become due.

The Sources and Uses of Funds statement reflects the flow of cash through a company's operations for a stated period. This analysis can be extrapolated from the statements previously considered. More importance to financial officers is the use of the statement's projections as a part of budget preparation to ensure that the company's financial obligations will be met promptly.

A single balance sheet provides little information other than the financial condition of the company as of a particular moment. It does not reflect the trend of the business. However, by comparing the balance sheets for the beginning and the end of a designated period, a great deal of information may be gleaned concerning the activities of the corporation during that period. These records, combined with the income and retained earnings statements, provide sufficient information to construct a cash flow statement for the period.

Assets represent uses of funds; liabilities reflect the sources of funds. An increase in assets or a decrease in liabilities during a period thus shows the net use of corporate funds during that period. Similarly, the sum of the decrease in assets and increase in liabilities reflects the net source of corporate funds for the period. Another type of Sources and Uses of Funds statement can thus be constructed by rearranging the net increase and decrease in assets and liabilities reflected in the change in the balance sheet for the period in question. In fact, there are actually many thousands of sources and uses for any particular accounting period. For an adequate picture of the company's transactions, however, it is usually sufficient to summarize the net effect of all these transactions. Although an analysis of balance sheets alone would provide such a picture, it would not be as nearly complete as can be obtained by considering also the income accounts for the period. In such an analysis, it is also common to regard the working capital accounts (current assets and current liabilities) as an entity. Thus, a net increase in working capital represents a use of funds and a net decrease indicates a source.

FINANCING CAPITAL NEEDS

Corporate financial officers are continually faced with the problem of how to finance the business's money needs. Municipal or governmental officers have similar financing concerns. Although government entities are able to increase taxes to fund interest and principal for issued debt securities, additional monies to fund debt cannot generally occur without the passing of a referendum, by popular vote, to fund additional debt. Once a taxing referendum is passed, additional municipal debt will be authorized by a governmental entity or municipal resolution.

Municipal finance officers must also be concerned about the balance sheet although such items as the inventory turnover are not applicable. Due to the ability to impose additional taxes to finance capital needs, municipalities were typically thought to be immune from financial difficulty. But in recent years several cities and towns have declared bankruptcy due to general financial and economic conditions which made it difficult to collect needed taxes. Since that time, governmental entities have faced additional balance sheet scrutiny from public investors. Because concern over financing capital is not a problem that directly concerns the corporate trust administrator, we need not deal with it in detail here. An understanding of the basic principles is, however, helpful in understanding the reasons for some of the negotiations involved in the drafting of particular indenture provisions.

We noted that short-term working capital needs are customarily financed by short-term bank loans. An additional and important source of short-term funds for companies of strong credit standing is the sale of *commercial paper*. This refers to short-term promissory notes, usually unsecured, which are typically written in multiples of $5,000 with maturities of from three days to nine months.[3] These notes do not bear interest, as such. Instead, an effective interest rate is established by the sale of the notes at a discount from face amount. Municipalities also use short term note financing for immediate needs or to manage debt issuance to take advantage of anticipated lower interest rate markets, as discussed in chapter 4, "Municipal Trusts."

When the issuer needs additional security to obtain a top credit rating for its commercial paper, a bank issues an irrevocable letter of credit, on either a standby or direct-draw basis.

Medium-term needs (e.g., the purchase of equipment that can be paid for in four to five years) might be financed through a bank term loan or an equipment lease transaction.[4] In recent years corporations and municipalities have turned to the use of medium term notes to address medium-term financing needs. Medium-term financing is described later in this chapter.

Corporate capital requirements are normally supplied from the capital markets or through the medium of retained earnings. Since this is the type of financing with which the corporate trustee is concerned, discussion will be confined to an analysis of its elements.

Capital requirements can be financed in any one of four principal ways: (1) through some form of borrowing--the issuance of debt securities; (2) through the issuance of preferred stock (while this is a form of equity or ownership security, the holder is entitled only to a fixed return from the earnings of the company--as opposed to a possibly larger return to owners, of common shares--but has a claim prior to common stockholders in the event of liquidation); (3) through the sale of additional common stock; or, (4) through retained earnings. Even though conservative management normally retains a portion of earnings for use in the business (and this might be said not to be financing in the true sense), the retention of earnings is in effect a forced investment by existing stockholders, and many of the considerations applicable to other types of capital financing are pertinent to the question of what portion of earnings should be retained, particularly if a change in the dividend policy is contemplated.[5]

Many factors affect a decision on the type of financing to be used for a particular project. Among the more important are: (1) the nature of the project or expansion to be financed, how speculative it is, and its relationship in size, cost, and, profitability to the existing business of the company; (2) the prospective earnings from the proposed investment and how precisely such earnings can be forecast; (3) the quality and durability of a company's existing earnings, or the taxing ability of a municipality for government entity borrowing, and the extent to which they are affected by cyclical changes in the general economy; (4) the company's existing capital structure, the government entity's financial condition, and the effect that alternative financing methods would have on this structure; and (5) the cost of alternative methods of raising the needed capital. These factors reduce themselves generally to a consideration of the risks involved in relation to the cost. It is assumed that the different types of capital are available at a price. If a particular method of financing is not available because of a prohibition in an existing contract, the quality of the borrower's credit, or for other reasons, choices are either more limited or nonexistent.

It is axiomatic that--from the point of view of the borrower--the less expensive the method of financing, the more risk it involves. Even though debt is usually the cheapest form of capital, there is some risk inherent in every type of debt financing since debt financing entails fixed commitments that must be met regardless of the earnings or taxing power of the borrower at the particular time. From the viewpoint of the common stockholder, issuing preferred stock is riskier than selling additional common stock, for it creates a class of holders with claims ranked higher than its own.

The cost of debt is the rate of interest that must be paid, but since interest paid by corporations is deductible under present tax laws in computing income tax, the actual cost of debt financing is less than half the nominal interest rate under present tax laws. The cost of using preferred stock is the *fixed dividend rate*. Because of lower priority in case of insolvency, this rate will usually be higher than the rate on debt for the same company. In addition, and possibly of greater significance, preferred dividends are not, with some exceptions, deductible for income tax purposes.

Another factor that is sometimes of considerable importance is the effect on existing capital structure that the proposed financing may have[6]. Thus, maintaining a proper debt ratio is important not only because of the safety of having a sound equity base but also because of the adverse effect that excessive debt may have on the borrower's credit standing. There is no approved ratio, and anyway, each financial analyst uses a different measure for every class of borrower. Accordingly, a fairly high debt ratio might be acceptable for a particular industry, whereas the same ratio in another would be cause for serious concern. Historically, few companies have been able to justify a debt ratio over 50 percent, and for most, the maximum is 35 percent. When the ratio begins to exceed the theoretical ceiling, the company's security rating is affected, which makes additional debt financing more difficult and more expensive. Thus, the proper proportion of equity to debt should be maintained at all times, and it is advisable to include a certain amount of equity financing while keeping a degree of flexibility, to take advantage of changing market conditions.

As stated earlier, security analysts consider the ability of governmental entities to impose additional taxation, as well as the short, medium and long term debt outstanding and the general economic condition of the governmental entity's geographic area. For example, some municipal debt is issued as revenue producing such as toll ways. In this case, the general need for a toll way and the projected traffic usage are taken into account when determining the issuer's ability to repay the borrowed funds.

Corporate and municipal finance is a volatile and constantly changing field, innovation and "creative financing" being the hallmark of aggressive investment bankers. The expert of twenty years ago emerging from a time capsule would find a strange world today. A number of factors introduced into the economy during this period have contributed to these changes. One, of course, is the tremendous expansion that has taken place in the economy and that has created an unprecedented demand for investment funds, including the vast sums borrowed by states and municipalities. Another factor of equal or greater importance is the impact on corporations of the tax laws and regulations on their everyday activities. In addition, the global economy has changed the economic rules for borrowers. Big government and, especially, big taxes are always present, and it is no longer possible to make important decisions based on the economics of only the particular situation

Private Placements

One of the most important trends that has taken place in the area of debt financing is the growth in the number and volume of *direct* or *private placement* contracts. Originally this was the direct result of concentrating funds in the hands of institutions that provided the bulk of available investment dollars--not only in savings bank and life insurance assets but also in both private and public pension funds, including the significant growth of individual retirement plans, such as IRAs and Keoghs.

Even though avoiding the uncertainties and expense of a public offering and compliance with the registration requirements of the Securities Act of 1933 (33 Act) are frequently cited as the motivating factors, more important considerations are the ability to achieve greater flexibility--to tailor each financing to fit the particular circumstances--and the greater ease of securing amendments to the contract necessitated by changing conditions. Some institutional investors prefer this customized type of investment. They not only may be able to secure a somewhat better return but also can plan their investment operations more accurately by making commitments for fixed amounts at negotiated rates.

The private placement assumed major importance during the 1970s and 1980's when these placements accounted for approximately 50 percent of total capital debt financing of corporations. By 1991 the market had shrunk to less than 3.0% of the total taxable market, but since the mid 1990s, this sector has hovered around 10% of the market. The adoption of certain initiatives by the SEC in April 1990 set the stage for another renaissance in the use of this financing sector. In 1990, the SEC adopted Rule 144A, which permits institutional investors having a minimum of $100 million invested in securities to trade in privately placed securities, eliminating the requirement that such securities be registered with the SEC as "public" securities under the 33 Act.[7] The effect of this new rule and the amendment to Rule 144, permitting the required holding period (usually two years) for private placements to begin the original issuance of the securities, in effect sets the stage for the creation of a secondary market in such securities.

These actions constituted the first step in the liberalization of the private placement market which has significantly increased its liquidity, making it more attractive to investors and reducing the cost to issuers of such financings. It has also increased the number of foreign issuers into this market--issuers that had been reluctant to subject themselves to the full registration requirements of the 33 Act.

Direct placement financing falls into three broad categories:

    1. Issues that are secured by the traditional form of corporate indenture--either an existing mortgage or a new bond or debenture issue. Except for the number of holders and the likelihood of a home office payment agreement,[8] such an issue is almost the same as a publicly offered issue.

2. Special-purpose and third-party corporation financing. The variations are legion, and the security is more likely to involve leases, charter hires, throughput agreements, government-guaranteed home mortgages, or some form of contractual arrangement other than the traditional corporate mortgage. In this type of financing, the credit of the obligor issuer is seldom important, for in most cases it will be a corporation specifically created for the purpose of issuing the debt obligation. The loan is made on the credit of the lessee or other contract party and its agreement to perform under its contract with the obligor issuer.

3. Note issues involving a direct unsecured loan without a trustee. Initially, these loans were similar to bank agreements, except they were for longer terms and normally for capital purposes. The borrowers were corporations with high credit ratings and usually little or no other funded debt. Frequently, only one institutional lender was involved, very seldom more than four or five. The loan agreements were uncomplicated, with few, if any, security covenants.

Inevitably, there was an increase in both the number of borrowers using this device and the variety and purpose of the loans. Credit agreements have become more complicated, with wider participation in individual loans. Eight to ten investors are fairly common, and many issues have had twenty-five to fifty participants. In private placement financing, these note agreements often replaced debenture financing, but without the flexibility, marketability, and uniformity of administration provided by the traditional debenture agreement with a competent and experienced corporate trustee.

We also note, though without extensive discussion, several other significant trends in recent years:

1. The volatility and changing character of the domestic market. In an environment of economic uncertainties, wide swings in interest rates have prevailed, with innovative factors built into the particular financing vehicle. These, together with the issuance of short – and mixed-term maturities, have ensured investors' continued interest in providing funds to both corporate and public sector borrowers. Today's spectrum of financing structures includes floating-rate notes, deep discount and zero coupon issues, auction-rate securities, convertible securities (both mandatory and optional), variable-rate demand obligations, put/demand options, medium-term notes, and asset-backed securities. Asset-backed securities are collateralized by a wide and growing variety of asset classes, including mortgages, home equity loans, credit card receivables, auto and mobile home loans, student loans, trade, and medical receivables.

There are also real estate mortgage investment conduits (REMICs) and collateralized mortgage obligations. The variations are almost endless, limited only by the imagination of investment bankers and the perceived appetite of the investing public.

2. Shelf registration under SEC Rule 415. This rule, permanently adopted as of December 31, 1983, permits top-tier corporations to register the offering or sale of their securities on a delayed or continuous basis in the future.[9] The effect of this rule is to allow such issuers almost instant access to the marketplace--whenever a "window" is available.

3. The increased popularity and rapid growth of medium term notes (MTNs), an instrument modeled

on commercial paper issued by corporations to obtain short term operating funds. The majority of MTNs are not sold through the traditional underwriting process, but under a continuous offering procedure in which the issuer, acting through an investment bank(s) as sales agent(s), makes securities available to investors desiring specific maturities ranging from nine months to as long as fifteen years. The most important feature of an MTN program (i.e., issue) is the sales agent's ability to tailor the maturity date to satisfy the issuer's need for funds to the investor's need for a specific investment period. Most MTN programs provide for fixed, semi-annual interest payments, although some issues have used a variable rate feature with interest being paid either monthly or quarterly.

4. The tremendous volume of public financing, including not only the continuous financing by the federal government in the management of the public debt but also the enormous amount of tax-exempt securities issued by states, state and local authorities, and municipalities. In addition to the increase in revenue bond financings for toll roads and bridges, the broad-scale use of industrial development bonds (IDBs) had a major impact on the market during the 1980s and 1990s. The primary purpose of IDBs was to make attractive the financing of new plants and/or the construction of pollution control facilities through use of the tax-exempt privilege. There has also been dramatic growth during the last two decades in the issuance of industrial revenue bonds, hospital and health-care revenue bonds as well as public housing bonds.

5. Globalization of the securities markets is presenting new opportunities to corporate trustees.

Although international project finance is by no means a new concept in funding construction of infrastructure, there is an emerging trend requiring the services of a trustee. Previously, such financings were arranged and handled by a bank or syndicate of banks, with the operational needs filled by the lead bank. Increasingly, project finances are more complex in structure, more diverse in investor base, and more limited in recourse. Project sponsors and investors now are willing to risk capital in the international emerging markets in search of higher returns. There is also a strong need to diversify portfolios, forge alliances and cultivate new relationships with international partners to compete effectively in the global marketplace. The flurry of activity is fueled by fundamental disparity between the demands of the emerging markets and their ability to meet these demands. New projects are being developed in Latin America, eastern Europe, and the Pacific Rim. Although power projects lead the way for new project financings, there is a great need for other infrastructure development such as toll roads, bridges, pollution control projects, airports, transportation, and industrial and manufacturing facilities.

As we move further in the new millennium fundamental changes are occurring in the international debt markets. Key among these are the following:

Changing Population Dynamics:

Countries all over the world are facing the need to support aging populations, and this need will drive fundamental changes in the capital markets. As life expectancy increases at the same time that younger people are postponing marriage and having fewer children, the age profile in virtually all developed countries is changing dramatically. In the United States, where sixteen people were working for every person retired in 1950, the ratio will be two working for every one retired by the time our youngest workers turn age 65. Similar changes are occurring throughout Europe, Asia, and Latin America. They will put tremendous stress on state-sponsored retirement plans, especially in Europe and Asia, where the retirement systems are largely state financed and have been built on a "pay-as-you-go" basis. In addition, these demographic changes will force fundamental changes in current pension schemes, including the increasing possibility of privatization and a continuing search for higher-yielding investments with a greater emphasis on equities as opposed to debt instruments. National and local governments that have long been dependent on using the state-run pension systems as a source of funding must now compete more aggressively for funding in the capital markets. This action will, in turn, force all issuers to broaden their search for debt capital, both geographically and by type of instrument.

More Cross Border Financings:

Needs for investable funds, for both governmental and corporate projects, will grow across the globe, especially in the lesser-developed areas where funds are desperately needed for building basic infrastructure. The sources of capital, however, will remain concentrated in countries with large, stable economies and large pools of investable assets such as pension funds, mutual funds, and life insurance company assets. Financing will necessarily become more cross border as underwriters work to match needs with sources. Large, well-established borrowers, whether governmental or corporate, can be expected to increase their issuance of foreign currency issues as well as global issues with separate tranches of the same security issued in different markets and denominated in different currencies.

More Complex Financings:

The increasing need for cross border financings--with the greatest need for financing in some of the higher-risk locations--will generate demand for more complex financings to attract limited investor capital. Underwriters can be expected to make greater use of more complex debt instruments such as securities with government guarantees or with "equity kickers", securitized instruments, instruments tied to specific revenue streams, instruments with obligations segmented into discrete portions for income versus principal an/or short versus long maturities, and multi-currency issues with debt service payable in different currencies.

Transition To A Common Currency:

The conversion of many European currencies into the Euro has led to more complex instruments. We have seen multi-currency issues with income and principal payable in different currencies as well as "currency optional" securities wherein the holder chooses which currency he/she wishes to receive payment in. A common currency in Europe has provided for reduced processing and accounting complexity as country-specific currencies have been gradually eliminated. The growth of these securities as well as other variations will continue to increase.

Underwriting Concentration:

The more complex financing vehicles will include derivatives and migrate outward from the United States and the major centers in Europe and Asia. But the underwriting will remain localized in a limited number of key centers because many, if not most, local markets will not have the internal capital and industry expertise to support these types of securities. Furthermore, the secondary markets for these securities, because they are dependent on liquidity and trading efficiency, will be concentrated in a few number of markets where the capital and the investment expertise can be brought together in one place.

---

[1] Model Simplified Indenture, 38 <Bus. Law.> 741 (Feb. 1983)

[2] Most states provide for the creation of limited partnerships, which limit the liability of the limited partners (as opposed to the general, or managing, partners) to the amount of money each has invested in the business.

[3] When the issuer needs additional security to obtain a top credit rating for its commercial paper, a bank will issue its irrevocable letter of credit, on either a standby or a direct–draw basis. In such instances, a bank is normally appointed as trustee and depository for the letter of credit.

[4] For a discussion of this type of financing and the role of the trustee bank, see chapter 15.

[5] On the assumption that the company is viable, such decision is not whether to pay a dividend but when and how much to pay. Such companies usually increase dividend payments some time after an improvement in their internal cash generation becomes apparent, and the payment is raised only to an amount that the management believes they can reasonably and safely maintain.

[6] A common assessment of the creditworthiness of an obligor with respect to any debt issue is based on: (1) the likelihood of the obligor paying the interest and repaying the principal, (2) the nature of and provisions of the obligation, and (3) the protection afforded by the relative position of the obligation in the event of a bankruptcy or reorganization.

[7] SEC Release 33-6862 and 34-27928 (Apr. 1990).

[8] Such an agreement provides that in consideration of payments of principal being mailed to the holder without requiring the presentation of the obligation for notation of payment, the holder, before disposing of the note, will surrender it to the obligor (or its agent) for such notation or issuance of a new note for the unpaid balance.

[9] SEC Release 33-6499 (Nov. 1983).

TWO

THE TRUST INDENTURE

The *trust indenture* is a device by which a corporation or governmental entity borrows money from the general public or large institutional investors to issue securities. Securities issued by corporations are known in the industry as *corporates* and securities issued by governmental entities are termed *municipals*. The indenture provides the terms and conditions on which credit is extended; restricts the activities of the issuing corporation or governmental entity so long as the indenture securities are outstanding; sets forth remedies available to the security holders if there should be a default in payments on the debt securities or in the terms of the indenture contract; and otherwise defines the rights, duties, and obligations of the obligor company or governmental entity, the security holders, and the trustee or trustees named in the instrument. If the indenture obligations are to be secured, the indenture creates or pledges the security and sets forth the terms and conditions for dealing with the security.

The use of a mortgage to secure the repayment of money is an ancient one. Likewise, the concept of a *"use"* or *"trust"* was developed at an early period in the common law, whereas the development of the *corporate mortgage*, or *trust indenture*, is fairly recent. It was first introduced around 1830 but until the latter part of the nineteenth century was used infrequently. The reasons for this are many. First, early corporate financing was primarily by *stock* rather than by the issuance of debt securities known as *bonds*. Also, the earlier corporations were generally created for special purposes and by special charter and their power to incur debt or mortgage their properties was strictly limited. The growth and development of trust indentures closely parallel the growth of the corporate form of business enterprise. With the passage of general incorporation laws in most states, the organization of corporations became relatively simple, and as a result, use of this form of business organization became common. The latter part of the nineteenth century was also a period of tremendous expansion and growth in the United States. Accordingly, there was a phenomenal increase in both the number and size of business corporations and the amount of capital required for their development.

The transaction of business by these vast enterprises came to involve both large stock financing and heavy borrowing. It became impractical to secure this financing through one bank, or even a group of banks, so a system of borrowing from the public at large was established through a multitude of small loans, each evidenced by the issuance of bonds of the corporation, and all secured by the same mortgage to one individual or a small group of individuals. The corporate mortgage was at first used almost exclusively by railroad corporations, but with the growth of the corporate form of business enterprise and the development of large corporate systems, the practice was extended until now there are corporations and corporate and government bond issues that include terms and conditions for almost every type of business undertaking.

Although the indenture has become a necessary and important factor in the economic life of the country, there is still a great deal of confusion about its essential nature. Whereas many court decisions have been rendered regarding particular problems, there is a lack of uniformity among the courts concerning the overall significance of the contract. Because the indenture contract has been in general use only since the latter part of the nineteenth century, and its real development achieved during the past seventy years, there has been no opportunity for a slow and gradual development of legal precedents. The courts have looked for guidance to cases that had only a superficial similarity to the problems at hand, although the legal relationships appeared to be the same. The trust indenture is an instrument sui generis, combining elements of several other legal relationships but being identical with none. Although most courts now agree that the indenture does not create a trust relationship in the customary sense, some cases have indicated that the full extent of fiduciary responsibility may be imposed upon the trustee. Indeed, it has been suggested that such measure of responsibility should be imposed by statute, even at the risk of seriously impairing its effective use.

Although every form of indenture has elements of similarity, the various types are designed for the different kinds of obligations to be issued, each with peculiarities of its own. The title of the indenture usually describes the type of obligations to be issued and the nature of the security, if any. For example, a mortgage indenture indicates that the security consists primarily of a mortgage on the obligor's fixed property and that the obligations outstanding are mortgage bonds. A first mortgage indicates that the bonds are intended to be a first lien on such properties, a second mortgage a second lien, and so on. Normally, an indenture securing junior lien obligations contains provisions for refunding the prior lien bonds, and in that event, the indenture and the obligations issued thereunder are called respectively a *refunding mortgage* and *refunding mortgage bonds*, terms that sound more attractive than *second* or *third mortgage*. If the obligations have a first or prior lien on any property at all, the title *first and refunding mortgage* is frequently used. In some jurisdictions the term *trust deed* is preferred to *mortgage*, although in most cases this is simply a variation in title. A *collateral trust agreement* usually denotes an indenture under which the obligations have a collateral rather than a direct lien. A *debenture agreement* usually, although not necessarily, indicates unsecured obligations. There are many other variations, combinations, and different forms of designation depending on the type of obligation, the type of security, and other considerations. Although for most purposes these distinctions do not affect the fundamental nature of the indenture or of the rights and obligations of the parties, they do involve different types of provisions and covenants and undoubtedly account to some extent for the confusion and contradictions existing in the relevant law.

The legal relationships of those features most common to the trust indenture are that of the mortgage, trust, and contract. It is important to compare the ways in which they are similar and dissimilar to the commonly accepted meanings of these terms in order to get a better understanding of the true nature of the relationships created.

THE INDENTURE AS A MORTGAGE

Most secured indentures under which bonds are issued entail a mortgage of some kind. The nature and extent of the mortgage security depend on the particular circumstances of the issue, but the security usually involves a mortgage on the fixed property and equipment used by the issuer in its business. The property is usually described in detail by metes and bounds in the instrument, and the document is executed with great care to ensure that it conforms to the laws and customs of the jurisdictions where the property is located. The document is then properly filed and recorded at the respective county and state offices. All efforts are made to ensure that the indenture creates the lien that it purports to do. The net effect of all this effort, however, is usually quite different from that which the investor expects when told that they have a first mortgage security.

In the customary mortgage transaction, the borrower and lender are dealing with a security understood by both parties. In the absence of extraordinary developments, the property's intrinsic and realizable value usually is more than adequate to cover the amount of the loan, and if there is a default, the lender forecloses and realizes from the security the full amount of the loan.

A transaction such as this is entirely different from a mortgage on the property of a large business enterprise. The average investor who purchases bonds has no conception of the value of a large railroad system, for example, although a "mortgage" on the system may constitute the security. Even if an examination of each separate parcel could be made, the investor would still be unable to ascertain its value, for in this case the value of the whole may be greater or less than the sum of the values of all its parts. As real estate, a railroad right-of-way one mile long and thirty feet wide may have little value, although the railroad may have issued mortgage bonds to the extent of $300,000 or more per mile. Instead, the real value of the property of a business enterprise is the "going-concern" value. Considered separate and apart from its use for the purposes of the business, the right-of-way's inadequacy as security is readily apparent. In determining the value of securities, analysts concern themselves with balance sheets, profit and loss statements, competitive conditions, economic trends, and other factors that may influence the business as a "going concern", and only infrequently is the intrinsic value of the security considered separate and apart, to be of substantial importance. A proper mortgage position is important, not only for the value that may be realized on a possible future foreclosure and sale, but also for the prior claim on earnings or preferred position in the event of default, bankruptcy, or reorganization.

THE INDENTURE AS A TRUST

There is another important distinction between the trust indenture and the ordinary mortgage. In the latter, the mortgagee is usually the real party in interest, holding the mortgage as security for credit it has extended. In the indenture, or corporate mortgage, immediately following the granting and habendum clauses, is a paragraph beginning with the words "In Trust, Nevertheless," which converts the mortgage into a trust deed and defines the terms and purposes for which the conveyance was made.

The trust so created, however, differs substantially from the usual *inter-vivos* or *testamentary* trust with which courts and practitioners are more familiar. The fundamental characteristic of the ordinary personal trust is possession by the trustee of a specific trust res that he or she holds and administers for the benefit of designated and usually well-known beneficiaries.

The trustee under an indenture, however, has no possession, or right to possession, of the mortgaged property until after a default occurs, and even then, the trustee's rights are usually circumscribed and limited. It has no control of the obligor's business (and if it did, it would be disqualified from acting) or, except for infrequent and unusual circumstances, any voice in the management of its affairs. Efforts to subject it under these conditions to the same degree of care with respect to the security as is required of an ordinary trustee with respect to a specific trust res would make the position of the indenture trustee untenable and render financing of this type almost impossible. It would be unwise indeed, even if practicable, to try to substitute the judgment of the indenture trustee for that of the management of the issuing corporation.

In the case of an ordinary trust, there is usually a close and intimate relationship between the trustee and the beneficiaries. The trustee is normally acquainted with their needs, and necessary actions can be patterned accordingly. Substantial discretionary powers are normally given to the trustee by the trust instrument with the resultant duties arising as much from the relationship with the beneficiaries as from the specific provisions of the trust document. In an extreme or doubtful case the trustee can usually secure the directions of a court--or obtain the consent or waiver of all parties in interest--before proceeding in a given transaction. It is also possible for periodic accountings to be submitted so that administration can be kept more or less up-to-date.

An indenture trustee is in the position of both a stakeholder and trustee.[1] Its administration covers a long period of time, and it is frequently called upon to make important and far-reaching decisions without the possibility of consulting the security holders or seeking instructions of a court. In most cases, the beneficial owners of the indenture securities may be unknown to it and are changing frequently, so that an effort to secure their unanimous consent to a particular action is extremely difficult.[2] In addition, the indenture trustee normally has no pre-default discretionary power and only limited authority. For instance, it is entirely without authority to deal with or compromise the debt itself no matter how desirable such a compromise might appear to be.

The trustee of a personal trust is responsible only to the beneficiaries, such duty being to administer the trust solely in their interests. While the indenture trustee's primary responsibility runs to the indenture security holders, it also owes to the obligor important practical duties, and in the interest of all parties it must be able to work cooperatively with the obligor.

A final and important distinction lies in the amount of compensation received by the two types of trustee. The fees of the trustee of an ordinary trust are measured by the amount of the trust res or the income therefrom. Although the trustee can be surcharged for a wrongful act or failure to exercise due care, the possible consequences of any particular course of action can normally be estimated with reasonable accuracy. The fees received by the indenture trustee are nominal in relation to the amount of indenture securities outstanding or the value of the trust estate. If it were to be held accountable for the full measure of discretion and fiduciary responsibility common to the ordinary trust, the amount for which it might be potentially liable would be out of all proportion to the compensation the obligor company or government entity could pay.

THE INDENTURE AS A CONTRACT

Even though it is similar to other legal relationships, the trust indenture is most of all a contract, and courts have been in almost unanimous agreement in applying contractual principles to the relationship.

The parties to the contract, or the indenture, are the obligor company or government entity and the trustee, and only these parties execute the instrument. However, there is another party or class of parties--the indenture security holders--essential to make the contract operative. Three distinct and separate sets of contractual rights and obligations are created by each indenture: those between the obligor and the trustee, those between the obligor and the indenture security holders, and those between the trustee and the indenture security holders.

It is important to distinguish between the contractual rights, duties, and obligations relating primarily to the debt itself and those relating principally to the security for the debt. The indenture provisions that define the trustee's principal rights, duties, and obligations and its relationship with the obligor relate primarily to the security for the obligations issued or to be issued, whether it be the specific security conveyed or pledged by the indenture or the "negative" security determined and defined by the indenture covenants. These provisions contain the trustee's authority for dealing with this security and define the limitations and restrictions on such authority. They also place restrictions on the issuing obligor in dealing with its property or in the conduct of its business. Since both the obligor and the trustee have an opportunity to read and examine the indenture before it becomes effective, and both are signatory parties, some of the features of a true contract may be said to be present. Many are lacking, however, and it is of particular importance to bear in mind that until the contract is executed, the trustee is acting not as a principal but only as a prospective administrator or fiduciary. The trustee does not negotiate the substantive terms of the contract, and if it objects to particular provisions, it can only suggest and not demand that they be deleted or amended. Its only recourse is to refuse to act, for it does not and cannot become an active participating party until the contract is actually signed and delivered.

The obligations issued under the indenture run directly to the security holders and not to the trustee and are looked to primarily to define the relationship between the obligor and the security holders. It is therefore important that any provisions of the indenture that modify or affect this relationship, or place limitations on the rights of the holders of these obligations, also be set forth or sufficiently described in the bond or debenture that runs to the holder. If there is any conflict or discrepancy between the indenture and the bond, the terms of the latter will be controlling in any suit by the holder. Since the indenture sets forth in detail the rights, duties, and obligations of the parties (including the security holders) and the limitations on those rights, it is important that the security itself embody those provisions by adequate reference. It is obvious that the whole indenture cannot be fully set forth in the bond, and it is usually sufficient to make specific reference to the indenture in general terms. This is done by including in the bond (or other obligation) language substantially as follows:

> This bond is one of a duly authorized issue of bonds, issued and to be issued under, and all equally

secured by a Mortgage and Deed of Trust dated as of_____, executed by_____Company to the_____Trust Company as Trustee, to which Indenture reference is hereby made for a description of the properties and franchises mortgaged, the nature and extent of the security, the rights of the holders of said bonds and of the trustee in respect of such security, and the terms and conditions under which the bonds are issued and secured.[3]

Although language like this is usually adequate to put the security holder on notice about the existence of the indenture and to make its provisions binding on the holder, it is desirable to make specific reference to such provisions that directly affect the rights of the holder of the obligation itself. Such provisions include subordination and redemption provisions, sinking funds, transfers and exchanges of securities, any provisions permitting substantial modification of the indenture by fewer than all security holders, and waiver of default.

The substantive provisions of the indenture that must be referred to in the bond are printed on the reverse of the certificate, as a continuation of the bond form. An alternative procedure made possible by the flexibility provided by Article 8 of the Uniform Commercial Code (UCC) is to print a summary of the pertinent indenture provisions in less formal and more easily understood language.

Even though the holders of the indenture securities are parties to the indenture contract and bound by its terms, it is more difficult in their case, to find all the essential elements of a true contractual relationship. Because the holders cannot exist as such until after the contract has been executed and delivered, they cannot have a part in negotiating the terms contained therein, although counsel for underwriting houses that acted for the "purchasers" may do so in their behalf. In addition, the indenture is like a unilateral contract to which the security holders become parties by purchasing their security. But here, too, the analogy is somewhat strained, for the indenture is seldom read by the investor before the purchase of the securities. In fact, except for the institutional or professional class of investors, the indenture is almost never read by the security holders and, if it were, many would not understand it. Nevertheless, for the proper functioning of these financing arrangements, it is essential that contractual principles be applied and that the indenture provisions be binding on the security holders as parties, even though in dealing with the obligor, the individual holder is at a distinct disadvantage if there should be a default in payment of the principal or interest on the obligation held.

These considerations have led many courts not only to construe indenture provisions strictly against the obligor but also to try to find some other legal theory or precedent with which to protect the interests of the security holders. Such decisions have contributed to much of the confusion that exists in the law, particularly as it relates to the third set of contractual relationships--those existing between the trustee and security holders. The existence of a "trust" is necessary to create and define the trustee's interest in and relation to the security and the contract, but its relationship to the security and the security holders is essentially contractual rather than fiduciary. The trustee's principal function is to administer the contract in accordance with its terms. It has only the authority and powers granted by the indenture and is subject to all its restrictions and limitations. Except to the limited extent specified, the trustee has no right or authority to represent or act for the security holders or to substitute its judgment for theirs. The trustee should be held accountable for failing to carry out its duties properly, but there is no basis for holding, as some courts have endeavored to do, that the trustee owes to each individual holder duties or obligations not specifically undertaken by it in the contract[4], or required of it by statute or regulation.

Where the trustee's obligation with respect to a particular subject matter is spelled out in the contract, no particular difficulty is encountered if the obligation has been carried out. There is danger, however, that where the indenture is silent on a particular point, an implied obligation will be found in either the other indenture provisions or legal precedents evolved under entirely different circumstances. It is therefore important to the trustee that the indenture clearly indicate its responsibilities in regard to all significant matters relating to the security or to the obligations, even if it merely indicates that no responsibility exists. For example, in a mortgage indenture it is important that the trustee's obligations, or lack thereof, with respect to maintenance, insurance, payment of taxes, and the like be clearly set forth to prevent the possibility of finding a substantial responsibility in the absence of any provision at all.[5]

TYPICAL PROVISIONS OF AN INDENTURE

Although the more important provisions of the indenture are discussed in later chapters in detail, we summarize them here. These examples have been taken from a mortgage indenture of an industrial corporation. However, the general provisions for a municipal indenture are similar. Provisions of other indentures may differ in various respects, depending on the nature of the company or municipality, whether the obligations are secured or unsecured, the structure of the financing, and whether the indenture is qualified under the Trust Indenture Act of 1939, as amended in 1990 (TIA).[6] Municipal securities are not subject to the TIA.

Recitals

Each indenture begins by naming the parties and usually contains a recital of the various factors that led to its creation. These recitals declare the purpose of the issue and state that all legal requirements and authorizations have been fulfilled or obtained. It is important that such recitals be included because they may constitute an estoppel against a later assertion by the obligor that the mortgage or debt was not properly authorized.

The form of bond, interest coupon if a bearer bond,[7] and trustee's (and authenticating agent's if any) certificate of authentication are also customarily set forth in full. As stated above, it is important that the form of bond contain all the essentials of the contract, either specifically or by appropriate reference to the indenture. Only obligations conforming substantially to the form prescribed in the indenture should be authenticated by the trustee.

Granting Clauses

Following the recitals come the granting clauses that set forth the specific security for the obligations to be issued. These clauses include a recital of the consideration, a specific grant to the trustee, and a description of the property to be mortgaged in sufficient detail to enable the indenture to be properly recorded as a mortgage. If any securities or other properties are to be pledged, they are fully described. The specific property descriptions are usually followed by descriptions of other properties intended to be included in the conveyance, such as appurtenances, franchises, and fixtures. The indenture should also set forth in detail the extent to which it is intended to become a lien on after-acquired property. It is also customary to enumerate the types or classes of property exempted from the conveyance and any other provisions that might aid in defining the exact nature and scope of the security intended to be granted. The granting clauses conclude with the habendum and trust clauses, which create the trust relationship and specify the purposes and conditions on which the grant is made.

Definitions

All the important terms used in the indenture are customarily defined, clearly and carefully, in a separate article. Not only is this a convenience for those who will later work with the indenture but also makes the job of drafting much easier. Defined terms throughout the indenture will typically be capitalized to make reference to the specific definition article.

Amount, Form, Execution, Delivery, Registration, and Exchange of Bonds

Whether under this or a similar heading, these sections contain important mechanical provisions for dealing with the obligations themselves and deserve careful attention at the time of drafting, particularly by representatives of the trustee who will administer them. Included here are any limitations on the principal amount of bonds that may be issued or be outstanding at any one time under the indenture; the form of the bonds (if not included in the recitals), or authority for the board of directors or municipal entity to determine the form, and other provisions with respect to any subsequent series; provisions with respect to the manner in which the bonds are to be executed; a statement of who may sign; authorization of the use of facsimile seal or facsimile signatures if permitted by the law of the particular jurisdiction; authorization of temporary bonds in appropriate cases and provisions for their exchange for definitive bonds; appointment of a registrar and authorization of the issuance of bonds in registered form; provisions establishing the various denominations in which bonds may be issued and prescribing the conditions on which bonds of one denomination may be exchanged for a bond or bonds of other denominations; provisions with respect to the issuance of bonds in replacement of mutilated, destroyed, lost, or stolen bonds and the evidence and indemnity required; provisions with respect to treasury bonds or bonds reacquired by the obligor; language establishing and providing for the negotiability of the bonds; and similar provisions that may be deemed desirable to authorize and facilitate the efficient servicing of the obligations as long as they remain outstanding.[8]

Because most modern indentures, particularly open-end indentures, remain in existence for a long period of time, it is important that these provisions be made as broad and as flexible as possible so that both the obligor and the trustee can take advantage of changing and more efficient methods for processing and handling the indenture securities.

Issuance of Bonds

Included in this section are the terms and conditions on which bonds may be issued under the indenture and the documents that must be furnished to the trustee on the basis of which it is authorized to authenticate and deliver the bonds.

Redemption of Bonds

If the obligor desires to reserve the right to retire the obligations, in whole or in part, before their stated maturity, this right must be reserved in the indenture. These provisions are included in a special article and set forth conditions on which bonds may be prepaid; the premium required, if any; the method of giving notice to the holders; and other pertinent requirements.

Sinking Fund

If the obligor is required to provide a sinking fund for retiring a portion of the outstanding bonds from time to time, this article will set forth the amount of such sinking fund, how it is to be paid, and the manner in which it must be applied by the trustee.

Particular Covenants

Covenants are an important part of each indenture contract and are normally set apart in a separate article. Most indentures, whether secured or unsecured, include covenants of some kind. They are both affirmative--requiring performance of certain things by the obligor, either continuously or at specified times--and negative--placing restrictions on particular activities of the obligor, such as incurring additional debt. These covenants provide additional security to the holders of the indenture securities, and the trustee has particular duties with respect to their enforcement.

Provisions in Regard to Pledged Collateral

If the indenture is in the form of a collateral trust, in which the security consists in whole or in part of securities or similar collateral pledged with the trustee, the indenture must set forth in sufficient detail just how this collateral is to be administered. Matters such as the following should be covered: the form in which the collateral is to be held (whether bearer or registered and, if registered, in what name or names); collection and disposition of income; voting of stock; disposition of principal collected; enforcement of rights as a holder; action to be taken on default in payment or under the indenture securing bonds or debentures held; release, substitution, replacement, etc.; and any other matters deemed to be pertinent to proper administration to achieve the purposes for which the pledge was made.[9]

Remedies of Trustee and Bondholders

This article will include the default and remedial provisions. Events that constitute a default under the indenture must be spelled out in detail, including grace periods, if any. Since the trustee has only the powers specifically granted by the contract, there must always be included alternative remedies available on default, with a grant of sufficient authority to pursue such remedies. The article must include a statement of the rights of security holders under the indenture, individually or collectively, and particularly, any limitation on the rights of security holders.

Immunity of Incorporators, Stockholders, Officers, and Directors

Since the obligations are corporate and municipal obligations, a provision is almost always included that specifically grants immunity to the stockholders, directors, officers, elected officials, and so forth, with respect to the indenture or the securities to be issued thereunder. A similar provision is usually included in the form of the bond. Although this immunity is now fairly well established as a matter of general law, the provision is intended as a protection against the possible application of some remote statutory or implied liability in a particular jurisdiction. It is doubtful that the protection would be applicable if fraudulent misrepresentations were involved. In fact, the 33 Act[10] includes specific penalties for misrepresentations or misleading statements in a registration statement or prospectus.

Consolidation, Merger, and Sale

This article will set forth the conditions under which corporate obligors may sell or lease all or substantially all of its properties or may merge into or with another corporation. If the corporate obligor has subsidiary companies, they should also be specifically covered in these provisions, for the conditions affecting subsidiaries may be quite different from those applicable to the parent company. In many indentures, particularly debenture agreements, this article is an additional negative covenant. Typically, municipal or other governmental entities are not involved with the merger provisions or subsidiary entities.

Releases

If the indenture is a secured indenture, and particularly if the security is a mortgage or collateral is held by the trustee, the obligor must be permitted to dispose of or substitute particular segments of the property as may be required or desirable from time to time. The indenture will describe the conditions under which such disposition or substitution may be made and the documents and consideration that must be furnished to the trustee.

Possession Until Default--Defeasance

Since the trustee's interest in the property is simply a security interest, the obligor is entitled to remain in possession, at least until default, and this article confirms such right. It is also important to provide for a reconveyance to the obligor, and the terms and conditions on which it will be made, if the obligor performs all the terms and conditions of the indenture.

Concerning the Trustee

This article concerning the trustee is the most important and is explored in the next chapter. The trustee's specific duties, responsibilities, and liabilities are explained in detail, and the necessary and appropriate exculpatory and protective provisions are examined.

Requirements Regarding Evidence of Compliance with Indenture Provisions and Certificates

The TIA requires that certain statements or reports must be furnished the trustee as evidence of compliance with particular types of provisions and the contents of certificates and opinions with respect to compliance with conditions and covenants.[11]

Supplemental Indentures, Bondholders' Meetings, Bondholders' Acts, Holdings, and Apparent Authority

The provisions for supplemental indentures, bondholders' meetings, bondholders' acts, holdings, and apparent authority explain the manner in which the indenture contract may be supplemented or amended. Some amendments may be made by the obligor and trustee without reference to the security holders, and these are usually enumerated. In general, any provision that does not affect a substantive right of the security holders may be added without their consent. Other provisions may be changed with the consent of a specified percentage of the holders, while others require 100 percent consent. If the consent of the holders is required, the manner in which such consent is to be evidenced will be spelled out, as will the nature of evidence on which the trustee may rely in establishing ownership of particular obligations. Various miscellaneous provisions will be embodied in a final article.

MODEL INDENTURES

Since the indenture was first used approximately 180 years ago, it has developed into the largest and, in many respects, the most complex of legal documents. Language was added through the years in response to frequent court decisions interpreting particular provisions, but until 1962, little effort was made to reduce the excess verbiage or standardize its provisions.

In 1962, the American Bar Foundation announced the adoption of the Corporate Debt Financing Project--A Project to Develop a Model Form of Corporate Debenture Indenture and Mortgage with Annotations and Comments.[12] The basic format adopted in 1965, after extended discussions by the project committees, contains two documents. One document called Model Provisions consists solely of the traditional boilerplate provisions common to most corporate debt indentures. The second document, sometimes called the Incorporating Indenture, incorporates by reference the Model Provisions, or as many thereof as are agreed to by the parties to the particular financing.

The Incorporating Indenture also contains the negotiated provisions, which usually include the principal amount, the interest rate, the stated maturity and the terms of redemption of the debenture issue, certain covenants, and other special provisions, all as negotiated by the parties. These documents were the result of many meetings and discussions participated in by counsel who had frequently represented issuers or investors or investment bankers, a representative group of corporate trust officers, the SEC (with particular reference to conformity with the TIA), the New York Stock Exchange, and an Ad Hoc Consultative Committee of the American Institute of Certified Public Accountants. The final product inevitably contained many compromises. Nevertheless, it represented an important contribution by simplifying those provisions that were generally subject to negotiation in the drafting of indentures and providing standardized boilerplate for non-negotiated provisions.[13]

The use of the 1965 Model Provisions (which provided for both bearer and fully registered debentures) was limited by the fact that by the time of publication, a majority of new issues were being offered in registered form only. In the latter part of 1964, while the 1965 Model Provisions were still in the drafting stage, the corporate trust group urged the project's directorate to prepare Model Debenture Indenture Provisions for "all-registered" issues. This corporate trust group undertook the task of securing general agreement on the basic procedures that should be incorporated in the model provisions, and early in 1966 the group published its recommendations.[14]

The result of this cooperative effort was the publication of a companion Sample Incorporating Indenture and companion Model Provisions tailored to all-registered issues of debentures, but whose text was otherwise substantially the same as the two 1965 documents.[15] The Model Provisions do not constitute an instrument but were intended as an exhibit to be attached to an indenture in the form recommended by the Sample Incorporating Indenture. It is, therefore, possible in the incorporating indenture to express specific deviations from the Model Provisions or to omit certain provisions entirely by not incorporating them in the Indenture.

The practice recommended by the project of incorporating the Model Provisions in the indenture by reference has rarely been used in practice because of its complexities, but the substantive provisions of the Sample Incorporating Indenture and the Model Provisions are very often used as part of the modern indenture and are seldom modified or changed.

The publication of the Commentaries on Indentures[16] marked the third major step in accomplishing the project's objective. The Commentaries were intended to accomplish a number of things: to outline the Model Provisions and how they were to be used; to explain why the particular form used was adopted and why certain traditional but outmoded provisions could be safely eliminated; to deal with the theories underlying the negotiable positions of the indenture; and to offer sample alternative provisions that might be suited to particular requirements.

With the publication in 1981 of the Model Mortgage Bond Indenture Form, the Project completed its objectives established nineteen years earlier.[17]

The Model Mortgage Form is structured as an integrated mortgage indenture, instead of following the two-part technique used in the earlier models. It contains standardized model provisions and the negotiable provisions and includes many footnotes referring to the Indenture Commentaries, providing illustrations of alternative texts.

The next effort to streamline the trust indenture was the publication in 1983 of a Model Simplified Indenture.[18] The model developed by the American Bar Association's Committee on Developments in Business Financing, is relatively short--thirty-one pages--and written in "plain English." The simplified model proceeds on the assumption

> that (except for provisions specifically required by the TIA) nearly all portions of an indenture are subject to negotiation in varying degrees, but seek to prescribe the language of frequently encountered provisions in such a way as to achieve a consensus generally acceptable to counsel accustomed to analyzing indenture terms from the points of view of debenture holders, corporate borrowers, lending institutions, investment bankers and indenture trustees.[19]

The extensive notes to the model are often explained with a comparison to the American Bar Foundation's model indentures and commentaries or with reference to stock exchange listing requirements or prevailing administrative practice.

The next endeavor was the Sample Uncertificated Debt Indenture, which provides for the issuance of corporate debt securities in either certificated or non-certificated form at the holder's option.[20] Developed under the aegis of the Business Law Section of the American Bar Association by a group of distinguished securities lawyers with advice from several corporate trust professionals, the indenture attempts to provide for the issuance of corporate debt instruments in pure uncertificated (i.e., dematerialized) form, as contemplated by the 1977 UCC Article 8 revisions, and the recommendations of the U.S. Working Committee of the Group of Thirty that "it is both desirable and achievable to eliminate use of the physical certificate by 1995 for the settlement of securities transactions".[21] In its report, the Ad Hoc Committee of the Business Law Section recognized that the application of this approach to municipal securities might be a problem, since

> many state laws require that municipal securities receive approval from local or state agencies other than the issuer thereof. Even when such statutes contemplate uncertificated securities, there may be a problem in the approving agency delegating its certification responsibility to the indenture trustee. Certain of such statutes could be construed to require approving agency signatures (albeit facsimiles) on each transaction statement

sent by the trustee to the seller and buyer involved.

In 1995, a subcommittee on the ABA's Committee on Developments in Business Financing began work on a revision of the 1983 Model Simplified Indenture. The focus was on the non-covenant provisions of a "standard" convertible, subordinated indenture and incorporating the 1990 amendments of the TIA. The new Model Simplified Indenture was published in 1999.[22,2]

The sum total of these efforts produced important and valuable additions in the field of corporate finance and particularly in the simplification and standardization of the corporate trust indenture.

---

[1] See Sklar, The Corporate Indenture Trustee: Genuine Fiduciary or Mere Stakeholder? 106 Banking L. Journal 1 (1989).

[2] Even with securities in fully registered form, such registration may be in nominee or street name. This is especially true of securities held in a depositary or by bank custodians, brokerage firms, and trust fund accounts.

[3] For a plain language version, see para. 4, 38 Bus. Law. op. cit. supra, at 776.

[4] See page 86, chapter 3, *infra*.

[5] For a discussion of the expanding scope of the trustee's potential liability, see chapter 3, and discussion covering secondary market disclosure in chapter 13.

[6] 15 U.S.C. sec. 77aaa et seq. (1990), as amended by the Trust Indenture Reform Act of 1990, P.L. 101-550 (TIRA). References hereinafter are to TIA section numbers, 301 through 328. For complete text of the amended act, see the appendices.[7] The Tax Equity and Fiscal Responsibility Act of 1982, Pub. L. 97-248, 96 Stat. 324, 576., effectively eliminated the issuance of corporate bearer bonds (as of January 1, 1983) and tax-exempt bearer bonds (as of July 1, 1983) by imposing adverse tax consequences on both issuer and investor.

[8] If the issue provides for book-entry-only certificates, the authorization for such should be included in this section. For specific sample provisions, see Article Two, Sample Uncertificated Debt Indenture, American Bar Assoc., Business Law Section, draft dated January 28, 1991. See also Report of the Ad Hoc Comm. on Uncertificated Debt Securities, Bus. Law. (May 1991).

[9] For discussion of collateral represented by pools of assets, see chapter 15.

[10] 15 U.S.C. sec. 77a (1976).

[11] TIA, secs. 314(c), (d), (e), and (f).

[12] For a detailed discussion of the background of the project see Rodgers, The Corporate Trust Indenture Project, 20 Bus. Law. 551 (1965).

[13] American Bar Foundation, Sample Incorporating Indenture--Model Debenture Indenture Provisions--1965.

[14] Corporate Trust Activities Committee, American Bankers Association, Recommended Procedures For Registered Bond Issues (1966). See also Kennedy and Landau, Recent Developments in Debt Financing and Corporate Trust Administration, 22 Bus. Law. 353 (1967).

[15] American Bar Foundation, Model Debenture Indenture Provisions--All Registered Issues--1967.

[16] American Bar Foundation, Commentaries on Indentures, 1972.

[17] American Bar Foundation, Model Mortgage Bond Indenture, 1981. See also Brown, Review of Mortgage Bond Indenture Forms, 36 Bus. Law. 1917 (1981).

[18] See note 1, chapter 1, *supra*.

[19] Id. at 742.

[20] See note 8, *supra*.

[21] See, Status Report and Request For Comment, U.S. Working Committee, Group of Thirty, Clearance and Settlement Project, at 8 (August 1990).

[22]. American Bar Foundation, The new Model Simplified Indenture, (1999)

THREE

THE CORPORATE TRUSTEE

DEVELOPMENT OF THE TRUSTEE CONCEPT

The development of a concept of the duties and responsibilities of the indenture trustee has closely paralleled the growth and development of the trust indenture itself. In the very early history of corporate mortgages, there are cases where the mortgage ran directly to the bondholders themselves, without a trustee being named. The difficulties presented by such an arrangement became apparent when the first default under such a mortgage occurred. The court ruled that for the mortgage to be foreclosed, all bondholders had to join in the petition. Consequently, the practice of using a trustee to whom the mortgage would run for the benefit of all the bondholders was adopted at an early date.

In the first years of this development, the trustee was usually a single individual, frequently an officer of the issuing corporation. Although such an individual's interests were obviously adverse to those of the bondholders, it made little practical difference, for the trustee at that time was simply a convenience for the mortgagor and had few, if any, actual duties to perform. The trustee was, in almost every sense, a mere stakeholder.

With the growth in the number of indentures and the gradually increasing intricacies of corporate borrowing, criticism began to be directed at this officer-trustee device and it soon became impractical. The next step was the designation of an independent individual as trustee. To give added status to the issue, individuals selected were usually outstanding citizens in the community.

The first instance of a bank being designated as an indenture trustee occurred in 1839, but the use of the institutional, as opposed to the individual, trustee did not become general practice until the latter part of the nineteenth century. The initial reason for the change was undoubtedly to avoid the problems presented by the death or incapacity of an individual trustee. After initial authentication of the bonds, there were still few duties to be performed, and responsibilities were not onerous.

As the use of the corporate indenture became more common and numerous problems were presented as a result of defaults, it was inevitable that greater power should be placed in the hands of the corporate trustee. As corporations grew and the size of their bond issues increased and became more complex, it became difficult for bondholders themselves, either individually or collectively, to enforce their security in the event of default. Consequently, more and more restrictions were placed on suits by individual holders, and most rights of action were concentrated in the trustee. It was much easier to create an appearance of protection, however, than it was to provide remedies adequate in fact. Several factors operated to impede an orderly growth and development of the trustee's duties and responsibilities.

Corporate trusteeships were regarded by many banks as being in the nature of escrows and were accepted, usually without compensation, as a service to corporate banking customers. Laissez-faire was the guiding economic theory of the day, and it was not surprising that in this, as in other areas of corporate practice, a real sense of responsibility was slow in developing.

The growth in the trustee's duties was accompanied by an equivalent growth in the number and scope of exculpatory clauses. Early efforts to raise fees for trustee services met with stubborn resistance, and the resulting reluctance of the trustee to undertake lengthy, expensive, and time-consuming legal proceedings was understandable.

As indicated previously, there were no clear-cut legal precedents, but rather considerable confusion in the minds of courts about the exact nature of the indenture and the legal responsibility of the trustee for preserving and enforcing the security. Reliance by courts on different precedents and concepts led to many conflicting opinions and to the introduction of new and unusual provisions into each indenture. After each court decision, indenture drafters devised new language for the protection of the obligor and the trustee. As a result, the corporate indenture developed rapidly into one of the most complex of all legal documents, without offering a real solution to the basic problem of how to provide reasonable protection to security holders without exposing the trustee to undue and unwarranted liability.[1]

A start had been made, however. Many of the more responsible banks began to express concern over the losses suffered by bondholders and the apparent ineffectiveness of remedies after default. The volume of corporate trust business was now sufficient to warrant the establishment of separate corporate trust units in the larger institutions, and this led to a reexamination of policies and practices. The sense of responsibility grew, and more attention was paid to all phases of corporate trust activity. Even among the older indentures, which contained little more than the basic mortgage provisions, advantage was taken of the "further assurance" clauses to secure continuing up-to-date information on the status of the security and the condition of the obligor's affairs. In newly drafted indentures, trustees began to insist on the inclusion of additional protective provisions and covenants. A new pattern of responsibility rapidly emerged, and by the late 1920s the corporate trustee had begun to be recognized as an important party to these financial transactions.

The pattern thus established by the more responsible institutions was not universal, however, and the practices still followed in a number of cases brought continued criticism by courts and recognized authorities in the field. The financial collapse of 1929 and the ensuing Great Depression resulted in an increasing number of defaults and led to a critical examination of all phases of security practice. Although the broad generalities embodied in the conclusions and recommendations of the SEC report[2] were neither impartial nor fair, no serious student of the subject could question the desirability of the establishment of minimum standards to which the trust indentures and the conduct of corporate trustees should conform. The TIA, in effect, codified the more important practices that had been developed and were already being followed by the leading corporate trust departments. As indicated, the essential provisions of this act are now fairly standard for all corporate indentures whether required to be qualified under the act or not, although private placement agreements usually do not impose the "prudent man" standard upon the occurrence of a default.

Whereas by 1940 the practice of using an individual--as opposed to institutional--trustee was practically obsolete, the act required the designation of an institutional corporate trustee meeting certain minimum standards of eligibility under all indentures to be qualified under the act.

ESSENTIAL FUNCTION OF THE CORPORATE TRUSTEE

In succeeding chapters, we will examine the duties of the trustee with reference to specific indenture provisions and the issuance and servicing of the indenture securities. First we consider briefly the principal areas of the trustee's responsibility.

As indicated in the preceding chapter, the essential function of a trustee is the administration of the security provisions of a contract between the issuing corporation and the holders of the indenture securities. There are three principal areas of responsibility.

First, if the issue is secured in any way, the trustee holds and deals with the security. If the security consists in whole or in part of a mortgage on corporate real property, the trustee will be the mortgagee and must concern itself with problems related to maintenance, insurance, taxes, release, and replacement and, within the scope of the powers granted, must see that the security is maintained in the agreed manner. If the security for the bond issue is personal property, such as equipment, the trustee will normally "perfect" its security interest in the property by filing a financing statement pursuant to the Uniform Commercial Code of the applicable state.

Second, as administrator of the contract, the trustee has the responsibility of making sure that the covenants and other indenture provisions are performed in the agreed manner. This it does in large part through examining reports and certificates it receives from the obligor or independent accountants, engineers, or other experts.

Finally, in the event of a default, the trustee has a primary responsibility for enforcing the remedial provisions of the contract. As we will explain in greater detail in a later chapter, the nature of this responsibility has been substantially changed by the enactment of federal and state laws dealing with bankruptcy and creditors' rights. In addition to the performance of specifically enumerated duties, the modern corporate trustee contributes a great deal more to the relationship. Most larger institutions have a trained staff experienced in handling many types of indentures and the innumerable problems concerning them that have arisen over the years. By virtue of this experience, corporate trust officers are able to make substantial contributions during the indenture-drafting process and frequently can suggest an appropriate course of action whenever difficulties arise. These professionals are also continually devising new and more efficient methods of handling the many administrative and operational details involved in the processing and servicing of securities through automation as detailed in part II, "Management", thus achieving substantial savings to both issuers and security holders.

In many instances an issuer will sell long-term debt obligations to a limited number of institutional investors under a "direct placement" contract. This practice eliminates the necessity of registering such securities under the 33 Act or of qualifying an indenture. Occasionally such securities are issued under purchase contracts with the separate investors, and no indenture or trustee is involved. Such a procedure is quite proper in the appropriate case. When security is involved, or where more than a few investors purchase a single issue, when complicated sinking-fund or similar provisions are involved, or, again, when the terms of the contract are unusual and require frequent checking, the use of a trustee is recommended. From the point of view of the investor, the activities of the trustee supplement rather than supersede those of the investor institution. From the obligor's point of view the convenience and service obtained usually outweigh the fairly nominal fees involved.

The terms of these issues are usually set in consultation with an investment banker and after discussion with one or more of the principal prospective purchasers. Special counsel appointed by the issuer to represent the purchaser traditionally drafts the financing documents. Although the flexibility available as a result of direct negotiations between issuer and purchaser is regarded as a major advantage of private placements, patterns of inflexibility developed as the major institutional investors established their own set of required covenants, sometimes without regard to the structure of the financing or the needs of the obligor. As a result many of the existing note purchase agreements follow a more or less rigid pattern, which is not always in the best interests of either issuer or investor. For public and many private issues, an experienced corporate trustee, familiar with all types of financing arrangements, is an important addition to the team of experts who work out the details of the financing document. A similar contribution can be made in the case of privately placed note issues.

The use of a corporate trustee for such issues also contributes to the solution of problems encountered in the past and, on the positive side, provides numerous benefits, such as:

1. Uniform administration of the security provisions of the contract.

2. Identification of the holders of notes entitled to the benefits of the contract, provided by the trustee's authentication of the notes issued,

3. Improved marketability of the obligations. To qualify for exemption from the registration requirements of the 33 Act, the notes must be purchased for investment and not for distribution. However, for an institutional investor, it is necessary that any obligation purchased be marketable; indeed an increasing volume of obligations originally placed privately are being sold by the original investors. This trend has grown with the development of the secondary market for private placements facilitated by SEC Rule 144A. Obvious problems are thus created, not only in consummating these transactions but also in determining rights of the transferees in the absence of an indenture and uniform provisions governing transfers or assignments.

4. Improved marketability should also reduce the interest cost to obligors. Institutional investors

usually insist, because of limited marketability, on a premium of ten to twenty basis points in the rate of interest paid on notes acquired in a private placement. Anything that would tend to improve marketability should reduce this spread.

5. Efficient servicing of the debt obligations, particularly in the application of the amortization formula to assure continuation of the relative interests of the investors vis-à-vis the total debt. Many issuers now employ a bank as agent to render these services.

6. More efficient communication. Each investor usually receives a complete set of all documents delivered at each note closing, although it is difficult to understand what real purpose is served by the dissemination of this volume of paper. If a complete set of documents were provided the trustee acting on behalf of all investors, all that any investor should require would be the note itself, a copy of the purchase agreement, and opinion of its special counsel. This should represent a considerable saving to most institutional investors, as well as to issuers.

ELIGIBILITY REQUIREMENTS

Section 310 of the TIA sets forth the requirements that an institution must meet in order to be eligible to serve as indenture trustee. The act requires that there be at all times a trustee which must be a corporation organized and doing business under the laws of the United States or of any state or territory or the District of Columbia. Such trustee must be authorized under such laws to exercise corporate trust powers and be subject to supervision or examination by federal, state, territorial, or District of Columbia authority. It must have at all times a combined capital and surplus of not less than $150,000. Foreign institutions are now permitted to serve as corporate trustees under certain circumstances.[3] The act prohibits any obligor on the indenture securities or any person directly or indirectly controlling, controlled by, or under the common control with such obligor, from acting as trustee on the indenture securities.[4]

These requirements are minimal and enable almost any banking institution normally exercising trust powers to act. Many qualified indentures impose much more stringent requirements. For example, a customary minimum capital and surplus requirement is $5 million.[5] Many indentures require much higher capital and surplus amounts. It is also frequently required that the corporate trustee have its principal office in one of the large financial centers. This requirement is no longer of major importance, for many institutions throughout the country are now fully qualified and have the technology to act under most indentures. The experience and qualifications of the prospective trustee are important factors that should be considered.

Inasmuch as the trustee will have been selected and will be acting at the time of the execution and delivery of the indenture, the purpose of the eligibility provision is to govern the selection of a successor trustee in the event the original trustee resigns or becomes incapable of acting.

Because this is a substantive provision, a successor trustee that does not meet the specified standards cannot be named without the consent of all the security holders or a specified percentage thereof. In the unlikely event that no other trustee can be found that meets the requirements of the indenture and is willing to act, it has been held that a trustee not meeting such requirements can be appointed and can exercise all the rights and powers granted by the indenture. If such a situation should develop, however, it is recommended that judicial sanction for such an appointment first be obtained.

PROHIBITION OF CONFLICTING INTERESTS -- QUALIFICATION OF THE TRUSTEE

The problem of conflicting interests is a troublesome one and one of which the trustee should always be conscious.[6] Issuing corporations often select one of their principal banks to act as indenture trustee. The familiarity such an institution has with the corporation's affairs and the close continuing relationship will enable the institution to do a more thorough job for the security holders, and the issuing corporation. The administrative officers should familiarize themselves thoroughly with all relationships between their bank and the obligor corporation and ensure that no possibility arises for the fairness and impartiality of the trustee's acts to be questioned. Although many corporations and municipalities do select their primary bank to serve as trustee, competitive pricing for trustee services has eroded some of the obligor loyalties to these banks.

One of the innovations introduced by the TIA in 1939 was the setting down of certain rules that would disqualify an institution from acting as trustee under a qualified indenture. In recognition of the fact that prior to default the duties of the trustee are essentially administrative and ministerial in nature, the TIRA suspended the requirement of resignation for conflict of interest until a default occurs. These provisions are set forth in Section 310(b) and are now incorporated by force of law in all qualified indentures. This section does not, however, cover the whole field of conflicts or prohibit any interest that might possibly be a conflict. The trustee is deemed to have a potential conflicting interest if it has one or more of ten different relationships. We next look at these relationships from the viewpoint of prohibited general interests or affiliations.

Trusteeship Under More Than One Indenture

Section 310(b)(1) identifies as a potential conflicting interest the same trustee acting under more than one indenture of the same obligor "or is trustee for more than one outstanding series of securities . . . under a single indenture of an obligor". The latter provision, which was unfortunately included in the TIRA, appears to mandate that there be separate trustees for each series of defaulted bonds issued under secured indentures, e.g., utility and railroad mortgages. The SEC's broad exemptive powers, as well as the stay-of-resignation provisions absent a payment default will resolve this problem, except in two situations. The first occurs where the qualified indenture is a collateral indenture, in which the only collateral consists of obligations issued under the other indenture. The second exception is where both issues are unsecured and confer upon the holders substantially the same rights. It is required, however, that the qualified indenture specifically refers to the obligations under the other (prior) indenture. Exception is allowed where the second indenture is subsequently qualified under the act. On application, the SEC may permit a trusteeship under more than one indenture subsequent to a default if it finds that such trusteeship is not likely to involve a material conflict of interest.

The significance of the same trustee acting under separate indentures is apparent. Although before default the trustee might act under two indentures of the same obligor without encountering difficulty, the happening of an event of default will usually create a conflict and prevent the trustee from adequately representing holders under both indentures, for their interests are quite likely to be adverse. The difficulty in acting under separate indentures upon default can be realized when attempting to locate a successor trustee. Large corporations often name a number of trustees for their debt security issues. The recent consolidation in the corporate trustee industry and the general banking industry, which is more fully discussed in part II, may make it difficult to locate a qualified trustee who is not already serving as trustee for the obligor. The importance of having independent representation in proceedings after default was recognized in an 1895 decision of the federal court in New York, which permitted intervention of individual bondholders in a foreclosure suit where the trustee was acting under several indentures. Also, it was suggested that the trustee should be subjected to a higher standard of care where it was acting under more than one indenture.

The term *obligor* is defined in the TIA as every person (including a guarantor) who is liable on the indenture securities.[7] Trusteeship under indentures of affiliated companies is permissible provided the same company is not liable on the indenture securities issued under more than one of such indentures.

A difficult question is presented where no guaranty in fact exists but where the credit of one corporation is the primary security for obligations issued by another. Such a situation would arise, for example, if corporation A issued securities for the construction of certain facilities to be leased to corporation B, the rental payments being sufficient to service the securities and the lease, and the right to rents being pledged under the indenture. These facts alone are not sufficient to constitute corporation B an "obligor" on the securities, but greater care should be exercised in such a situation, and all the facts surrounding the proposed transaction should be considered to determine if an actual, as distinguished from a technical, conflict is likely to arise.

Ownership of Securities

Subdivisions (5) to (9) of Section 310(b) set down certain rules for the disqualification of the trustee based on affiliations through security ownership. Disqualification under these subdivisions does not depend on the existence of actual control of or any conflicting interest in fact, but beneficial ownership of the specified percentage of securities is required to be made a conflicting interest as a part of the contract between the parties. A potential conflicting interest is deemed to exist, and upon default, the trustee will be disqualified from acting as such, if any of the following situations exist:

1. Ten percent or more of the voting securities of the trustee is beneficially owned either by an obligor or by any director, partner, or executive officer of an obligor; 20 percent or more of such voting securities is owned, collectively, by any two or more of such persons; or 10 percent or more of such voting securities is beneficially owned by either an underwriter for any such obligor or by any director, partner, or executive officer thereof, or is beneficially owned, collectively, by any two or more such persons.

2. Beneficial ownership by the trustee or the holding by the trustee as collateral security for an obligation that is in default as to principal for thirty days or more of: (a) 5 percent or more of the voting securities of the obligor; (b) 10 percent or more of any other class of security of the obligor, excluding all securities issued under an indenture for which the trustee is acting as trustee; (c) 5 percent or more of the voting securities of a person who, to the knowledge of the trustee, owns 10 percent or more of the voting securities of, or controls directly or indirectly, or is under direct or indirect common control with, an obligor; (d) 10 percent or more of any class of security of a person who, to the knowledge of the trustee, owns 50 percent or more of the voting securities of an obligor; or (e) 10 percent

or more of any class of security of an underwriter for an obligor.

Since a conflicting interest by reason of the trustee's ownership of the above percentage of securities is predicated on the existence of an adverse interest in the trustee, ownership of securities issued under the particular indenture in question, or under any other indenture for which the trustee also acts as trustee, has been excluded.

3. Ownership by the trustee of securities in a fiduciary capacity. The trustee is required to make a check of its holdings promptly after the date of a default on the indenture securities, and annually as long as the default continues, of the types of securities enumerated above in its capacity as executor, administrator, testamentary or *inter-vivos* trustee, guardian, committee, conservator, or any similar capacity. A potential conflicting interest is deemed to exist if, on such date, the trustee holds in such capacities an aggregate of 25 percent or more or any class of security, the beneficial ownership of a specified percentage of which would constitute a conflict. In order to eliminate the possibility of an inadvertent conflict arising by reason of acquisition of securities in new estates, the act provides that the conflict provisions will not apply, for a period not to exceed two years from the date of such acquisition, to the extent that such securities do not exceed 25 percent or more of the particular class outstanding.

In the event that there is a default in the payment of principal or interest under an indenture that continues for thirty days, the trustee is required to make a prompt check of its fiduciary holdings, and thereafter any ownership in such capacity of securities over which it has sole or joint control is to be deemed beneficial ownership for the purpose of determining whether a potential conflict exists.

Excluded from the operation of subdivisions (6) to (9) of Section 310(b) is any security held by the trustee as collateral security for an obligation not in default; held as collateral security under the indenture, irrespective of any default thereunder; or held by it in the capacity of custodian, escrow agent, depositary, agent for collection, or any similar representative capacity.

Other Affiliations Between Trustee and Obligor or Underwriters

Four other situations are specified in Section 310(b), the existence of any one of which will constitute a potential conflict of interest.

First, if the trustee or any of its directors or executive officers is an underwriter for an obligor. The TIRA defines an *underwriter* as any person who, within one year prior to the time the determination is made, was an underwriter of any security of an obligor.

Second, if the trustee or any of its directors or executive officers is a director, officer, partner, employee, appointee, or representative of an obligor or of any underwriter (other than the trustee itself) for an obligor. One individual may be a director and/or executive officer of the trustee and a director and/or executive officer of an obligor, provided such individual is not at the same time an executive officer of both. Also, if, and so long as, the number of directors of the trustee in office is more than nine, one additional individual may be a director and/or executive officer of the trustee and a director of such obligor.[8]

Third, if the trustee directly or indirectly controls, is directly or indirectly controlled by, or is under direct or indirect common control with an underwriter for an obligor. The control referred to here is actual control, whether or not it involves ownership of a prohibited percentage of the securities referred to above. The question of whether or not actual control exists must be determined by the circumstances of each case.

Finally, a potential conflict of interest arises if the trustee is or becomes a creditor of the obligor. This new potential conflict codifies the existing practice of most major corporate trustees to resign a trusteeship for a financially troubled obligor when it is also a creditor. The credit policies for some banks prohibit acting as a corporate trustee if the bank is a lender. During the past decade many banks have increased their credit policy focus on situations where a dual trustee/creditor relationship may exist. Despite the fact that there is no prohibition for a bank to act in such dual capacity, some bank credit officers have misinterpreted the TIA to prohibit such a dual role.

ADMINISTRATIVE RESPONSIBILITY UNDER CONFLICT PROVISIONS

Under a qualified indenture, if a conflict of interest as outlined above exists or develops, the trustee, within ninety days after default must either eliminate such conflict or resign. The trustee should therefore establish procedures and checks that will bring to light any conflict that may develop. No established routine is required but the trustee should be in a position to show that it has exercised reasonable care, and it must report annually any change to its eligibility and qualifications to serve as trustee, and the creation of or any material change in any of the potential conflict of interest relationships set forth in TIA section 310(b)(1) through (10). A *material change* is any change that would cause the trustee to resign (if a default occurred), or would permit the bank to remain as trustee if there were an existing default under the indenture. It is recommended that an annual report be obtained from the obligor as to the latter's holding of trustee's securities, if any; as to the outstanding securities of such obligor; and as to firms that have acted as underwriters for such obligor within the preceding year. Procedures within the trustee's office should be established to ensure the prompt reporting of such security holdings as might constitute a potential conflict. Although the obligor may only report to the trustee annually regarding potential conflicts, it is recommended that formal procedures be implemented by the trustee to review potential conflicts quarterly. Larger trustees typically have implemented automated methods to assist the review of potential conflicts through the use of standard industry codes, comparative data bases between the corporate trust department and the bank's credit databases and general staff training emphasis.

The Chinese Wall

Under trust law, the general rule is that a trustee owes loyalty to the beneficiaries of a trust and normally is flatly opposed to self-dealing transactions. This means that a trustee should not favor its interests over the interests of its beneficiaries. The scope of the application of this rule is often narrowed so that, for example, an indenture might permit a trustee to invest moneys held in a bond reserve account through its own bond department or in its own paper. The TIA, as amended by TIRA, identifies conflicting interests that do not prevent qualification of the trustee but that must be eliminated in the event of default or else the trustee must resign. Liability comes not from having such interests, but from what one does within the context of those relationships that may breach the duty of loyalty. Trustee banks have sought to erect a "Chinese Wall" between the fiduciary area and the credit area of the bank so that, for a company for whom the bank also serves as trustee, information derived in the bank's fiduciary capacity will not form the basis for action on the lending side.

In the administration of registered, qualified public financings where a conflict of interest exists and, particularly, the account becomes financially troubled or defaults, it is possible that the account officer and others in the fiduciary area will know information that could influence actions taken in credit areas. If the fiduciary side and the credit side need to discuss, for example, the establishment of a preferential claims account, use of counsel on both sides helps to limit the discussion so that additional claims are not created.

PROBLEMS OF QUALIFICATION IN FOREIGN STATES

A corporation is a creature of the state in which it is incorporated but is a foreign entity insofar as other states are concerned. Although it is regarded as a "person" for many purposes of the law, it is not entitled to the protection of the "privileges and immunities" clause of the U.S. Constitution. Accordingly, with certain exceptions relating to interstate or foreign commerce, a state may exclude a corporation of another state from doing business within its borders and from suing in its courts with respect to any prohibited transactions or otherwise engaging in activities over which the state has jurisdiction. It may also impose such terms and conditions as it deems proper for the granting of permission to do business within its borders. Most states have general statutes, whether on a basis of reciprocity or otherwise, relating to the conduct of business by foreign corporations.

In 1994, legislation was enacted which effectively paved the way for full interstate banking by mid 1997.[9] Banks are thus able to acquire other banks in any state or to establish branches in any state, unless a particular state "opts out", as permitted by the 1994 legislation.

In addition, the Comptroller of the Currency in late 1995 rendered its opinion that

> a national bank that has been granted fiduciary powers may offer fiduciary services in, and have trust powers in, multiple states. . . Such a national bank may exercise any of the fiduciary powers granted in section 92(a)[of 12 U.S.C.]in any state unless that state both prohibits national banks and restricts its own state institutions from exercising that fiduciary power".[10]

It should be noted that this interpretation does not necessarily apply to state chartered banks and trust companies.

Trustees may still be presented with a problem with respect to the "holding" of a mortgage on real property in a different state. Most of the larger corporations do business and own property in a number of different states. When such a corporation wishes to execute a mortgage on its fixed properties to secure a bond issue, the question arises of whether the designated trustee may properly hold a security interest in property in all of the states in which such property is located. It is impossible to set down a general rule as a guide in these situations because the law differs from state to state. The following may be taken as a basic guide: (1) where there is a specific statute prescribing conditions for the exercise of trust powers by foreign banking corporations, the trustee may need to qualify under such a statute before accepting a mortgage or security interest in fixed property within that state; or (2) where there is no statutory provision, the trustee may normally hold such a security interest unless such act contravenes the general "doing of business" statutes. These are suggested as general guides only, however, because the statutes, and judicial interpretation of statutes, vary from state to state. Counsel should therefore be certain of the proper authority of the corporate trustee in each such situation.

If a corporate trustee undertakes to act without authority, it may not only subject itself to heavy penalties but, from the viewpoint of its fiduciary responsibility, it may also be denied access to the courts of the state for enforcement of the security if such becomes necessary.

The usual solution to this problem is to designate an individual to act as a co-trustee under the indenture. When only one state is in question, it would also be appropriate to designate a banking corporation in that state as a co-trustee.

Under the U.S. Constitution, an individual citizen of a state is entitled to all the privileges and immunities of citizens of other states and cannot be excluded from holding property or doing business as can a foreign corporation. In any situation in which there is a question on the authority of the corporate trustee, an individual co-trustee should be named.

Care must be exercised in drafting the appropriate indenture provisions. The usual provision, and a requirement of the TIA for qualified indentures, is that all rights, powers, duties, and obligations conferred or imposed upon the trustees shall be conferred or imposed upon and exercised by the institutional corporate trustee, or the institutional trustee and the co-trustee jointly, except to the extent that under any law of any jurisdiction in which any act or acts are to be performed, such institutional trustee is incompetent or unqualified to perform such act or acts, in which event such rights, powers, duties, and obligations shall be exercised and performed by the co-trustee.

Since all rights, powers, and duties are to be performed by the corporate trustee, except only such functions as it is incapable of performing, the corporate trustee is usually given the right, either alone or jointly with the obligor, to remove the designated individual trustee at any time and to appoint another individual to act. It is also a common practice to reserve to the corporate trustee and obligor the right to designate a co-trustee or an additional co-trustee at any time in the event such designation is necessary or desirable for the carrying out of any specific duty. This is done even though in the first instance a co-trustee may not be required, for it avoids the possibility of a situation arising where the corporate trustee cannot act and no mechanism is available for resolving the difficulty.

Although any individual citizen may be designated as co-trustee, the usual practice is for an officer of the corporate trustee to be designated as the individual co-trustee. This facilitates the exercise of powers or the performance of duties, such as the execution of releases or supplemental indentures, that the trustees are required to perform jointly.

Two states (Florida and Missouri) prohibit the exercise of trust powers by other than a corporation or individual citizen of such state. Although such statutes probably do not exclude an individual citizen of another state from holding or enforcing a security interest in property, it is advisable to comply with the letter of the law and designate an individual or a bank in such a state as the co-trustee. When administering indentures with an individual co-trustee it is important to obtain a signed, undated co-trustee notice of resignation and retain it on file. As indentures typically involve the issuance of debt securities with maturities as long as thirty years, individual trustees can be difficult to locate after many years. The signed resignation in file can facilitate the appointment of a replacement individual co-trustee.

These problems do not arise in the case of an unsecured debenture or note agreement, or in other indentures where no property is mortgaged or pledged, for the trustee normally performs no acts outside its principal office.

SPECIAL PROVISIONS RELATING TO TRUSTEE

In addition to the matters just discussed, certain general provisions relating to the trustee should be incorporated in all indentures. These are usually found in the separate "Trustee" article.

First is the acceptance by the trustee of the trusts and obligations imposed upon it by the indenture. Although the act of execution undoubtedly constitutes a sufficient acceptance, it is customary to include an affirmative statement to this effect.

Second is a provision relating to the compensation and expenses of the trustee. Rather than setting specific rates of compensation, the common practice is to provide that the trustee shall be entitled to reasonable compensation that shall not be limited by any statutory provision governing compensation of trustees. The practice avoids the possibility that statutes, which exist in many states, that fix the maximum compensation for executors and trustees of testamentary or inter-vivos trusts would be held applicable to these agreements. It is also desirable for the trustee to include a provision under which the obligor agrees to indemnify it with respect to any liability incurred or damage suffered by it resulting from other than its own negligence. The trustee should also be permitted, but not required, to make advances to preserve the mortgaged property, pay taxes, or for other purposes. All these items, including all expenses and disbursements made by the trustee, should be payable by the obligor on demand (with interest in the case of any funds advanced by the trustee). If the indenture is secured, the trustee is usually given a lien on the security (prior to that of the indenture securities) to assure payment of its compensation, expenses, advances, and liabilities. This is desirable, although one would be hard pressed to find a case in which the full implications of such priority of lien have been upheld.

Third, the trustee should be given authority to act through agents or attorneys in carrying out its duties, and it is customarily provided that the trustee will not be liable for the acts of such agents or attorneys if reasonable care is exercised in their selection.

Finally, the indenture should contain appropriate provisions relative to the resignation or removal of the trustee. As we indicated, a conflict of interest may develop requiring the trustee's resignation. The trustee should also be permitted to submit its resignation at any time for any reason it deems sufficient, or for no reason if it no longer wishes to serve. The indenture should provide appropriate procedures for such resignation and for the appointment of a successor, which must be eligible and qualified to act. A majority in principal amount of the holders of the indenture securities are usually given the absolute right to designate the successor trustee, but until such right is exercised, any successor appointed by the obligor has full authority and power to act. As a practical matter, a successor trustee is usually appointed by the obligor and seldom by the bondholders. If the trustee is involved in a merger or consolidation with another institution, the surviving corporation, if it is eligible and qualified, usually succeeds to the trusteeship without further act.

A majority in principal amount of the indenture security holders are customarily given the absolute right, at any time and with or without cause, to remove the trustee. Because the latter is supposed to serve their interests, it is quite appropriate that they have the power, by majority action, to remove the trustee and substitute another if for any reason they believe their interests are not being served properly. The obligor, however, should never be given the right by unilateral action to remove the trustee. Starting principally in the 1990s, but continuing in the new millennium, municipal obligors have with increasing frequency requested the right to remove the trustee, provided no known potential or event of default is in existence. The trustee should resist this request, as it appears in conflict with the general principles of a corporate trustee appointment for the benefit of the investors.

If the trustee submits its resignation and no successor is appointed within a reasonable time, the trustee or any security holder may petition a court for appointment of a successor, and an institution so appointed will be qualified to act.

EXCULPATORY PROVISIONS

Among the provisions that were the subject of a great amount of comment, criticism, and controversy in pre-TIA days were the "exculpatory clauses," which had come to be more or less standard in all indentures. The general legal effect of these provisions was to exempt the trustee from liability for any act or failure to act, short of willful misconduct or gross negligence. Much could be written pro and con on this matter, for these clauses were enlarged and expanded over a lengthy period. This was due in no small part to the misunderstandings on the part of security holders and courts concerning the essential nature of the trustee function and to attempt to hold the trustee accountable in some way for every unfortunate and unwise investment. Under these conditions it was essential for even conscientious trustees and their counsel to endeavor to protect themselves. Notwithstanding the validity of arguments that could be, and were, made in favor of these provisions, they had two unfortunate results. First, they provided protection even to a trustee indifferent to its responsibilities, and second, they subjected all trustees to criticism, even those who were diligent and conscientious in the performance of their duties, these latter comprising the great majority of trustees.

One result of the enactment of the TIA was the prohibition of such broad immunity provisions.[11] A qualified indenture may not contain provisions relieving the trustee of liability for its own negligent action, its own negligent failure to act, or its own willful misconduct, although the trustee must be protected from liability for any error of judgment made in good faith by a responsible officer, when the trustee was not negligent in ascertaining the pertinent facts. This has become the accepted practice for almost all modern indentures, whether qualified or not.

Certain exculpatory provisions are still perfectly proper and permissible if they do not contravene the foregoing prohibition. Trustees should endeavor to have them included to prevent a court reading into an indenture an implied covenant or duty on the part of the trustee where none was intended. Several cases make it apparent, however, that trustees can no longer be absolutely assured that such exculpatory provisions will provide the protection intended. These cases seem to fall into two categories: those holding that only a trial can determine whether the trustee's duties extended beyond the provisions of the indenture,[12] and those that question the trustee's protection in relying on information and advice given it by the obligor, bond counsel, and even by its own legal counsel.[13]

Despite these cases, trustee's counsel should ensure that in the absence of any express duty in the indenture, or only to the extent of any duty specifically imposed, the following provisions be included:

    1. The trustee has no obligation or duty to record the indenture.

    2. The trustee has no responsibility for the truth or

accuracy of the recitals in the indenture.

3. The trustee has no responsibility in regard to the application of the proceeds of any bonds, or with respect to the use or application of any property or monies released or paid out in accordance with indenture provisions. An exception can exist for municipal indentures that direct the trustee to accept bond proceeds, invest and distribute them upon written direction of the obligor.

4. The trustee may consult with counsel and be held harmless for anything done, in good faith, in accordance with the opinion of such counsel.

5. The trustee is not responsible for the validity of the indenture or of any securities issued thereunder, or for the obligor's title to, or the value of, the security held.

6. In the absence of bad faith, the trustee may rely on any certificates, opinions, documents, or other papers furnished to it and believed by it to be genuine and to be signed by the proper party or parties; the trustee is under a duty, however, to examine any such instruments furnished to it in accordance with an indenture provision to make sure that they comply with such provision.

7. The trustee shall not be liable for any action taken at the request or direction of holders of a majority in principal amount of the indenture securities.

PRESCRIBED STANDARDS OF CONDUCT

What should be the prescribed standard of conduct for an indenture trustee?[14] A clear distinction should be made between the duties before a default and those existing after a default occurs, when the security holder's investment is in jeopardy. In the normal case the obligor will perform its obligations and covenants, and the investor's principal concern is in receiving interest and principal when due. Under these circumstances the duties of the trustee are largely administrative. It is important, however, that the interests of the security holders be protected at all times, no matter how solvent or secure the obligor may appear. The trustee's active and vigilant administration is necessary at all times to ensure, if possible, that there is no default, or, if default occurs, that the bondholders will have the security for which they bargained from which to recover. If the trustee is concerned about a potential default, or is uncertain as to an appropriate course of action, it should consult with competent counsel or other experts. The overriding standard of conduct, in accordance with custom and practice in the industry, is that the trustee must act reasonably under the particular circumstances.

By offering its services to the public, the trustee undertakes an inherent obligation to perform such services in good faith, in a professional and competent manner and, where appropriate, in accordance with the custom and practice of other professional corporate trustees.

In this connection, corporate trust administrative officers should refer to the established trustee bank's policies and procedures governing the conduct and performance of the bank acting as a corporate trustee.

The nature and extent of the duties of the trustee will vary with each indenture, depending on its terms. Because the indenture is a contract between the obligor and trustee, it not only prescribes rules of conduct for the former but also defines the limits of the trustee's authority, and the trustee may do only what the indenture either in express terms or by necessary implication authorizes it to do.

As authorized by the TIA before default: (1) the trustee shall be liable only for the performance of such duties as are specifically set forth in the indenture; (2) the extent of such duties shall be determined solely by the express provisions of the indenture; and (3) no implied duties or covenants on the part of the trustee shall be read into the indenture.[15]

Most early court decisions dealing with the issue of fiduciary responsibilities relate to indentures that did not contain this language, and many courts found duties implied, but not expressed, frequently basing their decision on the nature of the agreement itself. The majority of indentures still contain language that imply, but do not specify, certain duties. For example, usually a trustee may on its own initiative, make independent investigations or require further evidence of the performance by the obligor of its covenants. Such a provision is highly desirable, but it is recommended that an express qualification be inserted to the effect that the trustee is under no duty to do so. Some courts have indicated that the trustee is under an implied duty to do whatever may be necessary to preserve the trust estate and that to this extent such duty cannot be abridged even by agreement.[16]

A real problem exists whenever the trustee deems it necessary to act beyond the scope of its express duties and powers. It is quite possible that an even higher standard of care may be imposed with respect to any such action, and the trustee may lose the benefit of the exculpatory clauses. If a situation arises where it is imperative that action be taken, the trustee should consult with counsel, and every effort should be made to find an indenture provision on which to base such action.

The TIA requires that upon the occurrence of an event of default, the trustee shall exercise such of the rights and powers vested in it by the indenture and shall use the same degree of care and skill in their exercise, as a prudent man would exercise or use under the circumstances in the conduct of his own affairs.[17]

Despite some earlier court cases that held that trustees may have pre-default obligations beyond those set forth in the indenture,[18] it is generally accepted now that prior to a default under an indenture the trustee's responsibilities are defined and determined solely by the terms of the indenture.[19] In *Meckel v. Continental Resources Co.*, the court concluded that "unlike the ordinary trustee, who has historic common-law duties imposed beyond those in the trust agreement, an indenture trustee is more like a stakeholder whose duties and obligations are exclusively defined by the terms of the indenture agreement."[20] Further reinforcing this doctrine, the court in *Elliott Associates v. J. Henry Schroder Bank & Trust Co.* stated that "we therefore conclude that, so long as the trustee fulfills its obligations under the express terms of the indenture, it owes the debenture holders no additional, implicit pre-default duties or obligations except to avoid conflicts of interest".[21]

It does not appear however, that this is a settled issue in all jurisdictions, since the TIA recognizes,[22] and courts have held that states may regulate trust indentures as long as such regulation does not conflict with the TIA.[23]

OTHER RELATIONS BETWEEN TRUSTEE AND OBLIGOR

Historically, a trustee was generally selected from among the banks with which the obligor had a banking relationship However, as discussed earlier, competitive fee pricing for trustee services has made this loyalty less of a common practice. This is perfectly proper, and the indenture usually contains provisions specifically permitting all other normal and customary relationships. The trustee, in its individual capacity, may own indenture securities and, as a holder, have the same rights and privileges as other holders. It may act as depositary, custodian, transfer agent, registrar, paying agent, fiscal agent, escrow agent, or in any similar capacity.[24] Subject to the qualification provisions of the indenture, it may also act as trustee for the obligor, whether under an indenture or otherwise.

Although the existence of a creditor relationship between the obligor and the trustee had not been a conflict of interest under the TIA as originally enacted, the TIRA added such a relationship as a potential conflict of interest. This was a logical step in view of the suspension of the conflict of interest provisions until default since it is obvious that the bank as creditor of an obligor may be in a position adverse to the bank as trustee for security holders of the obligor whenever the obligor is in a difficult financial position or faces insolvency.

Section 311 of the TIA as originally enacted, represented an effort to address the creditor relationship in a different way, and, in view of the TIRA, it remains as something of an anachronism, although presumably it will serve to govern the contractual rights of a trustee that has received payment on debt of the obligor within three months of an indenture default, or those of a former trustee/creditor that has resigned upon an indenture default. This section provides that if the trustee shall be, or shall become, a creditor, directly or indirectly, of an obligor upon the indenture securities within three months before a default in the payment of principal or interest on the indenture securities, it may not enforce any preferential collection of its claim against the obligor except on the conditions therein specified. The trustee bank under these circumstances must set aside, in a special account, for the benefit of itself and the indenture security holders: (1) an amount equal to any and all reductions in the amount due and owing upon any claim as such creditor with respect to principal and interest effected after the beginning of such three-month period and (2) all property received in respect of any claim as such creditor, either as security therefor or in satisfaction or composition thereof, after the beginning of such three-month period, or an amount equal to the proceeds of such property if it shall have been disposed of. The trustee bank is entitled: (1) to exercise any right of setoff it could have exercised if a petition in bankruptcy had been filed by or against such obligor upon the date of the default; (2) to retain for its own account payments made on account of its claim by a third person, and/or distributions made in cash, securities, or other property in respect of claims filed against such obligor in bankruptcy or receivership or in proceedings for reorganization pursuant to a bankruptcy act or applicable state laws; (3) to realize for its own account on any property held as collateral security for such claim before the beginning of the three-month period; (4) to realize for its own account on any property received as security simultaneously with the creation of such claim if the trustee bank became a creditor after the beginning of such three-month period and had no reasonable cause to believe that a default would occur; and (5) to receive payment on any claim against the release of any property held as security therefor to the extent of the fair value of such property. Property substituted after the beginning of the three-month period has the same status as property released to the extent of the fair value of the latter, and any renewal effected after the beginning of such period has the same status as the preexisting claim.

The language in Section 311 relative to the disposition of any funds or property segregated in such a special account is somewhat laborious. It appears that the property in the account cannot be apportioned until the obligor has gone through bankruptcy, receivership, or reorganization proceedings. The court having jurisdiction of such proceedings is given the right to apportion the property in accordance with TIA Section 311(a) or, in lieu of such apportionment, to give due consideration to such provisions in determining the fairness of the distributions to be made to the security holders and the trustee bank in such proceedings.

The formula according to which the property in the account is to be distributed is quite simple. Secured portions of the claims of both the security holders and the trustee bank are to be disregarded, and the respective claims are to be reduced to the extent of distributions with respect to such portions. The funds in the special account are then to be allocated so that the security holders and the trustee bank will receive the same proportion of the unsecured portions of their claims from such account and from dividends paid from the obligor's estate with respect to such unsecured portions. The problem will be one of applying the formula. Anyone familiar with reorganization proceedings will appreciate the difficulty of even approximating the value of any particular lien position or of the securities and interests distributed in reorganization. Calculating these values so as to allocate a fund according to an exact mathematical formula is all but impossible.

If the trustee resigns or is removed after the beginning of the three-month period, it is still subject to these provisions. If the resignation or removal was prior to such period, the trustee bank is subject to such provisions only if the property was received, and the claim occurred after the beginning of the three-month period, and within three months after the resignation or removal.

Certain creditor relationships may be excluded from the operation of this section. These consist of creditor relationships arising from: (1) the ownership or acquisition of securities issued under an indenture, or any security having a maturity of one year or more at the time of its acquisition by the trustee; (2) advances for the purpose of preserving the trust estate, or discharging taxes, prior liens, etc. authorized by the indenture, or by a bankruptcy or receivership court, if notice of such advance is given as provided in the indenture; (3) disbursements made in the ordinary course of business as trustee under an indenture, transfer agent, registrar, custodian, paying agent, fiscal agent, depositary, or similar capacity; (4) indebtedness created as a result of services rendered or premises rented, or as a result of goods or securities sold in a cash transaction; (5) the ownership of stock or of other securities of a corporation organized under the provisions of Section 25(a) of the Federal Reserve Act, as amended, that is directly or indirectly a creditor of the obligor; or (6) the acquisition, ownership, acceptance, or negotiation of any drafts, bills of exchange, acceptances, or obligations that fall within the classification of self-liquidating paper.

The use of the subordinated debenture issue raises special problems for a bank that is also a creditor of the issuer. In addition to prior funded indebtedness, these issues are usually made subordinate to all existing bank indebtedness and all future bank indebtedness up to specified amounts.

What is the status of a trustee bank that is or becomes the holder of preferred indebtedness to which the debentures issued under the indenture are specifically subordinated? The intent is clear, but an ambiguity is created by the provisions of TIA Section 311, unless there is specifically excepted from its operation the preferred indebtedness to which the debentures are subordinate. Indebtedness to the bank with a maturity in excess of one year at the time of its creation is undoubtedly exempt from this section, for a note is a "security" within the meaning of the TIA, and securities having a maturity in excess of one year are exempt from the provisions of Section 311. As to shorter term indebtedness, a court might well consider the expressed intent of the parties in making an allocation in a bankruptcy or reorganization proceeding, although there is no assurance that this would be done.

Although the SEC has not conceded that the Section is not operative, historically they have permitted the inclusion of a provision qualifying the preferential collection of claims provisions to the extent that the trustee is entitled to all of the rights (in the indenture) with respect to any senior indebtedness at any time held by it to the same extent as any other holder of senior indebtedness and that no other section of the indenture should be construed to deprive the trustee of any of its rights as such holder. Now that the TIA provisions are deemed incorporated into every qualified indenture and will no longer be set forth, trustees should specifically include such a qualifying provision in the subordination provisions.

Despite the possible inequitable treatment on a basis different from that accorded other holders of the same indebtedness, until this question has been clarified by statutory amendment or judicial decision, trustees should be well advised to assume that they will be required to account in accordance with Section 311 even though they hold an obligation that by its terms is superior to the indenture securities. If they are unwilling to continue on the basis of such an assumption, the alternative is to refuse an appointment as trustee under a subordinated indenture.

THE TRUSTEE'S ROLE IN RULE 144A PRIVATE PLACEMENT TRANSACTIONS

As noted in chapter 1, the growth in Rule 144A issues since 1992 has been steady, and has assumed a useful and established part of the securities markets. For corporate trustees, this has presented an opportunity to provide services even though the TIA does not apply to such issues. In particular such services would include: record keeping, collateral custody and investments, interest and principal payments, covenant monitoring and post default administration.

The technical features of Rule 144A issues as they impact the corporate trustee can be summarized as follows:

1. Purchasers of Rule 144A securities must be eligible as Qualified Institutional Buyers (QIB's). These include banks, brokers and private institutions meeting certain capital requirements;

2. Transfers of Rule 144A securities will be monitored by the trustee to ensure that the transferee is a QIB. Many trustees require that a purchaser which may not be a well-known institution provide a simple certification that it meets the rule requirements as a QIB. It is recommended that Trustees for Rule 144A issues have operational procedures in place to monitor the QIB requirements in order to avoid any potential liability issues.

3. Rule 144A securities can be traded at any time, and are exempt from the two year trading restriction applied to other, non-qualified private placements.

4. No unusual duties for a trustee are present simply because the private placement issue is qualified under Rule 144A. It is however incumbent on the trustee to be especially mindful of any monitoring responsibilities imposed on it by the institutional holders in the financing documents.

LITIGATION AND DISCOVERY

Although it is not within the scope of this book to cover litigation in any detail, it is important for corporate trust professionals to appreciate that they work in an environment fraught with litigation risk. This risk is due, in large measure, to the fact that when an obligor is unable to redeem its debt obligations, security holders will seek to recover on their loan from as many participants in the financing as possible. The list of potential defendants includes the obligor's underwriter, financial advisor, law firm, and accounting firm, as well as bond counsel, the corporate trustee and its counsel and agents.

The bank acting as the corporate trustee for a defaulted bond issue is an attractive target for law suits. This results from the nature of the trustee's duties and responsibilities in a post default situation. The trustee's performance (i.e. both its actions and its non-actions) will be measured, in hindsight, against three "standards": (1) the provisions of the indenture covering the trustee's post default duties and responsibilities; (2) the custom and practice in the corporate trust industry in similar defaults; and (3) when applicable - the "prudent man" rule, which may result in very different opinions by attorneys, experts, and ultimately judges and juries. In addition, the trustee's pre-default performance, and even its activities leading up to the date it legally becomes the trustee may be subject to examination and review by plaintiffs against both the trustee's policies and procedures, as well as custom and practice in the corporate trust industry.

From the trustee's perspective, it is unfortunate but the better its records are, the more thorough and complete are its written policies and procedures, the more requirements it has to create paper trails and document audit concerns, the easier it is for plaintiffs to measure actual performance against a standard of care that may not have been adhered to completely. Much of this information is obtained through a litigation process, known as *discovery,* which includes the deposition testimony of the trustee's employees and managers. The discovery process often elicits information which results in plaintiffs either propounding new allegations of negligence or breach of fiduciary duty, or supporting allegations set forth in the original complaint.

While it is not feasible to address all of the concerns of which trustees should be aware, the following are among the most important:

    1. Account Acceptance. Make sure the bank's

policies specifically authorize designated "positions" to accept a new trusteeship; and that no departmental document indicates any exception to this policy. Under the Comptroller of the Currency's Regulation 9, all fiduciary accounts must be accepted by the Bank's Board of Directors.[25] It is therefor essential that the corporate trust department have a process in place whereby the minutes of the Corporate Trust Committee (or similar committee) are reviewed and approved, in writing, by a committee of the board, or other entity specifically authorized by the board to accept fiduciary business.

2. Document Review. In connection with a new appointment, the trustee should read only those documents that relate to the trustee's duties and responsibilities. Trustee's counsel, however, should read every document related to the financing, and advise the trustee as to the impact or implication of any relevant statute or regulation. From the trustee's perspective, its duties and obligations should be limited to those contained in either the indenture or other specifically identified document. It is essential that the trustee completely understands all the words, phrases and terms of the proposed indenture or associated document. One should not accept a term or phrase on the basis of: "don't worry, it doesn't apply to you", or "it will never happen" or "it's required by some law or regulation".

3. Pre-Closing Activities. Ensure that care is exercised in the level of involvement in the financing transaction prior to the closing. An overly active role will create the risk that the trustee will be treated as a substantial participant in the offer and sale of the securities.[26] Chapter 4 has more to say about the trustee's reliance on information in the preliminary and final offering statements.

4. Conclusive Reliance. This is one of the most important trustee protection provisions in the indenture, with the language of the TIA version being the preferred one to use. It should be remembered that the negligence standard requires the trustee to examine each certificate or written opinion to ensure that: (a) it is responsive to the requirements of the specific indenture provision, or other document; (2) that it is understandable and unqualified in any way; and (3) that it is signed by an authorized person. It should also be understood that the attendant good faith requirement means that the trustee does not have actual knowledge that contradicts the information in the particular certificate or opinion.

5. File Documents. Keep only those documents and papers which are essential to the acceptance and administration of the account. All the trustee's files are subject to discovery in litigation, even handwritten notes which may be in the document files. This includes the minutes of trust committee meetings, which should be drafted accordingly, as well as the reports of any internal audits and responses thereto.

6. Counsel Fees. Subject to the bank's own requirements, the trustee should agree on the parameters of any engagement with counsel, including the basis for its billing (e.g. fee/hour). It is important to get periodic bills including the backup data to support all billed hours. This is essential if the bank expects to seek recovery of its ongoing legal expenses in a bankruptcy proceeding or other litigation. If additional counsel is required, particularly from another jurisdiction, the trustee should ensure that is has written justification for such retention in its files, with the same fee monitoring process in place.

7. **Fees.** Ensure that your fee letter (or fee schedule) is explicit as to the fees for each service or activity. All contemplated services or operational activities, as well as provisions for reimbursement of out-of-pocket expenses, should be covered. If the bank is to receive the value of any float on balances, this should be noted in your letter or schedule. Also make sure that you retain sufficient data to support your bills and reimbursable expenses.

---

[1] Not entirely whimsically, the corporate indenture has been defined as ``the crystallized fears of five generations of lawyers.''

[2] See SEC, *Report on the Study and Investigation of the Work, Activities, Personnel and Functions of Protective and Reorganization Committees*, Part VI (1936).

[3] TIA, sec. 310 (a)(1).

[4] TIA, sec. 310 (a)(5).

[5] Many major corporate issuers insist on a potential trustee bank's having at least $25/50 million of combined capital and surplus.

[6] Even if the issue is exempt from the TIA, this does not necessarily mean that the trustee is exculpated from adherence to conduct that would be prohibited if the issue were qualified.

[7] TIA, sec. 303(12).

[8] The SEC has indicated that "it is now our view that the term "director" as defined in Section 303(5) of the (Trust Indenture) Act would not include emeritus, honorary or advisory directors who are appointed rather than elected and who serve merely as advisors without any other customary responsibilities or duties, including the right to vote, of directors." SEC letter, dated June 22, 1981, to James D. McLaughlin Government Relations Counsel, American Bankers Association.

[9] Riegle-Neal Interstate Banking and Branching Efficiency Act of 1994 (P.L. 103-328)

[10] Interpretative Letter No. 695, December 8, 1995 addressed to Banc One Corporation.

[11] TIA, sec. 315(d).

[12] Cronin v. Midwestern Oklahoma Development Authority, 619 F.2d 856 (10th Cir. 1980); Nelson v. Quimby Island Reclamation District Facilities Corporation, 491 F. Supp. 1364 (N.D. Cal. 1980).

[13] Matthew's v. Fischer, 1979-80 Fed. Sec. L. Rptr. para 97,336 (S.D. Ohio 1978); Woods v. Holmes & Structures of Pittsburgh, Kansas, 489 F. Supp. 1270 (Kan. 1980).

[14] It is the board of directors which is ultimately responsible for the proper exercise of fiduciary powers by every national bank. All matters pertinent thereto, including the determination of policies, the investment and disposition of property held in a fiduciary capacity, and the direction and review of all officers, employees, and committees utilized by the bank in the exercise of its fiduciary powers, are the responsibility of the board. See 12 CFR sec. 9.7(a)(1) (1989).

[15] TIA, sec. 315(a).

[16] See generally, Schreiber and Wood, Caveat Indenture Trustees: Avoiding the Expanding Scope of Sutton's Law, 121/1 *Trusts and Estate* 48 (Jan. 1982).

[17] When the TIA was initially introduced in the Senate, it required inclusion of a provision in every qualified indenture that the trustee had to discharge its pre-default duties and obligations in a manner consistent with that which a "prudent man" would assume and perform [S.2065, 76th Cong., 1st Sess., sec. 315(a) (1939)]. The version of the Act introduced in the House of Representatives excluded the imposition of a pre-default "prudent man" duty on the trustee [H.R. 5220, 76th Cong., 1st Sess., sec. 315 (1939)], which was ultimately the version enacted as Section 315(c).

[18] Dabney v. Chase National Bank, 196 F.2d 668 (2d Cir. 1952), *appeal dismissed*, 346 U.S. 863 (1953), Van Gemert v. Boeing Co., 520 F.2d 1373 (2d Cir. 1975), *cert. denied*, 423 U.S. 947 (1975).

[19] Meckel v. Continental Resources Co., 758 F.2d 811 (2d Cir. 1985), Elliott Associates v. J. Henry Schroder Bank & Trust Co., 838 F.2d 66 (2d Cir. 1988). In Lorenz v. CSX, 736 F. Supp. 650 (W.D.Pa 1990), involving a non-TIA indenture, the court reached the same conclusion.

[20] 758 F.2d at 816.

[21] 838 F.2d at 71.

[22] TIA, sec. 326

[23] See, e.g., United States Trust Company v. First Nat'l City Bank, 410 N.Y.S.2d 580(1980)(holding that the TIA does not abrogate an indenture trustee's common-law, pre-default, fiduciary duty of loyalty). For an excellent discussion of the complexity and confusion that courts have demonstrated in this area, see *In re* E.F. Hutton Southwest Properties II, Ltd., 953 F2d 963 (5th Cir. 1992).

[24] TIA, sec. 310(b)(4)(C).

[25] 12 CFR 9.4(a) *(revised* Jan. 29, 1997)

[26] See generally, Robert P. Varian, The Demise of the Aider-And-Abettor Liability Under Rule 10b-5: The Implications for Banks and Trust Companies, 112 *Banking L.J.* 246 (March 1995)

FOUR

MUNICIPAL TRUSTS

During the past decade a major portion of tax-exempt financing has continued to be in the form of revenue bond issues. In such instances, it has become customary to appoint a bank as trustee pursuant to a bond resolution of a municipal authority. Often, trustees in close geographical proximity to the financed project are given the opportunity to bid for the trustee appointment. The growth in local trustee bidding opportunities has resulted in local and regional banks growing their corporate trust businesses. In Part II, we will explore how the expansion of the business during the past two decades has resulted in increasing numbers of corporate trust acquisitions and divestitures. Larger corporate trustees have placed increased focus on tax exempt financing appointments.

Three of the more common types of tax exempt financing have been for the construction of hospitals, educational facilities (including dormitories), and single and multi-family housing units. In addition, issues of industrial revenue bonds have been used for multiple purposes under legislation permitting the use of the tax-exempt bonds to build or modernize plant facilities of private corporations.

As with any document related to the particular financing, the trustee should carefully examine, in conjunction with its counsel, the relevant bond resolution, the opinion of bond counsel, and the bond purchase agreement. Even though it is not a document that the trustee needs to read, the preliminary official statement can be useful in gaining an understanding of the business intent of the financing, and in understanding the general cash flow of the financing. The governing indenture or resolution must always serve as the source document for administering the trust. The trustee or agent is not a party to and should not rely on the preliminary or official statement in administering the trustee duties. From time to time there will be areas of conflict between official statements and the governing indenture or resolution.

In addition to the trustee appointment, the trustee is generally appointed as paying agent. As the result of TEFRA,[1] the trustee may also be appointed as registrar. This last appointment entails the traditional registration of transfer services and the accounting for and, where physical certificates have been issued, the destruction of canceled certificates.

The traditional long-term, fixed rate, semiannual interest payment transaction consisting of serial maturities and term bonds, once referred to as a *plain vanilla deal*, gradually changed shape during the 1980s, soon after trustees and paying agents managed to enhance system capabilities to service the addition of capital accumulator or zero coupon bonds. Fixed rate transactions rapidly became a vehicle of the past as variable rate securities, with demand features, grew in popularity. With the enactment of the Tax Reform Act of 1986 (86 Act),[2] restrictions were placed on municipal debt issuers, including (among other things): restrictions on the amount of tax-exempt debt that any tax-exempt organization[3] could have outstanding at any one time; the introduction of state volume caps for "private activity bonds"; requirements for issuers to perform complex arbitrage rebate calculations; and restrictions on the percentage of gross proceeds allowed to be applied to the costs of securities issuance.

During the 1990s, municipal revenue bonds began to closely resemble securities generally associated with the corporate sector. Multi-modal, variable rate, variable term, variable interest and principal payment instruments (similar to commercial paper), medium term notes (MTN's), and even taxable municipals emerged. The proliferation of changes placed extraordinary demands on software providers while also demanding increased use of the personal computer at the corporate trust administrative officer's desk.

MUNICIPAL POOL FINANCING

The basic objective of any borrowing entity is to raise funds at the lowest possible cost. Three key factors in achieving this objective for issuers of tax exempt or taxable debt securities are: (1) to obtain the most favorable interest rate possible, (2) to structure the financing to appeal to a wide market and (3) to limit the costs associated with the actual issuance of the securities. One way of lowering the cost of borrowing is for entities to apply for a loan from a state, county, or city tax-exempt bond issuing authority, such as a state bond bank. The proceeds from the sale of bonds by the issuing authority are loaned to the entity at a more favorable tax-exempt rate than if it had borrowed in its own name. Loan repayments, as provided for in the loan agreement between the issuer and the borrowing entity, are deposited in a bond fund established in accordance with the trust indenture and used to pay the debt service on the bonds.

Smaller entities making application to the issuing authority could be at somewhat of a disadvantage as the interest rate it could obtain may not be as favorable as a larger issuing entity. The cost of issuance charges could at times actually be prohibitive for a smaller issuer. Additionally, market interest in purchasing the securities could be relatively limited, if for no other reason than little may be known about the issuer.

A financial structure designed to address the needs of both the smaller and larger borrowing entities is the *loan pool vehicle* in which proceeds from the same pool of bonds are lent to multiple similar entities with comparable financing needs. A group of hospitals or school districts are examples. Each issuer obtains approval for a loan by the issuing authority, then draws (borrows) against the pool of funds. The costs of issuance are distributed pro rata among the borrowing entities and a more favorable rate is generally obtained.

The 86 Act eliminated "blind pools." In many cases, a large percentage of the proceeds from the bond pool issuance were not lent, resulting in early calls for redemption of the bonds and arbitrage on the bond proceeds. Under the 1986 regulations, the issuing authority must have a reasonable expectation that a major percentage of the proceeds will be expended (lent) within a specific time frame. Consequently, the issuing authority must obtain firm commitments from the issuers wishing to borrow funds from a specific pool before the bonds may be issued.

Pool financing transactions place additional accounting and recordkeeping responsibilities on the trustee. Many trustees developed computerized sub accounting and management-reporting vehicles to meet the demands of the bond pool financing. In addition to the routine accounting functions involving the custody of collateral and the maintenance of funds established in accordance with the indenture, the trustee must also provide a loan administration and accounting function. Each borrowing entity's loan must be administered and accounted for separately. The loan repayments are collected from each entity and the aggregate funds are then transferred to the appropriate debt service accounts. Currently, twenty-two states have legislation authorizing bond banks, some of the more active ones are Maine, New Hampshire, Vermont and Indiana.

ANTICIPATION NOTES

In chapter 1, we examined the problems corporations encounter in financing the short-term working capital needs of corporations. Municipalities face similar cash flow challenges. Although operating expenses must be paid throughout the year, major income items such as property taxes are often collected at stated intervals during the year. Through the issuance of tax anticipation notes (TANs) and other types of revenue anticipation notes, the municipality is able to finance working capital during periods of cash flow shortfall. Generally, if the anticipation note is not outstanding for more than thirteen months and the principal amount of obligations issued is less than the anticipated maximum cumulative cash flow deficit,[4] the issuer is permitted to invest all the proceeds of the TAN sale at an unrestricted yield.

Anticipation notes are issued in accordance with a resolution generally requiring the services of a paying agent, since a trustee appointment is not typically utilized. As discussed later, the benefits of pool financing combined with unrestricted yield from the investment of the proceeds of anticipation notes, among other things, have resulted in programs that may require the services of an indenture trustee.

MASTER TRUSTEE

Another way of pooling like entities to borrow to meet capital needs is through the formation of an obligated group. There is no requirement that the members of such a group be affiliated entities; however, for practical reasons this is usually the case. Health institutions, with multiple facilities, are the predominant users of this type of structure. Individual entities become members of the group (i.e., obligated issuers) by executing a note issued in accordance with a master trust indenture. By executing the note, each obligated issuer agrees that it will duly and punctually pay the principal, interest, and any applicable premium in accordance with its terms. Additionally, each obligated issuer jointly and severally guarantees and promises to pay any and all amounts payable under any note issued in accordance with the master trust indenture.

The master trustee is responsible for performing the note registrar function, enforcing the covenants of the master indenture, and, in some instances, collecting the principal and interest payments on the notes. Master notes are frequently issued in conjunction with one or more revenue bond transactions. The master notes are then registered to the issuer of the revenue bonds in the same aggregate principal amount as the bonds issued under the indenture. All the right, title, and interest of the issuer in the master notes is then placed and assigned by the issuer to the bond trustee. If there is more than one related revenue bond financing, the same procedure applies to each of the issuers and bond trustees. The payments by the obligated issuers in accordance with the provisions of the master note are then made directly to the bond trustee or trustees to provide for debt service. Because the master trustee must take prompt action in the event of default, it is of utmost importance that it establishes procedures with the related trustees to ensure that it receives prompt notification of a default on any note payment. Because there is a potential for conflict between the role of the bond trustee and that of the master indenture trustee, the same entity generally should not act in both capacities.

ADVANCE FUNDING PROGRAM NOTES

Tax-exempt issuing authorities also pool similar borrowing entities through the issuance of advance funding program notes. The proceeds from the sale of the program notes are advanced to participating entities to resolve cash flow deficiencies in the current fiscal year. Entities participating in the program issue TANs that are purchased by the issuer. Each participating entity pledges to the issuing authority a security interest in all revenues derived by it from taxes and other revenues, by executing an advance-refunding agreement. The program notes issued through the authority must comply with the anticipation note regulations (referred to previously) in order for the proceeds to be treated as invested during a temporary period in accordance with the Internal Revenue Code.[5] The repayments by the participating entities of the tax and revenue anticipation notes plus the interest earnings on any funds held in accordance with the trust indenture are transferred to the debt service fund to provide for the payment of the principal and interest on the program notes as they become due.

As with other types of pooled arrangements, the trustee may be required to perform loan administration and loan accounting functions in addition to its duties as indenture trustee, registrar, and paying agent.

VARIABLE RATE SECURITIES

Since the early 1980s, different forms of this type of security have been popular investment vehicles in the tax-exempt market. They are designed to approximate interest-rate changes to keep the value of the security at or as close to par as possible. The earliest issues paid an interest rate based on a percentage of an established index, often tied to a particular bank's prime lending rate. These issues were typically private placements.

The next development involved bonds that allowed bondholders to tender their bonds back to the issuer at par through a "put" or "demand" feature. The benefit to the issuer was that it only had to pay a short term interest rate (largely based on the time period between tenders) instead of the usual long term rate based on the maturity of the bonds. The spread between the short term variable rate and the long term fixed rate results in savings to the issuer, which can be offset by the fees of the various agents required to run the program. Cleary, the greater the spread between short term and long term rates in the credit markets, the more likely is the issuance of variable rate securities.

Securities with a "put" or "demand" feature will typically involve a remarketing agent, a liquidity facility provider, and a tender agent. The *remarketing agent*, usually an investment bank, is responsible for setting new interest rates, for remarketing or reselling any securities that are tendered, and for providing the new registration information and remarketing proceeds to the tender agent. Except in unusual circumstances, the remarketing agent is usually successful in selling the tendered securities to new investors.

The *liquidity facility* can be provided in various forms, including letters of credit (L/C's), insurance, or standby purchase agreements. Letters of credit are the most popular liquidity vehicles. Letter of credit banks in effect guarantee that in the event of failure by the remarketing agent's failure to remarket the securities, the L/C bank will step in and purchase the securities. This "guarantee" of liquidity on a tendered security helps to keep the interest rate low. Note that the rating of the securities is usually the same as the rating of the liquidity facility provider. The "guarantee" is only as strong as the ability of the liquidity facility provider to make payments if called upon to do so.

The *tender agent* receives notices of tender from security holders; notifies the remarketing agent, liquidity facility provider, issuer and trustee of receipt of the notice and the securities being tendered; pays the tendering holders with the appropriate funds; and in a co-registrar capacity, reissues new securities to the new purchaser. The tender agent functions may also be performed by the trustee.

Tender bonds come in two types. The first is a *put bond*, which the bondholder can tender only during certain preset times, usually between fifteen to thirty days prior to the payment date. Semiannual and annual tender bonds are the most common examples. In some security issues, the "put" option is only permitted to operate in designated years.

The other type of tender bond is the *demand bond*, whereby the bondholder can demand payment at any time upon giving the appropriate notice. These are often called v*ariable rate demand bonds* (VRDBs), of which weekly demand bonds are the most popular. Others include daily and monthly demand bonds. A weekly VRDB is structured with an interest rate that is reset each week by the remarketing agent at a rate that will allow the bonds to be remarketed at par. This ability to reset the rate helps the remarketing agent resell bonds that are tendered.

Commercial paper mode bonds are a hybrid of the two types of tender bonds. During their existence in a commercial paper mode, bonds can be issued with maturities ranging anywhere from 1 to 270 days, as in typical commercial paper programs. An issuer benefits with commercial paper mode securities by gaining the flexibility to use shorter or longer mandatory "tender" dates. These dates would be determined during remarketings based on buyer demand and current or anticipated changes in the interest rate. An interesting feature of most variable rate securities is the ability to convert from one rate mode to another. For example, a weekly mode security can be converted to a fixed rate mode or a daily rate mode. Some issues allow for only a single conversion, to a fixed rate, but most provide the flexibility to change into any one of several different modes. This change in modes is accomplished through a mandatory tender. When a security issue is offered, there may be portions of the issue in different modes at the same time. The issue is designated a *multi-modal structure instrument*.

A typical tender by a holder occurs as follows. Security holders choosing to tender their bonds provide the tender agent or trustee with a notice or demand. This notice which is usually available from the trustee, states the holder's irrevocable intention to tender a specific principal amount of bonds for settlement on a specific date. This notice usually includes the numbers of the securities being tendered. The tender agent or the trustee then notifies the remarketing agent, liquidity facility provider and the issuer of the receipt of the notice. At this point, the remarketing agent looks for a new buyer of the securities. If successful in selling the securities, the proceeds are forwarded to the tender agent or trustee to pay the tendering holder upon presentation of the securities. In the case of an unsuccessful remarketing, the tender agent or trustee will draw upon the liquidity facility provider to pay for the tendered securities. New securities are then registered in the new buyer's or the liquidity facility provider's name, whichever is appropriate. Variable rate security tenders must be carefully planned and orchestrated by all parties to the transaction. Failure to process a tender timely can result in trustee and/or agent operating losses. Preparation of notices, remarketing the securities and arranging for the liquidity draw are usually timed to occur within short periods of time. To ensure the transaction is processed accurately and timely, the trustee and its counsel must closely review the timing, administrative and operational requirements during the initial governing document preparation and review.

[1] See note 7, chapter 2, *supra*.

[2] Pub. Law 99-514 (1986).

[3] See Internal Revenue Code, sec. 501(c)(3) for specific types of organizations.

[4] Maximum cumulative cash flow deficit is defined as the sum of: (1) the amount the issuer will expend, from the beginning of the period to the computation date, that would ordinarily be paid out of or financed by anticipated tax or other revenues, plus (2) the amount of the anticipated expenditures for a period of one month after the computation date, minus (3) the sum of the amounts (other than the proceeds of the issue in question) that will be available for the payment of such expenditures during such period.

[5] Sec. 1.103-14(c).

FIVE

PREPARATION, EXECUTION, AND RECORDING OF INDENTURES

SELECTION OF METHOD OF FINANCING

It is the responsibility of corporate and municipal financial officers to secure the necessary funds for the expansion and operation of the corporate enterprise and governmental entity, in the amounts and at the times they are required. If these funds are not generated from operations of the business, or, in the case of a municipality through its general taxing powers, they must be obtained in the highly competitive and often volatile financial markets. Finance officers must try to secure the most favorable terms with the fewest possible restrictions placed on the obligor's freedom of action.

Of the many reasons for capital financing, the most common is providing new facilities in the form of plant and equipment for the expanded needs of the business, such as a new office building to house the executive and administrative staffs. If additional working capital is required or funds are needed for a maturity, existing indebtedness may be refunded on more favorable terms. During the 1980s and 1990s, and into the new millennium, much of the corporate debt financing was fueled by the rapid growth and widespread use of leveraged buyouts and mergers. Because capital financing is an expensive operation even for large municipalities and major corporations with a high credit rating, careful planning is required so that there will be no necessity for too frequent recourse to the capital markets.

Many companies resort to their commercial banks for interim financing, with the understanding that at periodic intervals or within an agreed period funded debt will be issued and the bank loans paid off.

Many factors enter into determination of the form and method of financing, including the purpose of the loan, the credit standing of the issuer, existing capital structure, availability of investment funds, and market conditions. Although the exact terms are determined by negotiation, the obligor's officials, usually with the assistance of qualified financial advisers, make a preliminary determination of the amount of the issue, whether it will be secured or unsecured, the approximate amount that can be repaid annually by way of a sinking fund, the restrictive provisions that will be permitted, and the final maturity date. Decision must then be made on how the issue will be marketed or distributed. Although there are a myriad of investment bankers with innovative and creative financing ideas in the financial marketplace, there are essentially three methods by which financing needs are met: negotiated transactions, public bids, and direct placements.

In a *negotiated transaction*, an investment banking firm is selected to underwrite the issue, and the substantive terms of the issue are negotiated with this firm. When this method of marketing is used, the investment bankers usually, although not necessarily, act for all issues of the particular obligor and are thoroughly familiar with the obligor's financial affairs and programs. In addition to underwriting the company's public offerings, the firm may be retained as a general financial consultant and is able to render substantial valuable collateral services to the corporate officials. The investment bankers usually participate in discussions from the earliest date; their familiarity with security markets, as well as the obligor's affairs, will enable them to tailor the issue to meet the obligor's requirements and current market conditions.

Compensation of the underwriters is provided by the "spread" between the wholesale price they pay for the entire issue and the retail price at which the securities are sold to the investors (often referred to as *underwriters' discount*). Usually the principal or lead underwriter will bring together a number of other firms (called a *syndicate*) to market the issue, with each firm being responsible for, and assuming the risk involved in, a percentage of the total issue. The amount of the underwriter's "spread" will vary, but it is calculated to provide a reasonable profit based on the work involved and the risk assumed in the particular financing.

Another method for marketing debt securities issues is through a *public invitation for bids*. Public bodies having jurisdiction over regulated industries may or may not prescribe or influence the manner in which securities are offered, but they must approve the method selected and the terms of sale. Under the method of public bidding, the issuing corporation will engage experienced independent counsel to represent the prospective purchasers of the securities, and the terms and details of the offering will be negotiated between the company and such firm, except for the price, which will be determined by the public bids. Occasionally the company will retain investment bankers as advisers who work for a fee and who will not participate in the bidding. Usually the company and counsel will know the investment houses that head the various syndicates likely to participate in the bidding, and these firms may be consulted in advance about some of the proposed terms of the issue. Since market conditions determine the price at which securities can be offered successfully, most bids are very close to one another, and competition revolves around the amount of the underwriter's commission. The use of public bids, as opposed to the negotiated method, has certain advantages and disadvantages. Some regulatory bodies feel that the obligor obtains a better price through public bids, although experts differ on this matter. This advantage can be weighed against the value placed on a continuing relationship with, and the advice received from, investment bankers in a negotiated transaction. A third method of marketing that is frequently used by more mature companies with a high credit rating is *direct placement* (i.e., private placement). Under this method the issue is not underwritten at all, but negotiations are conducted with a group of institutional investors who are the actual purchasers of the securities. The corporation usually retains an investment house or the corporate finance department of a major bank as an agent to find interested purchasers and negotiate the terms, although it may elect to do this itself. Such an issue does not have to be registered under the securities acts, and the indenture is not qualified. In some instances where the issue is unsecured only a few purchasers are involved, the terms are not complicated, and an indenture and trustee are not used. The company will execute separate but identical agreements with each purchaser, embodying all the terms of the contract.

These three methods outlined are the principal ones used in distributing debt securities, but others are sometimes used, such as offering convertible debentures, which may or may not be underwritten, to existing stockholders. Mergers, acquisitions, recapitalizations, reorganizations, and similar transactions usually involve the offering of securities to existing security holders of either the issuing or a different corporation. The corporation itself may elect to market its securities publicly without the assistance of an underwriting firm, although this practice is rare. Moreover, under SEC Rule 415 permitting shelf registrations to be filed, a corporation gains tremendous flexibility in its issuance of debt securities as well as almost instant access to the capital markets.

PREPARING THE INDENTURE

Because the indenture, when executed, becomes a contract binding on the security holders, the obligor, and the trustee, establishing the obligations and rights of the parties, and setting limitations on the rights of all, it follows that the preparation of the indenture is one of the most important steps in the whole process. It is here that the security holders stand in the greatest need of protection, and it is here that they frequently lack adequate representation. The substantive terms are established by agreement between the issuer and the underwriter, or counsel appointed to represent the underwriter. Although this process offers some protection -- for the leading investment houses feel some moral responsibility for issues they sponsor--the underwriter's primary concern is in securing terms that will make the issue readily marketable and not necessarily terms that a security holder, in retrospect, might have considered desirable.

Over the years a number of developments have substantially resolved this problem, with the result that the typical indenture is a fairly sound financial document with reasonably adequate safeguards designed to protect the investor. Among such developments are the following:

    1. The significant influence of the institutional investor. Whereas the direct placement contract is the only situation in which the investors actually negotiate the terms of an issue, the institutional purchaser is also important in publicly distributed issues, and both issuers and underwriters endeavor to style the issue and the terms of the contract so as to attract professional investors.

    2. The minimum standards set forth in the TIA. They are now applicable, as a matter of law, to every qualified indenture, and should not be written into the indenture itself. It may be helpful however to include

a TIA section reference page at the beginning of each qualified indenture.

3. The disclosure provisions of the 33 Act. Most public corporate issues of securities are required to be registered under this act, which requires full disclosure of both the history and current financial condition of the issuer and all important terms and provisions of the indenture and the securities to be issued. This information, or summary of it, is required to be set forth in a prospectus, preliminary offering statement, or offering memorandum that must be furnished to all prospective investors. Thus, the investor has available all pertinent information, necessary to make an informed investment decision. If the investor fails to use or comprehend this information (assuming it is accurate), he or she has no one else to blame.

4. The regulatory powers of the SEC and other regulatory agencies. These agencies have set certain minimum standards required in cases where they have the authority to approve or prescribe the terms and conditions of a proposed financing.

5. The patterns for typical indentures that have become established among investment houses, institutional investors, and bond counsel.

6. The influence of the more experienced corporate trustees and their counsel.

Once the essential terms of the indenture have been agreed upon, drafting it is relatively simple. An earlier indenture, frequently of the same obligor, is selected as a model. Many of the provisions remain exactly the same. Clauses not appropriate to the current transaction or that experience has shown to be troublesome are eliminated; new provisions that embody the terms of the contract are added, as are any new clauses that the evolutionary process has revealed as beneficial or desirable. Once an initial draft of the new indenture is ready, copies are distributed to all interested parties, and the document is modified until all parties are reasonably satisfied.

THE TRUSTEE'S FUNCTION

At some point, the corporate trustee must be selected, usually by the issuer itself but, in many instances upon the advice and recommendation of its investment banker, underwriter, or attorneys. This should be done at the earliest possible moment, for the trustee can make important contributions to the process of finalizing the terms of the indenture. Although it has no responsibility for the substantive provisions of the contract and, under normal circumstances, should never undertake to alter the terms of the basic contract, it is the party that will have to administer the agreement for the life of the debt securities issued and so should be allowed to participate fully in all discussions relative to translating the contract into indenture language.

Given the importance of all phases of the indenture preparation process, the trustee should always be represented by experienced legal counsel and should work closely with such counsel until the indenture has been executed and the initial bonds delivered. Although some corporate trustees follow the practice of relinquishing to counsel the conduct of all matters during this preliminary process, this is inadvisable. A number of business and operational, as well as legal, considerations are involved, and the trustee cannot delegate, nor should it permit counsel to usurp, the trustee's responsibility for making decisions. The corporate trustee, however, should consult with counsel on all legal questions.

It would be difficult to describe the exact procedure the trustee should follow in its examination and review of the terms of the proposed indenture, but the following are some of the general principles:

1. Since the recitals constitute no part of the substantive contract and the trustee has no responsibility for them, there is a tendency to skip over these clauses. It is important, however, that the due authorization by the obligor of all acts relating to creation of the indenture, issuance of the securities, and mortgaging or pledging of property be stated. Whereas appropriate evidence of such authorization should be obtained and examined, the recitals may constitute an estoppel against the obligor if it should subsequently claim lack of proper authorization.

2. The form of bond as set forth in the indenture should be examined closely. Since the bonds, when executed, become separate instruments and constitute separate contracts and obligations running directly to the holders thereof, the bond form should contain specific reference to the indenture and should also set forth in sufficient detail any provision of the indenture that modifies or affects the obligation contained in the bond or imposes any limitations upon the rights of the holder. In any suit by a bondholder, if the provisions of the indenture conflict with the provisions of the bond itself, the provisions of the bond are controlling.

3. The adequacy of the granting clauses to convey the property and create the lien (or "perfect" the security interest) intended is a legal matter and should be a concern primarily for counsel. The trustee should secure appropriate legal opinions covering these points. A detailed examination of the property descriptions would serve no purpose, for the trustee usually has nothing against which to check or compare such descriptions and must rely on the obligor and its counsel, although the use of a title

company can be helpful. The trustee should make sure, however, that it is qualified to hold property as mortgagee in the various jurisdictions in which the property is located. If there is any question, a qualified co-trustee might be appointed. When the ownership of franchises, rights, or permits is essential to the obligor's business, the trustee should make certain that these are included with the mortgaged property. The same care should be taken with regard to any important leases, easements, contracts, rights of way, etc., the purpose being to ensure that the lien covers the obligor's property as a "going concern." If any important franchises, leases, contracts, etc. expire before the maturity date of the securities to be issued, any renewal privileges or the securing of alternative rights should be investigated to avoid the possibility of a substantial diminution of security or of a default. If an after-acquired property clause is included, the trustee should ensure that it expresses clearly the intent as to what subsequently acquired property is to be covered. If any property is to be assigned or pledged, proper record should be made so that an executed assignment or physical delivery of such property is obtained at the closing. If any part of such property is in the possession of another trustee, proper notification should be given to the other trustee and a tickler record prepared to obtain possession of such property on satisfaction of the other lien. If any leasehold estate is mortgaged, the last day of the term of each such lease should be specifically excluded. This avoids the creation for the trustee of an estate identical with that of the obligor-lessee, and the possibility of a claim that the trustee is liable for performance of the lessee's obligations under the lease. Finally, consideration should be given to the possible applicability of any special laws or regulations in the jurisdictions in which the property is located, or the mortgage contract executed and delivered, or where a financing statement is to be filed.

4. Although the trustee has no responsibility for the substantive provisions of the contract or for the covenants that may be included, it should review these provisions carefully to make certain that they are clear and unambiguous and adequately set forth the intent of the parties.

5. The trustee should examine carefully the evidence it is to receive of compliance by the obligor with the various indenture covenants to ensure its adequacy. Note that section 314(a)(4) of the TIA requires the obligor to furnish the trustee annually, a certificate "from the principal executive officer, principal financial officer or principal accounting officer as to his or her knowledge of such obligor's compliance with all conditions and covenants under the indenture" (i.e., a "no-default" certificate). This should be in addition to specific evidence on the more important covenants. Although municipal indentures are not qualified under the TIA, it is wise to request a similar annual certificate from a principal municipal official.

6. It is the obligor's and not the trustee's responsibility to see that an indenture to be qualified does not contain provisions contrary to the TIA. A diligent trustee, however, will carefully review the indenture language and advise the obligor (or its counsel) of any inconsistent language.

7. The trustee has a particular responsibility for the operational provisions that relate to the servicing of the indenture securities. It should verify that they are workable and not in conflict with its established

practices and procedures as well as applicable state law (e.g., escheatment). The greatest degree of flexibility consistent with clarity should be retained. Whenever possible the manner in which a particular operation is to be conducted should be left to the discretion of the trustee rather than set forth in detail. This permits a change in procedure to conform to evolving and more efficient methods and system developments and is not only proper but also desirable so long as substantive rights are not affected.

8. Particular attention should be given to the remedial provisions and to the trustee article. The rights, powers, duties, and responsibilities of the trustee, and any limitation on its rights and powers, will be governed by the general provisions of these articles. The trustee should ascertain that it has all requisite power and authority to carry out its duties. It should also make sure that appropriate exculpatory and protective provisions are included, for the potential liability is substantial.

9. Finally, after appropriate attention has been given to each separate section, the contract should be considered as an entity. It is important that the various provisions and covenants be consistent, for the indenture must be considered and construed as a single document. The trustee should have a clear understanding of the essential purpose and intent of the transaction and the provisions of the indenture, considered together, should clearly express and carry out this purpose and intent.

THE REGISTRATION STATEMENT AND QUALIFICATION OF THE INDENTURE

Issuing securities is not only a delicate marketing operation but also a matter of careful planning and timing. The many different transactions that together constitute a unified operation must be initiated at the appropriate time so that everything will be completed on the date set for delivery of the securities. Time is usually of the essence, and the customary procedure is to select a date for sale of the securities and to relate all other activities to this date.

When securities are to be distributed publicly, they must be registered under the 33 Act. Unless the issuer has filed an SEC Rule 415 shelf registration,[1] it can take several weeks for a registration to be cleared and to become effective. A copy of the indenture must be filed as an exhibit to the registration statement, and the indenture should be in as complete and final form as possible in order to minimize the number of amendments that have to be filed.

The contents of the registration statement and the prospectus are the responsibility of the obligor and not the trustee. It is advisable for the latter to review copies of these documents, however, to ensure that no information is disclosed therein that might affect its rights or obligations or that might be contrary to its understanding of the transaction. In particular, the sections summarizing indenture provisions should be carefully reviewed. The trustee must exercise caution during the review of these documents to make sure it is not deemed to be participating in the offering of the securities.

The TIA requires any information and documents that the Commission may prescribe to be filed with each registration statement, to enable it to determine whether any person designated to act as trustee is eligible and qualified. The SEC has prescribed the form in which this information is to be furnished. Form T-1 is required for domestic institutional trustees, Form T-2 for individual trustees, and T-6 for foreign trustees. Form T-1 requires the filing, among other documents, of the trustee's most recent report of condition, a copy of its articles of association or incorporation, a certificate of authority to commence business, a copy of its bylaws, and the consent of the trustee that copies of reports of examination by federal, state, territorial, or district authorities may be furnished to the Commission. Forms T-1, T-2, and T-6 require information sufficient to enable the Commission to determine whether the proposed trustee is qualified to act under section 310(a) of the TIA.[2] Electronically filing the documents associated with the registration of a new corporate security issue has cut the amount of time required to receive approval from the SEC. The trustee is expected to conform to electronic filing requirements. Bond counsel often assumes the responsibility for collecting the electronic media information from all parties to the financing.

EXECUTION, DELIVERY, AND RECORDING OF THE INDENTURE

As soon as the registration statement has become effective and all other authorizations and approvals have been obtained, the indenture may be executed and the securities delivered (often referred to as the *bond closing*). The trustee should make certain that the officers or officials of the obligor who execute the indenture have been authorized to do so. The trustee is also usually requested to furnish an appropriate certificate of the authority of its officers who join in the execution of the indenture (i.e., trustee's certificate of incumbency).

The indenture customarily contains an express statement that the laws of a particular state will apply with respect to all questions that may arise in its interpretation. This is important, for the laws of different states may vary substantially in important respects. It is desirable, although not essential, that the state specified be that in which the office of the trustee is located, for its laws are the ones with which it is presumably most familiar. In the absence of an express provision the law applied is that of the state in which the contract is executed and delivered. If delivery takes place at the office of the trustee, there is no problem. If the laws that are to govern are those of another state a problem may be presented, since the trustee may not be qualified to do business in that state. More important the trustee may be barred from bringing an action in that state against the obligor if this should be necessary. If it is impossible to negotiate a change in the language of the "governing law" provision, the trustee should make every effort to have additional language inserted stating that the rights, duties, liabilities, and obligations of the trustee be governed and construed in accordance with the laws of its state of incorporation or principal place of business. The parties to the indenture must also agree that any action by the obligor against the trustee be brought in the district or state courts in the state where the trustee is located, and that the parties consent to such forum.

When the indenture is delivered, the trustee should receive documents establishing the authorization of all proceedings in connection with the indenture and the securities. Counsel should be consulted about the documents required and the form and content.

If the indenture grants a mortgage or lien on any property, one of the first steps to be taken after it has been executed is to have it recorded in all jurisdictions in which the property is located. Sometimes this is done before or simultaneously with delivery of the securities, but it is usually sufficient if done promptly thereafter. Whereas the contract is binding on the obligor when delivered, the importance of recording is to give public notice of the lien and prevent a third party from obtaining a lien prior to that of the trustee. Recording is the responsibility of counsel to the issuing corporation. If a number of jurisdictions are involved, local counsel familiar with the laws of each jurisdiction are used to ensure strict adherence to recording requirements.

If the indenture creates a security interest in real estate, including a lease or rents thereunder, and in any personal property or fixtures, the filing provisions of Article 9 of the UCC will be applicable to "perfect" the security interest in the personal property. The appropriate filing must be done even though the mortgage or supplemental mortgage creating the lien on real and personal property is properly recorded as a real estate mortgage. (If, however, the mortgage or supplement creating such lien was properly recorded as a mortgage of real property prior to the effective date of the UCC, no filing is necessary.)

If all the collateral under an indenture is in the possession of the trustee, that alone will "perfect" the security and no filing is necessary. In the usual collateral trust indenture, this consists of negotiable instruments or securities such as stock and bonds.

When filing is necessary, the UCC prescribes the formal requisites for the financing statement. Most states have adopted a standard form for this purpose. Completion is merely a matter of filling in the blank spaces and having it signed by the obligor (the debtor) and the trustee (the secured party). Although the indenture itself may be filed if it meets the particular state's requirements, as a practical matter it is simpler to use the prescribed form of this purpose.

The trustee should obtain appropriate evidence of such recording and/or filing. The recorded counterparts of the indenture and/or a filing counterpart of each financing statement showing the recording or filing data are usually returned to and retained by the trustee. In addition, the obligor must furnish the trustee with a legal opinion or opinions on the sufficiency of such recording and/or filing. This requirement provides that the obligor will furnish the trustee (1) promptly after the execution and delivery of the indenture and of each indenture supplemental thereto, an opinion of counsel either stating that in the opinion of such counsel the indenture has been properly recorded and/or filed so as to make effective the lien or security interest intended to be created thereby, and reciting the details of such action, or stating that, in the opinion of such counsel, no action is necessary to make such lien or security interest effective; and (2) at least annually thereafter an opinion of counsel either stating that in the opinion of such counsel such action has been taken with respect to the recording, filing, re-recording, and refiling of the indenture and of each supplement as is necessary to maintain the lien or security interest of such indenture, and reciting the details of such action, or stating that in the opinion of such counsel no such action is necessary to maintain such lien or security interest.[3]

Although a mortgage of real property usually need not be recorded to maintain the lien, a financing statement perfecting a security interest in personal property will lapse after five years from the filing date unless a continuation statement is filed within six months prior to the expiration of the five-year period. Some governing jurisdictions have varying lengths of time before the financing statement or continuation statement expires. After the timely filing of continuation statements, the effectiveness of the original statement can be continued for successive five-year periods or such other periods as prescribed by governing jurisdictions.

The revised Article 9, which took effect on July 1, 2001, expanded the scope of the property and transactions covered as well as the rules about where to file a financing statement.

Now, filing is in the state of incorporation of the obligor, not the location of the property as previously required. One of the first actions that should be taken by the trustee after execution and delivery of the indenture is to make a complete review of the indenture provisions and establish an appropriate tickler, or diary note, record in relation to all actions that the obligor or trustee have to take in connection with administration of the indenture. These would include such things as dates on which the sinking fund is to operate, the date when certificates and opinions are required to be filed, and so on. No particular form of record is required, provided the form used is adequate to ensure that appropriate timely reminders will be brought to the attention of the administrative officers and that monitoring of uncompleted items can be followed up. Many trustees maintain automated ticklers, or diary notes, and follow up. Details of this automation are more fully described in part II.

SUPPLEMENTAL INDENTURES

In addition to the original indenture, supplemental indentures for various purposes may be executed from time to time. They may provide the terms of additional series of securities to be issued under the indenture; they may convey additional property or pledge additional security; they may modify or amend provisions of the original contract; they may impose additional restrictions on the obligor; or they may be executed for other reasons that require that the original contract be supplemented or amended.

The same care should be exercised as for the original indenture in regard to the proper authorization, execution, delivery, recording, and filing of these instruments. The trustee should also ensure that each such supplement is consistent with and is authorized, either explicitly or by necessary implication, by the original indenture.

Once the supplement has been executed and delivered, it constitutes a part of the contract and the original indenture, and all supplemental indentures must be read together to determine the rights, duties, and obligations of the parties.

Since the effect of many provisions in the TIRA is to relax restrictions previously imposed on the trustee, and since the act does not preclude the trustee from "agreeing" to more rigorous contractual provisions, it is wise to include in any supplemental indenture to a pre-November 15, 1990 qualified indenture, language substantially as follows: "Except to the extent specifically provided therein, no provision of this supplemental indenture or any future supplemental indenture is intended to modify, and the parties do hereby adopt and confirm, the provisions of section 318(c) of the Trust Indenture Act which amend and supersede the provisions of the [indenture] in effect prior to November 15, 1990."

---

[1] See chapter 1, note 9, *supra*.

[2] The text and instructions for Forms T-1, T-2, and T-6 are set forth in 17 CFR 269.1, 269.2, and 269.9, respectively. See also "Rules and Forms to Implement the Trust Indenture Reform Act of 1990." SEC Release Numbers 33-6892 and 39-2263 (May 8, 1991).

[3] TIA, sec. 314 (b)(1) and (2).

SIX

ISSUANCE OF INDENTURE SECURITIES

THE TRUSTEE'S RESPONSIBILITIES

Since the purpose of the indenture is to provide security for the outstanding securities and to set forth the terms and conditions upon which they can be issued, the proceedings surrounding the authentication and delivery of the indenture securities are among the trustee's most important responsibilities. The issuance of securities in uncertificated form (more commonly known as *book-entry securities*) and, as is less likely in the future, in certificated form is governed by the indenture provisions. The trustee is responsible for seeing that the necessary conditions precedent have been fulfilled.[1] When the trustee receives the documents called for by the indenture, it is entitled to rely thereon and is not required to make an independent examination of the facts certified. If it acts in good faith it will be protected even if it develops that such certificates were false. Where the requisite conditions precedent do not exist and the trustee fails to receive the requisite documents, when the documents are not in the required form, or when they disclose facts that put the trustee on notice that the requisite conditions do not exist, the trustee may be held liable by the security holders. The measure of liability has been held to be that which would be required to put the security holders in the same position as they would be if the requisite conditions existed.

All securities physically issued under the indenture must be authenticated by the trustee with original signatures. This is done by applying the trustee's signature to a certificate imprinted on each separate bond or debenture. The form of this certificate seldom varies from standard phraseology: "This bond is one of the bonds, of the series designated therein, described in the within mentioned indenture." The bond should provide that it will not become valid for any purpose until this certificate has been executed by the trustee.

The purpose of the authentication certification is to enable the trustee to control the amount of the issue outstanding and to prevent an over issuance. It ensures that the obligor corporation cannot sell bonds in excess of the amount authorized. The authentication certificate is not a guaranty nor is it an implied warranty of the sufficiency of the security or the regularity of the obligor's conduct in issuing bonds. The trustee should be careful that the certificate contains no representation, lest it be held to be under a duty to ascertain the accuracy of the facts represented. For example, a certificate stating that this is a "convertible subordinated sinking fund debenture" may be held to be a representation by the trustee. Although a diligent trustee will, to the best of its ability, ascertain that all representations made by the obligor are accurate, it is seldom in a position to check all facts, and a representation that it has done so is neither required nor advisable.[2]

THE FORM AND CONTENT OF SECURITIES

Because the trustee is authorized to authenticate only the securities provided for in the indenture, it must see that the securities do conform with the indenture provisions. The indenture provides the form and text of the securities authorized, and the trustee should carefully compare the text of the security itself with the text set forth in the indenture. Minor variations in detail are permissible, but each such variation should be noted and reviewed. To avoid possible embarrassment, the trustee should arrange to examine proofs of all securities before they are prepared in final form. As a practical matter, bank note companies that prepare these securities generally require approval by the trustee before they will prepare the final securities. Despite this preliminary check, a final examination should be made of one bond of each denomination before the securities are released, although as uncertificated bonds have increased in popularity, bonds are printed in "blank" unlimited form to accommodate all requested denominations permitted by the indenture and to assist the operational issuance of bonds.

Not only should the text be compared, but the securities must also be in the form required by the indenture. The various requirements for form are set forth in detail and will be designed to comply with stock exchange regulations for corporate securities or with general usage. The New York Stock Exchange has probably the most detailed regulations of any national exchange for the form of securities, whose purpose is to guard against duplication, alteration, or forgery. These regulations require that the border, vignette, denomination or "money" boxes, the promise-to-pay clause, and certain other standard provisions must be engraved. Variable parts of the text, including those that appear on the reverse side, may be lithographed or printed.

Municipal securities are not subject to the same strict bond form regulations since they are not listed on national exchanges. Accordingly, it is not uncommon for small municipal bond issues to be printed by local printers on pre-printed stock border paper. It has also become increasingly popular, with the advent of the personal computer, to prepare some smaller municipal bond issue bond forms on safety paper. Whether the bond forms are printed by local printers on blank border stock or on safety paper, they must still be authenticated by the trustee with an original trustee signature. Bond forms which are not printed by nationally recognized bond printers can be difficult to print by automation.

Before 1964 most corporate debt securities were issued in bearer form, for bearer bonds were the only security form that constituted a good delivery when sold. Municipal debt issues, on the other hand, were issued primarily in bearer form until July 1, 1983.[3] The indenture usually provided that the holder could have the bond registered as to principal, in which case, it could be transferred only by assignment of the registered holder. It was also customarily provided that bonds could be issued in fully registered form, without coupons, whereby both principal and interest were payable only to a registered holder. As the institutional investors became more important, a number of corporate trustees urged issuers to liberalize exchange provisions to encourage increased holding of large registered pieces by these investors. As the result of such efforts and the cooperation of the underwriters and dealers, as well as the increased awareness on the part of the investing public of the advantages, the number of corporate issues sold only in fully registered form grew steadily each year until, by the end of 1982, ninety-nine percent of the new corporate issues marketed were in such form.

The major exception to this change involved the sale of debt securities by domestic corporations to nonresident alien investors, the so-called Eurobond issues. Because of the reluctance of such investors to hold these debt obligations in registered form, almost all of these issues up until the end of the 1990s were sold in bearer form with coupons.[4]

Today Eurobonds are all in book-entry form. These bonds are not registered under the 33 Act and may not be offered or sold within the United States or to, or for the account or benefit of, U.S. persons (as defined in Regulation S under the 33 Act) except: (a) to qualified institutional buyers in reliance on the exemption from the registration requirements of the 33 Act provided by Rule 144A, (b) to persons in offshore transactions in reliance of Regulation S, (c) pursuant to an exemption for registration under the 33 Act provided by Rule 144A (if available), or (d) pursuant to an effective registration statement under the 33 Act, in each of cases (a) through (d) in accordance with any applicable securities laws of any state of the United States.

On November 15, 2007, the SEC approved major changes to Rule 144. Most significantly, the revisions will shorten the holding period for resales of restricted securities of reporting companies from one year to six months. Also, all restrictions on resale will end after one year for non-affiliates of both reporting and non-reporting companies. The rule changes will allow restricted securities to enter the public markets more quickly, thereby increasing the liquidity of privately sold securities for investors and reducing the cost to companies of raising capital through private placements.

The bonds are registered in the nominee name of Depository Trust Company or in the names of the nominees of the Common Depositories in Europe and held by the clearing systems of Euroclear and Clearstream. The bonds are initially issued as global bonds. However, some bonds in registered certificate form may still be issuable from time to time.

Also today, practically all bonds for new domestic financings, both corporate and municipal, are issued in book-entry form only.

However, the indenture still sets forth the denominations in which the securities may be issued, and no other denominations are authorized or should be authenticated by the trustee. The customary and recommended practice for corporate issues is to authorize these in $1,000 denominations and any denomination that is a multiple of $1,000. Municipal issues, however, customarily, are issued in minimum denominations of $5,000, and multiples of $5,000.

Historically, the huge volume of all registered issues, the greater use of automated equipment to process the certificates, and the ever-present storage problem, dictated the need for the use of the uniform "stock certificate size" approved by the American National Standards Institute (ANSI). As discussed earlier, the substantive provisions of the indenture or summaries of the pertinent provisions are printed on the reverse of the certificates as a continuation of the bond form. The use of certificates with preprinted denominations was very desirable, as well as "blank" or unspecified denomination certificates. In addition to the standard $1,000 denomination certificate, both $5,000 and $10,000 certificates were prepared for corporate issues in excess of $100 million. It was more common to use preprinted certificates when trustees did not have the sophisticated technology to utilize blank certificates. The inability to employ sophisticated technology often placed trustees at a disadvantage due to the added cost incurred by the obligor in printing additional denominations. However, for those bond registrars using computer-generated certificates, the use of only "blank" denominated certificates was especially attractive.

For a "good delivery" of bond certificates of issues listed on the New York Stock Exchange (NYSE), the denomination amount should be engraved in both upper corners of the face of the certificate, the bond number being printed directly below. "Blank" denomination certificates up to $100,000 are also acceptable, provided the numeric amount is macerated or "matrixed" on the certificate. Such blank certificates need only have the numeric dollar amount recorded in the upper right corner, the upper left corner being used for the bond number.

Bonds using a single global certificate may be listed on the NYSE if (a) interests therein may be transferred by book-entry on the books of DTC, and (b) the certificate is on deposit at DTC. The same requirements are also recommended[5] for unlisted corporate issues as well as municipal issues. The indenture will also specify the manner in which the bonds are to be executed by the obligor, and the trustee should see that this provision is adhered to strictly. All signatures should appear on the face of the certificate and, whenever possible, those of the obligor should be facsimile. A limited number of municipal issues require manual obligor signatures. This usually presents a processing delay as it can be difficult to locate appropriate municipal officials with an understanding of the bond issue. The trustee's authentication should, however, never be other than a manual signature. The corporate seal on the bond is usually a facsimile, but this also should be specifically authorized by the indenture.

Not only should the trustee compare the text of the bonds of each denomination with that set forth in the indenture, but each individual bond, if certificates are to be issued, should also be examined by the trustee to see that it is properly signed and sealed; that the text on both face and reverse is complete (to guard against a mechanical printing failure); that the bonds are numbered consecutively; and that the aggregate amount of bonds so executed is the amount authorized to be authenticated. Computer-generated certificates usually reprint the bond's certificate number on the certificate to verify the accuracy of data entry on the bond registration software.

The trustee is responsible for controlling the total principal amount of bonds authenticated and delivered. The records established to maintain this control should indicate each bond certificate received, authenticated, delivered, canceled, replaced for lost or stolen securities or otherwise dealt with by the trustee so that it will be in a position to certify the bonds outstanding.

UNCERTIFICATED SECURITIES

As the result of the back-office paper crisis that occurred on Wall Street in the late 1960s, several far-reaching innovations took place, the goal being to make the entire transfer process for securities more efficient. Among the most significant innovations was eliminating the use of the physical certificate as evidence of ownership in a corporation, and as evidence of indebtedness of both public and private corporations.

The U.S. Treasury was the first to eliminate paper certificates and in 1967 began the process of eliminating physical Treasury Bill securities. By 1986 all marketable U.S. Treasury obligations were in book-entry form, as are all securities issued by the Federal National Mortgage Association, the Student Loan Marketing Association, and the Federal Home Loan Mortgage Association.

By 1977 comprehensive revisions to Article 8 of the UCC were completed and promulgated, including provisions that permit the issuance of uncertificated securities and govern the legal relationships and liabilities of the parties dealing with such.

Despite these efforts over the past fifty years, the most visible real progress toward the eventual elimination of the security certificate has been the very successful development of the "immobilized clearance" system by the Depository Trust Company, which by 2006 accounted for over 90 percent of outstanding shares and public debt securities of companies listed on the New York Stock Exchange as well as practically all outstanding municipal securities. In most cases, DTC holds the physical certificates that are registered by the issuer's transfer agent/bond registrar in the name of Cede & Co., their nominee. The book-entry-only process for debt securities has been implemented, the difference between it and a pure book-entry system is that in this case one jumbo certificate is prepared and registered by the bond registrar in the name of Cede & Co. To avoid the necessity of issuing a new jumbo certificate each time securities move in or out of DTC's position, many bond registrars indicate on the certificate itself that the face amount of the certificate is "such amount as shall be shown on the securities registrar from time to time as the amount payable to Cede & Co."

The trend of the future is clearly the complete elimination of the paper certificate. The movement received reinforcement from the recommendations of the U.S. Working Committee of the Group of Thirty (an independent, nonpartisan, non-profit organization established in 1978 to address public policy issues around the world). In its August 1990 interim report, the U.S. Working Committee reached the preliminary conclusion/recommendation that "it is both desirable and achievable to eliminate the use of the physical certificate by 1995 for the settlement of securities transactions and transfers." Substantial progress was made in the 1994 Same Day Funds Task Force Recommendations to the Group of Thirty in which the following guidelines were recommended: "Effective January 1, 1995, all new issues must be made depository-eligible by meeting depository eligibility requirements and must be structured so that all payments to depositories of principal and income must be made in same day funds on payment date. Such issues can be in certificated or book-entry-only form."[6] Despite the initial slow progress, it is evident that the "certificateless society" has at last been achieved. Paper certificates may very well be found only in attics and antique shops!

DISPOSING OF BOND PROCEEDS

In the absence of express provisions in the indenture, the trustee is under no duty to see to the application of the proceeds of bonds, and the indenture will usually so provide.

There have been a few cases where courts have found an implied duty even in the face of an express provision to the contrary but these cases have all involved situations where a specific use was set forth and the facts indicated that the trustee had actual knowledge of misapplication.

Generally, when the indenture provides for bond proceeds to be applied to a specific purpose, it should require the furnishing of appropriate evidence to the trustee of such application. In such cases, the trustee should be authorized to retain possession of the bond proceeds and disburse them as required upon receipt of proper certificates. A typical example is a bond issue authorized for construction of a specific project. For a newly formed corporation that has no substantial property, or where the proposed expenditure is substantial in relation to the company's net worth, protective provisions are essential, and a trustee should not accept an appointment unless they are included. Normally, however, when all conditions for the authentication and delivery of bonds have been fulfilled, the trustee should not be concerned about the actual use of the specific proceeds.

TYPICAL PROVISIONS GOVERNING THE ISSUANCE OF BONDS

The indenture must specify the terms and conditions by which the indenture securities may be issued. The usual debenture or note agreement will provide for issuance of all authorized securities initially, so that each issue of such obligations is covered by a separate agreement or indenture. But this is not always the case, and it is proper for such an indenture to provide for the creation and issuance of additional series of obligations, provided that such obligations are of the same class. The condition for issuing additional obligations under such an agreement is the existence of no default, and if the indenture requires maintenance of specified financial ratios, such required ratios must exist after the additional obligations have been issued. As distinguished from the usual debenture or note agreement, a typical mortgage bond indenture is open ended and is designed to provide not only for the current financing but also for all future bond financing of the corporation. The reasons for this are obvious. Not only would the creation of a separate indenture for each financing be expensive, but also use of a separate mortgage indenture is the only way in which secured obligations, ranking *pari passu*, can be issued from time to time over a period of years. Because a first mortgage obligation normally commands a better price and be more readily marketable than one having a junior lien position, it is desirable to provide a vehicle under which senior securities can continue to be issued.

Such an indenture describes the provisions of the first series of bonds to be issued and stipulates the manner in which the terms and provisions of later series are to be established. This is done either by a resolution of the board of directors of the corporation or by a supplemental indenture, or usually by both, for such supplement must be approved by the board. It is recommended that a supplemental indenture always be used. Recording of the original indenture will give public notice only of the initial series of bonds. Although the lien created will probably be effective until specifically discharged, it is desirable that public notice be given of additional debt secured, particularly if the maturity date of the later series extends beyond that of the initial series. Such notice is given by the proper execution and recording of a supplemental indenture.

The indenture authorizes the initial authentication and delivery of a specified principal amount of bonds. These bonds are usually authorized to be authenticated and delivered upon request of specified officers of the corporation, without compliance by the corporation with any conditions other than execution and delivery of the indenture and the furnishing of the requisite documents and authorities to support such execution and delivery. Additional issuance can be secured only after specified conditions have been met. Bondholders contract for specific security coverage for their obligations as a condition to the extension of credit. Each additional creation of debt, ranking equally with that outstanding, will automatically deplete the security interest of each bondholder in the property existing at that time. The purpose of the detailed provisions governing the creation of additional indebtedness is to ensure that such security interest is not reduced proportionately (in regard to the aggregate value of the property) below the minimum contracted for in the indenture. This is the basic concept that the trustee should have in mind in reviewing these sections of every proposed secured indenture.

We cannot describe every purpose for which additional bonds might be authorized. The more common and customary purposes are:

1. To provide funds for the construction of property additions or to reimburse the company for expenditures made in such construction.

Property additions should always be specifically defined, but they normally include any type of property that is included in the company's fixed property accounts in accordance with accepted accounting practices. All property owned by the corporation at the date of the indenture (or frequently as of the end of the fiscal period next preceding or next succeeding such date) is regarded as "funded" and is not available for use as a basis for the issuance of additional bonds or for any other purpose under the indenture. Property acquired after such date can be so used. Under an after-acquired property clause, such property becomes subject to the lien of the indenture as acquired but remains "unfunded" until it has been used for a specific purpose under the indenture, at which time its character changes to that of being funded.

An active corporation is almost continuously adding property and retiring property that has become worn out or obsolete. For proper security to be maintained, only "net property additions" should be taken into account when considering the amount of property that can be "bonded" (i.e., used to support the issuance of additional bonds). Sometimes the computations to determine this become quite complicated, for frequently other indenture provisions and the use of property thereunder have to be taken into account. The general process, however, is to deduct from the gross amount of all unfunded property additions those additions from book value of all property retired to determine net property additions. The value at which the gross property additions may be taken into account is the lesser of the cost to the company, or the fair market value as of the date of the certification.

When the net value of property additions has been determined, it is then necessary to compute the amount of bonds that can be issued on that basis. Rarely are companies permitted to issue bonds to the full value of such property. The importance of the debt ratio has been previously mentioned, and bondholders should always insist on a reasonable margin of security. A frequent percentage found in utility mortgages, for example, is 60 percent, which means that for each $1000 of net value added to the fixed property account, a maximum of $600 of additional secured indebtedness is permitted.

    2. To retire prior lien obligations. When prior liens exist on all or any part of the property mortgaged, provisions should always be made for their retirement. Even if no such liens exist when the indenture is created, this problem should be considered, for often additional property is acquired that is subject to a lien at the time of acquisition. If such additional property is used as a basis for the issuance of bonds, the amount of the prior lien should

143

first be deducted from the bondable value of the property. It is then appropriate to permit refunding of the prior lien by the issuance of additional bonds under the indenture.

This is one of the situations in which the trustee is responsible for the proper application of bond proceeds. A common requirement is the surrender to the trustee of the prior lien obligations as a condition for the issuance of the bonds. Such is usually the case where the prior lien is only partially retired, and quite often the prior lien obligations are required to be held alive by the trustee. The desirability of such a provision is questionable, for it is unlikely that the trustee could claim a position *pari passu* with the remaining holders of prior lien obligations to the extent of such obligations held by it. A certificate of the prior lien trustee with respect to cancellation of a specified amount of prior lien obligations seems to afford the same protection as their delivery to the trustee, and an indenture provision to this effect should be acceptable.

When the prior lien is to be retired in whole, the trustee should be protected in paying over the proceeds to the prior lien trustee or to the company if it receives a duly executed and recorded counterpart of the satisfaction of the prior lien obligation.

3. Refunding of outstanding indenture securities. This is obviously a proper purpose, for it results merely in the substitution of one indenture obligation for another. When bonds are acquired by the obligor company by purchase or otherwise, their surrender to the trustee for cancellation is a sufficient basis for the authentication and delivery of an equivalent amount of bonds of another series. When a preceding series is to be redeemed in whole or in part, it is sufficient if the trustee holds, in trust, funds sufficient to effect such redemption and is authorized to take the necessary steps required. Any premium or interest

payable on the redemption must be supplied separately by the obligor. Previously issued bonds often are retired or redeemed without the concurrent issuance of additional bonds, but the obligor will wish to reserve the right to issue bonds on the basis of such retirement. This is perfectly proper, and it is unnecessary to require that such previously issued bonds be held alive in the company's treasury to preserve this right.

Bonds retired through operation of a sinking fund or similar provisions normally should not be permitted to be made the basis for the issuance of additional bonds under the indenture. This would result in an indirect depletion of the bondholders' security.

    4. Issuing bonds against deposit of cash. A common indenture provision permits the issuance of bonds against the deposit with the trustee of an equivalent amount of cash. The cash so deposited is subject to withdrawal upon the company's establishing its right to the authentication and delivery of an equivalent amount of bonds under other provisions of the indenture. Each separate bond financing is expensive. When a company contemplates a substantial expansion program or where such a program and a refunding may be under consideration, it may take down its estimated total requirements through one issue against deposit of cash with the trustee. As property additions are completed, it makes the necessary certifications to the trustee and withdraws cash in an amount equal to the principal amount of bonds it could issue on the basis of such property. The net result is the same. This was once a frequently used provision, although it is more common now for corporations to resort to interim bank financing to finance construction programs, deferring permanent bond financing until the program is substantially

completed. This practice tends to reduce interests costs. But bond financing rather than interim bank credit might be more advantageous during a period of a favorable bond market with low interest rates. One final point should be noted. If a default should occur after bonds have been issued under such a provision and before the cash is withdrawn, such cash is part of the general trust estate securing all bonds outstanding and cannot be set apart for the benefit of the holders of the specific series issued against its deposit. In the absence of express and specific provisions to the contrary, all indenture securities are on a parity in regard to their claims against the trust estate and the obligor.

EVIDENCE REQUIRED BY TRUSTEE OF COMPLIANCE WITH CONDITIONS

The indenture specifies the particular documents to be delivered to the trustee to establish the company's right to the authentication and delivery of the bonds requested. The trustee must examine all such documents carefully to see that they establish compliance with all the conditions, and it must also make sure that the documents are in the form required by the indenture. Because of the importance of these transactions, the trustee should always have such documents reviewed by counsel.

The documents received will be determined by the particular purpose for which the bonds are to be issued. Three documents should be received in all cases, however, including a resolution by the company's board of directors (or in the case of tax-exempt bonds, of the directors or governing body of the tax-exempt entity) authorizing the issuance of the bonds, describing the purpose for which they are to be issued, directing the execution of the bonds by specified officers, providing for execution and delivery of necessary documents to the trustee, and requesting authentication and delivery of the bonds by the trustee. The trustee should also receive a certificate executed by authorized officers of the company to the effect that there is no default under the indenture and that all conditions precedent to the authentication and delivery of the bonds requested have been performed. This should be accompanied by an opinion of counsel that all such conditions precedent have been fulfilled.

When authentication and delivery of bonds is on the basis of property additions, these property additions should be certified to the trustee by authorized officers in sufficient detail to permit their identification. The certification should also include an appropriate computation of the net bondable value of such property to establish the company's right to the issuance of the bonds requested. This certificate should be accompanied by a separate certificate from an engineer, appraiser, or other expert setting forth the value of the property additions. Under certain circumstances such engineer's certificate must be executed by an independent engineer or appraiser not under the obligor's control.

Frequently an earnings requirement is included as a condition. The customary form of such a condition is that for a specified period, the net earnings of the company available for interest (or the average earnings if the period is in excess of a year) must be so many times the interest charges on all indebtedness including the bonds to be issued. Compliance with this condition should be established by an accountant's certificate, which under certain conditions must be a certificate of an independent public accountant.

When property additions are made the basis for the issuance of bonds, the trustee should receive an opinion of counsel on the instruments of conveyance required to subject such property to the lien of the indenture, or assurance that no such instruments are necessary. As previously indicated, if the bonds to be issued are a new series, a supplemental indenture is desirable. A specific conveyance of the property is customarily included in the same supplement.

If the authorization of any regulatory agency or public body is required, evidence of such authorization should be secured.[7] If the bonds are to be issued publicly, registration requirements under the 33 Act must be completed, including the filing of a new Form T-1.

[1] Note the distinction between a pure "book-entry" system in which no physical securities certificates are issued and all transfers of ownership are made through entries on the issuer's books of record and an "immobilized clearance" system. In the latter case, a large portion of an outstanding issue is held in a depository facility represented by one or more jumbo certificates with record ownership changes effected by entry on the depository's books. The balance of the issue is held in certificate form by investors with certificates flowing in and out of the depository as the public's need for actual securities certificates fluctuates.

[2] For potential liability regarding additional representations, see Nelson v. Quimby, 491 F. Supp. 1371 (N.D. Cal. 1980)

[3] See chapter 2, note 7, *supra*.

[4] The sale of bearer bonds of issues sold after July 18, 1984 to off-shore investors has been affected by the repeal of the 30 percent withholding tax on interest paid. See sec. 127, Tax Reform Act of 1984, P.O. 98-369, 98 Stat. 552. To qualify for the exemption, certain procedures are prescribed by the Internal Revenue Service. See IRC sec. 163 (f)(2)(B) and IRS Regulations, sec.1.163-65(c)T.

[5] For specific recommendations on certificate format and paper quality standards, see American Bankers Association, *Recommended Certificate Standards For Registered Bond Issues, Corporate Trust Activities Committee*, (1974); American National Standards Institute, *Specifications For Fully Registered Municipal Securities*, X9.12-1983.

[6] "Implementing the G30 Recommendations", *Securities Processing Digest*, no. 25, Winter 1994.

[7] For a discussion of problems relating to public utilities bonding of nuclear generating facilities, see Corporate Trust Activities Committee, American Bankers Association, *The Bondability of Nuclear Facilities* (1977).

SEVEN

SINKING FUND AND MAINTENANCE PROVISIONS

A common type of covenant found in indentures is the sinking fund provision. This is a device for amortizing the debt, or a part thereof, over the life of the security issue. It is an important provision of the security issue and is almost always found in an unsecured debenture or note agreement. The provision is also common to bond indentures. If a security issue is created for the construction or purchase of certain fixed property or facilities, the holders' security will tend to be depleted unless the amount of the debt is reduced proportionately by the depreciation or loss in value of the property as it is used in the business. A common use for cash generated by the depreciation charge is reduction of debt incurred to purchase the property. Even though unrelated to specific property or security, a sinking fund is a convenient device for reducing corporate and municipal funded debt.

In mortgage indentures, particularly those of utility and railroad corporations - and hospital and housing related securities, a maintenance covenant is frequently included in lieu of, and sometimes in addition to, a sinking fund provision. The type of covenant referred to is not the simple maintenance covenant undertaken by the obligor to keep the mortgaged property in good working order and condition. A simple maintenance covenant should be in all mortgage indentures. A maintenance covenant is more in the nature of an undertaking to expend a stated amount of money to renew and replace the property. The theory of this covenant is that in lieu of retiring debt as the value of the property depreciates, the company will maintain the value of the security by expending an equivalent amount to construct or acquire additional property.

The operation and purpose of this covenant can be illustrated by a simple example. Let us suppose that a corporation acquires a new plant for $100 million with an estimated productive economic life of twenty-five years. For convenience we assume that the value will depreciate on a level basis, or at the rate of $4 million per year. The plant is financed with $40 million of equity money and $60 million of bonds, secured by a mortgage on the property. Clearly, for the bondholders to maintain their margin of security, $2.4 million in bonds would have to be retired each year. This would be done through a sinking fund. An alternative method would be for the company to maintain the security at $100 million, by mortgaging entirely new facilities, by additions to the existing plant, or by replacing of portions of the plant as they become old or worn out. Such an alternate undertaking would be set forth in a maintenance or a renewal and replacement covenant. The common term for the retirement and replacement of mortgaged property is *property deletions and additions*. Schedules to denote the appropriate changes are typically maintained by the trustee and obligor to substantiate the current value of the collateral underlying the outstanding securities.

SINKING FUND COVENANTS

A *sinking fund covenant* may take any of a different number of forms, and the exact terms included will result from the negotiations leading up to the issue. Some indentures do not contain a sinking fund, although investors usually insist upon the inclusion of an orderly procedure for retirement of debt. This is particularly true in the case of the unsecured debenture or note issue. It is uncommon for an agreement of this kind not to include a sinking fund. An alternate method for retirement of debt is to provide for the serial maturity of securities. Serial maturities usually are scheduled annual maturities, rather than all maturing at the same time. Serial issues are very common in state and municipal bonds. Purchasers of corporate bonds, however, prefer term bonds with a sinking fund rather than serial maturities. Consequently serial maturities are not often found in issues of industrial companies.

The trustee has substantial duties and responsibilities for the proper operation of the sinking fund. The indenture provisions should receive its careful attention during the drafting of the indenture and in connection with each sinking fund operation since, if the trustee misapplies the funds it may incur substantial liability. The trustee should review its role as the paying agent to verify the sinking fund provisions can be managed efficiently within the capabilities of the operating system and with sufficient notice to the bondholders.

Method of Computation

A sinking fund may operate annually, semiannually, or even at more frequent intervals. Because each separate operation may be quite expensive, it is not advisable to provide for an operation more often than is needed to carry out the basic purpose of the contract. There are many different ways in which computation of each sinking fund payment may be made, and there is no particular preference or advantage for one method over another. The method of computation should be the one best suited to obtain the desired result.

The most common methods are: (1) payment of a fixed dollar amount; (2) payment of an amount calculated as a percentage of the maximum amount of securities that have been at any time authenticated and outstanding; or (3) payment of an amount sufficient to retire a fixed percentage of such bonds. The last might be the preferred method in any case where a redemption premium on a declining scale is involved in any sinking fund operation, for it ensures retirement of a level rather than a variable amount of bonds.

Although most sinking funds are fixed in some definite amount or according to a specified formula, a variable sinking fund is often used. Such a sinking fund might be measured by a percentage of net earnings, either of the total company's net earnings or from a specified source. It also might also be a combination of several factors; for example, a minimum fixed sinking fund might be provided, to which is added a percentage of net earnings over a specified amount. This type might be particularly desirable for a company whose earnings tend to fluctuate substantially with cyclical changes in the economy, ensuring greater retirement of debt during financially successful years and providing some measure of protection in less successful years.

It is also common for the amount of the fixed sinking fund payment to vary from year to year, for instance retiring a smaller percentage of bonds during the earlier years and an increasing percentage during later years. This method is almost always used where the principal security is a lease or contract obligation. Level amortization payments are provided to cover both interest and sinking fund. The amount required for interest decreases with each payment, leaving a greater amount available for retirement of principal.

When several series of bonds are outstanding under the same indenture, different procedures may be followed. A separate sinking fund may be created for each series and a number of separate payments will be made, either at the same or different times. Each requires an entirely separate operation related to the securities of the particular series involved. Or a single sinking fund may be established that can be applied to the bonds of any or all series. The only change that takes place when a new series is created is that the amount of each such sinking fund is usually increased.

When a single sinking fund payment is made for bonds of different series with different interest rates and maturity dates, the trustee should apply the monies carefully and should always endeavor to see that the indenture spells out the exact procedure to be followed. The usual provision requires the retirement of bonds that, computed on the basis of the price to be paid, provide the highest yield to maturity. Such application is the most advantageous to the obligor company, results in the greatest reduction in annual fixed charges, and thus might be said to be the most beneficial to the trust estate. Whereas the usual effect is to eliminate certain series of bonds from any participation in the sinking fund and thus might be said to be unfair in this respect, it should be kept in mind that it is part of their contract, and theoretically at least, the holders of such series could have bargained for a separate sinking fund allocable to their series of bonds if they had so desired.

The trustee does have a duty to carefully review the sinking fund provisions to avoid conflicts with securities to be issued. The trustee should make certain that the indenture is clear about how the interest and premium (if any) required to be paid in connection with any sinking fund retirement are to be provided. It may be evident from the manner in which the sinking fund is computed, but if such is not the case, language should be included specifying whether the company is to provide these amounts separately or whether they are chargeable against the sinking fund.

Inasmuch as bonds can usually be retired through operation of a sinking fund without premium, or at a lower premium than for optional redemption, the obligor company has no right to increase the amount of a sinking fund or to anticipate sinking fund payments unless such right is especially reserved. If the indenture includes this reservation, there should also be no doubt about whether the obligor is entitled to a credit against subsequent sinking fund payments for any amounts so anticipated or paid beyond normal requirements.

Method of Application of Sinking Fund Monies

The trustee should ensure that the method for application of sinking fund monies is clearly set forth in the indenture and, if alternate methods are provided, that the indenture is specific as to the order in which such alternate methods are to be used or the conditions that determine selection of the particular method.

Once specific bonds have been selected for purchase or redemption by the sinking fund and all steps necessary to effect the purchase or redemption taken except the actual surrender of the bonds, the funds in the hands of the trustee cease to be general trust estate funds and become specifically allocated to the particular bond or bonds so selected. In the event of a subsequent default, the holder is entitled to payment upon surrender of his or her bond, regardless of what may be realized by other indenture security holders.

A more difficult problem is presented, however, when a default occurs before there has been any application of such monies or before all steps necessary to retire specific bonds have been taken. The problem is complicated if the sinking fund payment was made for a particular series of bonds or if the trustee has selected specific bonds for retirement but has not mailed the notice of redemption.

The law applicable to such a situation is not clear, and the trustee's action should be guided by counsel. As a general rule, all further action should be suspended, any preliminary steps that may have been taken be revoked, and the funds be retained by the trustee without application until the default has been cured or waived or until the trustee receives judicial direction on disposition of the funds. Even when only one series of bonds is involved, application of funds to retirement of specific bonds with knowledge of a default might involve participation by the trustee in an unlawful preference for which it might be held liable. Aside from the question of the trustee's liability, such an application would be obviously unfair if, as a result of the default, the remaining security holders received less than their full claim.

The obligor company is frequently given the right to receive credit against its sinking fund obligation for any bonds it surrenders to the trustee for cancellation. (This right may, in the case of a convertible debenture issue, also include the principal amount of debentures already converted.) This enables the obligor company to acquire bonds throughout the year in the open market, taking advantage of favorable market conditions, and some companies continuously satisfy their entire sinking fund obligations in this manner. The amount of the credit the company receives for bonds so surrendered may be the par value of the bonds, the actual cost of the bonds to the company not in excess of the par value, or the current sinking fund redemption price if more than par.

In the absence of a specific right of the obligor to surrender bonds against credit or in lieu of a sinking fund payment, a question arises about the trustee's right to acquire or purchase bonds held by the obligor company in its treasury in applying sinking fund monies. It is preferable to have this right specified, although such actions are a more or less accepted practice and, in the absence of an express prohibition, would seem to be entirely in order. But such acquisition should be at or below the price at which equivalent bonds could be obtained by purchase from other holders.

The trustee may be directed to apply sinking fund monies to the purchase of bonds in the open market at a price not higher than the current redemption price. If the bonds are non-callable a more or less arbitrary price is fixed by the indenture. Interest and commission paid on such purchases are usually, although not necessarily, separately reimbursed by the obligor. If not, then such amounts may be added when computing the maximum price that can be offered. A time limit is customarily set for this method of operation, and if the funds cannot be exhausted within this time, a different method must be followed for the remaining funds.

Another method of operation is for the trustee to invite tenders of bonds. This is regarded by some as a fairer method of operation, although it usually results in payment of a higher average price than would be the case in an open-market operation. When the current market price is in excess of the maximum price at which tenders can be accepted (usually the sinking fund redemption price), an invitation for tenders is essentially an idle gesture, and where the trustee has discretion about the method to be followed, this fact should be considered.

The procedure to be followed when tenders are invited is relatively simple but it still requires the exercise of care. A date is selected for the submission of tenders, with both the hour and the day specified. The invitation is then mailed in accordance with the indenture's provisions to all registered holders of securities. (If bearer bonds are outstanding the notice must be published, and copies mailed to all holders who may have filed their names with the trustee for the purpose of receiving reports and notices.) It is desirable to request submission of sealed tenders, and all other conditions should be clearly set forth in the notice. The right to reject tenders in whole or in part should always be specifically reserved. To avoid error it is recommended that some form of dual control be established for all tenders received. A record of their receipt should be kept and the tenders deposited in a locked container. If any are received unsealed, they should be examined to see that all necessary information is included and then immediately sealed and deposited. No record of prices should be made, and until the tenders have been opened and examined at the appointed time, no information should be disclosed to anyone, including the obligor company.

When the appointed hour has arrived the tenders should be opened, examined, and listed and a recapitulation made in the order of the prices at which bonds are offered. In the case of different issues with different interest rates and maturity dates, price should be computed on the basis of yield to maturity, the higher the yield the lower the price. Sufficient bonds should then be accepted at the lowest prices offered to exhaust the monies available. Mailing of notice of acceptance completes the contract.

A final method of operation is through selection of bonds for redemption through operation of the indenture's redemption provisions. Bonds are usually redeemable at par for the purpose of the sinking fund or at prices lower than would be required for an optional redemption. The particular bonds to be redeemed are selected according to the indenture. It is customary for such selection to be made by the trustee. When drafting these provisions it is desirable for the trustee to retain flexibility, and so it is better to have a provision allowing for the selection to be made in such manner as the trustee shall deem equitable, rather than have the mechanics spelled out in detail. Once the particular bonds to be redeemed have been selected, the trustee arranges to mail an appropriate notice in the manner prescribed by the indenture.[1] Once the notice has been mailed, the designated bonds become due and payable on the date specified, and the necessary funds should be segregated by the trustee and held in an account specifically allocated to their payment.

In the case of direct placements, in which all securities are held by institutional investors, it is customary to provide that in lieu of application by lot, sinking fund monies proportionate to their holdings must be allocated among the owners. Care must be exercised both in drafting and administering the provision, the objective being for each holder to retain its proportional percentage of the debt obligations as nearly as possible. Normally, bonds must be retired in even multiples of $1,000 for corporate securities and in multiples of $5,000 for municipal securities. There is a problem when the sinking fund percentage is applied to each holding resulting in an uneven multiple of the permitted denomination of $1,000 or $5,000. This seldom happens, however, and it is necessary for the trustee to devise an appropriate formula for each operation. No particular formula is required so long as the same formula is applied consistently year after year and produces the desired allocation. Although operating systems in use by most trustees and agents perform pro-rata redemptions, it is helpful to understand the processing routine they perform to complete the redemption process – the basic premise being the same or equal proportionate rate or percentage being redeemed for each holder for the particular sinking fund.

Bonds retired through the sinking fund are usually canceled by the trustee and cannot be reissued or used by the obligor as a credit under any other indenture provision.

MAINTENANCE AND REPLACEMENT COVENANTS

As we said earlier, a maintenance and replacement covenant is sometimes used in lieu of, or in addition to, a sinking fund. This is more common in the case of a regulated company, such as an electric utility, which requires a more or less continuous supply of funds for capital purposes and for which a somewhat higher debt ratio is permissible. The fund established pursuant to such a covenant is more properly a renewal and replacement than a maintenance fund. Every corporation is expected to provide funds for normal maintenance of its properties, and these constitute expenses chargeable to its income account. The fund we are considering here is a capital fund and the expenditures are normally chargeable to fixed property accounts.

There is no fixed formula by which the amount of such fund is to be computed, and it varies with the type of company involved, the nature of its properties, and other considerations. In the case of regulated companies, the regulatory authority may require application of a particular formula, or it may otherwise be determined as part of the negotiations relating to the drafting of the indenture. Ordinarily, it should be closely related to the amount of the obligor's annual depreciation charges and in any event should be designed to provide such amount as will enable the company to preserve the value of the property securing its outstanding bonds.

As an illustration, a more or less arbitrary rule of thumb was at one time applied to electric utility operating companies. As a general average, the investment of $4 in fixed plant was required to produce $1 of gross annual revenue. Also, as a general average, using those amounts for the entire property account resulting from the application of required depreciation percentages to specified classes of property indicated an annual average depreciation charge of 3.75 percent. Using these figures, a covenant to expend 15 percent of annual gross revenues from operations for maintenance and replacement purposes was frequently used in indentures of these obligors. This percentage might vary when the character of an obligor's property differed substantially from the norm. Most indentures now pattern the covenant to fit the circumstances of the particular obligor rather than to follow a preestablished percentage.

The indenture requires annually filing with the trustee of a certificate, in sufficient detail, to show compliance with the covenant. All computations should be shown, and the trustee should check them carefully against the governing indenture covenants, and also check the data included against the financial statements and other information it may receive from the obligor.

It is important to note that all property acquired by the obligor and certified to the trustee in compliance with this covenant becomes funded property and cannot be used as a basis for the issuance of bonds or for other purposes. Accordingly, the trustee should receive all the supplemental documents with respect to such property as it would receive if the property were being used as a basis for the issuance of bonds. These documents include an engineer's certificate of value, an opinion of counsel and an officers' certificate as to the company's title to the property and as to the lien of the indenture thereon, and any required instruments of specific conveyance.

As distinguished from the case of the issuance of bonds, property additions can be taken under this covenant at 100 percent rather than at the bondable percentage of their value. If any such property is subject to a prior lien, it is necessary to deduct an amount equivalent to the bondable property value of such prior lien. For example, if the bondable percentage of property additions under the indenture is 60 percent, 166 2/3 percent of any prior lien bonds are deducted in such a computation.

Usually the maintenance covenant is combined with a renewal and replacement covenant, to allow the obligor to take expenditures for normal repairs and maintenance as a credit. It is also necessary, as it is when issuing bonds, to deduct the book value of property retirements from the gross property expenditures to determine the net credit to be allowed.

One of the difficult administrative problems is dealing with property certificates under a number of different indenture provisions.[2] Although the value of a particular addition can be used only once, the value of the addition may be in excess of the amount certified for a particular purpose and the excess can be used for another purpose. Similarly, it is necessary that deduction for property retirements or prior liens be made only once. The certificates should be so drawn as to enable the trustee to check these facts.

During any year, if the obligor expends more than the required percentage for maintenance and replacement, it is normally allowed a credit for such excess against the requirement of subsequent years. This credit may be unlimited in that it can be taken at any time, or it may be required to be used within a specified time. If the latter is the case, a word of caution is necessary. For example, if the use of such a credit is limited to the three succeeding years and the company has excess expenditures for four successive years, the amount of the credit for the first of the four years is no longer available. This would seem to be obvious, except that the certificates may be so drawn as to indicate that in each year the company first uses the credit for the preceding year and that the resulting larger credit for the current year is allocable to that year and not to both years. The result may be to carry forward indefinitely a substantial credit that would otherwise have lapsed.

If the computation indicates that the company has not expended the required percentage during the year, a deficit for the year results. This deficit may be offset by the amount of any credit the company was entitled to carry forward from previous years. To the extent not so offset, the obligor must deposit cash or bonds with the trustee, which may be subsequently withdrawn against certification of property additions or on the basis of a credit shown in a subsequent maintenance certificate. If the company desires, any bonds so deposited may be canceled as a credit against the maintenance requirements. The bonds so canceled have the same status as sinking fund bonds and cannot be reissued or used as a basis for any other action under the indenture.

[1] If bonds are outstanding in bearer form, an appropriate notice must also be published.

[2] See chapter 6, note 7, *supra*.

EIGHT

RELEASE AND SUBSTITUTION OF PROPERTY

Another major segment of the indenture contract dealing with maintenance and preservation of the bondholders' security is the section dealing with the release and substitution of property. These provisions are not, of course, pertinent to the unsecured debenture or note agreement, but in almost every case in which specific property is mortgaged to or pledged with the trustee, the indenture contains detailed provisions for how the obligor should deal with its properties and prescribes conditions for the release and substitution of specific properties on which the indenture is a lien. During the early history of the corporate trust business, most provisions for release and substitution of property were contained in utility company indentures. Most of the utility indentures were served by financial center trustees. Now municipal securities for hospitals and single and multi-family housing utilize trustees located outside of financial centers requiring them to become familiar with related property clauses in governing indentures.

The necessity for and importance of such provisions become clear when one considers that in the usual case the real security is the business of the obligor as a going concern and not the aggregate of the individual parcels of property. It is customary for mortgage indentures to continue for an indefinite period, and the needs of the mortgagor obligor are likely to change considerably while the indenture is in operation. Also, many parts of the original property wear out and become unfit for use in the obligor's business. The primary purpose of the release provisions is to enable the obligor to dispose of such obsolete and unproductive properties, free from the lien of the indenture, and to use the proceeds to acquire additional properties or improvements necessary or useful in its business operations. Because it is desirable to provide for almost every contingency, the release provisions cannot be limited to mere disposition of worn out or obsolete properties but usually cover any property that the obligor may sell or otherwise dispose of.

Inasmuch as the trustee's primary responsibilities revolve around the preservation of the bondholders' security, the duties discussed in this and the two preceding chapters might be regarded as the tripartite base on which most of the pre-default administrative provisions of a secured indenture are founded. The sections dealing with the issuance of bonds limit the creation of additional debt to a prescribed percentage of the additional value added to the security and are designed to insure that the requisite equity is maintained. The sinking fund and maintenance provisions have as their purpose, the continuation of the predetermined minimum ratio of security value to debt. The minimum ratio is ensured through the retirement of debt in proportion to the effect of depreciation and obsolescence factors on the obligor's properties. Finally, the release provisions enable the obligor to deal with its properties efficiently and expeditiously, provided that equivalent value is substituted for properties sold or otherwise disposed of. Once this basic concept is thoroughly understood, a proper foundation is laid for the intelligent consideration of applications or certificates filed under any of the various indenture sections. Although the entire indenture constitutes, and must be considered as, a single contract, it is important that these three segments be complementary. In reviewing the terms of a proposed new mortgage indenture, the trustee should make sure that the various provisions are entirely consistent and designed to carry out the essential purposes outlined above.

From the viewpoint of both the obligor and the trustee, the release provisions are of the greatest importance, and some of the most intricate problems involved in indenture administration have to do with the release of property. It is simple enough to state the basic proposition that the trustee's duty is discharged if equivalent value is received for value surrendered, but how is "value" in such an instance to be determined? If a piece of property is sold as a result of arm's length bargaining, isn't the sale price fairly conclusive in relation to the "value" involved? But this means that we are dealing solely with intrinsic values. What happens to the concept that the important consideration is the maintaining of the value of the business as a going concern and not the intrinsic value of the individual pieces of property? Given the "going concern" theory, is it ever proper for the trustee to accept less than the intrinsic value of the specific property being disposed of? In particular situations, should it insist on receiving a great deal more?

The problem is further complicated by the trustee's dual responsibilities. Preserving the security is the trustee's fundamental responsibility, and to this end, its duty to the bondholders is absolute. Conversely, before default, the obligor has the right within the terms of its contract to deal with its property in a manner that seems to be in the best interest of all parties, and the obligor is in a much better position than the trustee to make such a determination. The release provisions constitute a part of the contract between the obligor and the trustee, and if the necessary conditions are fulfilled, the trustee must assent to a requested release and may be liable if it refuses to do so.

This essential problem may be illustrated by considering a specific situation. Assume that two extensive railway systems--Railroad A and Railroad B--serve exactly the same territory between two points on their lines approximately two hundred miles apart and that for this distance their lines roughly parallel each other. The property of each is heavily mortgaged. As a result of detailed studies and with approval of the Interstate Commerce Commission (ICC), the companies agree that railroad A will grant to railroad B the right in perpetuity to use A's tracks between the points in question and that the latter will abandon its trackage and right-of-way. The remaining single line is capable of handling all traffic and no revenue loss will be occasioned. In fact. a saving of several million dollars annually will result from reductions in property taxes, maintenance, and terminal expenses. Railroad B makes application to its mortgage trustee for release of its entire two-hundred-mile line, the consideration being the mortgaging of the trackage right from railroad A and the deposit of all proceeds of salvage, with the proceeds to be used to enlarge and improve certain facilities on the new joint line to facilitate the handling of the increased traffic. What should be the attitude of the mortgage trustee? Despite the economic desirability of effectuating the agreement, isn't the value of the trust estate being diminished? Does the trust estate benefit at all by the savings realized, unless they are set aside and used to reduce outstanding indebtedness? It is doubtful that the trustee could successfully impose this as a condition to the release, if it receives an engineer's certification to the effect that the value of the trackage rights is at least equal to the value of the right-of-way to be abandoned.

Railroad A's trustee also has a problem, although possibly not so great as that of the railroad B trustee. The latter would have to insist that the rights granted be superior to all mortgages on the railroad A property, although this would result in a substantial encumbrance ranking ahead of the lien of railroad A's mortgage, requiring a consent or release by the trustee. Again, the consideration could only be the savings in expense, which might or might not directly benefit the trust estate.

In administering the release provisions the trustee must always insist upon receiving the certificates and other documents required and must examine them to see that the proper statements and certifications are made. The question is the extent, if any, to which the trustee should examine the practical aspects and possible consequences of the proposed transaction and interpose its independent judgment. The matter is further complicated when the action requested is unusual, and there is uncertainty about whether it is specifically authorized by the indenture provisions. The trustee has a difficult decision to make in these cases, even though the contemplated action appears to be clearly in the interest of the bondholders. If it assents to the proposed release without requisite authority and loss results, it may be liable for acting beyond the scope of its powers. Conversely, if it refuses to execute a release and loss results, it may be liable both to security holders and to the obligor if in fact the transaction was within the scope of the indenture. All too frequently, time is of the essence, and it is impossible in these situations to obtain a judicial construction of the indenture language.

The problem of releases has been the subject of considerable comment over the years, both in judicial decisions and by writers on the subject. Unfortunately, no consistent pattern has been established that might serve as a guide to the trustee. The cases considered have for the most part involved situations where substantial losses resulted, and the trustees involved were subjected to severe criticism even though the facts indicated that the terms of the indenture had been followed strictly.

In other cases where trustees departed from indenture restrictions and logically might be subject to criticism, their actions were upheld. A striking example of the latter situation is presented by the numerous cases involving the substitution of buses for municipal railway systems. Few of the railway system indentures provided for the release of lines of railway, and in fact, many contained an express prohibition against it. Most companies, however, would have faced serious financial trouble and possible loss of franchises if a way had not been found to effect a change in the method of transportation. Almost without exception, the courts were able to find enough implied authority in the indenture sufficient to permit the transactions. One court held that bondholders acquired their obligations with implied knowledge of a possible change in methods of conducting business and that this was implicit in the agreement.[1] Another found the requisite authority in the provisions reserving to the company, before default, the right to possess, manage, and operate the mortgaged properties.[2]

The extent to which a trustee may go in refusing to execute a release where it appears that the bondholders' security will be impaired, even though the necessary conditions precedent exist, is problematic. Two cases on this point, both decided by New York courts, illustrate the problem.

The first case involved a collateral trust indenture in which the collateral consisted largely of bonds secured by real estate mortgages. The indenture provided that such bonds could be accepted as collateral only when accompanied by appraisals showing that the unpaid balance was not in excess of 75 percent of the value of the real estate. The indenture further provided that whenever the principal amount of bonds outstanding under the indenture was less than 83 1/3 percent of the par value of collateral pledged, the excess collateral could be withdrawn until the percentage was reached. The case involved application for withdrawal of $8 million of excess collateral computed on this basis. The trustee refused to comply, arguing that, despite the fact that the collateral bonds were adequately secured at the time of deposit, depreciation in real estate values had wiped out the 25 percent margin and that in many cases the value of the underlying real estate was less than the face amount of the bonds. The trustee's position was upheld by the court, which ruled that the release provisions were qualified by an implied intent that a 25 percent margin in security for all collateral be maintained.[3]

The second case involved a mortgage indenture that contained a rather unusual provision permitting releases upon deposit with the trustee of a stated proportion of the consideration for which the property was sold, the percentage varying with the gross sales price of the property. On December 18, the obligor notified the trustee that it would default on the interest installment due on the succeeding January 1. On December 30 it applied for the release of certain property, tendering 20 percent of the sales price, which was the required percentage under the applicable indenture clause. The trustee refused to release the property, but the courts upheld the company's suit for specific performance, holding that, since a default did not exist on the date of application, the trustee had no right to refuse.[4]

Under the TIA the trustee is protected if it relies in good faith on certificates furnished to it pursuant to the indenture provisions, but it must examine the certificates to ensure that they do conform to such provisions.[5] In most situations, no problem will be encountered if the trustee follows this rule. No hard-and-fast rule can be established, however, to guide the trustee in the unusual or special situation. The requirement of good faith means that it cannot free itself from considering the practical aspects and potential consequences of the proposed transaction.

In considering the usual and customary provision of the indenture relating to these matters, we will deal separately with the mortgage indenture and the collateral indenture. Although the essential purpose is the same in both, different problems are presented.

DEALING WITH PROPERTY UNDER MORTGAGE INDENTURES

Before default, the mortgagor obligor has the absolute right to possess, manage, and operate its properties free from restriction or interference, provided only that it complies with the covenants and provisions of the indenture. It is customary for this right to be specifically affirmed in general terms by the indenture. The first sections of the release article enumerate specific rights retained by the mortgagor in furtherance of this general affirmation.

The first provision deals with the company's right to remove and dispose of property and equipment that has become obsolete or unserviceable or is no longer useful in the company's business activities. This can be done without the necessity of release or other action by the trustee. The only condition is that the property so disposed of be replaced by other property of at least equal value or that, to the extent of any deficiency, cash be deposited with the trustee. Mechanically, the most feasible method of ensuring compliance is to require the filing with the trustee an annual certificate of the aggregate value of property so retired, the value of property substituted, and the amount of the cash deficiency, if any.

A second section gives the obligor the right to relocate machinery or equipment; to move any of the property from one location to another; to alter, remodel, or change the location of any building or structure; or to make any similar change or alteration so long as the aggregate value of the mortgaged property is not diminished. Because these rights do not affect the lien of the indenture, no accounting to the trustee is necessary.

Finally, the mortgagor is given the right to alter or amend any lease, contract, easement, license, franchise, or similar right, or to enter into any such agreements. This right is usually conditioned on a finding by the obligor's board of directors that the alteration or amendment will not prejudice the obligor's activities or the trust estate or that it will be in the best interests of the obligor and its bondholders. Other conditions may be imposed as may be appropriate to the obligor's circumstances. For example, if the obligor is given the right to grant leases or other interests in its property, it is usually provided that these must be made expressly subject to the prior rights of the trustee as mortgagee.

This reservation of rights in the obligor is a necessary and integral part of its right to possession and use of the property and is to be exercised without reference to or action by the trustee. Normally, however, on the obligor's request, the trustee executes the release or other documents that may be necessary or desirable to confirm the company's action in any particular situation.

Because the trustee has no control over dealing with its security, these sections should be carefully examined by it to ensure that the security will not be prejudiced by any such action. Likewise, the restrictions on and qualifications for the obligor's unilateral action under these sections should not be so broad as to prejudice the action the obligor can take with the concurrence of the trustee, under the general release provisions. In one situation, a provision prohibiting the granting of leases, except subject to the prior lien of the indenture, raised a serious question. A trustee was presented with an application for the release of a leasehold estate to enable the separate financing of substantial improvements to a particular property, in the absence of a clear right to execute such a release. It would have been simple to make the restriction applicable only to unilateral action by the obligor, carrying out the obvious intent of the parties.

Whereas the sections permitting unilateral action by an obligor should be fairly restrictive, a great deal of flexibility is desirable with respect to the action that may be taken with the consent and concurrence of the trustee. As long as the essential character of the security is preserved, the obligor should be given the right to obtain the release of any property it wishes to dispose of, upon the substitution of property of equivalent value or upon an appropriate reduction in the amount of the secured indebtedness.

The conditions for the obligor's right to secure a release of property and the documents required to substantiate compliance with such conditions are set forth in Section 314(d) of the TIA.

Many indentures provide that property cannot be released unless the obligor has sold or contracted to sell the specific property in question. Although this appears not to present a problem, sometimes it has proved to be too restrictive. Occasionally it may be desirable to effect a change in the terms of a lease, contract, easement, or other property right where no actual sale is involved and under circumstances requiring the consent or participation of the trustee. Any such general limitation or restriction should be questioned.

One of the basic documents required is a resolution of the obligor's board of directors reciting the essential facts surrounding the transaction, containing an adequate description of the property, and requesting execution of a release by the trustee. Though seldom required, it is desirable also to have the resolution specifically state that the obligor is not in default and that the requested release will not impair the security of the indenture in contravention of the provisions. These are required conditions and must be covered in other certificates. The basic purpose in requiring a resolution, in addition to seeing that requisite authority is given the obligor officers, is to ensure that the transaction has been referred to and authorized by the senior responsible body of the obligor, and it is desirable to require affirmative consideration of all aspects of the transaction.

The value of the property to be released is determined by the certificate of an engineer, appraiser, or other expert. This certification must also state affirmatively that the proposed release will not impair the security of the indenture. Under certain circumstances, when the value of the property to be released is in excess of a specified amount, this certification must be made by an independent engineer, appraiser, or expert having no affiliation with the obligor. The certificate must recite in sufficient detail the scope of the examination and investigation that formed the basis of the opinion certified. Normally the obligor is given the right to select the engineer or appraiser, but the selection should be made subject to the trustee's approval. In view of the importance of this certificate, the trustee should insist upon receiving an adequate statement of the expert's qualifications and should make an evaluation of such qualifications.

Two additional documents are always required--a certificate of designated officers of the company and an opinion of counsel, each of which must state that all conditions for the requested release exist or have been performed, and recite in sufficient detail the examination and investigation made by the signers to ascertain the necessary facts. In addition to this general statement, it is customary to require the officers to certify affirmatively to all pertinent facts--that there is no default, that the property has been sold or that a release is necessary for the reasons set forth, that the release is desirable in the conduct of the company's business and will not impair the security of the indenture, and such other facts as may be appropriate to the particular situation.

Finally, a consideration for the release must be furnished. This should equal the greater of the fair value of the property released or the consideration received by the company on its sale. This consideration is normally in the form of cash or other real or personal property, but occasionally it may be purchase-money obligations secured by the property released. If the latter, it should be limited to a fixed percentage (usually 66 2/3 percent) of the value of the property. It is also desirable to limit the aggregate amount of such obligations that may be held. Even though they may be perfectly good security, they diminish the working capital of any corporation that is not in the business of investing in mortgages.

Any cash received is deposited with the trustee and may be withdrawn by the company to reimburse itself for any additional property acquired and subjected to the lien of the indenture, in an amount equal to the lesser of the cost or the fair value of such property to the company. The indenture should be reviewed before any investment of cash is considered. Municipal mortgage indentures are likely to provide for the investment of proceeds from the sale of mortgaged property. Corporate indentures are often silent and any investment of proceeds from the sale of property should only be made upon written approval and appropriate indemnification from the obligor. When investing these proceeds, consideration should be given to the length of time funds will be on deposit by consulting with the obligor. Written direction should be received from the obligor even if investment is specifically allowed by the governing indenture. Whenever any property is subjected to the lien of the indenture, either as the basis for the release of other property or for the withdrawal of cash, substantially the same documents must be filed as in the case of the issuance of bonds on the basis of property additions. These must include an engineer's or appraiser's certificate of the fair value of such property to the company; an opinion of counsel that all conditions for the withdrawal have been complied with and that the property is subject to the lien of the indenture; and an officers' certificate that such property is useful and desirable in the conduct of the company's business and that all conditions for the transaction have been met. If counsel indicates that instruments of conveyance are necessary or desirable to perfect the lien of the indenture on such property, such instruments must be executed and recorded and become supplements to the indenture. Some confusion is frequently created in the mind of the inexperienced administrator by complex provisions, that may be included in open-ended mortgages, which try to classify properties used as a basis for releases and to permit their re-use at a later date under other provisions of the indenture. The reason for this becomes clear if the distinction between *funded* and *unfunded* property is borne in mind. The distinction is of paramount importance. *Funded* property is property that has been bonded or used as a basis for credit under a sinking fund, maintenance, or similar provision, or used to secure the issuance of additional bonds. *Unfunded* property, though subject to the lien of the indenture, is excess property that is available for use by the company in certifying compliance with the pertinent indenture sections. Property substituted for other property released should retain the latter status, and when this is unfunded, the new property still remains available for use for other purposes, even though it is certified to the trustee as a basis for releasing other unfunded property.

It is desirable also to include a provision that, although used infrequently, permits the trustee to apply any cash deposited to the purchase or redemption of bonds. Normally, the application should be at the option of the obligor.

Miscellaneous Provisions

For the general purposes of the release clauses and for special situations or contingencies, it is customary to include a number of general sections in the release article, most of which become operative only for particular events.

When frequent sales of property are likely, it is desirable to include a provision permitting the obligor, without application to or release by the trustee, to consummate sales up to a specified aggregate amount each year. Preparing individual release applications is time-consuming and expensive, and such a provision results in substantial savings in time and expense. The obligor must provide a single annual accounting to the trustee. Although it is seldom required, it would be desirable to have a single release covering all such properties executed annually. The conveyance of property without a specific release of a mortgage lien creates a possible cloud on title that may require expensive proceedings to remove at a later date. Sometimes it is difficult to identify a particular parcel as one that was properly sold under such a general section, and the trustee is placed in an embarrassing position when it is requested, years later, to join in a confirmatory release.

A statement should always be included to the effect that the purchaser of any property released by the trustee is protected and under no duty to inquire into the particular circumstances or the propriety of any such release. When the trustee executes a release improperly or without the requisite authority, it is not clear what the effect on the title of the purchaser may be. Some cases have held that a release so executed is invalid, and the purchaser does not acquire good title. Other courts have held, however, that when the indenture contains such a provision protecting the purchaser, the provision is controlling and the purchaser is protected even though the trustee's action was *ultra vires*. No one should question the desirability or equity of such a rule.

There should always be included provisions dealing with the disposition of property taken through the exercise of the power of eminent domain, or by the exercise of any right of any government, bureau, or agency, or any public or quasi-public body to condemn or take possession or title to any property or interest in it. The award granted for any such taking will be paid to the trustee. As discussed earlier, the governing indenture provisions should be reviewed if the proceeds are to be invested and appropriate authority and indemnification should be obtained from the obligor. It is desirable to include a greater degree of flexibility, however, and the procedure will be simplified if the obligor is given the right to compromise or settle its claim in such a situation. The practice usually followed is to proceed under the general release section, but sometimes the conditions are not completely satisfied, and because it is a special situation--not subject to the company's control--it is better to deal with it as such. An appropriate certificate of the fairness of the proposed settlement can serve as a basis for the release of the property. This enables the obligor to use the proceeds promptly to acquire substitute property and avoid the delay and expense of pursuing the condemnation route.

The normal release provisions are operative if no default exists under the indenture. There may be a problem if there is a default. It is customary to provide that the rights of the obligor under the release article are exercised by a trustee appointed in bankruptcy or reorganization proceedings. As a practical matter, this official operates under the orders of the court having jurisdiction, which may direct the sale of particular property whether or not there is indenture authorization, but it is desirable nevertheless to provide for this contingency.

Of more significance is the situation that exists when no formal proceedings have been instituted. Here the trustee is required to exercise more discretion and judgment, and the release sections are usually made permissive. If in the judgment of the trustee the proposed transaction seems desirable, it is granted authority to execute a release but is permitted to refuse to do so. The trustee should receive the same certifications and documents as in the case of a pre-default release and may require such additional evidence as seems indicated to enable it to reach an appropriate conclusion.

Finally, provisions should be inserted to deal with any special situation or special properties that may be significant in the case of the particular obligor involved. The nature of such provisions, if any, will depend on the special circumstances existing. Certain property or classes of property may be of such significance in the financing arrangement as to warrant a prohibition against their disposal or a provision that the proceeds can be applied only to retirement of the debt. Acquisition particular classes of property with trust monies may be forbidden or may be limited to a fixed aggregate amount or to a percentage of the indenture securities outstanding. The trustee should ensure that it understands the purpose intended and that the provisions inserted are designed properly to effectuate such purpose.

PROVISIONS AS TO PLEDGED COLLATERAL

The traditional collateral trust indenture does not now occupy the importance in corporate financing that it did during the period of the 1920s and 1930s.[6] This was the era of the growth and influence of the large holding company systems, particularly in the public utility industry. The parent companies in these systems, and often the companies on the second and even third tiers of the intracorporate structure, owned no physical operating properties at all but merely held securities of subsidiary and affiliated companies in the system. Capital debt financing by these corporations was arranged through the collateral trust device, under which securities of affiliated companies constituted the sole security for the outstanding obligations. The rapid expansion of these systems and the numerous recapitalizations resulted in substantial pyramiding of the debt and frequent withdrawals and substitutions of collateral under the various indentures. A number of events greatly lessened the relative significance of these arrangements. Of the greatest importance was the enactment of the Public Utility Holding

Company Act of 1935 under which the giant systems either disappeared or were substantially curtailed. In the process the old indentures were satisfied through the exchange of securities during the reorganization process.[7] The companies' capital structures were simplified and their valuation became more realistic. Debt securities of the system are not usually issued by the subsidiary operating companies where operating properties rather than collateral constitute the security. Public financing by the parent holding company is normally done through sale of equity. When debt securities are issued, it is on an unsecured basis. When securities are held as part of the trust estate, the requirements governing their release are now substantially the same as those relating to real property. Important is the requirement of certificates of value for collateral being released as well as collateral being substituted for other property. These certificates must be made by experts who cite the criteria for their appraisal, which can be subjected to objective scrutiny. In particular situations, these certificates must be furnished by independent appraisers.

Despite the decline in importance of the traditional collateral trust indenture as such, the handling of collateral security is a significant factor in many mortgage indentures and asset-backed financing vehicles. Numerous companies still conduct a portion of their business through subsidiary or affiliated companies. To provide security on the complete business operation, it is necessary to create a combined mortgage and collateral trust indenture. The significance of the pledge of securities, however, lies not in their current market value but in the granting of a collateral lien on the parent company's allied or subsidiary operations conducted through the companies whose securities are pledged. The pertinent indenture provisions should therefore be designed for this purpose.

It is important that all securities of such affiliates or subsidiaries owned by the obligor be included in the pledge.

This need not necessarily cover open-book advances, although these too are frequently included through a requirement for execution and pledging of an unsecured note. In the case of a real property mortgage, creation of a prior lien is effectively prevented by recording requirements. A collateral lien can, however, be impaired by the issuance of senior securities ranking ahead of those pledged. Without a specific requirement for the pledging of any such securities, protection should be obtained in the form of negative covenants controlling the amount of such securities that can be issued. Before default no particular action is required of the trustee other than the custody of the securities pledged. The obligor is entitled to all income thereof and should be permitted to exercise all voting rights except on matters that might affect the value of the collateral lien. Enforcing the principal of any debt obligations pledged is not important, and the trustee may properly be freed from any duty in this connection. Despite the lien nature of the pledge, however, any payments made on account of principal or received on retirement of equity securities should be sent to the trustee. This requirement is roughly equivalent to the maintenance requirement for mortgaged property.

Adequate provisions should be included to facilitate any exchange, recapitalization, merger, or other type of intracompany transactions that may occur from time to time. These should authorize the trustee--upon receipt of appropriate resolutions and certificates establishing the desirability of the proposed arrangement--to execute the documents or give any consent that may be required.

By reason of the special purpose of this collateral pledge, normally no part of the securities of any particular company held (except on payment, exchange, or for a similar reason) should be released unless all the securities of the particular company involved are disposed of simultaneously. As in the case of real property, any special situations should be dealt with specially, and appropriate authority should be included in the indenture for the trustee's guidance.

After default, the trustee should have all rights of ownership with respect to pledged securities, including the right to receive and return income, the right of sale or other disposition, and the right to exercise full voting control.

---

[1] Mayor et al. of City of Baltimore v. United Railways and Electric Company of Baltimore City, 108 Md. 64, 69 Atl. 436 (1908).

[2] New York State Railways v. Security Trust Company of Rochester, 135 Misc. 456, 238 N.Y.S. 354 (1929).

[3] Prudence Company Inc. v. Central Hanover Bank and Trust Company, 261 N.Y. 420, 184 N.E. 687 (1933).

[4] Indian River Islands Corporation v. Manufacturers Trust Company et al., 253 App. Div. 549, 2 N.Y.S. 2d 860 (1938).

[5] TIA, sec. 315(a)(2).

[6] For discussion of various types of collateral used in asset-backed transactions, see chapter 15.

[7] The Energy Policy Act of 2005 repealed the Public Utility Holding Company Act of 1935, thus deregulating the utility industry. The new Public Utility Holding Company Act of 2005 took the Securities and Exchange Commission out of the utility regulatory business and shifted a more limited regulatory prerogative to the Federal Energy Regulatory Commission.

NINE

INDENTURE COVENANTS

In addition to provisions relating specifically to the trust estate or to the debt and the rights of the relevant parties, most indentures contain a number of covenants designed to restrict the obligor's activities. The number and nature of the covenants included result from negotiations between the obligor and the person or persons representing the prospective purchasers of the securities (in a public issue, normally counsel to the underwriters). The type of covenants included depends to a large extent on the nature of the business of the obligor, the term of the loan, the purpose for which it is being made, whether it is secured or unsecured, the extent and nature of other outstanding obligations, and other, similar considerations.[1] Corporate indentures will typically contain more financial covenants than municipal indentures.

The trustee is not, of course, responsible for what covenants are or are not included in a particular indenture, for this is part of contract between borrower and lender. Even though the trustee does not draft the covenants, it should carefully review all of them and insist on language that gives it the options to exercise its duties and responsibilities in a timely and flexible manner to protect the bondholders' interests. Once the contract is executed, however, the trustee has the primary duty of enforcing it and therefore must be concerned with all its provisions. A more effective job can be done if there is a clear understanding, not only of what the language means but also of the purpose it is intended to accomplish and why the provision was included in a particular indenture. Unfortunately, some drafters have special provisions they like and sometimes insert them without regard to their relevance to the contract. An astute trustee will examine these provisions closely and make sure their relevance and purpose are clearly understood by the parties to the contract. Once the indenture is executed and delivered, it is difficult and expensive—and sometimes even impossible--to have it modified. It is unfortunate when a particular covenant, designed to enhance the credit and protect the investor, actually threatens the security primarily relied on and places the obligor in a difficult situation. When faced with such a development the trustee finds itself in an unenviable position that might have been avoided by the exercise of greater care when the contract was still in draft form.

Of paramount importance, of course, is the cardinal rule applicable to all indenture language--that its meaning be clear and unambiguous. One of the trustee's most difficult tasks is interpreting and applying a particular provision to a situation not contemplated at the time it was drafted and that the covenant was not designed to address. No matter how sincere and honest corporate financial officers may be, they tend to interpret provisions in light of the particular problem with which they may be faced from time to time, the language taking on different shades of meaning as the circumstances of a particular obligor undergo change. Since many covenants require only unilateral action on the part of the obligor, default may occur unintentionally because of an incorrect or slightly distorted interpretation on the part of the obligor officials.

Of equal importance is that the covenant be drafted so that any violation can be easily detected. Where the existence of particular facts or prohibited acts or situations is solely within the knowledge of the obligor, and not likely to be readily disclosed by the financial statements or other information furnished to the trustee, every effort should be made to obtain periodic certification of compliance with the covenant. Compliance should be stated either as part of a general certification or with adequate detail about the facts indicating compliance or noncompliance with the specific provision. In general, covenants should be related to and designed to facilitate the carrying out of the purpose of each loan contract. It is impossible to detail or recite all covenants that might be desirable, and so the following enumeration is intended to present only the covenants more commonly used. Many of those listed would not be applicable to particular indentures, but a thorough understanding of the uses and purposes should be useful to indenture administrators in most situations.

Covenants may be classified in a number of ways, but probably the simplest classification is to distinguish between *affirmative* covenants, which require specific action on the part of the obligor, either continuously or at specified periods, and *negative* covenants, which are prohibitive or restrictive and require, not the taking of actions, but the refraining from certain actions.

AFFIRMATIVE COVENANTS

As the name implies, an affirmative covenant requires some positive or definite action on the part of the obligor. It requires the taking of specific action, either continuously, from time to time, or at specified times. A sinking-fund covenant is, of course, of this type, although it is almost always covered in a separate section of the indenture and is not included in the enumeration. Many affirmative covenants are pertinent only to mortgage indentures and relate to the mortgage security, while others are equally applicable whether the issue is secured or unsecured.

Some provisions are frequently included in the covenant section, although they are more in the nature of warranties. Typical of such provisions are the following:

1. Covenant that the obligor has complied with all legal requirements and is duly authorized to execute and deliver the indenture and to issue the indenture securities and that the indenture securities in the hands of the holders thereof will be valid and enforceable obligations.

2. Covenant that the obligor is lawfully possessed of the mortgaged and pledged property and has good right and lawful authority to mortgage and pledge it.

3. Covenant that the obligor will warrant and defend the title to the property and the trustee's security interest therein against all claims and demands.

These provisions may be included as recitals in the indenture instead of, or in addition to, being included as specific covenants. It probably makes little difference where they appear, for the conditions recited go so obviously to the essence of the contract that a violation would provide a basis for immediately prematuring the debt and bringing the remedial provisions into play. Their inclusion as specific covenants provides a direct relationship with the default and remedial section and is to be preferred for that reason. Whether included as covenants or recitals, or both, they serve as an estoppel against the corporation and prevent its questioning the validity of its acts, even though there may have been some technical failure to secure due and proper authorization of the indenture, the indenture securities, or the mortgage. An estoppel would not be effective against third parties who obtained rights for value and in good faith. Its inclusion in the indenture, therefore, does not mean that the trustee and its counsel should be less diligent in assuring themselves about the due and proper authorization of the indenture and the obligations issued thereunder.

Other types of affirmative covenants are applicable only to secured indentures and are usually to be found--in one form or another--in most mortgage indentures. Some of these may be included as parts of other covenants or undertakings, but are listed separately for clarity.

> 4. Covenant to maintain and preserve the lien of the indenture.
>
> 5. Covenant to give further assurances.
>
> 6. Covenant to subject to the lien of the indenture, by supplement, if necessary, all property acquired after the date of the indenture and intended to be covered thereby.

All these covenants are meant to give further assurances and provide a basis for a trustee's demand that additional documents be executed or things be done that will better ensure maintenance of the security the indenture purported to create, and extend the lien thereon to additionally acquired property should any question exist about the effectiveness of an after-acquired property clause in any jurisdiction. For example, the further assurances covenant has been used as a basis for a request, in a nonqualified indenture, for an annual certificate of after-acquired property and an annual opinion on the timely recording and filing of the indenture and the necessity for any periodic re-recording or refiling.

> 7. Covenant to record the indenture and all supplements, and to furnish opinions of counsel, after each such recording and annually, as to the due recording thereof and the necessity for any re-recording or refiling to preserve the lien thereof.

Section 314(b)(1) of the TIA imposes such a requirement for all indentures qualified thereunder that include a mortgage or pledge of property. The matter of recording is of such obvious importance that this is a more-or-less standard provision in all mortgage indentures even if not qualified under the act. Because of the multiplicity of jurisdictions frequently involved and the diversity of recording statutes, reliance must be placed on counsel who are familiar with the laws of the various states where the property is located.

8. **Covenants with respect to prior lien bonds.** Where prior lien bonds are outstanding, it is customary to include provisions with respect to such prior liens. These provisions are designed to prevent a default under the prior lien and its extension or refunding thereafter with other prior lien obligations. The indenture will therefore usually contain covenants to the effect that the obligor will comply with all provisions of prior lien indentures; that it will pay the obligations when due and will not consent to the extension of the maturity thereof (the indenture will usually contain provisions for the refunding thereunder of prior lien obligations); and that upon satisfaction of any prior lien indenture, it will cause such trustee to surrender to the trustee all specific property pledged with such prior lien trustee. When prior lien obligations are retired in part or acquired by the obligor, the indenture often provides that they will be held alive and pledged with the trustee. The theory of such a provision is that, to the extent of the obligations so held, the trustee will acquire rights *pari passu* with the other holders of such prior lien obligations. The validity of this theory is doubtful, however, except to the extent of value actually paid by the trustee for such obligations.

Many other affirmative covenants are equally applicable to secured or unsecured indentures, although their context or purpose may differ, depending on the nature of the obligor and the indenture. Some of the more common covenants of this type are listed next.

9. Covenant that the obligor will duly and punctually pay the principal of and interest and premium, if any, on all of the indenture securities outstanding according to the terms.

Inasmuch as the obligations themselves contain an absolute

promise to pay, inclusion of such a provision in the indenture might seem unnecessary and redundant. The obligation in the securities, however, runs directly to the holders thereof and not to the trustee. The indenture covenant runs to the trustee and enables it to enforce the obligation for the benefit of the security holders if there should be a default in the payment of any installment of principal or interest.

    10. A covenant to maintain an office or agency where the bonds may be presented for payment and where notices and demands may be served on the obligor.

It is customary to provide that an office or agency will be maintained in one or more specified cities and that, if the obligor should fail to keep or provide such office, presentation may be made and such notices and demands served at the principal office of the trustee. As a practical matter the trustee's office is almost always designated as the office or agency, and in any event, any demands and inquiries by security holders are directed to the trustee.

    11. A covenant to pay all taxes, assessments, and other changes or claims imposed upon the obligor's property, or upon the income or profits thereof, or upon the lien or interest of the trustee in respect of such property or such income.

It is usually also provided that the obligor may delay payment of any such claim so long as it is, in good faith, contesting the validity thereof by appropriate legal proceedings. The purpose of this covenant is to prevent the creation of any lien or claim that might be given preference by operation of law to the indenture securities.

    12. A covenant to maintain its corporate existence and maintain, preserve, and renew all rights, powers, privileges, and franchises owned by it.

The purpose of this undertaking is obvious. Because the loan is based on the credit of the corporation as a "going concern," all rights essential to its continuing as such must be preserved. This covenant is usually made subject to the merger clause and occasionally to the release and other provisions of the indenture.

> 13. A covenant to maintain, preserve, and keep its properties in good repair, working order, and condition.
>
> 14. A covenant to set aside from earnings each year proper reserves for renewals and replacements, obsolescence, depletion, exhaustion, and depreciation.

These are customary covenants in most indentures, whether secured or unsecured, which emphasize further the importance of the "going concern" concept of the business and to maintenance of the security for the debt. In some types of mortgage indentures--particularly those of regulated companies such as public utilities and railroads--the covenants are combined and enlarged into an elaborate maintenance covenant as outlined and discussed in chapter 7.

> 15. Covenant to maintain insurance.

Some indentures require maintaining specific types of insurance; for example, in some businesses, public liability insurance may be of great importance, and failure to provide it in proper amounts might result in a severe loss to the obligor and prejudice to the security holders' claims. Needs and requirements tend to change over the years, however, and as a general rule it is unwise to try to be too specific. The customary and more desirable form is to provide that insurance of such kinds and amounts will be maintained as is customary in the industry or as is customarily maintained by other companies operating similar business. As long as the covenant requires maintenance of adequate insurance, it is desirable to permit as much flexibility as possible. The obligor should be permitted to select the insurance companies, to participate in an insurance pool, or if desired, to provide its own system of self-insurance. When properties are widely scattered, with no great percentage of the total value concentrated in one place, this last may be the most desirable arrangement. Other innovations may also be appropriate in particular cases, such as inclusion of a deductible clause of a substantial amount to avoid a multiplicity of small claims and correspondingly heavier premium charges. In any system of self-insurance, the trustee should insist that the indenture contain requirements for appropriate certification to it of the adequacy of such a system and the reserves maintained.

In many of the old type of indentures, the insurance policies were required to be deposited with the trustee. The modern practice is to provide instead for a periodic certificate to be furnished, usually annually. This certificate should set forth the kinds and amounts of insurance and the names of the companies and contain a statement of the adequacy of the insurance coverage. Although such a detailed statement is not as essential in an unsecured indenture, it is frequently provided for, or the trustee is given the right to request it. If the certificate indicates that policies expire before the next certificate is to be furnished, an appropriate tickler should be set up and a followed up to see that the insurance is renewed. It is common for municipal indentures to specifically indicate the amount and type of insurance coverage to be carried by the obligor. The insurance certificate should be carefully reviewed to the requirement of the indenture to verify compliance with the indenture covenants.

When the indenture constitutes a lien on the obligor's properties the trustee should be named in the policies as a named payee, so that it will receive any proceeds of the insurance. Usually the proceeds up to a specified amount are turned over immediately to the obligor, but amounts in excess thereof should be retained by the trustee until receipt of appropriate evidence that the property has been restored or replaced.

16. Covenant to honor obligations as lessee.

If an important part of the obligor's property consists of leaseholds or ground rent estates, it is advisable to include a covenant that the obligor will perform all covenants and obligations as lessee, will see that the lessor observes all its covenants and obligations in the leases, and will renew the terms of any leases that expire before the maturity date of the indenture obligations.

17. A covenant to continue to engage in a particular business or in the business in which the obligor is presently engaged.

This is an example of the type of covenant that should be examined carefully and used only if particular circumstances would seem to make it appropriate. If the indenture is to run for a long period of time, there is danger in such an undertaking, as any harness maker could verify. In a majority of indentures, it is obviously unnecessary. It might be appropriate to a situation where the loan is of relatively short duration and the principal security is a special inventory or special purpose machinery and equipment suitable only for a particular business.

18. A covenant to keep true books of record and account.

19. A covenant to file with the trustee balance sheets, income and surplus statements, and other pertinent financial statements.

20. A covenant to furnish copies of all reports forwarded to stockholders or filed with the SEC and such other information as may be prescribed from time to time by regulations of the SEC.[2]

21. A covenant to permit a representative of the trustee at all reasonable times, upon request, to inspect the obligor's books and properties.

22. A covenant to furnish such other data and information pertaining to the obligor's affairs as the trustee may reasonably request.

These covenants all relate to the keeping of proper financial and accounting records and the filing with the trustee of periodic reports relative to the obligor's financial affairs. Section 314(a)(1) of the TIA requires that the obligor file with the trustee copies of the reports required to be filed with the SEC pursuant to Sections 13 or 15(d) of the 34 Act. These sections require the filing of periodic financial reports and supplementary reports to keep current various data filed with the original registration statement. In addition, copies of the annual audited statements certified by independent public accountants required to be filed within a specified period after the close of the obligor's fiscal year.[3] Interim statements may also be required in particular cases, and it is usually sufficient to have these certified by one of the obligor's financial officers. In a situation where the condition of the business may be subject to rapid change and where the maintenance of certain ratios or a minimum amount of working capital is important, a more frequent check on the obligor's condition than is provided by the annual audited statements may be desirable.

How detailed an examination and analysis of the financial statements the trustee should make is not prescribed. Some corporate trust departments follow the practice of having all such statements reviewed by outside accountants. But this seems extreme and, except in a most unusual situation, should not be necessary. Finance is a bank's business, and a trust company that purports to act as a corporate trustee should have personnel sufficiently qualified to make whatever analysis would seem to be indicated. The trustee is charged with the knowledge of any facts that would be revealed by a reasonable examination, and the minimum requirement would seem to be a sufficient check to see that no violation of any indenture provision is disclosed. An experienced administrator or account officer will also review the pertinent footnotes and commentary, the latter often called "Management's Discussion and Analysis" or similar heading. Any unfavorable trend or situation that might warrant a more careful follow-up should be noted. The nature of the business, the financial standing of the obligor, the purpose of the loan, specific responsibilities of the trustee, and other similar considerations will serve as a guide to the degree of care and attention that should be devoted to the examination beyond the limits indicated.

> 23. A covenant to furnish to the trustee annually a certificate signed by "the principal executive officer, principal financial officer or principal accounting officer as to his or her knowledge of such obligor's compliance with all conditions and covenants under the indenture."[4]

For pre-TIRA indentures requiring a different certification or are required to be signed by different officers, it is recommended that both the requirements of the indenture and the section be complied with. In most cases, this can be satisfied by a certification reciting what the TIA requires and any other indenture requirement, to be signed by two "officers" (as defined in the indenture) one of whom is the principal executive, financial, or accounting officer.

Recognizing the importance of this certification, the TIRA converted what was a commonly used affirmative undertaking into a new legislatively mandated covenant. Not only does it give the trustee appropriate evidence on which it is entitled to rely, but more importantly by making such certification a Federal law requirement for all qualified indentures, criminal sanctions and civil suits are possible in the event of late, missed, or untrue certificates.

NEGATIVE COVENANTS

The difference between negative and affirmative covenants is not so much in the form of phraseology used, for almost any covenant can be expressed in the positive, as well as the negative. The distinction lies rather in the fact that the so-called negative covenants generally restrict the activities of the obligor in order to protect the interests of the investor or lender. Although some of these covenants are common to both bond and debenture agreements, the negative covenant is most commonly associated with the debenture indenture, or unsecured financing. Their essential purpose is to ensure, to the extent possible, that the investor for whose benefit they are made will remain in the same relative position (in regard to other creditors) as exists at the time of the extension of credit.

Their use has been severely criticized from time to time, particularly in an early report of the SEC.[5] The SEC's argument was that these covenants tended to lead the investor into a sense of false security and were of limited value because of the ease with which they could be violated and the lack of any effective legal remedy to prevent violations.

The statement that no effective remedy exists to prevent the violation of these clauses is also doubtful. Theoretically, an action for specific performance or for injunctive relief should be possible, although it is likely that these remedies will offer little protection in the usual case because the trustee will probably not know of the violation until the assets have been transferred or pledged or a prohibited loan or advance has been obtained. To have such a transaction set aside would require proof not only of the violation but also of knowledge on the part of the pledgor or transferee. There is one remedy, however, that can be effective: the right to declare a default under the indenture and premature the indenture obligations. Although this may not place the security holders in as good a position as formerly and therefore cannot be said to constitute full protection, it is a potent weapon that should deter all but the most callous. Faced with such a threat, the obligor is more likely to endeavor to resolve a difficult situation through frank disclosure and negotiation rather than through intentional violation of a restrictive covenant. In many cases an unsecured obligation under a carefully drawn indenture will provide as much protection and security to the investor as a mortgage bond does. The principal considerations in either case are the credit of the obligor as a going concern and the caliber of its management. In some cases the unsecured credit of the borrower is so good that few restrictions or covenants are necessary. When the investors are obtaining a senior creditor position, all that is reasonably required are provisions in the agreement that under normal conditions will assure the retention of such a position. It is impossible to protect against every possible contingency, and an effort to do so by placing overly restrictive conditions on the continued operation of the business is as likely to prejudice as to improve the security holders' position.

It is quite possible, however, that the lack of strong restrictive covenants can imperil the value of bondholders' investments. This became evident during the 1980s when the growth of complex and diverse financial instruments, coupled with the explosion of novel and debt-laden corporate capital structures, had a major impact on the holders of bonds issued during the preceding twenty years. During the past twenty years, there has been a continuous effort by major corporate issuers to reduce the number of restrictive covenants applicable to their new issues, particularly those which restrict the payment of dividends or the incurring of additional debt.[6]

The losses incurred by bondholders who had purchased high grade debt instruments and ended up with so-called junk bonds reinforced a reversal of that trend. Institutional investors, in particular, demanded much greater protection against recapitalization transactions, commonly called *event risk*, which can have a devastating adverse impact on the value of their investments. It is evident that

> the tension between restrictive financial covenants and business flexibility for the issuer has led the marketplace away from covenants which measure the "symptoms" of a worsening financial condition to covenants designed to identify the events which cause the condition and provide an immediate bailout opportunity for the holder upon the occurrence of those events.[7]

Public corporate issues offer the opportunity for monitoring obligor financial conditions through filings with the SEC, but municipal issues do not offer the same access to financial information and covenant satisfaction. There is much concern among investors and security analysts over the disclosure needs of the municipal marketplace. It is likely that the SEC will request Congress to legislate mandatory municipal issuer disclosure of financial information which would be made available to investors. The result of efforts to improve this information availability for municipal issues is discussed in Chapter 13 under the section on "Secondary Market Disclosure".

The original "poison put" provision was designed to ward off unfriendly takeovers and did not normally operate in the event of a friendly takeover (e.g., a management buyout). But the latter event can be just as disastrous to the bondholders as any hostile acquisition, with the result that institutional investors increased their insistence on the inclusion of "super poison put" covenants, which eliminate the distinction between friendly and hostile transactions. Such covenants include change of control tests and others directed at the obligor creditworthiness such as:

> 1. Net Worth Call. This provides for the acceleration of a sinking fund in the event that the obligor's net

worth falls below a specified level.

2. Poison Puts. An immediate tender can be made back to the obligor if there is an increase in the debt to equity ratio over a specified amount, or if there is a downgrade in the obligor's credit rating.

3. Interest Rate Reset. This provides for a set increase in the interest rate if certain specified ratios are not maintained.

4. Automatic redemption. This covenant mandates an automatic redemption with a premium, either fixed or based on a spread over long-term U.S. Treasury bonds.[8]

Because it is impossible to foresee every contingency, it is desirable to provide for some degree of flexibility, but this is difficult. When the notes or debentures are purchased directly by informed institutional investors, this situation can be resolved by an agreement among such holders to amend the indenture or to modify or waive a particular provision either permanently or during a temporary period of stress. A different problem is presented where an issue is sold publicly. The first principle to be observed is to include only such restrictive covenants as under reasonably foreseeable conditions are not likely to cause undue hardship or seriously impede the normal conduct of the obligor's business. If the credit is not good enough under those conditions, it is best avoided.

It is also desirable to include a provision permitting modification of the indenture by the holders of a specified percentage of the indenture securities. The customary percentage used is 66 2/3 percent. Although it may be almost impossible to contact all holders of a publicly held issue, consent of a reasonable percentage can normally be obtained if the modification proposed is reasonable and desirable and if adequate foresight and preparation are exercised.[9]

The trustee is frequently asked to consent to a temporary

waiver or modification of a particular provision or at least to consent to take no action for some period of time after a breach. Under the circumstances in which it is presented, the obligor's proposed action usually appears reasonable and often highly desirable from the security holders' viewpoint. Whereas a good argument can be made for granting such discretionary powers to a trustee, under the usual indenture it has no such power and no authority or right to give any such consent or waiver. Once a breach has occurred and matured into a default under the indenture, the trustee's conduct is subject to the prudent man standard of judgment. It is unfortunate that relatively few judicial precedents exist for the trustee's guidance in such situations, since, in their absence, the trustee may quite logically be inclined to take immediate action under the remedial provisions to avoid subjecting itself to substantial liability.

In many cases, though, patience and a reasonable degree of judgment and discretion enable the situation to be worked out without subjecting the obligor and the security holders to the substantial expense and virtually inevitable losses incurred in a reorganization proceeding. To avoid this, some indentures provide that a default will not occur for breach of an indenture covenant of this type unless and until the trustee has received notice thereof from a specified percentage of the security holders. But this type of provision is generally undesirable because it tends to restrict too greatly the trustee's right to take action. A more desirable provision, and one that is common in most indentures, permits a majority in principal amount of the security holders to waive a default or to direct the trustee's course of conduct in the event of a default.[10]

As in the case of affirmative covenants, the types of negative clauses are many and varied. It is desirable, therefore, to include restrictive provisions to fit the circumstances of each particular case rather than to endeavor to apply a set pattern or formula to each and every situation. The provisions discussed below are some of the more common covenants used. It is important to bear in mind that where the obligor conducts part of its operations through subsidiaries, or may subsequently do so, the covenants should be so phrased as to apply to subsidiaries, as well as to the obligor itself.

 1. Covenants relating to the maintenance of working capital.

Covenants of this type relate to maintenance of working capital (sometimes called *net current assets* and representing excess of current assets over current liabilities) at a certain minimum level. The covenant takes different forms. Sometimes the obligor is required to maintain working capital of a certain stated amount. Sometimes the current ratio (current assets divided by current liabilities) cannot fall below a prescribed minimum. Frequently the covenant requires maintenance of working capital as a stated percentage of funded debt. Occasionally, there will be a combination of several requirements of this type. It is common practice to combine this requirement with other negative covenants. For example, the obligor may be permitted to borrow additional funds so long as the net working capital is maintained at the required percentage of total funded debt.

This type of covenant is important and is almost always included where the principal purpose of the credit being arranged is for working capital, for such purposes as expansion of inventory. Regardless of the proposed use of funds, if the business requires a large amount of working capital, this is one indicator that should be monitored closely when examining the obligor's financial statements. It is desirable to provide some basis for action if there are signs that the obligor's position may be deteriorating.

 2. Covenant against creation of additional debt.

This is a covenant that is commonly found in most debenture agreements. Because the obligations to be issued are unsecured, it is obvious that continued unrestricted borrowing might seriously prejudice the security holders' position or impair the equity on the basis of which they undertook to extend credit.

The basic prohibition is against creation of additional funded debt (usually defined as that having a maturity in excess of one year at the time incurred), but it is sometimes extended to include current debt or current borrowings above a stated amount.

There are normally a number of permitted exceptions to this restriction that can be expressed in several ways. Always exempt from its operation are liabilities (other than for borrowed money) incurred in the ordinary course of business, accrual of taxes, claims for labor, and other similar accruals that are an essential part of the orderly operation of the business.

As indicated above, the restriction is frequently made inoperative as long as certain ratios are maintained. The ratios most frequently used are working capital to total debt and net tangible assets to debt. The latter restriction can be expressed in another way: aggregate debt is limited to a certain percentage of the total capitalization of the obligor. These requirements are usually combined with an earnings requirement. An example of this is a provision that the average profit before interest and taxes during the past five years--and for each of the two preceding years—that is available to pay interest must have been at least nine times the total interest requirements on all debt, including that proposed to be issued.

Finally, the limitation of debt may be merely a total dollar limitation, expressed either with or without the exclusion of liabilities incurred in the ordinary course of business.

   3. Covenant against sale and leaseback.

Under this type of financing, a obligor that owns substantial real estate, such as office buildings, warehouses, or retail stores, arranges for the sale of such property to one or more investors and takes back a noncancelable lease for a specified term at a rental aggregating the purchase price plus an amount equivalent to the going rate of interest on the unamortized purchase price. This not only provides a convenient method of raising funds but also enables the obligor to keep its capital invested in its primary business rather than in the ownership and operation of real estate.

The covenant is designed to prohibit or limit such arrangements during the terms of the loan. The limitation may be expressed in many ways, such as a dollar limitation on the gross value of property transferred, a limitation on the aggregate annual rentals equal to a percentage of net earnings for a prescribed period, or, as in the case of the preceding covenant, a limitation in terms of maintenance of certain ratios of working capital or net tangible assets to debt, where the aggregate of all leaseback sales is added to debt.

The purpose of the covenant is twofold. The first consideration is substantially the same as the restriction against debt. Rentals under the leases become fixed obligations, and a limitation on the incurring of such obligations is usually important. A second consideration is related to the "negative pledge" clause and is a prohibition against sale of productive facilities to which recourse might be had in event of a default. Thus, in some cases, sale of an office building or similar holding may be permitted while sale of factories, warehouses, or other essential productive property is restricted.

  4. A covenant against execution of lease of real property or equipment.

  5. A covenant against rental or lease of personal property sold by the obligor or acquired by an investor for rental or lease to the obligor

These covenants are similar and serve the same purpose as the restriction on sale and leaseback arrangements. Here again, the prohibition may be absolute or may be expressed in terms of certain limitations or exceptions. These limitations may be expressed in terms of a maximum dollar amount of annual rentals or aggregate rentals as a percentage of net earnings, or such leases may be permitted if the terms thereof (including renewals) do not exceed a stated period, usually not more than five years.

      6. Covenant against creation of prior liens (negative pledge clause).

This restriction is designed to prohibit the creation of claims or obligations paramount to those of the indenture securities, so as to insure maintenance of the holders' same priority position as existing at the time the credit is extended. This may be accomplished in either of two ways; the covenant is frequently expressed as either absolutely restricting creation of liens on obligor property or of permitting their creation only on condition that the indenture obligations are equally secured at the same time.[11]

To permit the orderly conduct of the obligor's business, certain logical exceptions to the restriction are usually permitted. These include the following: (1) liens for taxes not yet due; (2) liens existing on property at the time of its acquisition by the obligor or purchase money mortgages created in connection with the acquisition of additional property (these liens may be limited to a certain percentage of the value of such property, and it is usually expressly provided that they cannot extend to any other property of the obligor. It is customary to include a maximum dollar limitation on the aggregate of all such liens); (3) renewals or extension of liens referred to in (2), provided they are not increased and do not extend to other property; (4) liens incurred in the ordinary course of business not involving the borrowing of money; and (5) deposits of money or property to secure performance of a contract or obligation, such as deposits required by worker's compensation laws, under government contracts, in connection with self-insurance arrangements, and the like.

This covenant is frequently referred to as a "negative pledge" clause, which is actually a misnomer. The clause does not create a pledge of any assets nor does it give an equitable lien on any property that may be thereafter pledged or transferred in violation of the covenant.

>7. A covenant against loans, advances, and guarantees.
>
>8. A covenant against pledge or discount of receivables or their sale at less than par.
>
>9. A covenant against mortgage of patents, copyrights, or similar property.
>
>10. A covenant against ownership of securities, except stock or indebtedness of subsidiaries or obligations of the United States.

These covenants fall into the same general category as the preceding one and are intended to prevent the encumbrance, dissipation, or use of obligor assets except in the orderly conduct of its business. The covenant against loans, advances, and guarantees usually includes an exemption of intrasystem transactions if a portion of the obligor's business is conducted through subsidiaries, and the restrictive covenants in the indenture apply to both obligor and subsidiaries. Transactions in the ordinary course of business may also be excepted if guarantees are normally granted as a part of the conduct of the business.

>11. A covenant restricting payment of dividends or purchase or retirement of stock.

Equity capital, or the stockholders' investment in a business, is made up not only of the stated capital and surplus, which they have paid into the business as consideration for the issuance of their shares, but also of the amount of the earned surplus, which represents the aggregate of the earnings that the obligor has retained for use in the business. Generally speaking, earned surplus is not subject to any restrictions and could be paid out or distributed to stockholders at any time as dividends. This distribution could be in cash or in property. One of the principal concerns of an investor in extending credit is the amount of the stockholders' equity, particularly in relation to the amount of the debt that will be outstanding. Because debt represents a priority claim against the assets of the obligor, any excessive distribution to stockholders may be regarded as a preferential distribution to a subordinate claimant.

It is therefore quite common in all indentures, whether secured or unsecured, to include a provision that will prevent any unwarranted distribution. This is usually done by placing a substantial portion of the unrestricted earned surplus in a restricted category for the duration of the loan. A portion of such surplus is usually left in an unrestricted category available for dividends, the amount being a matter for negotiation, but quite frequently it represents a sum approximately equal to one year's dividends on the stock. In working out the other terms of the credit, the amount so unrestricted is usually disregarded by the investor and the amount retained provides an additional cushion to bolster the credit extended.

The covenant usually provides that no dividends will be distributed to stockholders or any funds of the corporation applied to the purchase, redemption, or other retirement of shares of stock in excess of the sum of (1) the amount of the earned surplus left in an unrestricted category, (2) the obligor's net earnings after a stated date (usually the end of the next fiscal year), and (3) the amount received by the obligor as proceeds of sale of additional shares of stock.

The payment of dividends or other distributions to stockholders is always made contingent on there being no default under the arrangement and, quite frequently, on the existence of certain minimum ratios at the time of declaration.

12. Covenants relating to subsidiaries, the most common being: (a) against the sale of stock or debt of a subsidiary, (b) against the issue of stock of a subsidiary except to the parent obligor or to another subsidiary, and (c) against permitting a subsidiary to issue preferred stock except to the obligor or to another subsidiary.

As indicated above, when subsidiary companies are important to a system operation, all general restrictive covenants, such as those against additional debt or against creation of liens, are made applicable alike to the parent company and subsidiaries. Because the companies are viewed as an entity for the purpose of the credit, intrasystem transactions are customarily excluded from operation of these restrictions. It is therefore necessary to add other restrictions to prevent the weakening of the entity by reducing the system percentage ownership of any subsidiary obligor.

The first of the covenants prohibits disposal of the investment in a subsidiary. In order to permit flexibility, the restrictive provision usually states that no stock or indebtedness of a subsidiary may be sold except as an entirety and then only if (1) the operations conducted by such subsidiary do not represent a significant part of system operations; (2) in the judgment of the obligor's board of directors, retention of the investment therein is no longer necessary for system operations; (3) the sale is for a cash consideration representing the full value of the system investment in the subsidiary; and (4) the subsidiary owns no stock or indebtedness of another subsidiary.

For subsidiary companies that are less than 100 percent owned by the system, covenant (b) above, is usually qualified to prohibit any issuance of stock that would decrease the system's pro-rata interest.

The reason for prohibiting a public issue of preferred stock of a subsidiary follows the same theory as the prohibition against prior liens. As far as the obligor itself is concerned, the indenture securities have priority over any preferred stock issue. The stock of a subsidiary company is, however, an asset of the obligor, and permitting the issuance of another class of stock having priority would be equivalent to subjecting the property represented by such asset to a prior claim.

> 13. A covenant against merger of the obligor or sale or lease of all or substantially all of its assets.

The indenture usually contains a separate section dealing with mergers, consolidations, and so on. It is included here because it is, in effect, a restrictive covenant. There is usually no absolute prohibition against mergers or consolidations or sale of obligor assets, but such activities are permitted only under certain conditions, which should be carefully and explicitly stated. The following conditions are usually included:

> (a) Either the obligor must be the surviving corporation, or the obligations under the indenture must be expressly assumed in writing (usually by supplemental indenture) by the survivor.
>
> (b) There must be no default under the indenture, and no default can exist after completion of the merger.
>
> (c) If any other debt will become a lien on any properties of the obligor upon completion of the merger, the indenture securities must be secured by a mortgage or other lien on the obligor's properties prior to the merger.
>
> (d) If the surviving corporation will have secured debt outstanding in excess of a given amount

(whether or not the obligor's property will become subject to such lien), the indenture securities must be first secured by a lien on the obligor's properties.

(e) If the indenture requires the maintenance of a certain specified ratios (such as minimum working capital, working capital to debt, or net tangible assets to debt), these ratios usually must exist in the prescribed minimum amount immediately following the merger.

In reviewing a draft of a proposed indenture contract, all the provisions should be read together as in the aggregate constituting a single entity. This is particularly true of all the covenants of the indenture. In addition, the administrator should ensure that none of them is inconsistent with any of the obligations/covenants mandated by the TIA. To administer a contract properly, the trustee must understand it. This means not only making sense out of the language of each provision considered separately but also understanding the meaning and purpose of the whole indenture as a single contract. The investor is willing to extend credit on certain terms and conditions that the borrower is willing to meet. The indenture contract should spell out those terms and conditions completely and unambiguously. All the provisions thereof should fit together as a pattern. Once the concept of the entire contract is understood thoroughly, each covenant will take on its proper meaning, and the job of administration will be rendered much easier.

---

[1] See TIA, sec. 314. The TIRA converted several frequently used covenants, designed to afford the continuing supply of information to the trustee about the obligor's affairs, into legislatively mandated obligations.

[2] See TIA, sec. 314(a)(2). The annual report of the obligor should be accompanied by a certificate or opinion of independent public accountants, as to the obligor's compliance with those conditions or covenants in the indenture which are subject to verification by accountants.

[3] TIA, sec. 314(a)(2).

[4] See TIA, sec. 314(a)(4). This certification need not include the four compliance statements set forth in sec. 314(e).

[5] See chapter 3, note 2, *supra.*

[6] McDaniel, "Bondholders and Corporate Governance," 41 *Bus. Law.* 413, 425-427 (1986).

[7] Patricia A. Vlahakis, "Old Indentures--New Transactions," 929 *Law J.* (Seminars Press) 19 (1989).

[8] See also Patricia A.Vlahakis, "Deleveraging: A Search for Rules in a Financial Free-for-All," *M & A and Corporate Governance Law Reptr.* 290 (Oct. 1990); Clemens, "Poison Debt: The New Takeover Defense," 42 *Bus. Law.* 747 (May 1987).

[9] See TIA sec. 316(a)(1)(B) and 316(c).

[10] Id.

[11] For an excellent review of this topic, see Morey W. McDaniel, "Are Negative Pledge Clauses in Public Debt Issues Obsolete?" 38 *Bus. Law.* 867 (May 1983).

TEN

PAYMENT AND REDEMPTION OF SECURITIES

Although the "perpetual debenture" without a fixed maturity has been used with success in the United Kingdom and certain of the Commonwealth countries, this practice never developed in the United States. Such obligations are frequently regarded more as stock than debt, and certainly they have many of the aspects of permanent equity capital. Almost without exception, corporate debt obligations issued in this country under indentures, have a fixed maturity. This is, of course, an essential condition to the negotiability of the securities.

The fixed obligation in the securities and the corresponding indenture covenants to pay the principal and interest as they become due are the obligor's most important undertakings. On or before the fixed maturity of the debt, funds must be provided to make payment thereof, although this is not always easy. As we noted earlier, one device is the use of the sinking fund in which a portion of the debt is retired each year over its life, thereby eliminating, or substantially reducing, the problem presented at final maturity. Another common device used in financings of states and municipalities is to provide for serial maturities, with a portion of the debt actually falling due by its terms each year. This practice has been seldom used in issues of business corporations, as market acceptance can make it more difficult to sell the securities.

It is unusual, and sometimes not prudent from a cash management perspective, for an obligor to pay off a large fixed principal maturity out of available cash. Even where a sinking fund covenant has been included, there is often a substantial portion of the obligations to be paid at final maturity. The obligor's financial officer must therefore plan the cash flow sufficiently in advance of the maturity date to ensure that funds will be available to pay the obligations at maturity. Some form of refunding that involves the issuance of other securities to provide the cash to pay off the maturing issue is usually necessary. As we pointed out in chapter 5, among the purposes for which additional securities are customarily authorized to be issued under open-end indentures is the refunding of prior lien securities or other series of securities outstanding under the indenture.

When the obligor enjoys a good credit rating and where adequate thought has gone into the drafting of the contracts involved in the obligor's financial undertaking, no serious difficulty is presented by an approaching debt maturity date. An important question may be, however, timing and cost. If an obligor is faced with the necessity of meeting a maturity during a period of higher interest rates, its annual fixed charges may be substantially increased. From the obligor's point of view, therefore, it is desirable that a considerable degree of flexibility be reserved in the indenture to facilitate its dealing with its debt obligations.

To provide this flexibility, the indenture's redemption provisions are important. These usually appear in a separate article of the indenture. The redemption provisions constitute the reservation by the obligor of the privilege of prepaying its securities, or designated portions thereof, at its option, before their stated maturity. To exercise this privilege the obligor may be required to pay a price, in the form of a redemption premium, in addition to the principal and accrued interest to the date of prepayment. The right of redemption before maturity is a significant right. The terms on which it may be exercised, including the amount of premium that must be paid, are important elements in the original negotiations. It is common, however, to set the initial redemption premium at an amount equivalent to one year's interest on the securities. This premium is then scaled down, in substantially equal amounts throughout the life of the issue. Generally, no premium is paid during the last year.

Because this affects the rights of the security holders, the redemption privilege must be set forth in the text of the securities, as well as in the indenture. The language should be in sufficient detail to put the holder on notice about the essential terms and conditions on which the obligation may be called for prepayment.

During periods of high interest rates, investors prefer to protect themselves against the possibility that the obligations they purchase will be refunded as soon as a change in market conditions makes it advantageous for the issuer to do so. When there is a rapid change in market conditions and a substantial decline in interest rates, obligors may call their securities, even if they have been outstanding less than a year. As a result investors may suffer substantial losses because they sold other securities (or passed up other investment opportunities) to purchase these obligations whose subsequent redemption necessitated reinvestment at much lower yields.

The protection against such a possibility takes the form of a noncallable or nonrefundable provision in the security and indenture. A *noncallable* provision means merely that the obligor may not redeem its securities (except for sinking fund purposes) for a stated period of time. A *nonrefundable* provision permits redemption, but specifies that this cannot be done with other funds borrowed at a rate of interest less than that borne by the indenture securities. These restrictions are usually limited to a specified period of time following the date of a security issue--commonly five or ten years.

A noncallable provision is easily administered, whereas a nonrefundable provision may present difficulties. The trustee should insist that the indenture include a provision for receiving a certificate from appropriate officials of the obligor. This certificate should state that a proposed redemption does not violate the restriction, and the trustee should be authorized to rely conclusively on such a certificate.

Some indentures provide that the obligor, at its discretion, may purchase securities on the open market and submit them to the trustee in satisfaction of mandatory sinking fund redemptions and in lieu of redeeming securities. Corporate obligors are particularly likely to do this during periods when current market prices for the securities are lower than the call price. Indentures permitting this alternative should clearly state that the obligor must provide a certificate to the trustee, well in advance of the date specified for the trustee to select securities to be called, stating exactly how a particular sinking fund will be satisfied. Typically the obligor's certificate is provided at least sixty days prior to the redemption date, to allow the trustee sufficient time to process the redemption and provide notice in accordance with the governing provisions of the indenture.

Whether or not an indenture provides for a sinking fund, it may permit the obligor to purchase securities on the open market and submit them to the trustee for cancellation. Many corporate obligors take advantage of this in periods of favorable market conditions to reduce the outstanding debt and related carrying costs. In this situation the trustee should receive an appropriate certification well in advance of the time when it would normally begin to select securities for redemption. It is important for the trustee to maintain accurate records of credits applied toward future sinking fund obligations. It is common for obligors to satisfy sinking fund requirements several years in advance, if market prices permit the purchase of securities below the redemption price.

Another alternative to a sinking fund call in some indentures, particularly municipal revenue issues, is the right of the obligor to instruct the trustee to use accumulated cash deposits in the sinking fund to conduct a tender offer for securities. The trustee selects sufficient securities from among all securities tendered to satisfy the sinking fund requirement. The indenture should spell out the mechanics of such a procedure, including the timing of and criteria for notifying holders and selecting security certificates.

A different form of redemption giving the security holder the right to sell the security back to the issuer, at par, has also been used. In issues with this provision, the holder receives a "put" or "demand" option, the difference being that in the *put option*, the security may be sold back *only* on a fixed date or specific dates. In the *demand* option, the right may be exercised at any time, usually on one to seven days' notice. In either situation the underlying agreement must carefully spell out the holder's option rights.

Put and demand options evolved during the late 1970s and 1980s in response to investors' desire for greater liquidity in periods of economic uncertainty and interest rate volatility, and is still in use today. Obligors have used one-to-seven day put security issues as alternatives to the issuance of commercial paper. Although initially, puts were associated primarily with municipal securities, they have been used in many forms by corporate issuers. One such variety, developed as part of a corporate anti-takeover strategy is the *poison put*, in which holders may put their securities back to the issuer, as for example in event of a significant change in ownership of the obligor (i.e., a hostile takeover).

Although some securities are issued without put or demand features, they have put options attached to them by investment bankers to improve the marketability in times of sharply rising interest rates. Certificates representing these *added on* options are separate from the security itself, and the terms will be specified in a separate option agreement. Usually the security holder pays a price--either deducted from interest payments or otherwise paid--for the right to the put option in these situations. Issues that provide the holder with a put or demand option also may entitle the obligor to the right of redemption of the issue on the put date or upon notice to holders in the case of a demand option. Generally, the right to redemption by the obligor can be exercised at its option. It is common for a tender agent to be appointed independent of the trustee. Managing a put feature requires extraordinary coordination among the tender agent, trustee, the paying agent and the applicable operations department, requiring each party to the transaction to understand the rules and the timing in which the put will operate. Puts require cautious interpretation as they often contain restrictions which may not be fully understood by the security holder.

RISK AND LIABILITY CONCERNS

Because of the great surge in the number and amount of security redemptions beginning in the late 1980s, trustees and paying agents have been subjected to ever increasing pressure from the investment community and the public to compensate holders for losses resulting from failure to present and redeem called securities in a timely manner. In seeking such compensation, holders frequently claim that the trustee/paying agent was "unjustly enriched" as a result of the holder failing to submit a called security until sometime after the redemption date. In such situations the holder may allege that he/she did not receive proper notification of the security call. To establish industry guidance for the payment of such claims, the American Bankers Association (ABA), through its Fiduciary and Securities Operations Division, developed a set of Compensation Guidelines covering processing time frames and conditions for payment of called debt securities. The Guidelines established parameters for payment of compensation in the event of error or noncompliance by the trustees and paying agents.[1]

These guidelines, apply to all corporate and municipal debt securities, and to the presentation of called securities either through physical or book-entry delivery.

Uniform standards for redemption notices and compensation claims are important in limiting risk to trustees/paying agents in processing calls of zero coupon security. Because these obligations do not pay periodic interest, a holder who misses a security call may not become aware that his/her security was called until presenting it for payment years later upon final maturity. At that time, upon finding that the security can be redeemed for only the accreted value as of the call date many years earlier, a holder may attempt to lodge a claim or file a lawsuit against the trustee/paying agent. The redemption standards approved by the American National Standards Institute (and discussed later), contain special provisions for zero coupon securities which requires one additional notice of an early redemption to be sent within a year's time after the redemption date, via secure means. But the ability to maintain current addresses of security holders for zero coupon corporate securities is hampered because fewer notices need to be mailed, under the reformation of the Trust Indenture Act. As an added service, trustees and agents may ask obligors to consider a special periodic mailing to zero coupon security holders to verify their current addresses.

Of related concern to the trustee/paying agent is liability that may result from the method of giving notice to security holders. Although an indenture for a fully registered or partly registered issue may require that notice be given by publication only, it is wise for the trustee also to mail notice to the registered holders to avoid claims and possible litigation. The redemption standards mentioned later in this chapter contain a provision for marking the outside of envelopes containing redemption notices with a notice reading "IMPORTANT NOTICE OF REDEMPTION ENCLOSED."

For both partial and full redemptions, an appropriate affidavit of mailing should be prepared by the trustee and filed as part of its records. This affidavit would include, as attachments, the redemption notice and a listing of all registered holders with called securities. In case of bearer security issues, the list of the serial numbers arranged numerically by maturity should be included as part of the redemption notice as published and mailed. Appropriate affidavits of both publication and mailing should also be obtained by the trustee.

Another area of concern in risk management is redeeming structured financing transactions. The trustee/paying agent must be careful to execute redemptions in accordance with the operative documents, because failing to do so may adversely affect cash flow coverage of future debt service and could destroy the integrity of nonrecourse financing. In financings requiring a "strip call" or involving zero coupon securities, failing to call the correct securities on just one occasion may have an escalating negative effect over future years. Credit enhancement providers and rating agencies monitor trustee/paying agent performance in these areas, and the trustee/paying agent may be held liable for damage to cash flows arising out of errors in redemption processing. Examples of structured financings where these concerns are critical include those involving multifamily housing, single family housing, and collateralized mortgage obligations.

MECHANICAL PROVISIONS

Terms and Conditions

The terms and conditions on which the securities may be called for prepayment should be carefully spelled out in the indenture. Although it is the obligor that theoretically exercises the right, as a practical matter the trustee will usually be called upon to carry out all details. Therefore, these provisions should receive careful attention by the trustee as it reviews the prospective contract. Under an open-end indenture, providing for different series of securities, the redemption terms (other than the amount of premium payable) are usually set forth in the original indenture and are made applicable to all series of securities including those to be issued in the future. As an alternative, the terms of the original indenture may be made applicable only to the initial series of securities, the terms and conditions for subsequent series being included in the supplemental indenture or board resolution creating each series. Although not frequently used, the latter practice is recommended as providing the greater degree of flexibility.

The first condition to which attention should be directed is the nature and extent of the right. Subject to any provisions for nonrefundability, this right should be as broadly based as possible. The right should be reserved to redeem all or any part, of the indenture securities at any time or from time to time. Occasionally redemption is restricted to a minimum principal amount, and such a restriction is proper from the point of view of both the obligor and the investor. Some indentures restrict the redemption to an interest payment date, while other indentures may not allow for redemption at any time.

The redemption premiums should be explicit. They are customarily expressed as a percentage of the principal amount. If a formula for a declining percentage is to be used, it should be worked out prior to execution of the indenture and the actual prices (by dates) set forth in the indenture and in the securities. This formula avoids any possibility of error or misunderstanding at a later date. For a sinking fund, the securities normally are callable at par, without premium.

From the practical handling of redemptions, two provisions are desirable for the trustee: for registered securities, no endorsement or assignment should be required if payment is to be made to the registered holder. The securities must be presented to obtain payment unless a home office payment agreement is allowed by the governing indenture. Home office payment agreements typically apply to private placement securities owned by institutional investors. When redemption is on an interest payment date, the interest check should be mailed to the registered holders as of the record date in the normal manner. In the case of bearer securities, the holders should be instructed to detach and present separately the interest coupon maturing on that date; otherwise a great deal of confusion may arise in subsequent accountings. Even though the principal amount of securities in bearer form has declined dramatically, unless redeemed, some bearer securities are expected to be outstanding for the next decade or so.

Notices

Notice of redemption must be given to the holders of the securities. The indenture must specify not only the method of giving notice but also the period of time before the redemption date when such notice must be given. A minimum of thirty days' notice is ordinarily required, and it is also common for a maximum period to be specified. The usual provision is to require the first notice to be given not less than thirty, nor more than sixty, days before the date designated for the redemption.

The indenture should specify the information to be included in the notice including a full description of the issue as printed on the security certificate: name, date of issue, maturity date, interest rates, date of redemption, redemption price, CUSIP number, certificate number and called amounts for each certificate (for partial calls), the place or places of payment to which the called securities should be presented, total principal amount called, if less than the entire issue is called, and if a new security will be issued for any unredeemed portion, and any other information that may be pertinent to the particular situation or required by law or regulation.

The notice should state that on the designated redemption date, the called securities (or portions thereof) will become due and payable, and that on and after this date all interest will cease to accrue and the holders will cease to be entitled to the benefits of the indenture, as their rights are limited to receipt of the redemption price in the hands of the trustee, or paying agent, upon presentation of their securities for cancellation. As we stated earlier, it is common for security holders to allege they did not receive a notice of redemption and to claim additional interest. An additional operational procedure to avoid future interest claims from security holders, is to cite the redemption or the final maturity on the interest check of each applicable security holder. The endorsement block on the check can state that the holder's endorsement includes acknowledgment of notice of the redemption or final maturity. This notice typically can be programmed into the operating system.

To overcome problems in the redemption notification process of securities, the SEC and the American Bankers Association established standards and guidelines based on a consensus of opinions expressed by major securities industry associations, the self-regulatory organizations, and federal regulatory agencies.[2] The standards were that:

> 1. Notices of security redemptions should contain the preceding information.

2. All notices should be sent in a secure fashion (e.g., certified mail or overnight express) to all registered securities depositories and to the national information services that disseminate such information.

3. Notices provide for a thirty-day period between notice date and redemption date.

4. Notices should be sent to the registered depositories in advance of the publication date (a guideline generally not acceptable to corporate trustees).

5. Second notices of advance refunding should be given thirty days prior to the redemption date.

6. The CUSIP number be indicated on all redemption payments (checks and wires).[3]

These guidelines were disseminated as "Recommended Guidelines for Processing Bond Calls" by the ABA's Corporate Trust Committee in the summer of 1989. To further encourage industry wide acceptance of these guidelines (with even greater specificity), the American National Standards Institute, working through its X9D Committee, developed a revised set of standards which were approved and published on December 11, 1992 as the *Called Securities Processing -- Securities Subject to Early Redemption.* These standards include: notice of redemption, publication of notice of redemption, follow-up notices, and suggested trust indenture language.

It is standard practice for all parties to a new financing to abide by these standards. During the indenture review period, trustees should monitor the redemption provisions to verify the standards are included. For older municipal indentures, it may be difficult to provide a thirty-day advance notice of the redemption as the standards require. Accordingly, some older indentures contain a shorter advance notice period.

The redemption notice standards have also been incorporated in the required procedures and operating arrangements of securities depositories. Trustees and agents should be familiar with the required procedures and should maintain current copies of procedures provided by Depository Trust Company (DTC) and by broker/dealers, if the securities are registered in "street name." For a partial call of a fully registered security issue, the traditional notice listing all the security numbers and applicable principal amounts called for redemption can be avoided by using a letter form of notice incorporating the required details of redemption. This notice should be accompanied by a special form addressed to each holder affected by the call setting forth the principal amount of holdings selected for redemption and the security number(s) against which the selection was allocated, to be presented for payment. Copies of this form can also be used for follow-up and posting operations. Such notice should be sent by mail to the registered holders at their addresses as indicated in the security register. The notice needs only to be sent to the registered holders of securities selected for redemption. Notice by registered or certified mail should never be required. A certificate of mailing should be prepared indicating that the notice was mailed on a specified date, that a count of notices mailed was reconciled with the number of registered holders whose securities were called, and that the notices were properly addressed and deposited in a postal facility.

The indenture should not contain any requirement for the publication of the notice, for this is expensive and unnecessary where all securities are registered. However, when an issue is actively traded, it is very desirable to have a list of the numbers of the called securities made available to any securities exchange on which the securities are listed, in addition to DTC and broker/dealers, which often require that this data be provided by the trustee.

When securities are outstanding in bearer form, notice is given by publication in an authorized newspaper. What constitutes an "authorized newspaper" should be defined in the indenture. Published notices should comply with the standards specified in the SEC and ABA guidelines. For corporate issues, copies should also be sent to any securities exchanges on which the securities are listed. In addition to publishing the required notice, which should also indicate the specific serial numbers of the bearer securities to be redeemed and the coupons that must be attached to them, a copy should be sent to each registered holder of called securities. The trustee should be most careful to see that such mailing is effected, and at the same time as the initial publication. Bearer security holders often have requested trustees and agents to maintain their names and addresses on file for future notices. Since the few outstanding bearer security issues typically allow for issuance of registered securities, trustees should consider abandoning the practice of agreeing to maintain bearer holder addresses for future notice, to limit potential compensation claims from holders.

If the redemption is for the sinking fund, or is achieved by use of special funds constituting a part of the trust estate, the notice should be mailed (or published) under the name of trustee (or sinking fund agent, if other than the trustee) unless the indenture specifies otherwise. If redemption is pursuant to an option right reserved to the obligor, it should be mailed (or published) under the name of the obligor, even though it was actually prepared and disseminated by the trustee.

Payment Provisions

Provision should be made for depositing with the trustee those funds required to effect the redemption. It is not necessary that this be done before the selection and mailing (or publication) of notice, although the funds should be deposited on or before the date of payment and in the full amount. The deposit should be made in trust, and the funds held in a special account specifically allocated to payment of the securities to be redeemed. Same day funds payment rules as recommended by the Group of Thirty became effective on February 22, 1996. The rules are a requirement for all dividend, interest and principal payments on securities and requires funds to be received at DTC early in the afternoon on the payable date. Meeting this deadline allows DTC to pay its participants on the payable date. Much has been done to educate municipal and corporate obligors to deposit federal funds early on the payable date in order to comply with the same day funds requirements. In the past, many municipal issuers preferred to make their debt service payments by check. Fortunately, this is no longer the case. Trustees and paying agents must carefully control the receipt of funds to determine if the funds are collected at the time they are paid to DTC. Monitoring receipt and disbursement of debt service funds avoids the potential for incurring daylight overdrafts. Trustees should consult the operating procedures of DTC to fully understand the rules, should a payment be made in error and it is necessary to retrieve the funds. On heavy redemption dates, the amounts being wired to DTC may exceed their bank's day-light overdraft cap. Thus each trustee must be aware of the daylight overdraft rules established by the Federal Reserve System.

Managing the timely receipt and immediate disbursement of funds is one of the many operating challenges of the trustee and or agent. If the deposit is made with a paying agent other than the trustee, it should be placed in a special trust account in the name of the trustee and should be under its control rather than the obligor's. An appropriate letter to this effect should also be obtained from the paying agent unless such an undertaking is included in a general letter at the time of execution of the indenture. If not deposited, or if the obligor acts as its own paying agent and retains the redemption funds under its control, the called securities should not be discharged from the trustee's records until they are actually received and canceled by it. If because of a refunding or for other reasons, funds necessary for the redemption are deposited before the date of the mailing (or first publication) of notice, an early payment is sometimes offered. This is an offer to pay the full redemption price upon presentation of securities at any time after mailing (or publication) of notice, even if presentation is before the redemption date. The making of such an offer is an acceptable, although seldom used, practice, but it should be made at the discretion of the obligor, and must be made if the indenture so requires. The trustee should not undertake, by agreement with anyone other than the obligor, to effect such a prior payment, even though the funds may be in its possession.

When payment is made for redeemed securities, the trustee/paying agent must ensure that proper procedures have been established in the operational area so that IRS Form 1099B will be issued for each payment made. These forms should be issued as of the redemption date and for the year in which the redemption date occurs, regardless of when redeemed securities are actually presented for payment. The issuance of the Form 1099B also serves as an additional notice to the security holder if the holder has failed to present their security timely. This, of course, applies to all securities redeemed, whether interest on such securities is taxable or tax-exempt. Since most municipal securities are tax exempt, it is common for municipal security holders to argue that no notice to the IRS is required. Notice to the IRS on Form 1099B can serve as notice of a potential capital gain or loss on a municipal security. If the trustee/paying agent has not previously received a certified taxpayer identification number for a payee on IRS Form W-8 or W-9, it must obtain such a certification prior to disbursing redemption proceeds.

As stated in the Interest and Dividend Tax Compliance Act of 1983, as amended, the trustee may be required to withhold 28 percent of the total redemption proceeds for a payment in the event such payee fails to provide certain certifications, or if the trustee/paying agent is ordered to withhold by the IRS. Most operating systems provide the functionality to maintain accurate filing information. Any required withholding of interest is generally performed by the trustee/agent's operating system.

With the passage of the Tax Increase Prevention and Reconciliation Act of 2005, trustees, paying agents, and broker-dealers were required for the first time to report to the IRS all tax-exempt interest paid to bondholders on municipal bonds, in the same manner as interest paid on taxable obligations. The provision was enacted retroactive to January 1, 2006. Although tax-exempt interest is not subject to federal income tax, it is included in the computation of taxable Social Security benefits, and "private activity bond" interest is taxable for the alternative minimum tax. Also, tax-exempt interest counts as investment income when determining eligibility for the earned-income credit. This additional reporting requirement was handled relatively smoothly by the corporate trust industry for the first time in 2007.

PARTIAL REDEMPTIONS

When fewer than all of the securities of an issue are to be redeemed, provision must be made for selection of the particular securities. This should be done by the trustee, and the method followed is the same as in the case of selection of securities for redemption by a sinking fund. As noted in chapter 7, the indenture should give the trustee the flexibility in the selection process. Rather than detail the particular procedures to be employed, indenture drafters should leave this entirely to the trustee's discretion. The only requirement should be that the method adopted be fair and equitable to all holders. In this way, the trustee can keep up with current practices rather than be bound by possibly antiquated procedures. The traditional method of selection has been by security number, with a basic unit of $1,000 for corporate issues and $5,000 for municipal securities. Securities of larger denominations being assigned as many unit numbers as there are multiples of $1,000 or $5,000. Other methods of selection may be equally fair depending on the particular case. For an all registered issue the indenture may require the trustee to make the selection pro rata by holder and then allocate the portions selected against a particular security or securities. The significance of this method is that each holder receives a portion of the redemption proceeds.

Some structured financings with serial securities require a partial call so that the aggregate annual debt service requirement will be reduced proportionately for each serial maturity. For this type of call, known as a *strip call*, securities must be selected across all maturities, including maturities comprised of zero coupon securities, so that proportionate reduction is achieved. The proper execution of these calls in accordance with indenture provisions can be critical to future cash flows.

The necessity for closing the security register during the selection period is obvious, and there is no way in which changes in the holders or numbers of outstanding registered securities can be permitted. The indenture should provide that the privilege of transfer or exchange of securities may be suspended for a period of fifteen days preceding the mailing or publication. It is incumbent upon the trustee, however, to use its best efforts to keep the suspension to a minimum period of time, especially for an active security issue, so that registration of transfers as a result of trading is not unduly disrupted. If the parties desire, an interim receipt can be issued for a security presented for registration of transfer or in exchange during the period the security register is closed. In such event, however, the registrar should place a legend on the receipt to the effect that the security register is closed for purpose of selection of securities for redemption at a designated price on a designated date; that the security presented for registration of transfer or exchange is subject to selection for redemption in whole or in part; and that in the event of such selection, a new security(s) registered, as indicated on the receipt, for the uncalled portion will be delivered in exchange for the receipt, together with a redemption ticket redeemable on the redemption date, for the called portion of such security.

Once the selection has been made and the notice mailed (or first published), the securities selected become due and payable on the date designated. On this date they cease to be outstanding for any purpose of the indenture except to receive payment and should be removed from the classification of outstanding securities by appropriate entry in the trustee's records. It is desirable to control them in a subsidiary redemption ledger, with appropriate entry being made as the securities are actually surrendered and paid.

Because some of the securities will not be presented promptly, care should be taken on the next record date for payment of interest that appropriate stop payments are noted on the registrar's records. For bearer securities, the stop payment should be noted against the coupons appurtenant to all such securities that remain outstanding. This will not only prevent the making of an unauthorized payment but will also facilitate notice to such holders who have not surrendered their called securities.

After the selection has been completed and the security register reopened, any security not affected by the call may be transferred, exchanged, or otherwise dealt with. When a portion of a security has been selected for redemption and such security is presented for transfer or exchange before the redemption date, it is perfectly proper to effect the requested transaction with respect to the uncalled portion of the security. The original security, now representing only the called portion, should be retained by the trustee (or forwarded by the registrar to the trustee or paying agent) for payment on the redemption date. It has been suggested that provision be made for registration of transfer of called securities between the date of selection and the redemption date. It is difficult to understand why this should be desired, for the status of the obligation has now been changed. It represents only the right to receive payment of the redemption price on the redemption date and can no longer be used in settlement of a contract to deliver a "security" of the issue.

If the entire issue has been called for redemption, it may be desirable to continue the registration of transfer process and permit the trading of "called" securities. In this situation any securities delivered should be overstamped with an appropriate legend of the redemption.

The process of selecting securities for redemption and special precautions to avoid future payments on called securities is delegated, in most trustee and agent offices today, to the operating systems. The redemption standards and increasing numbers of redemptions can best be processed with sophisticated operating systems.

CONVERTIBLE SECURITIES

Debt securities that can be converted, at the option of the holder, into other types of securities of the issuer, require the trustee to protect this privilege. The common practice when any securities are called for redemption is to continue the conversion privilege to and including the redemption date. The trustee should request that such a provision be included in the indenture. Some issues provide that a conversion privilege will terminate several days before the redemption date. No matter how carefully it is spelled out in the notice, many holders invariably miss the cutoff date and consequently sustain substantial loss. In preparing the redemption notice, it is recommended that the conversion privilege, if of value, be stated separately so that the holder's attention is drawn to it. It is inevitable that some holders will lose their privilege through misunderstanding or carelessness, but every effort should be made to keep such loss at a minimum.

For convertible issues, the trustee should insist that the indenture provisions contain specific time frames prior to a redemption date in which the obligor may notify the trustee of its election to redeem securities. Discretion for the trustee to determine that a shorter notice period is satisfactory may lead to claims or litigation by holders in the event that the economic return to the holders resulting from such conversion and redemption timing is effected.

Funds held in the redemption account for payment of securities converted are usually returned to the obligor. This is proper, for in effect payment for the securities has been made by the issuance of other securities (e.g., stock). The trustee should make certain that this is explicitly covered in the indenture.

---

[1] For recommended redemption notification guidelines, see this chapter, note 2, *infra.*

[2] SEC Release 34-23856 (Dec. 3, 1986), 51 Fed. Reg. 235 at 44398 (Dec. 9, 1986).

[3] See Van Gemert v. Boeing Co. 520 F. 2d 1373 (2d. Cir.), *cert. denied,* 423 U.S. 947 (1975).

ELEVEN

SATISFACTION AND DEFEASANCE

An important part of every indenture is the section pertaining to satisfaction and discharge, or defeasance. *Defeasance* related to the "undoing" or release from the lien of the indenture or the mortgage of property originally pledged or mortgaged to secure the payment of principal and interest, and to ensure performance by the obligor of its covenants. For any type of secured issue, including a mortgage bond indenture, defeasance will entitle the obligor or mortgagor to receive its pledged or mortgaged property free and clear from the lien of the indenture.

Such defeasance should not be confused with *in-substance defeasance* (also referred to as *taxable defeasance*, *de facto defeasance* and *effective defeasance*), which are transactions intended to satisfy debt obligations in substance although there is no legal discharge of the obligation. In effect, an issuer purchases U.S. government obligations at a discount and places them in a trust, pledging the future income and principal of the governments to pay off the interest and principal on its own outstanding security issue. This transaction may be advantageous to the issuer in that it can (1) enhance its financial statements, (2) upgrade its debt rating, and (3) result in effectively retiring an outstanding security issue without having to repurchase the securities.[1] Next, we examine special concerns with these transactions.

In most cases, the indenture covenants are included as additional security provisions to guarantee performance of the basic covenant, namely, to pay the indenture obligations as they become due. Accordingly, if all such obligations

231

have been paid, or satisfactory provision made therefor, the obligor is entitled to a satisfaction, even though a default may have occurred or may at the time exist under a particular security covenant.

The obligor must, however, have discharged, or provided for the discharge of, all its obligations to the security holders. For example, if the securities contain a convertible provision, an option to purchase stock, or any other condition or provision that constituted an additional consideration for purchase of the securities by the holders, it is not sufficient merely to provide for payment of principal and interest on the indenture securities. All other conditions must be performed or their performance provided for before the obligor is entitled to a formal satisfaction and discharge of the indenture.

The obligor must also have discharged all obligations owing to the trustee and other agents. These include payment of all disbursements, repayment of all advances (with interest if properly chargeable), and payment of all fees and other compensation due, including reasonable fees for execution of a satisfaction and any other duties required to be performed subsequently.

If the trustee executes and delivers a satisfaction improperly, it will be liable for legal damages to anyone injured by its action. Conversely, if it improperly withholds a satisfaction, it may be liable to the obligor. The trustee must therefore exercise due care in all matters relating to the satisfaction and discharge of the indenture.

It would be impractical and unfair to require actual payment of all the outstanding securities before the obligor could obtain a satisfaction. Over a long period of time some securities become misplaced or lost, or holders are slow in presenting them for payment. Occasionally, a small percentage of the obligations are never presented, and in many instances several years may elapse before all the obligations are actually retired. Nevertheless, the security holders are entitled to their security until they receive payment for their securities, and it is important that such payment be secured for them before the indenture is satisfied.

The usual provision is to require deposit with the trustee, in trust, of funds sufficient to pay all principal and interest on the securities to maturity date, or to the redemption date, if the securities have been called and for the indenture to provide that, upon such deposit, the obligor shall become entitled to a satisfaction of the indenture. If any facts must be established or any conditions satisfied, the indenture should provide that the trustee will be protected if it accepts and relies in good faith on an officers' certificate and opinion of counsel as to the existence of such facts or the performance of these conditions.

It is not essential that all steps be taken to effect the redemption before a satisfaction can be given. This fact may be important if the redemption funds are being provided through refunding under another indenture. In order that the obligor give a proper lien under the new indenture--which is essential to enable it to secure the necessary funds--it must at the same time be able to secure a legal discharge of the former lien. It is sufficient if the requisite funds are deposited with the trustee together with irrevocable instructions to perform all acts necessary to make the redemption.

ACCOUNTING ANALYSIS

For the trustee to determine what funds are required, an appropriate accounting may have to be prepared. This may take any form as long as it is reasonably detailed and accurate and includes all obligations that have become due under the indenture and the provision made for their discharge. If the appropriate records have been accurately maintained throughout the life of the issue (especially if bearer obligations are involved), the analysis for a final maturity (or full redemption) should not present a problem. But if this is not done or if the records are out of proof, then a major task may be involved.

Analyzing principal requires accounting for the total principal amount authenticated by the trustee at any time under any provision of the indenture. Because securities will have been issued because of registration of transfer, exchange, or replacement or for other purposes, the aggregate of obligations to be accounted for usually exceeds the amount outstanding at any time under the indenture.[2] Offsetting principal obligations so authenticated will be the aggregate of all such obligations that have been canceled by the trustee. Ordinarily, the evidence of a cancellation is the executed destruction certificate in the trustee's possession. If the trustee does not have destruction certificates or canceled securities for all the securities, the trustee should satisfy itself that proper disposition has been made of the canceled obligations. If the trustee's records do not disclose cancellation of such obligations, it should insist on surrender thereof so that proper disposition may be ensured. Subtracting the principal amount of obligations canceled from the aggregate amount authenticated will give the principal remaining to be accounted for. This may be offset by funds on deposit with the trustee, by monies to be deposited, or by satisfactory indemnity bonds on file.

In preparing any interest accounting, the principal amount of obligations outstanding on each interest payment date should be ascertained and the interest calculated for each such date. The amount of registered interest paid, the aggregate amount of coupons canceled, and the coupons paid against bonds of indemnity for each period should be shown separately. The sum of these subtracted from the interest due leaves the balance due for each interest date represented by outstanding unpresented coupons. The total of these amounts should represent the funds on deposit with the trustee or paying agent. If the trustee is not the agent for paying registered interest, it should receive an appropriate certificate of a responsible disbursing agent. This should be examined and proved to the total of the registered interest due, and a record kept for use on the subsequent accounting. When the trustee is not the paying agent, the trustee must remember to reduce the principal outstanding on its operating system at the time the agent provides certification of the payment.

Coupons paid are customarily destroyed by the trustee, and the destruction certificates provide the evidence necessary to support this phase of the accounting. When the paying agents are other than the trustee, they should arrange to have all interest obligations surrendered to them periodically for verification and destruction. In lieu of surrender, the trustee may accept a destruction certificate from a reliable agent, although good practice should prohibit acceptance of such a certificate of the obligor without independent verification.

Most indentures permit replacement of lost, stolen, or destroyed obligations, or their payment, in lieu of replacement, upon furnishing of evidence of such loss, theft, or destruction and provision of satisfactory indemnity. These replacement securities, however, constitute additional contractual obligations entitled to the security of the indenture. In connection with a final accounting, it is customary to give credit for all obligations covered by a satisfactory bond of indemnity, if an original counterpart is on file with the trustee and if the latter is named as an obligee. This is a matter for the trustee's discretion, however. If the security afforded by such bonds of indemnity is not in all respects satisfactory, the trustee is entitled to insist on the furnishing of adequate security or to the deposit of funds to cover such obligations.

DEPOSIT OF FUNDS

The trustee is entitled to, and should insist on, deposit with it of all funds due for all outstanding obligations before it executes a satisfaction. It is important to remember that if funds to meet matured and unpresented obligations are on deposit with other agents, arrangements have to be made for their transfer to the trustee, even if the deposit with the other agent is in trust. The fact that a statute of limitations may have run against particular interest obligations is immaterial unless the indenture contains a specific provision that no further claim may be asserted.

In the exceptional cases where deposit with the trustee is not feasible, either because the latter is not an authorized depositary or for other reasons, the depositary should be satisfactory to and approved by the trustee and the deposit should be under the exclusive control of the trustee. In this case the trustee is not liable if reasonable care was used in the selection of the depositary, even if the funds are subsequently lost through failure of the depositary.

The issuer's obligation contained in its securities runs directly to the holders. When the requisite funds for their payment are deposited with the trustee, however, it has been held that this is equivalent to payment to the holders, and the issuer is not liable if the trustee misapplies the funds or becomes bankrupt. This is true, however, only from and after the date on which funds in the hands of the trustee become available to the security holders upon surrender of their securities.

DOCUMENTATION

When all requisite accountings have been prepared and

checked and the trustee has satisfied itself that it has funds in its possession to pay all obligations shown to be still outstanding; when it has received an officers' certificate and an opinion of counsel on compliance by the obligor with all conditions precedent; and when it has received from the obligor irrevocable instructions to complete all conditions requisite to redemption of the securities not previously completed, it is then in a position to execute and deliver a satisfaction and discharge of the indenture.

The instruments of satisfaction are usually prepared by counsel for the obligor, but the trustee should check them carefully.

In the case of a debenture agreement or unsecured indenture, execution of a formal instrument of satisfaction is not absolutely necessary, for no property has to be reconveyed. It is good practice, however, to acknowledge formally the compliance by the obligor with its obligations, and this is almost always observed. Complete and final accountings should be prepared in any event, as in the case of a mortgage indenture.

Under a mortgage indenture, the instrument of satisfaction constitutes a reconveyance of all the trustee's interest in the mortgaged property.[3] It must, therefore, be in a form that can be recorded in the necessary jurisdictions to discharge the lien of the indenture of record. The instrument must be in the form of a release or quitclaim deed and contain no warranties. It is good practice to have included in the instrument a statement that the instrument has been executed without covenant or warranty, express or implied and without recourse against the trustee in any event. The instrument should always run to the obligor and never to a third party. As securities are paid in full, corporations typically incorporate a release of the lien of the indenture into their payment procedures. Municipalities often fail to request the release on such entities as hospitals and housing projects when the security issues are paid in full. Several years can pass until the municipal entity realizes the appropriate satisfaction document was not received, and it can become cumbersome to secure the satisfaction several years later. In general, the widespread consolidation of the corporate trust industry and banks in general can make records retrieval more difficult.

Typically when the need for satisfaction documents is realized, it is an urgent need.

"IN SUBSTANCE" DEFEASANCE

For various economic and financial reasons, and particularly during periods when short term interest rates are lower than those born by an obligor's securities, an obligor may elect to defease an indenture, with securities to be redeemed at a future date or dates. Indentures for tax exempt issues frequently permit this type of defeasance, and tax exempt obligors often use refunding securities to finance such a transaction. One reason for this type of defeasance is that the securities are "call protected," i.e., not subject to an optional redemption until a future date, if at all. Indentures may permit such a transaction, stating that cash or government securities be deposited with the trustee, provided that such securities and cash together with interest to be earned upon them will be sufficient to pay all principal, premium, if any, and interest upon the outstanding securities as they become due by their term or through redemption. Some indentures however, require that an amount of cash sufficient to pay all future debt service be deposited to effect defeasance. The trustee should be careful to distinguish this type of defeasance (sometimes termed *gross defeasance*) from the first type, which allows future investment earnings to be factored into the equation (*net defeasance*). For either type of "in substance" defeasance, the trustee should request that the obligor obtain and provide an accounting from a recognized accounting firm clearly showing that the cash, securities, and investment income, if any, will cover all debt service in future years, up to and including final maturity or redemption.

In most instances, for tax-exempt financings, the trustee and obligor enter into a separate escrow deposit agreement, setting forth the obligations and duties of both parties until all securities are redeemed or mature by their terms. The escrow deposit agreement should include all of the provisions from the defeased indenture with regard to registration of transfer and payment of the securities, as well as exculpation, indemnification, and protection for the trustee in its new capacity as escrow agent. Although structured as an escrow agreement, the funds are nevertheless held in trust by the escrow agent for the benefit of security holders. The agreement also should clearly spell out the agent's responsibility for future investment and reinvestment of cash, securities, and investment income, and the disposition of any excess funds not required to pay principal and interest as they become due.

When an "in substance" defeasance is for a tax-exempt issue, the trustee would be wise also to request an opinion from a nationally recognized municipal bond counsel whether the defeasance will adversely affect the securities' tax-exempt status, in addition to any other opinions required by the indenture as a condition precedent to the defeasance.

DISPOSING OF COLLATERAL, FUNDS AND RECORDS

For all defeasances arrangements should be made for return to the obligor of pledged collateral, unclaimed debt service funds, or other items of property that are physically in the possession of the trustee but not required to be held as part of an escrow or otherwise for future payments to security holders. In this connection, the trustee should make sure that no junior lienor is entitled to possess the property. If such lien exists, arrangements should be made to surrender the property to the trustee of the junior lien against proper receipt. This may include the right to proceeds of any released property, insurance proceeds, or similar funds in the hands of the trustee.

It is desirable for every indenture to provide for the return to the obligor of all unclaimed funds deposited to pay the indenture obligations after a specified number of years have elapsed following satisfaction of the indenture. The most common period used is three years, as is the case in the State of New York[4], but the length is not material as long as some period is specified. Without such a provision, the trustee may be required to retain a small balance on its books, for it is unlikely that each and every obligation will be presented to it.

In the absence of appropriate indenture authority, the trustee runs a risk in returning any unclaimed funds to the obligor, no matter how many years may have elapsed, for the obligor has no legal right to such return. Similarly, the obligor is not entitled to have such funds invested for its benefit, and if such an investment is made, the trustee may be liable if loss results.

Most states have complicated the problems of corporate financial officers, municipalities and corporate trustees and paying agents by the enactment of sundry escheat or abandoned property laws. The general purport of these statutes is to require the transfer to the state of all funds and, in some states, securities held unclaimed for a stated period of time. In 1981, the Uniform Law Commissioners on Uniform State Laws promulgated a Uniform Unclaimed Property Act, which had been adopted by 27 states. The

1981 Act incorporated a 1965 U.S. Supreme Court decision that the right and power to escheat belongs to the state of the creditor's last known address as shown on the debtor's books and records.

Since theoretically a state can seize only property belonging to its residents, a difficult problem was presented where funds were held for the payment of bearer securities. In a 1993 decision, the U.S. Supreme Court held that an intermediary which holds property in its own name will generally be deemed to be the "debtor"[5] and if the "debtor's" records do not reflect a last known address, then the unclaimed property should be escheated to the "debtor's" state of domicile. This decision was incorporated into the Uniform Unclaimed Property Act of 1995.

In addition to establishing that the state where the financial intermediary (e.g. trustee/paying agent) is located is entitled to the escheatment of unclaimed bearer funds and securities, the act also provides that both the principal amount of a registered bond and its interest become escheatable three years after the first interest payment is returned as undeliverable. In the case of bearer bonds and original discount bonds, the three-year dormancy period begins after their date of maturity.

The indenture provisions relating to disposition of unclaimed moneys should therefore be drafted in accordance with any applicable escheat or abandoned property law. When an appropriate indenture provision is lacking, the trustee is presented with a difficult decision when called upon to execute a satisfaction. For example, let us assume that during the life of a particular issue the obligor has paid over several thousands of dollars pursuant to an escheat law requiring transfer of all interest moneys held unclaimed for three years. The issue matures and the obligor tenders, to the trustee, funds to pay the principal and all unclaimed interest due within the preceding three years and demands execution of an instrument of satisfaction. Should the trustee comply or should it insist upon deposit of an amount equivalent to the funds previously escheated? This is not an easy decision, but unless the escheat law was sufficient to discharge the trustee's obligation with respect to such unclaimed interest, it may act at its peril if it executes a satisfaction without adequately securing such unpaid interest, the coupons for which may be subsequently presented to it. Under such circumstances, the trustee would be well advised to secure at least an appropriate indemnity from the obligor.

One final problem remains. Now that the indenture has been satisfied and appropriate provision made for payment of all outstanding obligations, what disposition should be made of the mountain of documents and papers that the trustee has accumulated during the life of the indenture? Obviously the answer will depend to some extent on any laws or regulations that exist in the jurisdiction of the trustee relating to the disposition of fiduciary records. Most corporate trustees tend to follow a very conservative practice and to hold on to papers and documents for many years beyond the time when they can serve any conceivable purpose. This is an expensive folly, and it is urged that each trust obligor give consideration to establishing a reasonable schedule for the systematic disposition of obsolete records.

Some records accumulated by a corporate trustee should, however, be retained permanently, including one original executed counterpart of the indenture and of the instrument of satisfaction; a copy of its final accounting with respect to all indenture securities; copies of all destruction certificates; originals of all bonds of indemnity or assumptions of liability of others with respect to any indenture securities or other obligations; and any document relating to an obligation or undertaking beyond the maturity of the indenture securities or essential to establishing the basic historical continuity of the trusteeship, such as an assumption agreement by a successor obligor.

Most other documents can be disposed of within a reasonable time after termination of the appointment or after the running of applicable statutes of limitation. Today, many trustees are imaging documentation to avoid storage costs in future years.

Once the indenture has been satisfied, the recorded counterparts of the indenture and all supplements are no longer of any value to the trustee. They may be returned to the obligor corporation if it desires them. Otherwise they should be destroyed.

The original counterparts of indentures executed prior to 1966 bear canceled federal documentary stamps evidencing payment of the original issue tax that was imposed at the time and should be dealt with carefully. Because this evidences payment of an obligation by the obligor, it may be returned to the obligor if the latter wishes. A receipt should be obtained that should recite the principal amount of canceled tax obligations affixed. If the obligor does not wish to have this document returned, which is usually the case, it may be destroyed by the trustee. The destruction certificates should include a statement of the face amount of such tax stamps so destroyed.

---

[1] See Financial Accounting Standards Board, *Statement of Financial Accounting Standards No. 76, Extinguishment of Debt* (Nov. 1983); and SEC Interpretive Release Nos. 33-6501, 34-20509, 35-23176, FR-15 (Dec. 22, 1983).

[2] If a data base system captures certificate cancellation data and is able to produce a report of such covering specified time periods, it should not be necessary to detail the reason for the certificate cancellation in the final accounting. See also chapter 16, *supra*

[3] In the case of a collateral trust indenture, where the trustee had perfected its security interest by filing a financing statement under the UCC, the release of its security interest is affected by the filing of a termination statement.

[4] See New York State Abandoned Property Law, Sec 303, Article 3, and Sec 501, Article 5.

[5] Delaware v. New York 113 S. Ct. 1550, 123 L.Ed.2d 211 (1993)

TWELVE

DEFAULT AND REMEDIAL PROVISIONS

The administration of indentures after default is the greatest test of the corporate trust officer's skill and expertise. In addition to the requirements of the TIA most indentures provide that before default the trustee shall be charged with performance of only such duties as are specifically set forth in the indenture. The instrument itself serves as the guide for the action to be taken on each problem that arises. However, there are often no applicable precedents to follow, and the trustee may find itself navigating in uncharted waters. The consolidation of the corporate trust industry has prompted most of the remaining trustees to create special default units with the purpose of navigating these waters.

It is impossible to prescribe an exact course of conduct to be followed in the event of a default. The indenture is essentially a security instrument and should reflect the premise that the trustee's primary objective, both before and after default, is to protect the security position of the indenture security holders. If liquidation or reorganization becomes necessary, the trustee should see that the security holders realize in full, or to the greatest extent possible, on their claims.

Except for the duties imposed by the TIA,[1] the trustee's rights and powers after default are derived from the authority granted by the indenture, or are such as may be properly inferred from the authority expressly granted. Before discussing the general principles of default indenture administration, we should consider the default and remedial provisions customarily included in trust indentures.

EVENTS OF DEFAULT

The events that constitute an *Event of Default* and give rise to the remedial provisions must be set forth clearly in the indenture.[2] Although there is occasional variance because of particular circumstances, the general provisions are fairly uniform:

    1. Default in the payment of the principal of any of the indenture securities when the same become due, whether at maturity, by call, by declaration, or otherwise. Because of the serious nature of this type of default, no grace period is provided, for it is unlikely to happen by inadvertence. Also, prompt action on the part of the trustee may be indicated and it should not be hampered by having to wait through a grace period.

    2. Default in the payment of any installment of interest on any of the indenture securities when the same becomes due. Most indentures provide a grace period, usually thirty to sixty days, within which the obligor may cure such a default. The remedies provided in the indenture are stayed until this period of grace has expired.

    3. If the indenture provides for any sinking fund or purchase fund, or similar payments to be made to the trustee, failure to make any such payments will constitute an *Event of Default*. It is desirable to allow a period of grace for the curing of such default and such a provision is customarily, although not always, included.

    4. If there are prior lien securities outstanding, or other obligations that constitute a lien prior to the lien of the indenture securities on the trust estate or some part thereof, a covenant to pay such prior liens and

comply with all provisions of the indenture securing it should be included in the indenture. Failing to discharge these prior lien obligations when due should be made a default under the indenture after a grace period. There is a sound reason for this. Although failure to discharge the prior lien will normally constitute a default under the prior lien obligation, its holder may take no action to enforce the obligation. Unless this also constituted an *Event of Default* under the indenture securing junior obligations, the holders of the latter might be unable to take steps to protect their equity in the property until it had been substantially dissipated.

5. It is an *Event of Default* if the obligor pursuant to or within the meaning of any federal or state bankruptcy law commences a voluntary case, consents to the entry of an order for relief against it in an involuntary case, consents to the appointment of a custodian of it or for all or substantially all of its property, or makes a general assignment for the benefit of its creditors, or a court of competent jurisdiction enters an order or decree under any bankruptcy law that is for relief against the obligor in an involuntary case, appoints a custodian of the obligor or for all or substantially all of its property, or orders the liquidation of the obligor and the order or decree remains unstayed and in effect for sixty days.[3]

6. Finally, the breach of any covenant or the failure of the obligor to perform any condition provided for in the indenture leads to a default. It is customarily provided that an E*vent of Default* will not occur for this reason until the expiration of a stated period of time after the trustee or a specified percentage of the indenture security holders have notified the obligor in writing of the breach of the covenant or condition.

Whereas both a notice and a grace period should be provided for in the event of a breach of most indenture covenants, circumstances may exist when either or both may be unwise. For example, in the case of certain negative covenants, such as those against the incurring of indebtedness, creating prior liens, transferring properties, or declaring dividends, time may be of the essence and the trustee should have the right to move promptly if such action seems warranted. This should include the obtaining of injunctive relief from an appropriate court. Although the trustee does not draft these provisions, it should insist on such flexibility during the indenture review and negotiation sessions with the issuer (or its counsel).

A trustee and the obligor may disagree about whether a default has occurred under the terms of the indenture. This may result from differing opinions of counsel (to the obligor and to the trustee) on the proper interpretation or application of a particular indenture covenant. In this case, the trustee should consider the possibility of instituting a declaratory judgment action against the obligor in federal court, seeking a judicial determination of whether a default has in fact occurred.[4] Thus, the trustee may be able to avoid future litigation, either by the obligor or the security holders, for it will have received judicial approval of its action or nonaction.

REMEDIAL PROVISIONS

The indenture contains various remedial provisions to which, theoretically, recourse may be had once an Event of Default has occurred. To the average security holder the powers of enforcement granted the trustee seem entirely adequate, and an investor may therefore be at a loss to understand why in many situations the repayment of securities is less than bargained for. Unfortunately, remedial action normally requires judicial proceedings of some kind, and the remedies included are those with which courts and lawyers are familiar. When the intrinsic value of the security is sufficient, these remedies might be adequate. In the case of the usual corporate obligor, however, such are often inadequate, unenforceable, or impractical.

The remedies found most frequently in secured indentures are the following:

> 1. The right to accelerate maturity of the indenture securities and to declare all principal due.
>
> 2. The right of the trustee to recover judgment in its own name and as trustee of an express trust.
>
> 3. The right to sue in equity or at law for specific performance of any covenant or agreement, or for enforcement of any rights of the trustee and security holders, or for the enforcement of any appropriate equitable or legal remedy.
>
> 4. The right of entry on and possession of the mortgaged property by a custodian, agents, or otherwise, such possession to continue until all defaults are cured.
>
> 5. The right to sell the trust estate at public auction, with or without entry.
>
> 6. In the case of a collateral indenture, the exercise of full rights of ownership with respect to any collateral held.
>
> 7. The right to the appointment of a custodian or receiver of the mortgaged property and to foreclosure thereon by appropriate judicial action.
>
> 8. The right to file proofs of claim on behalf of all the security holders in any judicial proceedings.

In the case of an unsecured indenture, the same remedies will usually be included, except for numbers 4, 5, 6, and 7 above, which relate to specific action for realizing on the indenture security. The unsecured indenture customarily contains a general provision permitting the trustee to have a custodian or receiver of the obligor's property appointed and to bring suit to foreclose on the property to satisfy its judgment for the amounts owing on the indenture securities. The advantage of the mortgage indenture is that the lien on the properties is already established.

To aid in the trustee's powers of enforcement, the remedial sections usually contain three covenants on the part of the obligor:

> 1. In the event of a default in payment of principal or interest (whether at maturity, on redemption, or by declaration), to pay to the trustee promptly all amounts then due and owing. Because it is obvious that if the obligor could do this no default would have occurred, the provision may appear meaningless. It is intended as an aid to the trustee's obtaining a prompt judgment on the basis of which it may proceed to the enforcement of other remedies.
>
> 2. Upon the commencement of any action, suit, or proceeding by the trustee, to waive the issuance and service of process and to enter its voluntary appearance in such action, suit, or proceeding and to consent to the entry of judgment in favor of the trustee for all amounts owing under the indenture.
>
> 3. As far as it lawfully and effectively may, to waive and relinquish the benefit and advantage of any and all valuation, stay, appraisement, extension, or redemption laws then existing or thereafter enacted.

THE TRUSTEE'S RIGHTS AND DUTIES UPON DEFAULT

The Trustee's Responsibility

Before the TIA was enacted, most indentures provided that the trustee was under no duty to take action to enforce the remedial provisions of the indenture until it had received an official demand by a specified percentage of the indenture security holders, together with whatever indemnity might be required to protect it against expense and liability. This provision was accompanied by broad exculpatory clauses that relieved the trustee of liability except for acts amounting to willful misconduct or gross negligence.

Despite the great amount of criticism directed against these provisions, there was a sound and logical basis for their existence. Initially, as has been noted, the trustee was a mere stakeholder and its function was limited to that of holding the specific security for the benefit of the bondholders. Despite the grant of broad rights and powers to the trustee, this concept did not disappear entirely. Even though the trustee was given the right to proceed on its own to enforce the remedial provisions, in practice it continued to be regarded primarily as the instrumentality of the security holders in exercising the right. Accordingly, the customary procedure whenever a default occurred or seemed imminent was for the trustee: (1) to confer with the obligor to ascertain the essential facts and, if possible, to work out some tentative program or course of action; (2) to take those actions, with the cooperation of the obligor, if possible, as might be necessary to preserve the status quo insofar as was possible; (3) to communicate the essential facts to the indenture security holders and, if indicated, to assist in the organization of a committee to represent the security holders; and (4) to work with the security holders and their committee and to take action to enforce the indenture remedial provisions decided upon by the trustee and the committee. Whenever possible, an effort was made to work out a compromise solution without recourse to the drastic indenture remedies.

This process was, of course, time-consuming. These indenture provisions were included to protect the trustee to enable it to delay pursuit of the indenture remedies until opportunity was afforded for consultation with the security holders on its action.

Whereas the procedure outlined above was the one most frequently followed, at times the trustee initiated action without awaiting direction of the security holders. It is possible, though by no means certain, that if this had been done more often, some of the serious consequences that resulted might have been ameliorated. In any event, the security holders were regarded as having the inherent right to decide for themselves whether their interests would be served best by compromise or by strict enforcement of the indenture remedies.

The trustee's position was made more difficult by incorporation in all qualified indentures, and in most other indentures since 1940, of certain provisions required by the TIA. Although no specific course of action was prescribed, the act established a new standard for trustees after default. Section 315(c), required the inclusion in each qualified indenture executed prior to November 15, 1990, of a provision that the indenture trustee shall exercise, *in case of default*, those rights and powers vested in it by the indenture and shall use the same degree of care and skill in their exercise as a prudent man would exercise or use under similar circumstances in the conduct of his own affairs. The TIRA has made this duty a legislatively mandated standard of care.

The "prudent man" standard was not a novel concept. It existed in the law of numerous states as the fiduciary standard for executors, administrators, or inter-vivos trustees, and under early judicial decisions.[5] Precedent is a significant factor in determining compliance in a particular case and, in relation to the various types of "personal" trusts, precedent is not too difficult to establish. By reason of the generally high level of economic activity from 1950 to 1987, there were relatively few defaults under qualified indentures. As a result, the indenture act provisions were not fully tested and adjudicated. Even with the significant increase in the number of defaults during the late 1980s, there has not been a major acceleration in the development of legal principles related to the trustee's role in this area. Many of the "precedents" that still exist for the conduct of indenture trustees are those of pre-TIA days. These should not be relied upon in the future, for it must be assumed that the primary reason for changing the rules was dissatisfaction with these precedents.

More important is the fact that the trustee still has only limited powers. It is axiomatic that imposition of responsibility should be accompanied by the grant of sufficient power and authority to discharge it properly. Yet what occurred was the establishment of a new standard of conduct for indenture trustees without any change in its limited authority. The prudent man in managing his own affairs can take *any* action that seems to be indicated by the circumstances, and the same is generally true with reference to the classes of fiduciaries to which the rule has been applied in the past. As applied to indenture trustees, the trustee is limited to the exercise of the rights and powers vested in it by the indenture. A review of the customary remedial provisions set forth earlier in this chapter shows that they contemplate action to be taken only for the most serious type of default. What course of action should the trustee follow when prudence dictates remedies or procedures not included within the rights and powers vested in it by the indenture?

This question will arise many times, and for purpose of illustration, let us consider two possible "defaults." The first is a default in a covenant to maintain working capital in a specified amount. The obligor's financial condition remains basically sound, but because of circumstances beyond its control, its working capital falls below the minimum required. No judicial action will remedy the situation. What should the trustee do?

The second situation involves a sinking fund default. Owing to depressed business conditions the obligor is unable to meet its large principal payments. It appears, however, that rearranging the maturity schedule by deferring a portion of the current installments will resolve the difficulty. Can the trustee properly cooperate in securing the necessary adjustment, especially when it may require a substantial period of time to secure the requisite consents?

The answer to these and other questions must await the course of future court decisions. In the meantime, indenture trustees should consider the following possibilities:

> 1. Because the limitations of liability to performance of duties specifically set forth in the indenture is, by the terms of the indenture, related to predefault activities, courts may very well find implied discretionary powers to perform acts or take action not specifically embraced within the indenture language.

> 2. Despite this possibility, the taking of any action for which express authority is not included within the indenture may subject the trustee to the highest degree of care or to a stricter level of liability.

> 3. The trustee's right to rely conclusively on certificates or opinions conforming to indenture requirements is limited to certificates with respect to predefault activities.[6] After a default occurs, these certificates and opinions may not constitute adequate

protection if an independent investigation would have disclosed a different state of facts or resulted in a different conclusion.

4. In appropriate situations, full advantage should be taken of the indenture provisions permitting amendment of the indenture with the consent of a requisite percentage of security holders. The two hypothetical cases cited above would seem appropriate situations for recourse to this provision. Because this would seem the prudent course, the trustee should be fully protected in cooperating with the obligor in presenting a proposal to the security holders and requesting their consent. Care must be exercised to see that no material adverse change in the situation occurs during the interim.

5. Where the default is merely technical, or seemingly temporary, or, in the trustee's judgment, it is capable of being cured or resolved through negotiation or adjustment with the obligor, the trustee undoubtedly has sufficient authority to take the necessary action without reference to the security holders or without recourse to the remedial sections. This authority is necessarily implicit in other provisions of the indenture. However, starting in 2006, trustees saw a dramatic increase in aggressive bondholder attention to possible defaults – including the pursuit of remedial action on technical defaults. Trustees were being directed by aggressive bondholders to immediately issue default notices, especially for failure to file timely financial reports with the SEC or to deliver those reports to the trustee and investors. Late filings were attributed to the new reporting requirements under the Sarbanes-Oxley Act of 2002 which require, for example, that the chief executive officers certify the accuracy of financial statements. The SEC agreed to the delays in filings in

some cases. But by delaying the filing of quarterly and annual reports, obligors ran the risk of violating the terms of their indentures. Hedge funds and other investors, facing pressure to generate large returns on investments, increasingly used such defaults, which in the past were viewed as relatively minor or technical in nature, as long as the obligor was in relatively sound financial health, to their advantage and profit. For investors who purchased their bonds at less than face value, acceleration may result in redemption at par or even at a slight premium.[7]

6. Upon the occurrence of a serious default, the trustee is under an affirmative duty to take appropriate action. It is doubtful that the changes imposed by the TIA were intended to alter the basic concept of the trustee's responsibility. Accordingly, if the trustee acts reasonably and in a manner calculated to preserve the status quo until it has an opportunity to consult with the indenture security holders, this should be sufficient in the normal situation. The circumstances of each case will, however, determine the degree of care and course of action that should be followed. Although the trustee is responsible for taking prompt and decisive action, no specific course of action can be prescribed for every situation, but each must be carefully considered at the time. It is unfortunate, but the trustee's action or lack of action is almost always judged in hindsight.

Notice of Default

One of the first problems with which the trustee is confronted is whether or not to notify the indenture security holders of the occurrence of a default. In qualified indentures the trustee is under a duty to give security holders prompt notice of all defaults known to it. This notice must be given within ninety days after the occurrence of the default. This giving of notice is mandatory with respect to any default in the payment of the principal of, or interest on, any security, or in the payment of any sinking fund or purchase fund installment.[8] The trustee is protected in withholding notice of other defaults as long as its board of directors, executive committee, or trust committee determines in good faith that the withholding of notice is in the interest of the indenture security holders.

Under most indentures, before the TIA, the trustee had no express duty to notify the security holders of a default. Although such a general notice was sometimes given, it was the exception rather than the rule. When action by security holders seemed indicated, the trustee frequently contacted institutional and other holders of substantial amounts of securities known to it and also consulted with any security holders who made inquiries. But a general notification of security holders was usually deferred until it was determined that organizing a committee was desirable, and then notice was given by committee representatives rather than by the trustee. In other situations when some arrangement or adjustment appeared feasible, the trustee would work out an appropriate proposal with the obligor, which would then be submitted to security holders.

The absence of a specific indenture requirement did not, however, always serve as full protection to the trustee in withholding notice. In one case, an indenture contained a covenant that the obligor would not consolidate or merge with another corporation. With the knowledge of the trustee, the obligor merged into another corporation and the latter continued to pay interest. Subsequently, bankruptcy ensued. The court held that the trustee was guilty of gross negligence and bad faith in failing to give notice of the default despite the fact that the indenture provided that the trustee need take no notice of a default unless notified by a specified percentage of the bondholders.[9] Another court held that a trustee, in a suit brought against it by bondholders, was under a duty to explain why it had permitted a default for several years without taking action to notify the bondholders or protect their interests.[10]

When the trustee advances its own funds to meet interest payments and thus prevents the bondholders from learning of the obligor's default, it may be liable for any reduction in the value of the security that subsequently results. It has also been held in such a situation that the trustee is not entitled to assert a claim for reimbursement or share pro rata with the bondholders in a subsequent sale of the property. Similarly, it has been held that where the controlling stockholder of the obligor, engaged in marketing its securities, personally advanced money to pay coupons to prevent notice of default, such coupons are paid and not purchased and are not entitled to either priority to or equality against the obligor's assets.

As we noted, when there is a paying agent for the obligor's securities other than the trustee, the paying agent is under a duty to notify the trustee in case the obligor defaults in any installment of principal or interest when it falls due.

Most indentures provide that the trustee may, at its sole discretion, advance moneys for the payment of taxes, insurance, rentals under leases, or other items for preserving the trust estate. It is also provided that to secure such advances the trustee is entitled to a lien on the trust estate prior to the lien of any securities issued under the indenture. This type of advance is, however, exclusively for the purpose of preserving the trust estate or to prevent the creation of a prior lien thereon. It should be distinguished from the type of advance referred to earlier, which prevents security holders from learning of a serious default.

In the case of advances by the trustee to preserve the trust estate, the trustee is required under the TIA to give notice within ninety days of the making of any such advance if the amount of advances remaining unpaid aggregates more than 10 percent of the principal amount of indenture securities outstanding.[11] The trustee must also include in an annual report to security holders a report of any advances made by it that remain unpaid on the date of the report, if the unpaid advances aggregate more than one-half of 1 percent of the principal amount of the indenture securities outstanding on such date.[12]

There is still some inconsistency in the TIA provisions in this regard. As noted, the report sections require notice of advances only when they aggregate certain specified minimum amounts. Section 311 appears, however, to protect the trustee's lien and right to prior repayment only with respect to advances that have been reported to security holders, regardless of amount. Except under special circumstances it is unlikely that the trustee would make advances unless the obligor had defaulted. Notice of such default would have to be reported, unless it was withheld for the reasons permitted by the indenture. If these reasons are sufficient for withholding notice, the trustee should not be penalized by losing its lien or right to prior repayment. It is likely that the omission in Section 311 is unintentional that the trustee would be protected if it complied with the specific requirements for reporting outlined in other sections of the act. If such a situation arises, however, these provisions should receive the careful attention of the trustee and its counsel.

It is important that the trustee be given broad discretion in the matter of withholding notice of default and that it be protected in the exercise of such discretion. The security holders are entitled to prompt notice if their security or their investment is prejudiced, and the trustee should be prompt in notifying them of any serious default. As indicated, such notice is mandatory in the case of a default in payment of principal or interest. The primary objective of all parties should, however, be to prevent a default or to remedy the situation. If this is possible, then too hasty action in publicizing the default can cause irreparable damage. The trustee should always have sufficient time to explore the possibility of curing a default or of working out some arrangement to prevent a serious loss to security holders. The duty to act with care includes responsibility for withholding, as well as giving, notice in appropriate situations. The trustee should consider that the withholding of notice of technical default may result in preventing the holders from exercising their rights (e.g., declaring an Event of Default) and therefore it may be held accountable for any resultant loss. In a doubtful or borderline case, notice should be given. All facts should be investigated promptly and weighed carefully. Whatever the conclusion of the administrative officer, it is recommended that the final decision in each case be made, with the advice of counsel, by the trust committee or, if there is none, by the executive committee or board of directors of the trustee.

The Trustee and the Indenture Remedial Provisions

Even though under modern practice, with certain special exceptions, recourse is seldom made to the specific remedial provisions set forth in the indenture, it is desirable to describe briefly the general principles applicable to their use.

1. Trustee's discretion regarding remedy. Subject to the right of a majority in principal amount of the indenture security holders to direct the time, method, and place of conducting any proceeding for any remedy available to the trustee--which exists under most indentures--the trustee has broad discretion with respect to the particular remedy to be pursued. As long as it acts in good faith and not in a wholly unreasonable and arbitrary manner, a court should not interfere with the trustee's exercise of discretion. This is true even though the trustee may have a conflicting interest. Likewise, the trustee will not be liable for any error of judgment made in good faith by a responsible officer, unless it can be shown that the trustee was negligent in ascertaining the pertinent facts.[13] Although the trustee's powers are strictly limited by the indenture, a court may find implied powers or responsibilities or, in a particular situation, may authorize the trustee to perform acts it would otherwise have no power to perform. Thus, in a case where depressed economic conditions had rendered it impossible for the obligor to perform a covenant in an indenture secured by real estate securities relating to the maintenance of certain value ratios, and where the only alternative was foreclosure, the trustee was permitted to enter into a working agreement with the obligor permitting the latter to retain possession.[14] In another case where the security consisted of various collateral, the court held that it had the power to authorize the trustee to secure a loan on the collateral and make a distribution to security holders rather than dispose of it at a forced sale.[15]

In pursuing a course of action not specifically authorized or permitted by the indenture, however, the trustee should obtain an outside legal opinion or expert opinion, and in appropriate cases the authority of a court or permission of a majority in principal amount of the security holders. If it endeavors to act on its own without authority, even though in good faith and in an honest effort to preserve the security for the bondholders, it may be liable for any loss resulting from its action.

2. *Rights incident to other remedies.* The first two remedies enumerated above are included primarily for the purpose of enabling the more adequate enforcement of other remedies.

The first of these is the right of acceleration of the maturity of the indenture securities. This right is given to the trustee alone and, frequently, to a specified percentage of the indenture security holders acting without the trustee's concurrence. The purpose of the provision is to enable conversion of the obligor's obligation into a matured debt so that foreclosure or other proceedings may be undertaken to the same extent as if there had been a principal default. If the indenture does not contain such a provision, the trustee may not be able to foreclose, in the event of a default in interest, except to the extent of past due interest. This would necessitate successive actions until maturity of the principal debt. It is therefore important that every indenture contain an acceleration clause.

Another provision in all qualified indentures is giving the trustee the right to recover judgment in its own name in the event of a default in the payment of principal or interest. Inasmuch as the trustee's duties relate primarily to enforcement of the security, and the security holders themselves own the debt, a serious question arose about the extent of the trustee's rights in the absence of this power. Some courts have held that on foreclosure the trustee could not recover a deficiency judgment in the absence of such a provision.

3. *Rights of entry, sale, and foreclosure.* Some of the powers given the trustee in case of default are seldom exercised. One of these is the right of entry and possession until the default is cured. The theory underlying the right is prevention of mismanagement of the property and the diversion of the rents and profits there from to purposes other than the paying of interest and principal on the indenture securities. The theory is that the trustee should be able to take possession, receive the rents and profits until all defaults are cured, and then return the property in good condition to the mortgagor. Although such a procedure might be feasible in the case of a real estate mortgage, it is not practicable in the case of the usual industrial or utility mortgage where management is highly specialized. When a trustee is in possession pursuant to such a provision, however, it has all the rights of a mortgagee-in-possession and is accountable to the mortgagor

only after all payments required by the indenture have been made to the bondholders. Another remedy seldom pursued any longer is that of sale without judicial proceedings. It is usually impossible for an outright sale of property to be made to an independent purchaser, and sale of the properties is therefore only an incident to some form of reorganization proceedings and actually is unnecessary under existing provisions of the bankruptcy statutes. This power has been used in particular situations, such as under a railroad equipment trust agreement. It may also be of value where the trustee holds marketable collateral securities. Except for such situations, however, the power of sale does not provide an effective usable remedy.

One of the important rights on default, which is incidental to the concept of the indenture as a mortgage, is the right of foreclosure. Before enactment of Sections 77 and 77B of the old Bankruptcy Act, this was the most important remedy available and was used frequently for an effective reorganization. For this reason courts customarily found sufficient power invested in the trustee to initiate foreclosure proceedings, even where the indenture provisions were not clear or seemed to qualify the right. For example, when the only provision was an authorization for the trustee to foreclose on request of a specified percentage in principal amount of bondholders, it was held to have the right to do so on its own initiative.

Incidental to foreclosure proceedings or other remedies, an application should be made for appointment of a custodian for the benefit of the indenture trustee and the security holders. This is important in connection with provisions relating to assignment of rents and profits. The usual indenture is so drafted that the indenture trustee has no right to rents or profits until it takes possession. It has been held that a provision stating that an Event of Default would act as an automatic assignment of rents and profits is valid and enforceable. In any case, however, it is desirable to apply for appointment of a custodian and the segregation of rents and profits for the benefit of the trustee and bondholders.

One of the problems that arose in connection with foreclosure proceedings was the trustee's right to bid in the property. When no such power was granted, the trustee's rights have been held to be limited to the taking of such steps as would lead to a cash distribution to bondholders, and therefore no right to purchase the property could exist. Other courts have held that such a power could be implied or, if not expressly given, could be authorized by the court. Unless expressly required by the indenture, the trustee cannot be compelled to bid in the property. Where the trustee does bid in the property, it has an implied power to resell it for the best price obtainable.

ENVIRONMENTAL LIABILITY

During the past several years, concerns had been raised over an indenture trustee's potential liability in dealing with possibly contaminated property. The basis of these concerns was the possible applicability of the Comprehensive Environmental Response, Compensation, and Liability Act of 1980 ("CERCLA"), to security issues which are secured by property on which there may be hazardous waste.[16] The law provided that a current owner or operator could be held liable whether or not it had caused the contamination[17].

The courts have occasionally extended the liability to those who lent money on the property where it was found that the lender had the ability to control the operation that caused the contamination[18], or where the lender foreclosed, thus becoming the "owner"[19]. Although the US Environmental Protection agency ("EPA") sought to limit such liability, inconsistent federal policy, state policy, and court decisions caused uncertainty by making it difficult for secured real estate lenders (and therefore trustees of secured bond issues) to evaluate potential liabilities.

This uncertainty for lenders and trustees was resolved by the enactment of the Asset Conservation, Lender Liability, and Deposit Insurance Protection Act of 1996[20] The 1996 Act which expressly adopted the policy of the EPA, protect real estate lenders and indenture trustees which only act to protect their security interest in the property[21]. This exculpation from liability will apply as long as the ownership is held primarily to protect the security interest and the trustee does not participate in the management of the facility.

In addition, the 1996 Act provides that the liability of a trustee for any environmental contamination is limited to the assets of the trust for which it is a fiduciary. No longer can a trustee be held personally liable for environmental contamination for simply serving in such a capacity. If however, the contamination is caused by or contributed to through the negligence of the trustee, its liability will not be limited to the trust's assets.

CERCLA still holds owners/operators who "participate in management" of the facility strictly liable for environmental contamination. However, the 1996 Act narrowly defines such participation as actual and active participation, not simply having the "capacity to influence". Simply holding an ownership/security interest, without "exercising decision making control over environmental compliance for the facility" or "exercising control at a level comparable to that of a manager of the facility", does not create personal liability.

Thus, trustees will not be liable if they (1) monitor or undertake one or more inspections of the property or (2) administer the provisions of an indenture/agreement covering a facility that was contaminated before the trustee relationship began, provided that they do not participate in the management of the facility.

INHERENT DIFFICULTIES OF DEFAULT ADMINISTRATION

Having considered the various indenture provisions relating to default, it might be well to summarize the essential problems that face the trustee on default and the difficulty in dealing with them effectively.

Although it is essential to include the broad remedial provisions in indentures, one of the unfortunate consequences is the false sense of security created in the minds of individual security holders. As we emphasized, the real security for holders of securities is the "going concern" value of the obligor and the income and profits realized from operation of its business. The indenture covenants constitute a strong deterrent, and, if the business is profitable, the obligor is most concerned to see that no default occurs so that it may remain in the undisturbed possession and enjoyment of its properties. If the business becomes unprofitable, this "going concern" value, and hence the bondholders' real security, is depleted. The obligor is unable to meet its obligations, and the realizable value of the property, as distinguished from its value in the operation of the business for which it was intended, is usually insufficient to discharge these obligations. This is particularly true when the default occurs during a period of general economic recession or when the industry of which the obligor is a part is undergoing strain or depressed conditions. These are economic facts. They are the risks that each investor must personally evaluate, and no contract provisions can afford the investor complete protection against them. This scenario is especially true for unsecured issues, whereas in a collateralized bond issue, the real security will depend almost entirely on the value of the collateral itself, independent of the obligor as a "going concern."

A serious indenture default will usually be accompanied by a general inability of the obligor to meet its obligations or by insolvency. Where such a situation exists, the obligor can protect itself against the strict enforcement of indenture remedial provisions by seeking protection under the Federal Bankruptcy Code.[22] This in fact is what usually occurs. The trustee is than enjoined by the court from instituting or continuing any proceedings for enforcement of the indenture provisions.

Of even greater significance than the rights, powers, and remedies available to the trustee, are those it does not have, either by express limitation or by the absence of a grant. The provisions customarily included that have become more or less standard are derived from traditional common law remedies developed in relation to small, readily identifiable properties having inherent intrinsic values. They were not designed for large industrial properties devoted to corporate rather than individual use. They contemplate some form of liquidation and sale, which in most cases is undesirable and impractical.

Even if it were possible to enforce the remedial provisions according to the letter of the contract, this is seldom desirable, at least during the initial phases of most defaults. What is called for is some form of cooperative working arrangement to enable the obligor alone, or in conjunction with its major creditors, to endeavor to resolve its financial problems outside of the Bankruptcy laws. It is in this area that the trustee can only act in a conciliatory mode, since it is almost without power or authority to act independently. It is true that action can be taken with the support and consent of certain percentages in principal amount of the indenture security holders, but the delay necessarily involved, as well as the occasional harassment by individual or minority groups of holders, is unfortunate. As a result, the trustee must frequently walk a rather tenuous path. As suggested previously, further obstacles may have been created by the imposition of a stricter standard without a concurrent grant of broader authority.

Whether an indenture trustee should be given additional or broader powers is debatable. It has been argued that it is important to have provisions in the default section which allow the trustee to take legal action even when no monetary or other default has occurred, but where the very security of the bond issue may be impaired (e.g., where there is an effort to transfer assets to another entity prior to a principal payment or redemption). In such situations the trustee should have the right to obtain judicial determination to prevent any such impairment of the rights or interests of the bondholders or the trustee under the indenture.[23] It is certain that such grant would be resisted by trustees themselves unless adequate provisions for their protection in the exercise of discretion were included, as well as assurance that their expenses and appropriate compensation would be paid. Most corporate trust organizations are not staffed to make the detailed studies and investigations called for, and employment of experts would be necessary in most cases.

This grant of power would also mean delegating authority that traditionally has been reserved to security holders themselves. Some authority for dealing with the situation during an interim period until security holders could be organized would be desirable, if accompanied by appropriate immunity, protective provisions, and compensation.

In general, the powers granted to the trustee relate solely to the strict enforcement of the contractual rights under the indenture. To the extent that the obligor can be compelled, through judicial proceedings or otherwise, to perform its covenants and obligations under the indenture, or to the extent that a sale or foreclosure under the indenture is indicated and can be effected, the trustee has requisite authority.

Because the usual corporate indenture involves important

and necessary operating properties, liquidation such as is contemplated by sale or foreclosure is seldom feasible. Security holders will usually realize more through a reorganization or readjustment of the obligor's capital structure than through liquidation, even if the latter were permitted. Accordingly, where a major default occurs the object of most proceedings is the reorganization of the obligor's financial structure.

Although trustee's authority in these proceedings is usually sufficient to enable it to take all preliminary steps, there are strict limitations on its rights to represent the security holders. A reorganization can generally be effected only if the security holders are willing to accept other securities of the reorganized obligor in satisfaction of their claims. This normally involves some compromise of claims.

The trustee has no power or authority to make such a compromise on behalf of the indenture security holders or to accept anything but cash in satisfaction of their claim. The trustee has no title to, or interest in, the debt secured, except to the extent that it may recover judgment against the obligor as an incident to enforcement of the security. The debt secured cannot be compromised or discharged except by appropriate judicial decree or, if specifically provided for in the indenture, with the consent of the security holders themselves.

Unusual circumstances may justify an exception to this general rule. In *United States v. Freeman*[24] the court held that indenture trustees had power and authority to consent to a compromise settlement binding on bondholders. The case involved a liquidation proceeding following a terminated unsuccessful effort to reorganize a railroad. One of the trustee's powers was the right to take possession, operate the properties, and pay taxes and other proper charges superior to the lien of the mortgage. Although the trustees were not in possession and had been specifically enjoined from enforcing indenture remedies, the court found that since the amount realized on liquidation was less than the claims alleged to be prior to the indenture lien, the trustees had a right to enter into an agreement compromising all claims and that "this right of the trustees to assent on behalf of the bondholders was unquestioned."

In view of the limitations on the rights and powers of the trustee, it is important to consider the rights and powers of indenture security holders, both individually and collectively. This will be done in the next chapter before the problems involved in bankruptcy and reorganization proceedings are discussed.

---

[1] Sec. 315(a) and (c) and 317(a).

[2] Note that a so-called lower-case default will ripen into an Event of Default when: there is no grace period; or the appropriate grace period in the indenture has expired; or upon the trustee's giving of notice as prescribed in the indenture. The remedial provisions of the indenture will become operative only upon the occurrence of an Event of Default.

[3] Derived from the Federal Bankruptcy Code, 11 U.S.C.A. sections 301 and 303 (h) (2), Pub. L. No. 95-598, 92 Stat. 2549 (1978), and the Model Simplified Indenture, 38 *Bus. Law.* at 756. See also Committee on Developments in Business Financing, "Structuring and Documenting Business Financing Transactions Under the Federal Bankruptcy Code of 1978", 35 *Bus. Law.*1645 (1980).

[4] This action may be possible under the Declaratory Judgment Act, 28 U.S.C.A. sec. 2201.

[5] See Sturges v. Knapp, 31 Vt 1 (1858); Harvard College v. Amory, Pick. 446, 461 (Mass. 1931).

[6] TIA, sec. 315 (a)(2).

[7] *Reading Indentures Strictly: The Rise of Delayed SEC Filing Defaults and Aggressive Bondholders*, ABA Trust & Investments, January/February 2007, by Harold L. Kaplan and Daniel Northrop.

[8] TIA, sec. 315(b). In practice, most trustees will give holders notice of such default within ten days of its occurrence or after the expiration of

any applicable grace period.

[9] Seelig et al. v. First National Bank of Chicago, 20 F. Supp. 61, (D.C.N.D. Ill. 1936)

[10] Bolyston v. Senate Apartment Building Corporation, 11 N.E. 2d 636 (1937).

[11] TIA, sec. 313(b)(2).

[12] TIA, sec. 313(a)(3).

[13] TIA, sec. 315(d)(2). The act does not define "responsible officer." However the Model Provisions (see chapter 2, note 13, *supra*) define the term to include senior officers and designated junior officers of the trustee and any other officer of the trustee customarily performing functions similar to those performed by the two designated officers, and with respect to any particular corporate trust matter, any other officer to whom such matter is referred because of his (her) knowledge or any familiarity with the particular subject.

[14] N.J. National Bank & Trust Co. v. Lincoln Mortgage & Title Guaranty Company, et al., 105 N.J. Eq. 557, 148 Atl. 713 (1930).

[15] Seigle, et al. v. First National Company, et al., 338 Mo. 417, 90 S.W. 2d 776 (1936).

[16] 42 U.S.C. sec. 9601, *et seq*. (1980).

[17] See, for example, Resource Conservation and Recovery Act ("RCRA") 42 U.S.C. sec. 6990 *et seq*.

[18] United States v. Fleet Factors Corp., 901 F. 2d 1550 (11th Cir. 1990), *cert. denied*, 498 U.S. 1046 (1991) (suggesting that a lender's mere power to affect or influence a borrower's operation might be sufficient to subject the lender to liability).

[19] See, for example, United States v. Maryland Bank & Trust Co., 732 F. Supp. 556 (W.D. PA. 1989);

[20] Asset Conservation, Lender Liability and Deposit Insurance Protection Act of 1996 (42 U.S.C. 9607)

[21] The liability amendments apply to both RCRA and CERCLA

[22] See note 3, *supra.*

[23] See James Spiotto, *The Problems of Indenture Trustees and Bondholders*, Course Handbook Series Number 343 at 671, Practicing Law Institute, New York (1990).

[24] D.C., S.D.N.Y. (1/25/60).

THIRTEEN

RIGHTS OF SECURITY HOLDERS

The primary purpose of the indenture is to afford protection to the holders of the securities issued under it. The covenants and remedial provisions are of no avail unless ample power of enforcing them is given. In the previous chapter we considered the trustee's rights and duties to protect the security holders' interests. We noted, however, that these rights are not all-inclusive but are limited to those expressly granted in the indenture. Therefore, it is important to consider the rights the security holders have under the indenture, the enforcement of these provisions, and the claims represented by the securities they hold.

These considerations present a difficult question, and one that still remains to be resolved fully and satisfactorily. It is important to remember a distinction already made. The obligation of the issuer or obligor to pay principal and interest on the individual securities runs directly to the security holders themselves and therefore is an obligation which may be enforced by the holders themselves. Indentures typically recognize the ownership of the debt represented by the securities rests in each individual. As a result, no one should be permitted to amend, modify, prejudice, or deal with such debt without the express consent of its owner.

The difficulty arises when it is necessary to distinguish between the claim of an individual holder, which may be represented by only one of many thousands of obligations identical in terms, and claims under the indenture, which secures the entire debt represented by all such obligations outstanding. From the viewpoint of the issuer, obligor and the trustee, the debt secured by the indenture is a single obligation and is dealt with as such.

The trustee's rights, duties, and responsibilities all relate to enforcement of the security provisions of the indenture that secures the entire debt. Its rights to sue and recover judgment for the debt are in furtherance of such enforcement. Although the trustee has a duty to each individual holder, its primary responsibility is to security holders as a class, and it cannot permit the claim of an individual holder to prejudice the rights of the holders as a group. In addition, even though the law is not settled in this regard, the trustee may have a duty to protect the interests of the minority holders, if their rights are being prejudiced by the actions of the majority. For example, if the obligor enters into a side agreement with several large holders to "take out" their securities in exchange for their consent to changes in certain covenants, the trustee must be alert to ensure that such actions do not result in the unfair impairment of the minority holders' interests.

This discussion assumes that the duties and covenants that may be enforced only by the trustee are limited to indentures under which the securities issued are collateralized, but not to unsecured debt. In reality, all covenants under all indentures, secured and unsecured, are enforceable only by the trustee, except for: (1) payment covenants or (2) when the holders have made a demand on the trustee and given it sixty days notice and indemnity and the trustee has refused to enforce a remedial provision, also known as the "no-action" clause.

Also, during the life of a security issue the obligor accounts to the trustee with respect to its duties and obligations under the indenture. One of the advantages to an obligor of the indenture-trustee device is that it has only one entity with which to deal on most problems that arise. Whereas most obligors endeavor to provide any reasonable information requested by an individual holder, they cannot, for practical reasons, deal with many thousands of such holders individually.

A distinction should be made between holders of obligations issued publicly and holders who acquire obligations through a "private placement". In the latter case, besides executing an indenture with the trustee, the obligor often enters into a separate "purchase agreement" with each purchaser of a part of the debt. In these agreements, the purchasers usually require filing of periodic financial and other information directly with them. These rights are, however, acquired under separate agreements with the obligor and not under the indenture. In such cases, these rights may also be "personal" in that they may not be transferred on sale of the obligations to a subsequent purchaser. These rights will depend on the transfer/assignment provisions in the purchase agreement. Rule 144 A securities are not easily transferred because of securities laws, so that in such transactions, it's not the "rights", but rather "securities" that cannot be easily transferred.[1]

Whereas in relation to enforcement, many of the rules that would apply to holders of a publicly sold issue would also apply to holders under private placement contracts, in the following pages we will be concerned only with the former.

RIGHTS PRIOR TO DEFAULT

Information and Disclosure Provisions

Adequate protection of the investor's interest involves factors over and above enforcement and remedial provisions of the indenture. Under the securities laws the investor generally is entitled to have complete information about the obligations offered for purchase. The investor is entitled to be kept reasonably informed of developments that may affect such investment so long as it is held. The investor is also entitled to have knowledge of his/her rights in the event that action is required to enforce the claim represented by such investment.

One purpose of the 33 Act was to require full disclosure of information relative to new securities being issued publicly. The provisions of the Act were expanded by the TIA, which requires "qualification of an indenture in connection with registrations of new securities." Summaries of important provisions of the indenture must be included in the registration statement. Pertinent financial and other information contained in such statement, including summaries of the indenture provisions, must be incorporated in the prospectus prepared in connection with the sale of the securities. Each purchaser must receive a copy of the prospectus so that the investor has available all information pertinent to making an intelligent decision.

The security itself refers to important sections of the indenture, particularly any that impose limitations on the rights of the holder. If further information is desired, the trustee will always make a copy of the indenture available for the holder's inspection or advise the holder about the contents of particular sections that are of concern.

While not directly related to the individual security holder, the activities of the SEC under the 33 Act, the 34 Act, and the 40 Holding Company Act (which applies to special situations, not bonds generally) are designed to afford protection to security holders generally. The rules and regulations of the Municipal Securities Rulemaking Board (MSRB), national securities exchanges, the National Association of Security Dealers, and other groups have the same purpose.

Secondary Market Disclosure

Much attention has centered on the lack of sufficient secondary market information for investors in municipal securities. This situation has become worse since 1986 when industrial revenue bonds, housing bonds, and nursing and hospital bond issues accounted for almost three-quarters of the total dollar amount of payment defaults of all municipal securities. Because municipal issues are excluded from the registration requirements of the 33 Act, and the disclosure regulations promulgated by the SEC for corporate issues, the patterns of information dissemination and disclosure that have developed over the years by issuers, underwriters, and trustees have been neither uniform nor consistent. In fact, often investors in municipal bonds were unable to obtain any information.

Since the corporate trustee is an essential party to the ongoing administration of the bond issue and may be in possession of information which is material to the financing transaction, it has been at the center of ongoing discussions by participants in the securities industry. Efforts to broaden the trustee's burden of disclosure of information beyond that required by the indenture have put the trustee in a very difficult position. Although it is universally accepted that the trustee owes a fiduciary duty to its bondholders subsequent to an Event of Default, including disclosure of relevant information in its possession, how extensive that duty is has not been settled, including the issue of what is relevant (other than the occurrence of a default or an Event of Default), or the timeliness of any such disclosure. Traditionally, indentures have provided very little guidance to trustees on what can or should be disclosed, other than that which is required by the TIA. Trustees have been reluctant to provide information which could be of financial benefit to those receiving the information without providing the information to all holders alike, and they have been deeply concerned about their potential liability for any disclosure.[2]

It is clearly the issuer (and in the case of a conduit financing, the ultimate obligor) that must have the primary responsibility for continuing market disclosure. The issuer has the most direct access to such information and is in the best position to evaluate its accuracy and materiality. When, however, the trustee has material information whose disclosure to the bondholders would effectively put it into the public domain, the trustee can - without violating any duty to its bondholders - release that information to the marketplace.

To assist participants in the securities industry, and those needing to develop consistent and uniform guidelines for the ongoing disclosure of information, corporate trustees acting through the corporate trust committee of the ABA have worked with other legal and securities organizations to establish workable practices and procedures, including draft provisions that can be incorporated into bond indentures providing for the public disclosure of material information on a periodic or ongoing basis by the issuer or the trustee. In addition, these provisions can describe the trustee's obligation to furnish the issuer with information uniquely in its possession, the means of distributing such information, the compensation to the trustee for the additional responsibilities, and the indemnification of the trustee by the issuer for effecting disclosure at the issuer's direction.

On July 3, 1995, the Securities and Exchange Commission adopted amendments to Rule 15c2-12 under the 34 Act to deter fraud and manipulation in the municipal securities marketplace by prohibiting underwriting and subsequent recommendation of securities for which adequate information is not available.

These amendments were adopted as a result of the municipal markets inability to successfully implement a voluntary disclosure process just described. Since the SEC's has little oversight or jurisdiction over the issuers of municipal securities, it promulgated these amendments for broker dealer firms for which they do have regulatory oversight.

The amendments prohibit a broker, dealer or municipal securities dealer from purchasing or selling municipal securities unless the participating underwriter has determined that an issuer of municipal securities or an obligated party, (the obligor in a conduit financing or in some cases a credit enhancer or some other party responsible for the payment of the debt other than the named issuer), has agreed in a written agreement or contract for the benefit of the holders of such securities to provide certain annual financial information and event notices to certain information repositories; and prohibit a broker dealer or municipal securities dealer from recommending the purchase or sale of a municipal security unless it has procedures in place that provide reasonable assurance that it will receive promptly any event notices with respect to that security.

The rule is effective for issues distributed after July 3, 1996, and is not retroactive to any issue brought to the market prior to the enactment of the rule, which means that issues distributed prior to July 3, 1996, are not subject to either the financial disclosures or event disclosures. However it is presumed that once an issuer begins disseminating information relating to event disclosures and annual financial disclosures that standards will be developed by the issuers to disclose on all issues regardless of the issue date, not just those required by the regulation.

The regulations list twelve specific event disclosures and the manner in which the event notices are to be disseminated. The twelve events are:

1. Principal and interest payment delinquencies
2. Non-Payment related defaults

3. Unscheduled draws on debt service reserves reflecting financial difficulties

4. Unscheduled draws on credit enhancements reflecting financial difficulties

5. Substitution of credit or liquidity providers, or their failure to perform

6. Adverse tax opinions or events affecting the tax-exempt status of the security

7. Modifications to rights of securities holders

8. Bond calls

9. Defeasances

10. Release, substitution, or sale of property securing repayment of the securities

11. Rating changes, and

12. Failure to provide annual financial information as required

Even though these twelve events require a disclosure, they do not encompass all material events, and certain types of financings may require more or less disclosure. Issuers and their financial advisors must stay abreast of the transactions and judge whether the materiality of the events occurring in their financing transactions and judge whether an event disclosure.

These amendments may change some aspects of trustees' roles and trustees must pay careful attention to its responsibility with regard to the disclosure process. Trustee's may have to judge the materiality of an event and may be called on from time to time by issuers and obligated parties to participate in the determination process. Trustees should attempt to limit their role to that of a dissemination agent to transmit or send information to the market on behalf of the issuers unless the governing financing documents specifically set forth the events which require disclosure and they are events which the trustee can determine without independent judgment.

There will always be debate on the delineation of responsibility for disclosure and the trustee will always be part of that debate. There will be debate also on the merits of disclosing. From a trustee's perspective, the corporate finance industry has adapted to the concept of event disclosure for more than eighty years. Even though this concept is in its infancy with regard to the municipal finance industry, the more information that is made available to the marketplace, the more informed the investors become and the more informed that the investor is, the less likely they will be to blame the trustee for their unwise investment.

When information reporting arrangements cannot be provided for within the context of the indenture itself, as in the case of existing municipal bond issues, it is possible for the issuer (and, in the case of a conduit financing, the ultimate obligor) to enter into a separate agency contract pursuant to which the trustee acts as an "information-reporting agent" for the issuer. Such an agency arrangement must be subordinated to the trustee's obligation to the bondholders. For example, information disclosed to the secondary market should not be more complete or different from that given to the bondholders, nor should it be given to the marketplace before being released to the bondholders.

On September 7, 2004, the SEC released an interpretive letter authorizing municipal issuers who make continuing disclosure filings under Rule 15c2-12 to use a new Internet-based electronic filing system - or "Central Post Office" - to satisfy their continuing disclosure obligations. The Central Post Office (CPO) is located at www.DisclosureUSA.org (DisclosureUSA). Filings with the CPO are voluntary and may be made also via paper documents.

The CPO/DisclosureUSA is operated by the Municipal Advisory Council of Texas (TexasMAC) which created DisclosureUSA in response to a Request for Proposals from the Muni Council, an informal group of approximately 20 municipal industry groups. The Request for Proposals was prompted by concerns that filing continuing disclosure documents and notices with the four nationally recognized municipal securities information repositories (NRMSIRs) and three state information depositories (SIDs) was not working well or efficiently. TexasMAC transmits electronically all document filings receive by the CPO to each NRMSIR and SID.

TexasMAC operates DisclosureUSA without charge for electronic filings and imposes a modest fee for scanning and filing paper documents.

In 2007, the SEC stated that Congress should clarify by way of regulations the disclosure responsibilities of municipal issuers, underwriters, bond counsel, and other industry participants. This was the result of a consensus in the industry that the municipal investor did not have as much access to information on which to make investment decisions as did investors of corporate securities. The SEC felt the new regulations should not include the full registration and review requirements that apply to corporations, but rather should focus on improving disclosure available to investors.

Reports of the Obligor and the Trustee

Each obligor that has any security listed on any national securities exchange is required to file with the SEC, with each such exchange on which any securities are listed, and with the trustees under any indentures of such obligor, periodic financial statements and other reports. All such reports are public information and are available for inspection by any security holder.[3] Each qualified indenture is also deemed to contain a provision requiring the obligor to transmit to indenture security holders summaries of such reports and other information as the SEC may prescribe by rules and regulations. No such rules or regulations have been issued; therefore, this provision is currently inoperative. Many companies, however, endeavor to forward to known holders of their debt securities, copies of annual reports forwarded to stockholders. It is likely that almost every obligor would forward copies of their annual reports on a bondholder's specific request.

Section 313 of the TIA requires the trustee to send an "annual" report to security holders under indentures qualified under the TIA if there has occurred within the previous twelve months: (1) any change in the continued eligibility and qualification of the trustee; (2) the creation of or any material change to one of the post-default "conflict of interest" relationships set forth in section 310(b)(1) through (10); (3) the character and amount of any advances made by it, as indenture trustee, that remain unpaid on the date of the report and for reimbursement of which it claims, or may claim, a lien or charge prior to that of the indenture securities, on the trust estate, or on property or funds held or collected by it, if such advances remaining unpaid aggregate more than one-half of 1 percent of the principal amount of the indenture securities outstanding; (4) any change to any indebtedness owing to the trustee in its individual capacity and the security therefor, if any[4] (5) any change to the property and funds physically in possession of the indenture trustee; (6) any release, or release and substitution, of property under the indenture, and the consideration received therefor not previously reported; (7) any additional issue of indenture securities not previously reported; and (8) any other action taken by it in the performance of its duties under the indenture that in its opinion materially affects the indenture securities or the trust estate.[5]

We have already discussed the notices the trustee must give of the occurrence of defaults or events of default under the indenture. There may be omitted from clause (8) of the "annual" report described above, however, notice of any default being withheld pursuant to appropriate indenture provisions for the reasons previously discussed.

In addition to the "annual" report the trustee must also submit special interim reports of important transactions.[6] Besides reports of default, these include the following:

> 1. A brief report of the release, or release and substitution, of any property subject to the lien of the indenture, and the consideration therefor, if any, if the fair value of such property is 10 percent or more of the principal amount of indenture securities outstanding on the date of the release. Such report must be transmitted to security holders within ninety days after execution and delivery of the release.

> 2. A report on the character and amount of any advances made by the trustee as such, for which it claims or may claim a lien on the trust estate prior to that of the indenture security holders, if the amount of all advances remaining unpaid aggregates more than 10 percent of the principal amount of indenture securities outstanding. This report must also be transmitted within ninety days.

Bondholder Lists

Under the TIA, the corporate obligor is required to furnish to the trustee, at intervals of not more than six months, all information coming into its possession, or that of its paying agents, about the names and addresses of security holders.[7] The trustee is also required to retain any information furnished to it or as it may receive in its capacity as paying agent. The indenture usually provides that such information will be preserved by the trustee until a new list is received and prepared (which typically is done in connection with payment of the next maturing interest installment) and that the previous list may then be destroyed. The purpose is to keep such information in as current a form as possible.

In the case of debt obligations outstanding in bearer form, the only way that current information can be obtained about the names of the holders is in connection with collection of the semiannual interest coupons. Under current law (i.e., effective January 1, 1984), presentors of corporate bearer coupons must indicate in their transmittal, their name, address, and taxpayer identification number.[8]

When the issuer or the trustee wants to communicate with holders of bearer tax-exempt securities in connection with a specific matter, such as an amendment to the indenture or other special matter, a procedure was developed whereby substantial information can be obtained in connection with the collection of interest coupons. This is done through use of a memorandum certificate of ownership. If notified at least thirty days in advance of an interest payment date, the paying agent can prepare and deliver to the collecting agents a supply of such certificates with the request that they be completed and submitted with the interest coupons. This can be an effective procedure and will provide a fairly complete list of holders as of the particular date.

A major drawback to this method of obtaining information is that it can be done only when interest is being paid. Once a default in interest occurs, no further coupons are presented, and the trustee should consider the publication of a notice requesting the owners of the defaulted issue to send it their names and addresses.

The most accurate list of holders is that obtained from the registration records. Whether the security be fully registered or registered as to principal only, the holder is assured of receiving all reports the trustee submits to security holders. Of more practical importance, the holder is promptly notified of any redemption call that affects his or her holdings. When the holder of an old corporate bearer instrument does not wish to have such security registered, another alternative is possible. The holder may advise the trustee of such holdings and request that his or her name be placed on file as the holder of particular securities. The trustee is required under the TIA to maintain the name on file for a period of two years.[9] In acknowledging any such request, the trustee should call attention to the two-year limitation and suggest filing of a renewal request on or before a particular date.

Although the trustee is required only to mail copies of reports to the holders on this special list, most trustees treat it in the same manner as lists of registered holders. This is good practice, and it is suggested that copies of all redemption notices or other material of special interest to security holders be sent to all holders on the two-year list maintained by the trustee.

The trustee's annual reports and notices of defaults or events of default must be submitted to all known holders of indenture securities, including the list obtained from the obligor, the list maintained by it as paying agent, the list of registered holders, and the special two-year list. Interim reports on releases or advances by the trustee are required to be submitted only to registered holders and holders on the special two-year list. As a practical matter, however, any such interim reports are usually submitted to all holders, regardless of the source from which information was derived.

Under current practice, the largest (and most often only) registered holder is DTC, through its nominee, Cede & Co. Information dissemination is further complicated as DTC only maintains the names of its participants, i.e. banks and brokers that hold the particular securities issue. It is therefore incumbent upon the banks and brokers to disseminate any information received from the trustee to the beneficial holders.

ACCESS TO CONFIDENTIAL INFORMATION

Information about names and addresses of security holders is of importance to the obligor and to the trustee, and occasionally it may also be important to the security holders. Whereas this is particularly true in the event of a default or a threatened default, it may be important in relation to other proposed transactions. For example, certain holders may oppose a proposed amendment to the indenture and desire to organize other holders in opposition thereto. When they feel that their rights may be prejudiced by any proposed action, they should be permitted to communicate their opposition and the reasons therefor to other holders. This right is recognized by the requirement that under qualified indentures three or more holders of the indenture securities may apply to the trustee and state their desire to communicate with other holders of indenture securities with respect to their rights under the indenture or under the securities.[10]

If such holders can establish by reasonable proof that they have been holders of indenture securities for six months or longer, and furnish the trustee a form of proxy or other communication which they propose to transmit, the trustee must afford to such applicants all information in its possession about the names and addresses of security holders, or inform them about the approximate number of holders on the list maintained by it and the approximate cost of mailing the proxy or other communication desired to be mailed by the applicants. Upon request of the security holders and payment of such costs, the trustee is required to:

(1) offer the applicant access to the address data or (2) mail copies of the proxy or other information to all security holders known to it. If the trustee determines that mailing of such information would be contrary to the best interests of security holders, it must, within five days after receiving the proxy or other material, file with the SEC, a copy of the material submitted, and a written statement specifying the basis for its opinion that mailing of such material be contrary to the best interests of security holders. The trustee then sends the applicant a copy of the statement sent to the SEC. The TIA provides for a hearing by the SEC and for a finding either sustaining or rejecting the trustee's contention. If rejected, the trustee must mail copies of such material with reasonable promptness to all security holders known to it.

The trustee is protected with respect to disclosure of information or mailing of any material in accordance with the provisions of the statute or the order of the SEC.

AMENDMENTS TO INDENTURE[11]

Quite frequently it is necessary to amend the indenture by an appropriate supplement. Most amendments can be made by agreement between the obligor and the trustee without reference to or approval of the security holders. The most common amendments of this kind are the following:

> 1. To create and provide the terms of additional series of securities authorized by the indenture to be issued.

> 2. To mortgage or pledge under the indenture specific property or additional property as security and to provide the terms and conditions upon which the property may be dealt with by the trustee, consistent with other provisions of the indenture.

3. To modify, amend, or add to the provisions of the indenture in a manner as to permit the qualification under the TIA

4. To add to the covenants and agreements of the obligor.

5. To evidence the succession of another corporation to the obligor, and the assumption of the securities and the covenants and obligations of the obligor by the successor corporation.

6. To cure any ambiguity, or any defective or inconsistent provision of the indenture, so long as the rights of the security holders are not adversely affected.

Although types of amendment do not adversely affect any substantive rights of security holders and so could be made without express authority in the indenture, it is desirable and good practice to prevent any objections to it being raised.

At times it is considered necessary or desirable to make other changes or amendments to the indenture, or eliminate specific provisions that may affect a substantive right of the security holders. In the absence of indenture authority such changes cannot be made without the consent of all of the security holders or of all holders whose rights might be affected.

It is therefore important to include in the indenture a section setting forth the manner how such changes should be made and the authority required to do so. It is customary to permit these modifications with the consent of the holders of a majority or two-thirds of the principal amount of the securities outstanding, excluding any securities held by or for the account of any obligor. The indenture should set forth in sufficient detail just how such consent is to be evidenced and the manner in which proof of security holdings is to be made.[12] Here again, it is best not to spell out such requirements in detail, but rather to permit the trustee to make rules and regulations for these administrative matters.

Executed consents should be delivered to the trustee within a specified period or, alternatively, the indenture could be modified by vote of security holders at a formal meeting called for such purpose. In the latter event, provision should be made for voting by proxy. When securities are outstanding in bearer form, notice of the proposed meeting should be made by publication sufficiently in advance. In addition, whether or not required by the indenture - and except for registered holders, it is proper for technical reasons for the indenture not to so require - the trustee should mail copies of the notice to all security holders on the list it maintains.

Even though the obligor may be able to obtain the required consents without a formal meeting or approach to all security holders, it is good practice that notice of the proposed amendment be published or otherwise communicated to all holders. This will apprise everyone interested of the indicated change and afford them an opportunity to express their opinion. The greatest communication problem is encountered when most of the issue is held in DTC's or street name, thereby making it more difficult to obtain the necessary consents.

When the trustee has received the required consents, it is then authorized to join in the proposed amendment.

Certain provisions should not be subject to change or amendment without consent of all holders, or at least all of those who may be affected. Such matters would include extension of the time for payment of principal or interest on any securities; reduction in the rate of interest; modification of any sinking fund or purchase requirement; alteration of the rights of holders of some securities without similar alteration of the rights of other holders; or reduction of the percentage of the holders required to consent to any future amendment, to waive any default, or to waive compliance with any provision of the indenture.

It should be noted that the trustee cannot be compelled to execute an amendment without its consent, which changes its own rights, duties, and liabilities under the indenture.

RIGHTS AFTER DEFAULT

Limitations on Rights of Individual Holders

Every indenture should contain limitations on the right of individual holders to institute an action to enforce the covenants provided in the indenture. One reason for appointing a trustee is to make it the "agent" for the enforcement of the security holders' rights as a class. To permit individual security holders to bring suit for the enforcement of their individual securities as soon as default occurred might prejudice the rights of the other security holders, as well as subject the obligor to an unnecessary multiplicity of suits.

The usual provision is that no individual holder can institute a suit to enforce the covenants provided in the indenture, or otherwise, unless after demand on the trustee by the holders of a specified percentage of the indenture securities and offer of indemnity, the trustee refuses or neglects to take action. The percentage of security holders usually required to make such a demand is 25 percent, although this may vary.[13] Holders purchase their securities subject to the provisions of the indenture, and such a provision restricting suits by individual holders has been enforced by the courts, even when it was established that it was impossible to secure the necessary percentage to make demands on the trustee. It has also been held that without showing compliance with the indenture provisions, a bondholder could not institute a suit for the foreclosure of a mortgage or for an accounting for breach of trust on the trustee's failure to foreclose; apply for the appointment of a receiver for the mortgaged property; accelerate the principal of the securities; or institute suit for the breach of a sinking fund provision.

These restrictions on a holder's rights of action are strictly construed, however, and must be clearly set forth in the bond or debenture itself. Accordingly, in one case where the only reference to the indenture in the bond was the description and nature of the collateral security, it was held that the bondholder's right of individual action could not be defeated by a restrictive provision in the indenture. In an early case, a corporation had an issue of securities outstanding when all of its property was taken over by another corporation for cash, debenture shares, and stock. The cash and debenture shares were applied toward the reduction of the corporation's liabilities, including purchase and retirement of securities. When all liabilities except $1.3 million of securities had been paid, and the corporation had $31 million of cash and debenture shares remaining, it proposed to distribute $26 million to its stockholders. A suit by bondholders for an injunction was sustained despite the fact that the corporation had $5 million left to apply to its securities and that no demand had been made on the trustee. The court held that the bondholders had an inherent right to protect their securities.[14]

When the necessary percentage of holders has made demand on the trustee and the latter has taken no action within the time required, suit may then be instituted by the holders themselves. If the indenture has been appropriately drafted, and the trustee has instituted action for foreclosure, or for enforcement of any of the other remedies, an individual holder cannot intervene in the proceedings as a matter of right.

Although the TIA neither requires nor prohibits restrictions on an individual holder's suits for enforcement, it includes a provision designed to prevent "strike suits" by individuals.[15] This provision authorizes any court, in its discretion, in any suit for the enforcement of any right or remedy under the indenture, or in any suit against the trustee for any action taken or omitted by it as trustee, to require the filing by any party litigant of an undertaking to pay the cost of such suit. It also provides that the court may, in its discretion, assess reasonable costs, including reasonable attorneys' fees, against any party litigant in such suit, having due regard to the merits and good faith of the claims or defenses made by such party litigant. The provision is not applicable to any suit instituted by a holder or holders of more than 10 percent of the indenture securities outstanding or to any suit by any holder for principal of, or interest on, the security on or after the respective due dates expressed in the security.[16]

Suit for Principal or Interest

Although provisions restraining suits by individual holders to enforce the indenture have been generally upheld, a different question is presented where the suit is for payment of the principal of, or interest on, the security.

It is clear that the indenture provision requiring demand on the trustee relates only to enforcement of the remedies and does not restrain an individual's right to sue for principal at maturity of such bond. Even though a substantial majority of the holders have consented to an extension of maturity, a nonassenter may still bring suit at the regular maturity.

The TIA expressly recognizes the right of an individual holder to sue for principal or interest "on or after the respective due dates expressed in such indenture security".[17] Though rarely incorporated in indentures today, a provision is permitted authorizing the holders of not less than 75 percent in principal amount of the indenture securities outstanding (or if specified in the indenture, of any series of securities) to consent to the postponement of any interest payment for a period not exceeding three years from its due date.[18] This consent binds all holders. With this one exception, however, the right of any holder to receive payment of the principal of, or interest on, his or her security on and after the respective due dates expressed in such security, or to institute suit for the enforcement of any such payment, cannot be impaired without the holder's consent.[19]

The only qualification on this absolute right is that the indenture may provide that the suit cannot be maintained if the institution or prosecution, or the entry of judgment, would result in the surrender, impairment, waiver, or loss of the lien of the indenture upon any property subject to the lien.

Collective Action by Security Holders

1. Right to direct proceedings. The restrictions customarily placed on actions by individual holders do not apply to action by security holders as a group and demand by a particular percentage can compel the trustee to take action or will give the holders themselves the right to do so.

Under every qualified indenture the holders of a majority in principal amount of the indenture securities outstanding have the right to direct the time, method, and place of conducting any proceeding for any remedy available to the trustee or of exercising any trust or power conferred upon the trustee under the indenture.[20]

Although this provision may be expressly excluded, it is a desirable one, and should serve in most cases for the better protection of the security holders' interests. It is customary and desirable from the trustee's perspective, that a proviso be included permitting the trustee to refuse to follow directions that are unduly prejudicial to those bondholders not joining in any direction to it, that may be against the law, or that may involve the trustee in potential liability. The right given to a majority to control the trustee's action should help the trustee determine the proper remedy to pursue. Because the trustee is subject to the "prudent man" standard after default, to protect itself from potential liability the trustee might decide prematurely to accelerate the principal and/or institute suit for foreclosure or file a petition under the Bankruptcy Code.[21] But these actions may, in fact, harm the holders' interests by, for instance, forcing the issuer or obligor to file for bankruptcy. In some cases the trustee may be able to prevent liquidation or reorganization by refraining from exercising any rights or remedies under the indenture. Because the trustee is protected in acting or refraining from acting in accordance with the direction of a majority in principal amount of the security holders, cooperation by the holders may prevent hasty suits or help determine the proper remedy to pursue and the time and method for instituting suit, if bringing suit is appropriate.

> 2. *Waiver of default.* In addition to the right to direct the time, method, and place of conducting proceedings for enforcement, a majority in principal amount of the security holders have the right to waive any past default and its consequences under the indenture, other than a default in principal or interest. This waiver will be binding on all holders.[22]

This provision can be helpful in working out a readjustment plan wherein waiver of existing defaults is essential and consent of all holders could not be obtained. Depending upon the indenture such waiver might also apply to past sinking fund or purchase fund installments, even though extension of maturity, change in interest rate, or other prospective substantive changes in the indenture could not be made, without the consent of the holders affected.

Any modification or amendment of the indenture can be accomplished only with the consent of the percentage of the holders required by the indenture. As previously indicated, this would not include extension of maturity of principal, reduction in interest, or change in future sinking fund requirements, which typically require consents from all affected holders.

> *3. Removal of trustee.* Another remedy available to security holders, acting collectively, is removal of the trustee. The indenture will customarily provide that the trustee may be removed, and a new trustee substituted, by the action of a specified percentage - usually a majority in principal amount of the security holders. When a new trustee is appointed pursuant to such action, the court will not disturb the discretion of the security holders and must recognize the new trustee.

Instances where this remedy would be beneficial are the trustee's neglect or refusal to take remedial action, or the existence of some conflicting interest that make appointment of a successor advisable.

The right may not always be an unmixed blessing, however. It may be possible for a group of holders to acquire a majority in principal amount of the securities for the purpose of obtaining control of the obligor in default and then use such control for purposes not related to protection and enforcement of their rights as security holders. The trustee, with the rights of the minority in mind, might refuse to accede to the demands of this group for a particular action. It could then be removed pursuant to the indenture and a new trustee appointed that would join in the action of the majority. The right of removal by the requisite percentage of holders is absolute.

Problems arise if there is not an appropriate indenture provision, or if demand by the requisite percentage cannot be obtained. Where a trustee refused to comply with an order of a court in a foreclosure proceeding, it was held that it could be removed at the suit of an individual bondholder. A trustee normally will not be removed, however, if minority holders merely disagree with its policy. After a default if the trustee is a general creditor, under the TIA it is deemed to have a conflict of interest and will have to resign, unless it is a non-monetary default and SEC grants it a waiver.

4. Protective committees. As a practical matter, organizing the security holders to gain or secure the consent or approval of a majority to direct or assist the trustee is not an easy task, unless the securities are owned by a small number of holders with large investments in the securities. The principal advantage in organizing a committee lies in the ability to obtain consents and permit some form of voluntary readjustment in cases where default is not too serious and where liquidation and reorganization can be avoided.

The delay necessarily involved means, however, that the trustee must determine for itself the initial steps that must be taken and must proceed to the initiation of such action.

The trustee represents all the security holders and must always be alert to the interests of the minority. Although it can help to create a protective committee and cooperate with it, the trustee should maintain its independence at all times.

The trustee should not be a voting member of such committee, although it clearly should be aware of its proceedings and support its efforts, and if possible work closely with the committee, but only to the extent that it does not conflict with the trustee's fiduciary responsibility to represent the entire class of security holders.

[1] See discussion on issuance of private placements under SEC Rule 144A, page 25, *supra*.

[2] With evolutionary changes taking place in the traditional role of the trustee, legal "safe harbors" will need to be developed to protect trustees from risk and liability it was never intended they assume, and for which the compensation they receive is grossly inadequate.

[3] Arguing that bondholders do not receive sufficient information, a learned commentator suggests that such holders should have the same right to receive information and reports as do shareholders of a publicly traded company. Morey W. McDaniel, "Disclosure for Corporate Debt Securities, S & P Corporation," 16 *Rev. of Sec. Reg.* 907 (May 4, 1983).

[4] A drafting error in the TIRA added the words "any change to" to subparagraph (6) rather than (4). The SEC has advised trustees to prepare their reports consistent with congressional intent, as indicated here. SEC Release 33-6892 (May 8, 1991).

[5] See TIA, sec. 313(a). In our opinion a similar report, as appropriate, should also be sent annually to holders of securities under non-TIA-qualified indentures, including municipal revenue bond issues (and particularly industrial development bonds).

[6] TIA, sec. 313(b).

[7] Id. sec. 312.

[8] Interest and Dividend Tax Compliance Act of 1983, Pub. L.98-67, 97 Stat. 369, sections 104, 105, and 108.

[9] TIA, sec. 313(c)(2).

[10] Id. sec. 312(b).

[11] When executing any supplemental indenture to an indenture entered into prior to November 15, 1990, the trustee must be exceedingly careful not to reaffirm the provisions of the original indenture that are now deemed included as the result of the TIRA. The unintended result could be to have a different (and higher) set of standards imposed on the trustee through a contractual agreement with the obligor. See also p. 129, *supra*

[12] See TIA, sec. 316(c).

[13] TIA sec. 316(b); Quirke v. San Francisco Railroad Company 277 F. 2d 705 (8th Cir. 1960); Friedman v. Chesapeake & O. Ry., 261 F. Supp. 728 (S.D.N.Y. 1966) *aff'd* 395 F.2d 663 (2nd Cir. 1968).

[14] Hoyt, et al. v. E. I. du Pont de Nemours Powder Company, et al., 88 N.J. Eq. 196, 102 Alt. 666 (1917. See also *In Re* Envirodyne 174 B.R. 986 (1994)

[15] But see TIA sec. 316(b) re bondholder suits for payment of principal and interest on the bonds [16] Id. sec. 315(e).

[17] Id. sec. 316(b).

[18] Id. sec. 316(a)(2).

[19] Id. sec. 316(b).

[20] Id. sec. 316(a)(1).

[21] See note 1, chapter 14, *infra*.[22] TIA sec. 316(a)(1)(B). See also sec. 316(c) for provisions relating to record dates for solicitation of consents.

FOURTEEN

BANKRUPTCY AND REORGANIZATION

A corporation may become a debtor under the Bankruptcy Code[1] either voluntarily, by reason of its insolvency, or an inability to pay its debts as they mature, or as the result of an involuntary bankruptcy petition filed by its creditors. Insolvency is not, however, a precondition to either a voluntary or involuntary bankruptcy filing. Whenever an issuer files for bankruptcy protection, this triggers an Event of Default under most indentures. Before enactment of the Bankruptcy Code, filing a voluntary petition usually triggered the remedial provisions of the indenture and could result in the actual liquidation of the business of the obligor and sale of any properties mortgaged or pledged for the benefit of the security holders.

From the perspective of a secured creditor (e.g., a mortgage bondholder), and a senior debenture holder, actual liquidation may represent the best opportunity to recover. But as a result of the diverse creditor and equity constituencies and the Bankruptcy Code's protective umbrella of the "automatic stay," an immediate liquidation upon bankruptcy filing is not typical. In fact, it is evident that many courts interpret the underlying policy of Chapter 11 of the Bankruptcy Code as to favor the debtor's rehabilitation even if such does not assure the maximum recovery by creditors holding senior debt.

Although the Chapter 11 process may not primarily benefit the security holders but, instead, the equity holders, and despite the initial loss in security values that may accompany the commencement of a case in bankruptcy, it is often in the interests of security holders, as well as the debtor, that the issuer's capital structure be restructured and its business continued on a solvent and viable basis. The object of most Chapter 11 proceedings is a significant readjustment or reorganization of the obligor's affairs, brought about by extension, conversion, compromise, or in some cases, expungement of the rights and claims of indenture security holders and other creditors (or a combination of some or all of the foregoing actions). Often equity interests are extinguished, and security holders receive equity of a solvent, restructured entity.

Restructuring of the obligor's debt may be accomplished either through an out-of-court compromise between the obligor and its creditors or through the process of a judicial reorganization. In light of the expense of the Chapter 11 process, as well as the drain of the process on the management's resources, every effort should be made to achieve a consensual workout without resort to court proceedings. However, even temporary relief may not be achievable in some cases without judicial intervention. While a non-judicial workout may be preferable, the indenture trustee usually does not have the authority to allow the debtor the necessary accommodations for any out-of-court voluntary adjustment without the express consent of the holders. As indicated in the preceding chapter, most indentures do contain provisions permitting certain percentages of security holders to waive a past default or amend certain indenture covenants. As such, permanent adjustments are usually difficult to accomplish unless the security holders are few and easily accessible. Where a permanent adjustment in the terms of securities is required, it is therefore usually necessary to have recourse to some form of judicial proceeding. It may be possible, however, for the security holders, to agree to accept new securities in exchange for the old without the intervention of a court proceeding. Much has been written on the various bankruptcy and reorganization statutes, and space will not permit a detailed discussion of this subject matter here. Most indenture administrative officers will at some time be faced with the very serious problems involved in these proceedings, and should therefore have an understanding of applicable statutory provisions and the position of the indenture trustee in such proceedings.

THE BANKRUPTCY CODE

The U.S. Constitution specifically grants to Congress the right to enact bankruptcy legislation.[2] This power was exercised with the passage of the first National Bankruptcy Act in 1800, the Bankruptcy Act of 1898, the Bankruptcy Act of 1934, the Bankruptcy Reform Act of 1978 (the "Code") which became effective on October 1, 1979,[3] and the Bankruptcy Abuse Prevention and Consumer Protection Act of 2005.

The Code has now nine chapters: 1. General Provisions; 3. Case Administration; 5. Creditors, the Debtor, and the Estate; 7. Liquidation; 9. Adjustment of Debts of a Municipality; 11. Reorganization; 12. Adjustment of Debts of a Family Farmer or Fisherman With Regular Annual Income; 13. Adjustment of Debts of an Individual with Regular Income; and the new 15. Ancillary and Cross-Border Cases.

The filing of a petition under Chapters 7, 9, or 11 operates as an automatic stay, applicable to all parties in interest, of any action against the debtor.[4] The purpose of the stay is to promote the equality of distribution among competing creditors, and in Chapter 11 in particular, to give the debtor the opportunity to focus on its rehabilitation. The automatic stay bars the continuation or commencement of any action, judicial or administrative against the debtor; the creation, perfection, or enforcement of a lien against the debtor; or any action to collect, assess, or recover a claim or set off a claim by a debt owed to the debtor. The stay continues until the case is closed, dismissed, or a discharge is granted or denied, unless a creditor or any other party affected by the stay successfully petitions the court for termination or modification. After due notice and a hearing, the court may continue the stay, or may modify or lift the stay to allow a lien or claim enforcement. In certain cases, the court may condition the retention of the stay upon the petitioning creditor being provided with adequate protection of its interest during the pendency of the stay.[5]

Thus, the bankruptcy court becomes the pivotal point for the resolution of all issues and differences involved in determining whether any particular creditor may move to protect or improve its position.

Chapter 7 contains the basic provisions governing the collection, liquidation, and distribution of the estate in a liquidation case. It takes the place of the straight or "ordinary" bankruptcy under the former acts. In such a case, a trustee will be elected by the creditors to collect and reduce to money the debtor's property and to close up the estate as quickly as possible as is compatible with the best interests of the creditors. If necessary, the trustee will examine proofs of claim and object to the allowance of any claim that is improper and will file a final accounting of the estate with the court.[6]

Chapter 9 gives municipalities[7] the sole right to institute a case. It has no provisions for the creditors of a municipality to institute an involuntary proceeding.[8] The municipality must, however, demonstrate that it is either insolvent or unable to meet its debts as they mature, that it is specifically authorized by state law to be a debtor, and that it desires to enter into a plan to adjust such debts. Under the Code, the municipality must show that it (1) has obtained agreement, or having negotiated in good faith has not been able to gain agreement, from the creditors who hold a majority of the amount of claims of each class that would be adversely affected; (2) is unable to negotiate with its creditors, because such negotiations are impractical; or (3) reasonably believes that a creditor may attempt to obtain a preference.[9] Notice must be given of (1) the commencement of a case, (2) the granting of an order for relief, and (3) any dismissal of a case. Such notice must be "published once a week for three successive weeks in at least one newspaper of general circulation published in the (judicial) district in which the case is commenced and in such newspapers having general circulation among bond dealers and bondholders as the court designates."[10]

Chapter 9 was amended in 1988 to overcome certain structural problems in public ownership of municipal facilities. A category of "special revenues" was defined that includes receipts derived from the ownership or operation of projects or systems of the municipality primarily used for transportation, utility, or other services, special excise taxes, incremental excise taxes, other revenues derived from special functions of the debtor or specially levied taxes, but excludes receipts from general property, sales, or income taxes levied for the debtor's general purposes. These special revenues are subject to a post petition lien notwithstanding Section 552, which ordinarily defeats such liens. In order to ensure continued operation of essential services, Section 928 provides that the lien on special revenues is subordinate to the operating expenses required, for example, for electric generating facilities. The amendments also insulate a bondholder's receipt of payments on its revenue bonds from the recapture provisions of Section 547, if such funds are received within ninety days of the filing of the municipality's Chapter 9 petition.

Chapter 11 is the sole reorganization chapter in the Code available to nonmunicipal corporations. It forms a single system for the rehabilitation of a debtor and the adjustment of all claims against the debtor and its assets, secured and unsecured, as well as equity interests. In attempting to balance more equitably the competing rights of debt holders, secured and unsecured creditors, and holders of equity securities, it strives to make the reorganization process itself more expeditious, less expensive, and consistent with the realities of the competing interests. Subject to judicial extensions and reductions, Chapter 11 affords the debtor an exclusive opportunity to file a reorganization plan during the first 120 days after the court has ordered Chapter 11 relief. But if a Chapter 11 trustee is appointed the debtor loses its exclusive right to file a plan. Any other party in interest, including an indenture trustee, may file a plan if (1) a Chapter 11 trustee has been appointed; (2) the debtor has not filed a plan within its period of exclusivity to file a plan; or (3) the debtor has not filed a plan that has been confirmed within the debtor's exclusive period to solicit votes on a plan, which is 180 days after the order for relief, unless modified by the court. Courts often, after notice and a hearing for good cause, extend both the 120-day filing period and the 180-day solicitation period.

Once a reorganization plan has been completed, Section 1125 requires that a written disclosure statement, together with the plan or a summary of the plan, both as approved by the court after notice and a hearing, be sent to all holders of impaired claims or interests, in cases under Chapters 9 and 11. No solicitation of acceptances (or rejections) of the plan may be made until the disclosure statement is distributed to each member of each impaired class. However, in rare instances, different disclosure statements may be sent to different classes, the test being whether the particular class has received adequate information of a kind and in sufficient detail that a hypothetical reasonable investor typical of that class can make an informed judgment about the plan.[11]

Although the statutory prerequisites to the confirmation of a plan are detailed and complex, when satisfied, a plan can be confirmed if each class of creditors has either accepted the plan by the required percentages[12] or if dissenting, the class of creditors will be treated at least as well under the plan as if the estate were liquidated under Chapter 7 or if secured creditors receive value equal to interests in property securing their claims. In any event, no class of creditors or equity holders that is junior in right is receiving any distribution by virtue of their prior claims or equity interests.[13] While acceptance by a class of creditors requires a specified affirmative vote, [14] if a class is not impaired under the plan, it is deemed to have accepted the plan. Generally, if the proponent requests and if all other confirmation requirements are met except that all impaired classes have not accepted the plan, the court must confirm the plan.

Impairment is a new statutory concept, although it does have antecedents in Chapter XII of the Bankruptcy Act of 1934. The Code deems a class of claims or interests to be impaired unless the plan treats such claim or interest in a manner that provides full and complete recovery, in cash, of the creditors' claims or interest, leaves unaltered the legal, equitable, and contractual rights of the holders of the claim or interest, or restores full rights of interest in the debtor's property.[15] In effect, plan proponents may continue unaffected existing credit relationships and by doing so, disenfranchise such creditors from voting on the plan. When a class does not accept a plan it may be confirmed over the objection of a class of creditors if it provides certain prescribed treatment for such nonaccepting classes. In particular, with respect to each nonaccepting impaired class, the plan may not discriminate unfairly and is fair and equitable to each such class. In any event, at least one noninsider impaired class must accept the plan. This concept of confirmation over nonaccepting classes has been aptly dubbed *cramdown* and essentially satisfies the dissenter's claims in accordance with the absolute priority rule, which provides that any nonaccepting class be satisfied in full before any junior class shares under the plan. The prospect of cramdown and the desire of existing management to retain equity in the reorganized entity have an unmistakable bearing on the development of a consensus in producing a final plan of reorganization. Some of the other significant provisions that directly relate to indenture trustees are (1) Section 364, which allows the debtor to incur unsecured debt in the ordinary course of business[16] as an administrative expense without a hearing; (2) Section 364, which also permits the debtor under certain circumstances to obtain credit or debt secured by a senior or equal lien on property of the estate that is subject to an existing lien;[17] (3) Section 503(b), which provides reasonable compensation to an indenture trustee for services rendered in making a substantial contribution in a Chapter 9 and 11 case, including actual, necessary expenses and reimbursement of its counsel's fees and expenses; (4) Section 547, which permits a debtor to avoid many transfers of property made to or for a creditor of an antecedent debt within ninety days before the filing of a petition (such preference period is extended to one year if the creditor was an "insider";[18] (5) Section 548, which permits the trustee in bankruptcy to avoid fraudulent transfers by the debtor of an interest in its property, if, at the time of the transfer, there was an actual intent to hinder, delay, or defraud an entity to which the debtor was or became indebted, or if the debtor received less than reasonably equivalent value in exchange for the transfer and the debtor was or became insolvent at the time of, or as a result of, the transfer; (6) Section 552, which appears to render after-acquired property clauses in indentures automatically inoperative as of the date of commencement of the bankruptcy case;[19] and (7) Section 1102(a)(i), which directs the U.S. trustee to appoint a committee of unsecured creditors as soon as practicable, it being intended that the committee oversee the debtor and the reorganization process, as distinguished from the court's involving itself in the everyday affairs of the debtor.[20]

The appointment of committee members, in Chapter 9 and 11 proceedings, rather than their election differs from the former Bankruptcy Act of 1934, and ensures that the committees are fairly representative and not solely controlled by attorneys seeking committee counsel representations. If a prepetition committee does not exist, the U.S. trustee is authorized to select a representative committee from among the largest creditors willing to serve. Even if it does exist, the U.S. trustee must appoint a committee, usually naming the pre-existing committee as the official committee, with or without additional members or changes in members.

Occasionally, multiple committees representing different classes of debt or equity may be necessary. The appointment of additional committees may not be automatic, however, but may require a conclusion by the court, upon application, that the particular committee requested is necessary to assure adequate representation.[21] The importance of providing for "official" or "statutory" committees is that the expenses of the members, and the professional fees of those employed by such a committee, e.g., attorneys, accountants, financial advisors, are entitled to compensation from the estate based on the time, nature, and value of their services in relation to the cost of comparable services in a nonbankruptcy case. In practice, it is unusual and difficult to get such a special committee appointed. Usually a representative of debenture holders is appointed to the prepetition committee along with other representative creditors.

Chapter 11 does not require the appointment of a reorganization trustee but assumes the continuation of the debtor-in-possession. Any party in interest may, however, apply to the court for the appointment of a Chapter 11 trustee to operate the business. The request will be granted if the court finds that there are reasonable grounds for the appointment, which might include substantial evidence of fraud or mismanagement on the part of the debtor, or that such appointment is otherwise in the best interests of the creditors or stockholders.[22] As we noted, the appointment of a Chapter 11 trustee automatically deprives the debtor of the exclusive right to file a plan. If such trustee is not appointed (i.e., the debtor remains in possession and continues to operate the business), any party in interest may request the court to appoint an examiner, which request will be granted if it is in the interests of the creditors or if the debtor's nontrade, nontax unsecured indebtedness exceeds five million dollars.[23] The examiner's role is to investigate the debtor with respect to any adverse allegations, such as fraud or dishonesty, the financial condition of the debtor, and any other matter relevant to the proceeding or formulation of a plan.

THE INDENTURE TRUSTEE AND SECURITY HOLDERS IN REORGANIZATION PROCEEDINGS

The rights and functions of indenture trustees in connection with reorganization proceedings still have not been completely defined. Whereas indenture trustees are recognized as representing the indenture security holders, such rights of representation are strictly limited. In general, any matter relating to the security lien or priority of the indenture securities requires the indenture trustee's vigilance.

But the indenture trustee has no power or authority to compromise the claims of the security holders, and so to the extent to which it may properly participate in the formulation or advocacy of a plan that affects such a compromise is debatable. Nevertheless, absent an actual bondholder on a creditors' committee, the public debt holder - apart from the trustee - often has no voice in the development of the plan.

Notwithstanding the broad limitations imposed by the automatic stay on actions to enforce contractual rights and the prohibitions against contract rejection based solely on filing a bankruptcy petition, the filing of such petition, voluntary or involuntary, is invariably an Event of Default under most, if not all, corporate bond indentures. Upon default, the trustee's standard of conduct with respect to its rights, duties, and obligations is thereby raised to that of a "prudent man". Although not legally or contractually required to participate in statutory creditor committees, many corporate trustees of public debt, in furtherance of their duties, do seek to serve on such committees.

The right of the indenture trustee to be heard on all matters arising during the proceedings has been specifically recognized in Chapters 9 and 11. The indenture trustee may file a petition against a debtor, may intervene in any such proceeding as a matter of right, and is entitled to receive notice of all important matters arising during the proceedings.[24] These rights are recognized by the Code and are independent of the trustee's decision to participate as a member of a creditors' committee.

The specific provisions of the Code and the TIA with respect to the rights of the indenture trustee have not enlarged its authority to represent individual security holders. These provisions have recognized the importance of the indenture trustee as an agency for the representation of the interests of security holders as a class during the proceedings, but the importance of representation by the security holders themselves has also been recognized and emphasized.

This emphasis on the individual holder has not, however, minimized the importance of collective action by security holders through committees. The right of any creditor to be represented in a Chapter 11 case by a committee is specifically recognized in Section 1102. Because of the complexity of the large corporate reorganization and the lack of information available to an individual holder, as well as the substantial expense involved, it is impractical for most individual holders to appear personally in the case. In addition to facilitating conduct of the proceedings by having the various classes of creditors represented by committees rather than by a number of individuals, an objection that may be raised will be more persuasive if it is entered collectively by a large number of a particular class. A committee will also be able, as a rule, to intervene in the proceedings, a privilege that offers a much greater opportunity for participation than the general right of individual holders to be heard. If anything, the impact of collective action has been enhanced by requiring acceptance of a plan by at least 50 percent in number and 66 2/3 percent in amount of the creditors of any class as binding upon the dissenters of that class. Therefore, a dissenting minority now has more at stake and should organize to protect itself. Since the activity of these committees is subject to court supervision, security holders should be better protected in being represented by a committee. However, although the committee "represents" holders, it does not have any rights that belong to the individual creditors.

GUIDANCE AND GUIDELINES

The following are a general guide to indenture trustee administration officers in connection with reorganization proceedings. The circumstances of each case will vary, but these suggestions should apply in most situations:

> 1. Despite imposition of the prudent man standard of conduct and an understandable inclination of the indenture trustee to protect itself by court proceedings, filing of a petition for reorganization by an indenture trustee should be the last step to be taken. Experience has demonstrated that with few exceptions such proceedings result in substantial

delays and losses to indenture security holders. Every effort should be made to reach an out-of-court work out with the obligor and, to the extent possible, with a majority of the security holders. Interim arrangements should be pursued whereby the business operations can be continued and the rights of security holders protected. Filing of a petition under the Code should be regarded as an act of no alternative and resorted to only when no other means are available for protecting the inherent rights of the indenture security holders.

2. When a bankruptcy petition is filed by the debtor or by other creditors, the indenture trustee should file an appearance promptly so that it will receive notice of all matters presented to the court, including the disclosure statement pursuant to which the plan solicitation occurs. The trustee should consider also, with the advice of counsel, whether and to what extent it should send periodic information updates to the bondholders. In any event, only such information as is both factual and "public" should be included in any such report. The trustee may wish to have the bankruptcy court approve any information which it determines should be made available to bondholders.

3. The administration officer should make certain that every department of the bank is aware of the pending proceedings and is familiar with the general prohibitions against any dealing in securities represented in the bankruptcy case by the indenture trustee.

4. A critical duty the indenture trustee should perform is the filing of a proof of claim on behalf of all indenture security holders. Express authority to do so is included in most indentures, but the indenture trustee undoubtedly has implied authority even in the absence of such provision.

5. Pursuant to Bankruptcy Rule 2019, in every Chapter 9 or 11 case, "every person . . . representing more than one creditor or equity security holder and, unless otherwise directed by the court, every indenture trustee shall file a verified statement with the clerk.[25] This statement must include the security holders' names and addresses, a description of the claims, including the time of acquisition and facts surrounding the employment of the indenture trustee, including a description of any claims or interests owned by the indenture trustee. The statement must be amended to reflect any changes in relevant facts after the initial statement is filed. One of the sanctions for failure to comply is that the court may refuse to permit the indenture trustee from being heard or from intervening in the case. The Code has replaced the concept of the Bankruptcy Act of 1934 of "provability of claim" with that of an "allowed claim." This basically means that, unless objected to by the debtor or a party-in-interest, the amount of the claim is allowed as filed. The trustee should keep in mind the problems created by an original issue discount, which is characterized as unmatured interest and is therefore disallowed under Section 502(b) of the Code.

6. Where the indenture is a lien on the principal fixed properties of the obligor and grants the trustee right to income after a default, a motion should be filed promptly seeking the segregation of all income for the benefit of the indenture trustee and the security holders. This is important, for it may seriously affect the rights of the security holders under the plan when it is presented or the right of the indenture trustee to object to the disposition of accumulated income during the proceeding. A motion for adequate protection and relief upon the stay

should be filed promptly, where appropriate.

7. Upon satisfying certain requirements, the Chapter 11 trustee or debtor-in-possession may present an application for an order authorizing it to sell or dispose of specific items of property free and clear of the mortgage indenture and without seeking a release from the indenture trustee. The indenture trustee should insist that there be included in the order approving this petition a provision that the proceeds of any sale be held in escrow subject to the same liens and priorities as existed on the property disposed of and that such funds should be used only for distributions to the appropriate security holders or for the purpose of acquiring additional collateral. On the petition for approving individual sales under the general order, the indenture trustee should require presentation of appropriate evidence of the sufficiency of the consideration for any such sale.

8. Every petition filed in the proceedings should be examined carefully. A majority of these will deal with routine administrative matters and will require no action or statement of position by the indenture trustee. If representing secured claims, the major objective should be to maintain the priority lien position of the indenture on the debtor's property until a reorganization is consummated. Any proposed action that seems to affect such a position should be examined carefully, and if it appears likely to prejudice such a position, it should be opposed vigorously.

9. The indenture trustee's primary responsibility is to the maintenance and preservation of the bondholders' legal rights and distribution priority. The trustee should initiate any action that seems appropriate or necessary for the protection of such rights. In particular, it should endeavor to prevent the

diversion of the proceeds of sale or liquidation of any of its security to purposes not of direct benefit to security holders. Where the indenture is unsecured, it is especially important that the indenture trustee be certain that the estate is not dissipated or, if it is, that as much of it as can be recovered is recovered.

10. Any application by the reorganization trustee for authority to incur debt or to issue certificates of indebtedness should be examined carefully. These obligations will constitute a claim with priority over any prebankruptcy obligations. If a substantial amount of post petition indebtedness is created, the security holders' position in the reorganized company may be compromised.

11. In the frequent event of multiple lien positions, it may be necessary for the Chapter 11 trustee to prepare segregation formulae for the allocation of earnings and expenses among the various segments of the business subject to different lien priorities. Any new securities issued on reorganization must bear a direct relationship to prospective earnings, and indeed development of proper formulae for allocation of such earnings is frequently one of the most important activities during the entire proceeding. Accordingly, the indenture trustee should participate actively in all discussions and hearings relating thereto. This is a matter for experts, and in an appropriate case the indenture trustee is well-advised to employ expert assistance to support its case.

12. Whereas committees representing security holders' interests directly are usually of great importance, for the reasons which were discussed above the indenture trustee should not organize a committee or take an active role in such organizational efforts unless, with the advice of

counsel, this is necessary or desirable under the particular circumstances.[26]

13. If the indenture trustee has lists of security holders, these should be delivered to the reorganization trustee or filed in court, and access of individuals attempting to form committees should be to lists on file with the court. The trustee should not make such information available directly except with the approval of the court.

14. Once a committee has been organized and has intervened in the case, the indenture trustee should try to work closely with the committee on all matters relating to protection of the security holders as a class. If the class does not include different levels of debt the interest of the indenture trustee and the committee usually will be identical. The interests of the unrepresented security holders are usually the same as those represented by the committee, for all will now participate to the same extent and in the same manner under the plan as finally approved. Normally, therefore, no position adverse to the committee is necessary for protection of the minority. The indenture trustee should always bear in mind, however, that it represents *all* the security holders. Each member of the creditors' committee has a duty to all members of the class and therefore an indenture trustee serving as a voting member of a committee has a conflict of interest which it must address. While cooperating with a committee in every way possible (including serving as a member of the committee), the indenture trustee should never surrender its position of independence or prejudice its right to take a contrary stand. This is particularly true when the principal creditors serving on a committee are interested in issues other than the indenture

securities. The indenture trustee must be mindful also of the potential conflicting interests between the professional bargain hunters (also referred to today as "bottom fishers" or "vulture funds") who acquire the securities at severely reduced prices, and those investors who were prebankruptcy debt holders.

15. The indenture trustee should take an active interest in all matters relating to preparation and adoption of a plan, including a careful review of the disclosure statement. Appropriate objections should be made if the indenture trustee believes the statement is inaccurate, incomplete, or inadequate for the class of creditors it represents. Many trustees, conscious of their lack of authority to compromise the claims of security holders, have taken the position that negotiations on a plan are a matter for the security holders and their committees and that the indenture trustee should play a passive role. This attitude is shortsighted and unrealistic. It is true that indenture trustees cannot make a commitment binding on their security holders, nor can anyone else. This is a matter for individual holders who must be given the right to express their approval or disapproval by vote once a plan is disseminated for acceptance. The indenture trustee has no right to vote on a plan, but should participate freely to the same extent as other parties, including committees, in all discussions leading to agreement on a plan. Participation in plan negotiations will not foreclose its right to object to confirmation of a plan that it believes is unfair or inequitable or that is rejected by the security holders. Under normal circumstances, the indenture trustee should not itself endeavor to prepare and file a plan. The only authority for it to do so is contained in Section 1121 of Chapter 11 when a Chapter 11 trustee is appointed or when the debtor

does not file a plan and obtain acceptances within specified time limits.

16. The indenture trustee should insist that the final order of the court directing and providing for consummation of the plan contain a specific discharge of the indenture and the trustee's duties. If the plan contains such provisions, the canceled indenture securities may be properly disposed of by the distribution or exchange agent appointed by the court without being returned to the indenture trustee for cancellation and discharge. Unless this is done, the indenture trustee may find itself called upon to perform a great deal of detailed work for which it may be unable to obtain fees and expenses unless the court has approved them as an administrative cost.

17. The Code specifically authorizes the court, in directing consummation of a plan under Chapters 9 and 11, to set a period of time during which all claimants must present their securities or claims for distribution or exchange. At the expiration of this period the estate is closed and all claims for unexchanged securities become void. Any property left in the hands of the exchange agent reverts to the debtor or to the entity acquiring the debtor's assets under the plan.[27] This is an important provision and is usually contained in all final orders of the reorganization proceedings. Failure to so provide may mean that an estate may never be technically closed.

18. Where a debtor has been through a previous reorganization without provision for a final termination of an estate, a current bankruptcy case provides an opportunity to secure an appropriate order and dispose of remaining property that may be

held for distribution or exchange for old securities still outstanding from the previous reorganization. At the time of entry of the final order in the current case, an effort should be made to secure court authority for terminating remaining matters in all previous proceedings.

19. In a Chapter 7 bankruptcy (Liquidation) rather than a Chapter 11 reorganization, a court order establishing a limited period within which claimants must present their securities to receive their distributive share of the proceeds should also be obtained. Because there is no reorganized company to receive the balance of proceeds, a procedure that has been used successfully is to provide for a second pro-rata distribution among those claimants which received the initial distribution. This enables the indenture trustee to close the estate within a reasonable period of time and is the most equitable disposition that could be made of the remaining funds. It is essential, however, that such a method of distribution be incorporated in the initial order for distribution. In one case where this was attempted by a subsequent order, a state successfully intervened and claimed a vested interest in the remaining funds under an abandoned property law. Where provision is contained in the initial order for complete distribution of all proceeds, no such rights can vest in the state.

The Bankruptcy Abuse Prevention and Consumer Protection Act of 2005 was passed principally to address consumer debts, and also included significant provisions amending the Bankruptcy Code. Chapter 7 previously addressed both personal as well as corporate liquidations. Under the 2005 Act, personal bankruptcies now fall under Chapter 13 where debtors formulate a plan of repayment over either a three or five year period. Chapter 9 filings still cover municipalities and Chapter 11 covers corporate reorganizations. The 2005

Act created a new Chapter 15 for international or Cross-Border insolvency cases.

Of concern to indenture trustees was that the 2005 Act added significant responsibilities to unsecured creditors committees. For example, such committees are now required to provide access to information to creditors who hold claims but who have not been appointed by the U.S. Trustee to the committee. The creditors committee must also solicit and receive comments from such creditors. The new rules were intended to open up communication with all creditors. There is concern that debtors may require non-member creditors to sign confidentiality agreements as debtors require of members before providing information. Since there have not been many bankruptcy filings since the 2005 Act was passed, it is unclear how this new responsibility will be handled.

The 2005 Act amended certain other provisions of the Code:

1. Exclusivity – The court will no longer be able to grant extensions of exclusivity to submit a plan of reorganization beyond 18 months after commencement of the bankruptcy case to submit a plan and 20 months to solicit acceptances.

2. Commercial Real Estate Leases – If a debtor does not assume or reject a commercial lease within 120 days of the case, the lease is deemed rejected.

3. Preferences – A debtor or trustee may avoid a transfer during the 90-day period prior to the case. The trustee may not avoid a preference to the extent that the transfer was for payment of a debt incurred in the ordinary course of business.

4. Fraudulent Conveyances – A debtor or trustee may avoid a transfer made within two years prior to the case and that otherwise has the elements of a fraudulent transfer.

5. Automatic Stay – Prohibits the commencement or continuation of most actions against the debtor or its property after a bankruptcy petition has been filed. Several exceptions have been expanded such as the continuation of criminal proceedings against the debtor and the delisting of the securities involved.

6. Reclamation Rights – The time of reclaiming creditors has been extended to 45 days before the case commenced. Employee Stay bonuses to insiders are not allowed as administrative expense claims without a finding by the court. An investment banker that was an underwriter of the debtor is not automatically prohibited from being retained by the debtor.

7. Dismissal/Conversion – Requests that a Chapter 11 case be either converted to a Chapter 7 liquidation or dismissed may be granted "for cause", which includes, for example, gross mismanagement and unauthorized use of cash collateral.

8. Financial Contracts – Clarifies the rights of non-debtor parties to certain types of securities contracts, repurchase agreements, forward contracts, commodity contracts, and swap agreements.

Section 801 of the 2005 Act added to the Bankruptcy Code a new Chapter 15 entitled "Ancillary and Other Cross-Border Cases" which incorporates into U.S. bankruptcy law the Model Law on Cross-Border Insolvency developed by the United Nations Commission for International Trade Law. The current provisions under Section 304 of the Code were completely repealed. Under Chapter 15, the "foreign representative" appointed and authorized in a "foreign proceeding" to represent a foreign debtor may commence an ancillary proceeding by filing a petition for recognition of the foreign proceeding. An order granting recognition may contain such relief as staying actions concerning the debtor's property, suspending the transfer or disposition of assets, authorizing the examination of witnesses and taking of evidence, entrusting the debtor's property to the foreign representative, and any other relief available to a bankruptcy trustee other than authority to bring avoidance actions.[28]

As of December 1, 2007, amendments to the Federal Rules of Bankruptcy Procedure became effective. Rule 1014 recognizes the authority of the bankruptcy courts to dismiss a bankruptcy case without a motion by a party in interest. Rule 3007 prohibits a party objecting to a claim from including in a claim objection a request for affirmative relief such as damages. Also, it limits the type and number of claim objections that may be brought by way of an omnibus objection. Rule 4001 requires more extensive notice to interested parties. Rule 6003 sets forth new guidelines limiting relief in the early stages of a bankruptcy proceeding. Rule 6006 governs the assumption, rejection and assignment of executory contracts and unexpired leases. Rule 7007.1 requires that a party file a corporate ownership statement in its first "pleading". Rule 9005.1 adopts Rule 5.1, which provides that a pleading questioning the constitutionality of a federal or state statute, and requires the party to file a notice of constitutional question on the Attorney General of the United States or of the particular state, and Rule 9037 which recognizes that any personal information not otherwise protected by sealing or redaction will be made available over the Internet.

COMPENSATION AND RECOVERY OF EXPENSES

Almost every indenture contains provisions giving the indenture trustee a contractual right to seek payment of its fees and recovery of its expenses from the obligor. Even where the obligor is in bankruptcy, there has been express recognition of this contractual entitlement.[29] Thus, the trustee should always file a proof of claim for its prepetition fees and expenses and also for any contractually based fees and expenses which are incurred post petition. When settled, such a claim would receive consideration at the same level as that of any other unsecured creditor. However, given the uncertainties of a recovery, the trustee should also pursue a claim under Section 503 of the Bankruptcy Code, which allows a court to reimburse the indenture trustee for the actual and necessary expenses incurred in making a substantial contribution to a Chapter 9 or Chapter 11 case,[30] and to pay the trustee "reasonable compensation for services rendered by [it] in making a substantial contribution in a case under chapter 9 or chapter 11 of this title, based on the time, the nature, the extent and the value of such services, and the cost of comparable services other than in case under this title."[31]

Unfortunately, indenture trustees often do not recover either their fees or their expenses (which are primarily counsel fees). The award of post-petition fees and reimbursement of post-petition expenses under Section 503(b) is deemed to be an administrative expense of the bankruptcy estate, and as such is given an administrative priority status. Because payment of these expenses will reduce the amount available to creditors and claimants, the section has been construed very strictly and narrowly.

Most troublesome of all the cases denying recovery to indenture trustees is an Eighth Circuit Court of Appeals decision which held that the indenture trustee by merely performing its duties to its bondholders, even in a satisfactory manner, pursuant to its obligation to act as a "prudent man" was not, as a matter of law, entitled to compensation or recovery of expenses.[32] The court also concluded that the "bankruptcy estate should not have to pay for services which primarily benefit the debenture holders and only incidentally benefit the bankruptcy estate".[33]

This decision places the trustee in a difficult (some argue "impossible") position. The trustee must, as a matter of law under the TIA, and contractually under most indentures, actively discharge its obligation under the indenture as an advocate for its bondholders even if it means that other creditors might receive less in any reorganization, but if it does so perform, the bankruptcy court may deny its claim for fees and expenses. It is also evident that the indenture trustee must do a great deal more than simply file a proof of claim on behalf of its bondholders and otherwise perform in a perfunctory manner. Presumably, if the indenture trustee can show (i.e., prove) that its services provided a direct, significant, and demonstrable benefit to the entire estate; were not of a routine nature; and did not duplicate services rendered by other parties in the proceeding, it would stand a much better chance of receiving payment of its fees and reimbursement of its expenses. It is essential that the administrative officer keep a detailed diary of the dates, time, and activities performed, including the writing of any letters, responding to telephone calls from security holders etc, and attendance at all conferences and meetings involving the obligor.

Existing cases do not provide a definitive answer to this problem, nor do they even articulate an understanding of precisely what the nature and extent of the trustee's performance must be in order to recover from the bankrupt estate. The SEC, however, has articulated a formulation of what it believes should be the appropriate legal standard, stating:

> The Commission urges that an indenture trustee be entitled to compensation as an administrative expense pursuant to the substantial contribution test of Section 503(b) if its satisfies the following test:
>
> (1) the indenture trustee has, through its representation of the interests of bondholders, made demonstrable efforts towards furthering the reorganization process; and

(2) the indenture trustee's services or those of its counsel do not duplicate the services of official participants or other indenture trustees.[34]

As a last resort, the trustee can attempt to recover under its lien against any distributions under an approved plan prior to distribution to the bondholders. However, the parties in interest may be authorized to review the proposed deduction for reasonableness. Since the amount of the proposed deduction may be material to the bondholders' decision to accept or reject the proposed reorganization plan, the trustee should include a description in the disclosure statement of its plans for obtaining compensation from the bondholders' distribution. This will avoid the very real possibility that after confirmation of the plan, the bondholders will be unpleasantly surprised by the indenture trustee's action. As long as any cash distributions exceed the trustee's claim for compensation, a dollar-for-dollar deduction will be easy to implement, if the court approves. However, when the available cash is insufficient and the distribution consists of new debt and/or equity securities, the trustee may be in the rather unpleasant position of having to initiate a procedure before the court to value the noncash consideration received and to determine the appropriate deduction to be made. Given the additional potential for dispute with bondholders over valuation, it is unlikely that most trustees would pursue this route.

---

[1] Pub. Law 95-598, 92 Stat. 2549 (1978), which codified and enacted Title 11 of the United States Code--Bankruptcy. Section numbers hereinafter referred to are to Title 11.

[2] Art. I, sec. 8, clause 4.

[3] Note 1, *supra.*

[4] 11 USC 362(a) and 922(a). Section 362(b) excepts certain actions from the stay, including: acts to perfect an interest in property of the debtor to the extent that the bankruptcy trustee's rights and powers are subject to such perfection; the commencement or continuation of an action by a governmental unit to enforce its police or regulatory powers; and the setoff by certain financial market participants of mutual debt or claim arising in connection with certain financial market contracts. Section 1168 expressly provides an exception for "rolling stock," which affects railroad reorganizations.

[5] Id. sec. 362(d). See, however, sec. 362(f), which permits the court, without a hearing, to grant relief from the stay, if "necessary to prevent irreparable damage to the interest of an entity in property. . . ."

[6] Id. sec. 702, 704.

[7] Id. sec. 101(29). Defined as a "political subdivision or public agency or instrumentality of the state."

[8] Id. sec. 109(c), 901(a).

[9] Id. sec. 109(c)(5).

[10] Id. sec. 923; see also Rule 2002, Rules of Bankruptcy Procedure.

[11] See Rule 3017, Rules of Bankruptcy Procedure, for court considerations of disclosure statements.

[12] The requisite majorities for acceptance by a class are at least two-thirds in amount and more than one-half in number of the allowed claims of such class that vote on the plan. Section 1126(c).

[13] 11 USC sec. 1126(c), 1129(a).

[14] Note 12, *supra*.

[15] Id. sec. 1129(a). <See> sec. 1124 for specific criteria for determination of nonimpairment.

[16] A court will allow such action only in extraordinary circumstances and only if the interests of the original secured creditors are protected.

[17] Post petition debtor-in-possession (or DIP) financing is of vital importance to the debtor to enable it to stabilize its operations in the very early days following the filing of the petition for relief. A debtor may also obtain unsecured credit upon order of the court, even if not in the ordinary course of business. Id. Sec. 364(b).

[18] Id. sec. 547, 548.

[19] The applicability of Section 552, in the event of a municipality bankruptcy, has been curtailed by the addition of Section 928(a).

[20] US Trustees generally have responsibility for administering the cases and have a significant amount of influence.

[21] 11 USC, sec. 1102(a)(2).

[22] Id. sec. 1104(a).

[23] Id. sec. 1104(b).

[24] Section 1109 and Rule 2202(f), Rules of Bankruptcy Procedure.

[25] Id. Rule 2019. The filing of the verified statement makes available to the Court and, consequently, to interested parties, the names of the debt holders. The requirement does not override the indenture requirements for obtaining bondholder lists prescribed by the TIA. Nevertheless, attempts to impound a list of creditors have been disallowed by the courts; see *In re* Itel Corp., 17 B.R. 942 (Bkrtcy. App., 9 Cir. 1982).

[26] For case law on the problem of the indenture trustee being on a creditors' committee, see Wood v. City National Bank & Trust Co., 312 US 262 (1941). Courts have also recognized that an indenture trustee may serve on a committee in a voting capacity; see *In re* The Charter Company, 42 B.R. 251 (Bkrtcy, MD Fla. 1984)

[27] 11 USC sec. 347(b).

[28] The Bankruptcy Abuse Prevention and Consumer Protection Act of 2005, by Romano I. Peluso, ABA Trust & Investments, July/August 2005

[29] *In re* Flight Transportation Corporation Securities Litigation, 874 F.2d 576, 583 (8th Cir. 1989); *In re* Revere Copper & Brass Incorporated, et al., 60 B.R. 892 (S.D.N.Y. 1986).

[30] 11 USC sec. 503(b)(3)(D).

[31] Id., sec. 503(b)(5), emphasis added.

[32] *In re* Fight Transportation Corporation, *supra*, note 29, at 581.

[33] Id. at 591.

[34] Brief of the SEC, *In re* Baldwin-United Corporation, Case No. C-1-88-0056 (S.D. Ohio 1988), *appeal settled and dismissed*, BR Case No. 1-83-02495 (S.D. Ohio 1989).

FIFTEEN

SPECIALIZED TRUSTS AND AGENCY APPOINTMENTS

In the preceding chapters, we considered the more important duties and responsibilities of trustees under the customary indenture and private placement contract. Even these vary, however, because of differences in types of financing, the nature of the security, particular indenture provisions, and other factors. In general, these differences constitute matters of detail rather than a change in basic function or responsibility.

From time to time, a bank performing the corporate trust function is called upon to serve in a somewhat different or more limited capacity. Some of the more significant specialized trusts and/or agency appointments are discussed in this chapter.

ASSET-BACKED SECURITIES TRUSTS

Asset-backed securities, a term generally used to describe debt issues secured by assets other than those securing the traditional mortgage bond issue, have become a major factor in the capital markets during the past several years. They can be grouped into four asset types: (1) credit cards, (2) motor vehicles, (3) residential mortgages, and (4) student loans.

The trustee needs to be concerned with who can act as back-up servicer. Before accepting the trusteeship of any type of asset-backed security issue, the trustee should completely understand the complexities of asset backed securities and the additional duties and responsibilities required.

Although the issues that are sold publicly must be registered under the 33 Act and are subject to the disclosure and reporting requirements of the 33 and 34 Acts, the structure of the particular issue will determine whether the TIA is applicable. If the underlying assets which are being securitized are sold to a trust, the debt securities issued by the trust constitute an undivided interest in the trust and are exempt from the TIA's provisions.[1] With this type of structure, where the trust is the issuer, a bank will be appointed as trustee under a Pooling and Servicing Agreement.[2] This agreement is not considered to be an "indenture", even though it contains many of the standard provisions of corporate indentures.

The pooling of mortgage loans by the Government National Mortgage Association (GNMA or "Ginnie Mae") in 1970 was the earliest use of the securitization of a pool of assets and the issuance of securities backed by that pool. *Securitization* is simply the process under which pools of individual loans or receivables are packaged, underwritten, and sold to investors in the form of negotiable securities. The theory behind this financing technique is simply that the cash flows (which are generally predictable) from the underlying assets are used to pay the interest and principal on the securities. Until 1985, almost all the asset-backed issues were basically mortgage-backed securities issued by GNMA, FNMA, and the FHLMC. Thereafter the market expanded rapidly as diverse asset pools were securitized. Although principally securitizing automobile loans and credit card receivables, other issues were backed by computer leases, loans against insurance policies (i.e., "death-backed bonds"), loans supporting employee stock option plans, home equity loans, hospital receivables, and even high-yield debt securities! In 1997, the total volume of asset backed securities exceeded $140 billion. In 2006, the volume was $1.042 trillion.

When the first asset backed issues were brought to market, investors scrutinized the issuing entities. Since most asset backed securities are highly rated with limited potential for downgrading, investors later shifted their focus from the issuer to the quality of the collateral, the loss protection coverage and the structure of the deal. Over the years, issuers have undergone increased scrutiny based upon the issuer's capabilities to service debt for such receivables as automobiles loans and home equity loans[3]. The rationale for this type of financing vehicle is that the issuer, sometimes referred to as the "seller" (primarily banks, finance companies, and insurance companies) can positively affect its balance sheet by reducing its assets, which are securitized, with a consequent reduction in the need for and cost of capital to support those assets. Second, asset-backed securities can usually be funded at a lower cost, as they are typically structured to receive at least an "AA" bond rating; thus the issuer is able to borrow at lower cost than if it borrowed on its own credit.

Generally, investment bankers identify the specific assets to be pooled according to two criteria. First, the assets must be homogeneous in order to facilitate structuring so that the cash flows are steady and generally follow projections. Second, collateral will be selected that spreads the risk by limiting geographic - or, in the case of high-yield debt, industry - concentrations. Spreading the risk of default, linked with an economic downturn in a particular industry or geographic region, enables the asset pool to better absorb payment defaults.

If the selection of assets alone is not enough to obtain a high rating, other forms of credit enhancement may also be used. These credit enhancements may come in the form of the issue structure itself, a senior/subordinate structure, over-collateralization and reserve accounts; or a third-party enhancement in the form of a letter of credit or some form of bond insurance.

Investors find asset-backed securities attractive because of the high ratings and the "bankruptcy remote" nature of the securities. The lower potential for default results from the absolute separation of the security holders' claims against the assets from the credit of the originator of the assets backing the bonds. The creation of an "issuer" of the asset-backed security is the mechanism that accomplishes this result. This issuer is usually a special-purpose vehicle created specifically for the purpose of issuing the securities. An essential part of initiating this transaction is the sale of the assets to the special purpose entity, which may be a corporation, a partnership, or a trust created to hold the assets on behalf of the beneficial owners of the asset-backed securities. If a grantor trust is utilized, the owners of the asset-backed securities are also the owners of undivided interests in the asset pool. Such trusts are usually issued in pass-through form. If an owner trust form is used, the trust itself owns the assets and issues the more traditional type of debt securities that are collateralized by the assets. By using a special purpose vehicle, the cash flows can continue to service the securities even if the originator of the transaction files for bankruptcy.

Asset-backed securities have been marketed in a variety of forms. The main forms are *pass-throughs*, in which the payments on the underlying assets go directly through to the bondholders and *pay-throughs*, where the payments on the underlying assets are the basis for the cash flows supporting the debt service on the outstanding securities. The cash flows are structured to meet investor needs. Collateralized debt obligations, represent debt of the issuer collateralized directly by the assets. The payments received on these assets are not dedicated to the payments on the securities.

Most asset-backed transactions require a servicer, which may either be related to the issuer or independent. The servicer is responsible for tracking and collecting the payments due on the assets, for making the tax and mortgage payments on the mortgaged property and for taking necessary collection measures against the borrowers who fail to make timely payments. The servicer is also responsible for forwarding reports documenting the performance of the assets to the trustee. The servicer's responsibilities may or may not include calculating the payment to be made to the security holders.

Some transactions have more than one servicer. In these situations, a master servicer will be appointed. The role of the master servicer is to aggregate the information received from the various subservicers and forward it to the trustee.

The Trustee's Role

Because there is limited recourse to an issuer for asset-backed securities, the trustee's role becomes more involved than in a traditional form of debt financing. For the same reason that the issue is "bankruptcy remote", it could also be considered to be "issuer remote". Once the bonds are sold, few entities remain connected to the transaction. This financing structure requires the trustee to assume responsibilities normally reserved for the issuer. Even though the trustee typically has little discretionary power and limited authority in a pre-default situation, trustees for asset-backed securities are frequently called upon to make decisions involving the collateral[4], to assume expanded responsibilities, and to advise, hire, and fire other parties to the transaction. For these reasons the account officer and administrator must understand all the details of the particular transaction, including the cash flows and the collateral involved. It is essential that the documents associated with the financing, including the trust indenture and the pooling and servicing agreement, be carefully reviewed to identify any nontraditional functions the trustee may be asked to perform.

When reviewing the documents, the account officer should prepare a "flow diagram" of the transaction to determine whether the required reports and cash flows will work operationally. For example, if the trustee is required to receive master servicer reports on the 18th of the month, but subservicers are not required to report to the master servicer until the 17th of the month, the parties will experience difficulties meeting debt service payment deadlines. All duties must be clearly identified, and there must be complete understanding as to which entity is responsible for each specific performance. In certain situations, trustees may be required to advance any shortfall in the cash flows. Although the trustee is allowed to make recovery out of subsequent cash flows, a credit facility is usually required for the trustee to perform its duties. The decision to serve as trustee for asset backed securities is often determined by the trustee bank's willingness to place itself in the position as a creditor.

The account officer must also review the reporting requirements and sample formats in the agreements. Underwriters usually require extensive reporting to the trustee. It is essential that the trustee receive sufficient and accurate information to enable it to perform the necessary calculation of payments to the bondholders, or prepare other required reports.

One critical responsibility of the asset backed trustee is tracking and monitoring the servicer's activities. An asset-backed financing will work only to the extent that the servicer performs its duties in a timely and accurate manner. The servicer's expertise is important to the financing. To ensure that there is no interruption in servicing the underlying collateral, if the designated servicer fails to perform or defaults, the trustee needs to find a back-up servicer. Although investment banks and rating agencies perform due diligence reviews of the servicer, the trustee should also review the servicer qualifications prior to acceptance of the appointment. Although most corporate trust organizations will perform some sort of "credit review" prior to accepting a new trustee appointment, for asset-backed transactions the servicer should be reviewed as to the feasibility of performing its responsibilities over the term of the financing. This review should include the servicer's management qualifications and its data processing and information systems. Other statistical information, including payment delinquency ratios, should be compared to other servicers in the same industry. The rating agencies and investment bankers tend to focus on the ability of the servicer to service the assets. More critical to the trustee, and often overlooked by other parties to the financing structure, is the servicer's ability to translate the servicing activity to meaningful data to report to the investors. An otherwise excellent servicer may prove to be a significant threat to the viability of an issue if it does not understand the issue structure or if its systems cannot generate required reports.

Once the issue is closed, the trustee must continue to monitor the servicer's performance by reviewing its reports and ensuring that the indenture covenants are met. If the servicer's parent organization is placed in receivership or its debt is downgraded or if the servicer is put up for sale, the trustee must be in a position to know exactly what action it can take. The trustee must also decide what information it can and should disclose to the security holders and the investors.

More complex transactions backed by short term assets, like credit card receivables or trade receivables, often have *Amortization Events,* in addition to Events of Default. Amortization Events typically involve credit quality issues such as delinquency ratios or inadequate over-collaterization. When the underlying collateral deteriorates in quality, the document may require the trustee to take immediate action to unwind the security issue. In comparison, Event of Default language often allows for periods of time to resolve problems, notice to holders, and trustee involvement. On December 22, 2004, the SEC published final regulations, referred to as Regulation AB, which updates and clarifies the registration requirements for asset backed securities. Regulation AB impacts trustees. For example, Regulation AB requires disclosure of the extent to which the trustee has had prior experience serving as trustee for such transactions, addresses factors such as the extent to which the trustee will independently verify cash flows, activity in account statements, compliance with transaction covenants, the addition, substitution, or removal of pool assets, and the underlying data used for such transactions. A trustee engagement other than a "naked trustee" or mere paying agent (not involving calculation of distributions or other administration of cash flows) may fall within the definition of "servicer" under Regulation AB.

All public asset backed offerings commenced after December 31, 2005, are subject to the new regulatory requirements. There are new Form 10-K requirements that each entity performing any servicing functions, including most trustees, must submit as exhibits (1) an annual compliance statement with the transaction documents, (2) an annual assessment report addressing the servicer's platform-level compliance with certain serving criteria, and (3) a registered public accountant's attestation report. The person signing the Form 10-K must make the Sarbanes-Oxley Act of 2002, Section 302 certification.[5]

Agency Functions

The usual appointments associated with asset-backed transactions include registrar and paying agent as well as collateral agent/custodian. They may also include responsibilities for security holder payment calculations and for the preparation and filing of certain tax returns. Asset-backed securities, such as federal agency-backed collateralized mortgage obligations (CMOs), mortgage pass-through obligations, and automobile and boat loan receivables, are backed by the same pool of assets over the life of the securities. Transactions backed by short-term assets, including credit card receivables, continuously pledge new assets to the pool as other assets are paid down. In both cases the trustee must periodically review the UCC financing statements or other appropriate documentation to ensure that the trust maintains its perfected security interest in the collateral.

In the case of home mortgages, government obligations (e.g., Sallie Mae's), high-yield debt securities, and boat loans, the trustee may be asked to physically hold the securities or loan documents, and to perform a due diligence review of the securities and the loan documents.

On or before the closing of a loan-backed transaction, the trustee or custodian may receive the loan documents which are pledged to the trust. The trustee must compare each loan file to the governing documents and the underwriter's listing and verify that all files have been received. Each file must be reviewed to verify that all required documentation is in the file; such documents usually include a mortgage note, mortgage, assignment of the mortgage to the trust, and title or other insurance policies. In credit card or trade receivables transactions, the collateral may consist of computer generated files, supplied on magnetic tape or computer diskettes.

After the due diligence is completed, the custodian must identify all discrepancies and work with all interested parties to "cure" the problems. Typically these problems must be resolved by a specific time frame. At the end of the allowed time, the seller must replace or repurchase any loans with incomplete or incorrect documentation. The loan document files are then deposited in the trustee/custodian's vault for safekeeping. During the life of the security issue, the trustee and the servicer process requests for mortgage assumptions, reamortizations, proofs of claim, satisfactions, easements, and other legal matters. The trustee must examine each request in the context of the relevant agreement, consult with counsel as required, and take appropriate action. When the trustee is physically holding securities as collateral, it will be responsible for collecting payments and for processing substitutions of collateral.

The assets in these transactions generate substantial amounts of cash that must be deposited in a collection account, held by the servicer or collection agent and invested within the terms of the governing documents. Payments received on mortgage backed bonds are typically processed using the servicer and master servicer's existing collection accounts, with a single remittance to the trustee prior to payment date. Payments received from assets, such as automobile and boat loans, credit card receivables, and trade receivables, often are paid directly to an established account under the trustee's control. The collection agent or servicer is responsible for reconciling the cash received in the control account to the amount expected to be received. It is also the collection agent or servicer's responsibility to ensure that funds received between specific designated cut-off dates are properly earmarked for the correct payment date. The governing documents should clearly define which party to the transaction will "advance" funds to the security holders not received on time.

Often the collection agent's credit rating will be considered in determining whether it is eligible to hold a collection account. The trustee must be diligent in monitoring the credit rating and take any required action (including replacing the collection agent) should its credit rating fall to an unacceptable level.

The trustee may also be asked to make extensive calculations to determine the amount to be paid to the security holders, based on the data furnished by the servicer. The trustee must ensure that the documents clearly define its responsibilities. Data in a usable format, with clearly defined calculation requirements, must be delivered to the trustee on a timely basis. Finally, the trustee must be comfortable with the level of expertise in its own organization to develop the necessary financial calculations.

One problem in performing these calculations is correctly determining that portion of the periodic payment which represents repayment of a portion of the principal and payment of interest on the security. Typically, these securities pay principal during the life of the issue. The principal is paid based on a factor, which is a percentage applied to the original principal amount. The remaining principal amount is reported in terms of a factor that, when multiplied against the original face amount of the security will reflect the current outstanding amount. There is usually little risk of a redemption on asset-backed securities. When there is a redemption it is commonly known as a *clean-up call*. This results when 90 percent or more of the principal amount has been paid down, i.e., the factor on the issue has fallen to .10 or less.

In addition to the usual Form 1099 tax reports, trustee may be required to perform REMIC[6] tax reporting. REMIC reporting involves the preparation and filing of the trust's initial information return as well as its quarterly and yearly tax returns.

Serving as trustee for an asset-backed security issue represents a complex appointment with greater risk and more liability than other debt trusteeships. Having to make decisions in shorter time periods and monitoring the daily cash flow require special expertise. The volume of new asset backed securities has grown substantially over the last ten years and is expected to grow even more significantly over the next several years compared to the level of unsecured debt financings. The competition (including pricing) among trustees for these appointments will undoubtedly increase as well.

EQUIPMENT TRUSTS

A special form of contract has been developed for the financing of the purchase of equipment by railroads and, since 1970, for the financing of aircraft by the major airlines.

The basic concept of the equipment trust is ownership of the equipment by the trustee during the life of the loan. The obligations are in the form of equipment trust certificates, executed by the trustee, which represent a pro rata interest in the rentals and other proceeds received by the trustee through lease of the equipment to the user corporation. The proceeds received from sale of the certificates are used to purchase the equipment, and a lease thereof is executed by the trustee to the user corporation. This is a net lease calling for payments of rental over an eight- to fifteen-year period sufficient to pay all interest and principal on the certificates. In the case of railroads, the certificates mature serially and the obligations are retired more rapidly than normal depreciation on the equipment. Because the corporation (or as more recently seen, an institutional investor) provides equity in an amount equal to 20 to 30 percent of the purchase price of the equipment, and because most of such equipment is considered salable, these obligations command a ready market and usually a better price than the credit of many railroads or airlines alone would warrant.

In addition to its obligation to make the rental payments under the lease, the user corporation executes a guaranty on each certificate that runs directly to the certificate holder.

Normally, administration of these trusts is somewhat easier than the average trust indenture, although the initial documentation tends to be much more complex and very special problems are created if a default or equipment loss occurs under the lease.

CONSTRUCTION AND BOND FUND TRUSTS

Although occasionally an indenture requires administration of a construction fund in connection with a new bond issue as part of the other duties of the trustee, the type of trust considered here is somewhat unique. It may occur in connection with a revenue bond issue of a state or municipality or a public or quasi-public body created for a special purpose. Power districts, sewer districts, turnpike commissions, and similar entities are typical examples. Inasmuch as the security for the bonds issued consists of the revenue to be derived from the project to be constructed, the bond proceeds are required to be segregated and held in trust solely to pay the project's construction costs.

The function of the construction fund trustee is to hold the proceeds, make investments in a manner as to provide the greatest return consistent with the requirement for paying them out over a predetermined period, and disburse the funds and the income thereon for the project's construction cost. The disbursement is made against certifications by the project engineers of actual expenditures made or obligations incurred for construction purposes. Although the trustee is entitled to rely on these certifications, it should check them in sufficient detail to satisfy itself that the expenditures listed are of the type properly chargeable against the construction monies. In addition, the trustee should ensure that the types of investments are those specifically authorized by the indenture or bond resolution. As a practical matter it is desirable to limit these to obligations of the United States or its agencies or to certificates of deposit in prime money-center banks. One important consideration in establishing a construction fund is to provide for a revolving fund in a sufficient amount to take care of ordinary day-to-day disbursements for a reasonable period of time. This permits all miscellaneous disbursements to be included in one certificate at monthly or other periodic intervals, at which time the revolving fund is replenished.

Once the project has been completed and an appropriate certificate to this effect received, the duties of the construction fund trustee are finished. Any disbursed funds are usually turned over to the bond fund trustee and used to retire a portion of the debt.

In addition to a construction fund trustee for a revenue project, it is also necessary to designate a bond fund trustee. These may be separate institutions, or one trustee may be designated to perform both functions.

The duties of the bond fund trustee relate solely to receipt and disbursement of the revenues of the project once operation commences. Varied types of special funds are usually created to provide for operating expenses, maintenance, bond service, reserves, and major replacements, additions, or extensions to the project. The revenues are received directly by the trustee and allocated to each fund according to the formula set forth in the indenture. The funds are then disbursed for the proper purposes either according to a predetermined schedule or against certificates of the proper officials of the district, commission, or authority.

A bond fund trustee has no power of enforcement or other rights in the event of default or insufficiency of the revenues. If the revenues or other payments due should be withheld wrongfully, it could undoubtedly bring suit to recover them. Its duties relate solely, however, to the revenues or other funds provided to be paid to it. It is not a representative of the bondholders for purpose of enforcement.

ESCROW AGENT

The significant growth in the number and type of innovative financings has also increased the need for an escrow agent in many transactions. Essentially, an *escrow agent* is a disinterested party that holds something of value for two or more other parties in interest, until a specified time has passed or until a specified event has occurred. The simplistic nature of an escrow appointment should not overshadow the fact that quite often the parties to the arrangement are either in disagreement or lack faith and trust in each other.

This type of "custody" arrangement has been used to hold the down payment toward a purchase of a plant facility, to secure a portion of the purchase price in a merger or acquisition transaction pending the execution of specified representations and warranties, to hold investor payments for subscription to securities, to hold life insurance policies covering the principals of closely held companies, and even to hold the source code documentation for computer software to assure users of continued software support by the developer.

An escrow agent does not want to hold title/ownership of the escrowed property. Therefore historically, like-kind exchanges of real property have been avoided. Recent change in IRS regulations allow the escrow agent to hold interest in the contract between two parties and does not require that the property be titled to the escrow agent. The title to the property goes directly from the seller to the buyer at the time of the exchange. These changes have made like-kind exchanges of real property more attractive to escrow agents.

An escrow agreement can be as simple or as complex as needs dictate. If not carefully drafted, tremendous, and sometimes costly, liability can be placed on the escrow agent. It is essential that the escrow agreement clearly identify the parties in interest, detail each party's duties and responsibilities, accurately describe the property to be held, and specifically set out the circumstances of the release of the property from the escrow. The terms *verbal* and *discretion* can be the cause of great concern and should be avoided. If the property consists of cash and/or marketable securities, the escrow agent's duties and responsibilities regarding investment, reinvestment, collection, and disposition of income, registration of the securities, voting rights (in the case of stock), valuations, and reports should be carefully spelled out. All directives should be specific and in writing. The escrow agent should perform only those duties outlined in the agreement, no more and no less. Otherwise the escrow agent's performance could be questioned should litigation occur.

Appropriate provisions should also be included covering notifications and required methods of delivery, resolution of disputes, the governing law, and the resignation, removal, and succession of the escrow agent. The escrow agent should also have the authority to deliver assets to a court of competent jurisdiction in case of unresolved disputes or failure of the parties to appoint a successor escrow agent should the need arise. It is equally important to provide for full indemnification of the agent against all loss, cost, damage, or expense that may arise or result from the performance of the agent's duties--its liability being only for gross negligence or willful misconduct.

Should a bank desire to expand the functions of their escrow department, there are other services that can be offered. Although the designation of "trustee" may replace "escrow agent", the responsibilities of the bank can essentially mirror the duties of an escrow agent. These functions are those that do not fit the typical trustee services provided by other trust areas of the financial institution.

For example, federal regulations require a nuclear power plant to set aside funds for cleanup that may result from a problem with their nuclear plant. These funds must be held by a disinterested party, generally appointed as a trustee. Although the bank is designated as "trustee", if duties relating to the securities are assigned to an outside investment manager and the trustee's duties are to hold funds, settle trades and prevent improper distribution of funds, the actual function performed is more in line with those of an escrow agent than a trustee. The financial institution may choose to place these decommissioning trusts in an escrow department.

Voting trusts are used to comply with SEC regulations regarding majority ownership of securities. In its simplest form, a voting trust is set up for a closely held security with limited stockholders (fewer than 10 are preferable) and no cash dividends. The agreement should be very specific regarding proxy voting and limit the trustee's discretion, but the function of the voting trustee need be no more that holding the securities and voting the proxies.

Of course the more complex voting trust arrangements involve numerous stockholders, cash and stock dividends and transfers of ownership. Before committing the bank to these more complex relationships, the administrator should make certain the software and systems are available to make dividend calculations, distributions, transfers and tax reporting. The functions performed imitate those of a stock transfer and dividend paying agent.

These last two examples of trustee relationships violate the escrow agent "rule" of not taking title/ownership of property. Thus, agreements must be closely reviewed and protection for the trustee provided.

The functions that can be performed and the services that can be provided by an escrow department are only as limited as the imagination. Focus should be on the ability to provide the service to the clients while protecting the bank.

UNIT INVESTMENT TRUSTS

With the increased interest of private investors in the bond market and the desire to provide for portfolio diversification, offerings of a "pooled" portfolio of bonds much like mutual funds for stock issues has increased dramatically.[7]

An investment firm acting as a sponsor buys a selection of bonds for a particular UIT portfolio, and then offers shares or "units" of the fund for sale to investors. Each unit represents a fractional, undivided share of all the bonds in the portfolio. This selection is determined by the type of fund the sponsor seeks to sell to investors. It may consist entirely of tax-exempt bonds of a particular state, or of debt obligations of a particular industry, or it may be funded with securities of "growth" companies or, conversely, with debt obligations that provide high-income yield. The nature and type of the underlying portfolio are limited only by the ingenuity of the sponsor and its perception of the needs of potential investors.

Over the last several years, a financing backed by a portfolio of municipal tax-exempt bonds has been referred to as a municipal asset-backed bond financing. When interest rates generally increase somewhat higher or even lower than the underlying rate paid by the bonds in the portfolio, the underwriter is allowed to "collapse" the financing, meaning it is redeemed. The underwriter will then form a new pool of municipal securities which bears interest generally matching the current interest rate and new bonds are sold.

Because a UIT both issues securities and uses the proceeds to buy the underlying portfolio, it falls within the definition of an "investment company" in the Investment Company Act of 1940 (40 Act).[8]

The structure of the trust is governed by a trust indenture that designates the trustee, the sponsor, and the evaluator and that delineates their responsibilities. The indenture will also set forth the duration of the trust and the conditions under which it may be terminated early.

Section 26 of the 1940 Act prescribes the minimum requirements for the indenture, stating that: (1) the trustee must be bank having aggregate capital, surplus, and undivided profits of not less than $500,000; (2) the trustee cannot resign until the trust has been liquidated or a successor trustee appointed; (3) the fees available to the trustee, sponsor, and evaluator must be stated, and; (4) the sponsor must maintain appropriate unitholder records and notify the holders in the case of substitution of any portfolio security.

The bonds are deposited with a bank as trustee that has a variety of duties, including safekeeping of the securities until redeemed or called; the collection of interest on the securities and their principal if called or redeemed; the issuance to each investor of a registered certificate of ownership or the provision for a book-entry record of such holdings; the distribution of checks representing income on the shares on a monthly, quarterly, or semiannual basis, or the reinvestment of such; and the redemption of the trust's shares upon request by the investor.[9]

PROJECT FINANCING

The trustee's role in a project financing presents new challenges because of added complexity. As acceptance of the project finance vehicles grow, investment bankers, project sponsors and attorneys are called upon to structure increasingly complex transactions that employ the latest finance and risk management techniques. Derivatives, swaps and options are routinely used to hedge interest rates, fuel costs, currency conversion and foreign exchange risks. The corporate trustee must understand the importance to the exchange of funds between multiple parties and must require the funds to be moved through various domestic and offshore project "waterfall" accounts in a timely and accurate manner. As always, the trustee must fully understand its responsibilities, rights and powers which are set out in the indenture or like instrument and exercise them with the level of care as required by applicable law and custom and practice.

On international project finance transactions, the trustee is presented with a variety of challenges including

1. *Increased complexity.* International deals generally involve multiple parties and are much larger in scope and size than domestic transactions. The parties involved include project sponsors, export credit agencies, bilateral/multilateral agencies, commercial bank syndicates and capital market investors. Due to the increased size of the working groups, the trustee plays a greater role in coordinating the various administrative and operational aspects of the transaction.

2. *Diverse legal/regulatory systems.* A critical feature is that certain project security documents may be governed by local laws which require an understanding of differing legal systems and regulation. The trustee is assigned security interests in project property for the benefit of the investors. Through local counsel, the trustee must fully understand the nuances of these laws and their effect on its rights and responsibilities.

3. *Global network.* For an international deal, the

project's cash flows and payments are received and paid out in multiple currencies. Generally, local costs, such as for operations, maintenance, salaries, fuel costs and other operational costs are paid out in the local currency and remaining cash is converted into a principal currency, such as US dollars. Having a local presence or an established banking network is critical to handling, processing and executing all the trustee functions. Furthermore the trustee should be able to transact foreign exchange currency transactions so that funds can be repatriated into the investors' currency.

4. *Investment execution.* The success of a project financing requires that all investments and trades be settled in a timely manner to achieve expected returns on project cash flows. Uninvested cash will negatively impact investor and project sponsors' returns. In addition, some financing may require specialized or customized portfolio management capabilities with which the trustee should be able to work with or offer to the participants.

5. *Trustee issues.* In project financings, amendments and changes are made frequently, to adapt to unanticipated circumstances before and after the construction phase. A small, private investor group can more easily deal with such occurrences than can a many-tiered or public market structure. In both instances, the trustee must play a key role in the management of the amendment process.

6. *Technology capabilities.* To administer complex deal structures effectively, the trustee must use technology to carry out its responsibilities and duties, including payments, investments, account administration, foreign exchange and currency trades, swap payments, letters of credit, project documentation and ticklers or diary notes.

Instructions and periodic reporting to and from project sponsors and investors benefit from on-line technology in international transactions.

Administration

The revenue stream that a project generates is the principal source of funds securing payment of all expenses incurred in the operation and financing of a project. Additional sources of revenue include, insurance proceeds, liquidated damages, judgment proceeds, and payments from fuel suppliers.

All project revenues, received in the local currency are received by or on behalf of the trustee as collateral agent. The collateral agent is responsible for the movement of funds and for properly funding the various project "waterfall" accounts. All revenues are initially passed through an operating account in the local host country. Usually operating costs, fuel changes and local taxes are paid out in the local currency out of the operating account.

After local expenses, the balance (after a foreign exchange transaction) is transmitted to the trustee's general account in the United States. All converted funds, now in the lender's currency are used to pay interest and principal incurred in the financing of the project. After the lenders are paid, a series of project waterfall accounts are funded with the remaining cash. Accounts will generally have reserves required to provide additional assurance in case of cash shortfalls or cash flow interruptions due to unanticipated events. Waterfall accounts include operations and maintenance reserves, and contingent reserves for the project. The collateral agent is responsible for properly funding the accounts and executing all related investment functions.

After all project expenses are paid out and the reserve accounts funded, the remaining cash is the profit that remains to be distributed to the project sponsors or equity investors.

The Trustee As Information Agent

As project finance structures increase in complexity, greater coordination is required among the various parties involved in the transaction. The trustee is the one party that remains throughout the life of the transaction and therefore is a central source for the exchange and communication of information among the various parties.

Increasingly, the trustee is called upon to play this role as a coordinator of information through an "information agent agreement". Information flows in from various parties such as independent engineers, financial advisers, project sponsors, fuel; suppliers, and contractors. This information is received, coordinated and distributed to lenders, institutional and individual investors and other related parties.

The trustee should make sure that it is not responsible for the accuracy of the information, but that it is only acting as a conduit in distributing information to particular parties. This function is vital in international transactions where due to geographic and time distances, it is impossible for various parties to communicate individually.

---

[1] The SEC has taken the position that such trust certificates are deemed to be equity securities, thus being exempt under TIA sec. 304(a)(1).

[2] A pooling and servicing agreement is executed by the seller (i.e., the entity selling the mortgage or receivables pool to the trust), the servicer or master servicer, and the bank as trustee.

[3] "Asset Backed Securities Face New Scrutiny," *Wall Street Journal*, Feb. 18, 1997, p. C1.

[4] Although the underlying documents usually indicate that the trustee is to work with the servicer and may rely on its recommendations, the trustee must nevertheless independently exercise its discretion, especially when asked to release its lien on property not paid in full.

[5] Reg AB Clarifies Asset-Backed Securities Registration, by Romano I. Peluso, ABA *Trust & Investments*, September/October 2007

[6] Real Estate Mortgage Investment Conduit, as provided for in the Tax Reform Act of 1986.

[7] This investor interest has also resulted from the liberalization of tax legislation and regulation related to the establishment and funding of investment retirement accounts (IRAs) and Keoghs.

[8] 15 U.S.C.A. sec. 80a-3(a)(1) and 3(a)(3). UITs are also subject to the 33 Act but are specifically exempted from the TIA by its sec. 304(a)(2).

[9] For a detailed discussion, see Jay B. Gould and Gerald T. Lins, "Unit Investment Trusts: Structure and Regulation Under the Federal Securities Laws", 43 *Bus. Law.*1177 (Aug. 1988).

SIXTEEN

INTERNATIONAL FINANCINGS

In this chapter, we describe the role of indenture trustees in the U.S. for international financings as well as the differences in the roles of the trustee here and in the United Kingdom.

U.S. Trust Law

The trustee function in the U.S. in the international marketplace has its origins in the Trust Indenture Act of 1939, as amended by the Trust Indenture Reform Act of 1990. Under an indenture, the trustee has three areas of responsibility:

1) The trustee holds and manages funds and any collateral if the bonds are secured.

2) The trustee maintains and administers the indenture, supplemental indentures, and other documents relevant to the bond issuance and monitors compliance with the covenants and other provisions of the indenture through periodic reports filed with it.

3) The trustee enforces the remedial provisions of the indenture in an event of noncompliance or a default.

This is still true in international financings. However, international financings are not as carefully regulated as in the United States. There are more concerns as a result of foreign historical concepts and cultural differences.

The decision makers are the investment bankers, not the issuers. Financings range from conventional straight debt, which may be convertible and subordinated, to very complex structures such as project finance, securitization, and repackaging of assets. Issuers range from governments to corporations to special purpose entities.

The Euro

The largest international market is still the Euromarket which began about 50 years ago, with now more than $1 trillion of debt outstanding. It is the one true global market, but there are other prominent markets as well: Latin America, Asia, the Pacific Rim, and Russia. The Euromarket is loosely regulated, multi currency, multi-jurisdictional, and its primary aim is flexibility and liquidity.

Payment of interest and principal range from U.S. dollars, euros, pound sterling, yen, etc., and commonly debt is paid in multiple currencies.

Thirteen European Union countries, out of the twenty-seven Member States, currently have adopted the euro as their common currency. The original eleven on January 1, 1999: Austria, Belgium, Finland, France, Germany, Ireland, Italy, Luxembourg, the Netherlands, Portugal, and Spain. Then followed Greece and, as of January 1, 2007, Slovenia. Cyprus and Malta will adopt the euro on January 1, 2008.

Denmark and the United Kingdom have a special status allowing them to decide, and if, they will join in adopting the euro.

The remaining Member States will join as soon as they fulfill the necessary conditions required by the "Maastricht" convergence criteria.[1]

Appointment of a Common Depository

Most international financings listed on foreign exchanges which use the major European clearing systems, Euroclear and Clearstream, require the appointment of a common depository. The common depository function requires a bank to:

1) Maintain records for the clearing systems;
2) Report daily changes in holdings;
3) Report material changes in a financing;
4) Maintain aggregate holdings versus nominal holdings; and
5) Maintain the status of global notes.

Registrar Function

The registrar function is basically the same as in the United States – a bank maintains the records of bearer certificates outstanding and certificates registered as to principal only and any in fully registered form and processes any transfers and exchanges.

Because of the reluctance of investors to hold debt obligations in registered form, almost all of these issues up till the end of the 1990s were sold in bearer form with coupons.

As mentioned in Chapter 6, today, Eurobonds are all in book-entry form. These bonds are not registered under the 33 Act and may not be offered or sold within the United States to, or for the account or benefit of, U.S. persons (as defined in Regulation S under the 33 Act) except (a) to qualified institutional buyers (QIBs) in reliance on the exemption from the registration requirements of the 33 Act provided by SEC Rule 144A, (b) to persons in offshore transactions in reliance of Regulation S, (c) pursuant to an exemption for registration under 33 Act provided by Rule 144A (if available), or (d) pursuant to an effective registration statement under the 33 Act, in each of cases (a) through (d) in accordance with any applicable securities laws of any state of the United States. The bonds are registered in the nominee names of Depository Trust Company or of Euroclear and Clearstream. The bonds are initially issued as global bonds.

Rule 144A, under the 33 Act, exempts from registration the resale of privately placed securities to QIBs. Regulation S is available only for offers and sales of securities outside the United States.

The custodian function is also similar – safekeeping securities for its customers; collecting dividends and interest, which may be payable in different currencies; and buying, selling, receiving, and delivering securities upon instructions.

A bank's role in such financings can vary widely. It may be trustee, issuing and paying agent, registrar, custodian, and/or common depository.

The Trustee's Role

The use of a trustee is not as widely used internationally as in the U.S. A trustee, however, is appointed if there is need to monitor the security interests or collateral on behalf of bondholders or there are fund accounts to be maintained.

There is need for much more caution in international financings, partly because of relaxed regulations, but also because of:

    1) fraud;

2) money laundering;

3) the requirement for a trustee/paying agent to make payment in multiple currencies around the world;

4) the ability to provide accurate and timely custodian services

The *Know Your Customer* and risk management policies and procedures of the trustee should be implemented carefully, and an exhaustive review made of the entire transaction as the governing laws of countries vary. Tax treaties in each country also play an important role in how a financing is structured, marketed, and sold. Investors range from individuals to institutional investors to governments.

Where there is no trustee appointed, an issuing and paying agent is usually appointed with a much reduced fiduciary role.

In pre-default situations, most indentures require the issuer to provide continuing information to the trustee, even if minimal in nature. Some affirmative covenants include a commitment to pay interest and principal, to maintain issuer existence, and to pay taxes. Providing a no-default certificate and financial statements is less frequently required under foreign indentures. Basic negative covenants may include restrictions in incurring additional or senior debt, the sale of substantially all of the issuer's property, or the sale or leasing of property.[2]

Foreign issuers selling debt in the United States must file an annual report on Form 20-F and a semi-annual report on Form 40-F pursuant to the rules and regulations of the 34 Act. Foreign governments must file an annual report on Form 18-K.[3]

There are two major concerns for trustees in international financings:

1) The political, currency, and other foreign risk. Political risk involves the possible instability of the country in which the financing is being done. Currency risk involves the fluctuations in currency that can imperil the ability of the issuer to pay for example U.S. dollar-denominated debt and to convert local currency to dollars and then to transfer the dollars offshore.

2) The collateral perfection and enforcement under foreign laws. The trustee must be sure that it has proper perfection of any security interest under local law, that it is able to and understands the limitations on its collecting or foreclosing in those countries, and that it has effective control of any accounts not held in the United States. Also, there are likely to be very different and unfamiliar bankruptcy or insolvency laws that should be understood.

Upon the occurrence of a default, the trustee must determine whether to notify the bondholders. The duty to act with a proper degree of care includes the ability to withhold as well as give notice. Bondholders are entitled to notice whenever their security or their investment is permanently prejudiced. The primary objectives of all parties should be to prevent a default or to remedy the situation. Hasty action in publicizing the default may be unnecessary or counterproductive. The final decision should be approved by the appropriate trust committee of the trustee.

In post-default situations, a trustee must rely on advice of local counsel that is familiar with that country's bankruptcy and insolvency laws. A trustee's pre-default duties are bound by the exact provisions of the indenture and are generally ministerial in nature. After a default, a trustee assumes responsibilities to act as a prudent person would on behalf of bondholders. Defaults include non-payment of interest and principal; failure to make a sinking fund, purchase, or redemption payment; failure to discharge prior lien obligations when due or default under other debt instruments permitting acceleration; insolvency; filing for bankruptcy; and the breach or failure of any other covenant or condition in the indenture. Grace periods are frequently included. Some defaults are non-financial, temporary, or capable of being cured through appropriate negotiation with the issuer and the investment banker. Amending provisions in the indenture need to be considered and reviewed very carefully. Some amendments may not require bondholder consents. Others, however, do if the amendments adversely affect the holders' rights as to payment of interest and principal.

As previously stated, there are still bond issues in the international markets in bearer coupon form. In default, as with redemptions, publication of notices in appropriate authorized newspapers in the specified cities in foreign countries is required. Bondholder meetings are commonly held with great care given by the trustee to attendance and quorums, voting concerning direction given by bondholders as to action to be taken and the exact tabulation and reporting of the votes cast. The trustee and its counsel need to work very closely with the investment banker and the issuer to make certain that the bondholders are properly represented and protected.

A trustee must have the knowledge, expertise, appropriate staff, local office presence, and very importantly, the technology to service these financings with all their many varied characteristics.[4]

U.K. Trust Law

In the United Kingdom, the English trust law for trustees (or commercial trusts) is pursuant to the Trustee Act of 1925, repealed and/or amended, in part, by the Trustee Investments Act of 1961, and the Trustee Act of 2000.

These Acts govern trusts but are directed more toward private trusts and have a largely unintended impact on corporate trusts. Custom and common law guide the activities of a trustee in the U.K. and the duties under English law derive from such custom or explicitly as the provisions dictate in the governing trust deeds. Unlike in the U.S., the trustee role in the U.K. is more discretionary and advisory.

Under traditional trust deeds in the U.K., there is usually a higher degree of interpretation and judgment required of the trustee in executing its duties and responsibilities on behalf of bondholders, particularly in the event of a default under its terms or in the event of the insolvency of an issuer. In general terms, a U.S. indenture contains more explicit provisions setting out the role of the trustee and the rights of bondholders. Whereas, English law trust deeds have wider and less stringent provisions.[5]

In the U.K., there is fierce competition driving down fees, so trustees are offering broader services to win business, but they are also under pressure to take greater responsibility. Pressure on the U.K. trustee to monitor transactions remains, as the rating agencies are being more vigilant in what they are allowing trustees to indemnify themselves against when drawing up the documentation for a transaction. Rating agencies are tightening up indemnity language and are not accepting previous provisions. The way in which trustees indemnify themselves is important because the fewer exclusions there are the fewer actions the trustee is likely to take without recourse to bondholders or the courts.[6]

Trustees in the U.K. are in an ambiguous position as they are appointed and paid for by issuers but are charged with protecting investors' interests. Bondholders are expecting more activism with the result that trustees are coming under closer scrutiny. In an English law-governed international bond issue, a trustee has discretion to agree to modifications, waive defaults, and accelerate bonds or take enforcement action. And because trustees in Europe take more responsibility, they are often exempt from actions for negligence.[7]

In the U.K., the trustee has fewer issuer covenants to monitor. A trust deed typically is written stating that a trustee may change a material term or approve/disapprove an action that impacts the bondholders. The English trustee has considerably greater impact on restructurings of debt or renegotiations that the issuer may want to undertake and which directly may impact the bondholder. The English trustee has an inherent direction from the bondholders to represent their interests. In the U.S., a trustee needs to obtain the requisite percentage of the principal amount of bondholders to consent to taking certain actions, such as acceleration of the bonds or to amend certain provisions of the indenture. It must obtain unanimous consent for any change to the payment terms of the bonds.

For non-defaulted financings, the standard of care for a U.S. trustee is "reasonable" and "prudent". In the U.K., the standard of care is negligence or breach of trust. The advisory role for a U.S. trustee is limited to the initial document review and to operational matters. The U.K. trustee plays an advisory role as to defining the scope of the trustee role in the trust deed.

In litigation involving non-defaulted financings, in the United States, investors as well as corporations initiate lawsuits for both minor and major claims. Most of the litigation involves attempts to impose additional duties upon the trustee not set forth in the indenture. In the U.K. lawsuits are mostly brought by those who claim the trustee has exercised its discretions negligently or in breach of trust. In the U.K., there is no distinction between negligence and gross negligence. In the U.K., a trustee is generally protected if it has acted on advice of legal, financial, or accounting experts. It could be at risk if it was careless in its selection of an expert. The English courts generally have been inclined to protect trustees, but there is a higher duty of care expected of someone who holds himself/herself out as an expert. Similarly, the U.S. courts have been generally in favor of trustees and are reluctant to impose duties not explicitly set forth in the indenture. Trustees here, to avoid liability for "gross negligence", have tried to adhere to the role defined in the four corners of the indenture.

Under English law, the trustee acts for holders of a class whereas under U.S. indentures, individual bondholders retain the right to sue for interest and principal. However, under English law, this right only applies if the trustee has failed to act.[8]

In default or bankruptcy in the U.S., a trustee acts as a prudent person and exercises discretion usually upon direction of a majority of the bondholders and with indemnification for its fees and expenses. If a trustee has a TIA conflict, it must resign within 90 days. In the U.K., it is unusual for a trustee to resign or to delegate its trust duties. The standard of care under English law trust deed is arguable higher, or more subject to interpretation under case law than that of a U.S. indenture. In global insolvencies, a U.K. trustee may bear a correspondingly greater risk of liability in representing bondholders in either restructuring negotiations or administrative proceedings in the courts than a U.S. trustee.

---

[1] The Internet, www.ec.europa.eu/economy_finance/euro, The Euro: Our Currency

[2] The Role of the Trustee in International Financings, by Romano I. Peluso, *ABA Trust & Investments*, July/August 2000

[3] The Internet, www.sec.gov, Securities Exchange Act of 1934, Rules and Regulations

[4] Id at FN 2

[5] The Cross-Border Trustee: From Behind the Scenes to Center Stage, by Daniel R. Fisher and Stephen W. Norton, *International Corporate Rescue*, Volume 1, Issue 5, 2004

[6] Surviving Under Scrutiny, by Neil Day, *Structured Finance International*, May/June 2004

[7] Trustees Face Up to Heavier Burdens, by Mark Brown, Euromoney, June 2004

[8] Id at FN 5

SEVENTEEN

SERVICING DEBT SECURITIES—AGENCY FUNCTIONS

Corporate trust officers must be concerned not only with protecting the security of the indenture and administering its provisions but also with providing facilities for performance of the many responsible and detailed duties involved in the handling of the securities themselves, from the time they are issued until they are finally retired and disposed of. In the larger institutions that handle a substantial volume of corporate trust business, these "operating" functions are usually performed by a separate staff under the management of a senior officer experienced in operating procedures and systems. In the smaller banks, however, which constitute a majority, a single officer may be responsible for both indenture administration and securities servicing activities. Even in the large institutions, an administrative officer cannot discharge the functions properly unless there is an understanding of the basic problems involved in servicing debt securities.

These functions are separate and distinct from the specific duties of the trustee, although their responsibilities necessarily overlap at many points. The functions are performed by the bank in an agency capacity, and it should receive separate appointing documents and instructions. Because the relationship is essentially that of an agency, it may be terminated by the issuer at any time without a change in the basic trustee relationship.

The security agent's obligation is to exercise good faith and due diligence--an obligation that under the UCC cannot be varied by agreement, although standards of performance may be subject to negotiations among the parties. The agent is also entitled to full protection and indemnity for any action taken or omitted to be taken on the instructions of the issuer, as long as the agent acts in good faith with due diligence and without negligence or misconduct.

In regard to any function which it performs, each agent has the same obligation to the holder or owner of the security and has the same rights and privileges as the issuer has in regard to those functions. The net effect is that the agent has the same liability as the issuer and is subject to suit by a holder regardless of whether or not the issuer is also sued.[1]

The bank designated as corporate trustee is usually appointed as the corporation's principal agent to service the indenture securities, and in most instances, this designation facilitates handling the many problems involved. The issuer may, however, and sometimes does, designate other banks to act in one or more agency capacities.

New York City is the principal financial center in the United States, if not the world, and many purchasers of securities in the past preferred to have facilities provided there for the servicing of their securities. The creation and growth of the Depository Trust Company (DTC) eliminated the need for a New York facility to provide immediate transfer and payment services. In a book entry only environment and with the FAST security service offered by most transfer agents through DTC, the need for a New York City location for a transfer agent for issues listed on the New York Stock Exchange also is no longer needed.

Because many millions of securities are held in custodial or depository arrangements in New York City, much money can be saved if they do not have to be shipped to other areas of the country or the world. Accordingly, many older indentures require the obligor to designate an office or agency in New York City where demands or notices may be served and where the securities may be presented for payment, registration of transfer, tender and exchange. There is no longer any need to designate a bank outside New York City as the principal agent to service the securities with a New York bank named as either co-agent to perform all requisite agency functions or as drop agent to receive items on behalf of the principal agent.

The agent's functions in the past included that of authenticating agent for the trustee to authenticate securities to be issued on registration of transfer, exchange, or partial redemption. Occasionally, a co-agent is named in one or more cities in addition to New York.

The use of a New York City agent, even for outstanding older securities, is of limited use with the services offered through DTC. Most of the older security issues have been qualified as depository eligible, which resulted in most New York banks depositing their security positions with DTC. The DTC in turn has submitted the older security issues, which often include bearer securities, to the transfer agent for registered securities, registered in DTC's nominee registration, CEDE & CO. The result is that the burden of safekeeping bearer securities has been shifted from the New York City agent and the depository to the transfer agent and trustee.[2]

In recent years, some trustees and transfer agents have made a business decision to cancel and destroy significant supplies of negotiable bearer securities held in their vaults against registered securities outstanding. Should a request be made for a bearer security, the trustee will have the certificate(s) printed at its expense. The decision is based on the limited liability for printing costs being substantially less than paying for expensive vault space and insurance coverage on the bearer securities. There are fewer and fewer bearer issues outstanding and a request for a bearer security is very rare today.

Procedures tend to vary widely, depending on volume handled, local practices, and in some cases, requirements of specific laws and regulations. This chapter focuses therefore on the more important aspects of the particular agency appointment, and the relevant duties and responsibilities incident to such appointments. These securities processing services are security registrar, interest paying agent, principal paying agent, exchange agent, conversion agent, tender agent, auction agent, and accounting and destruction agent.

APPOINTING DOCUMENTS

The only documents normally required to support an agency appointment are (1) a resolution of the company's board of directors; (2) a copy of the indenture or supplemental indenture creating the issue (or in the case of a municipal security issue, a copy of the security resolution or ordinance); (3) incumbency certificates; (4) a specimen of each authorized denomination of the bond or debenture; and (5) such supplemental instructions from the issuer as may be required to set forth the agent's specific duties and responsibilities. When the agent is also the trustee, most of these documents will have been received by the trustee and duplication is unnecessary.

When the agent is designated by name in the indenture itself, a general resolution approving the indenture is all that is required, although it is a desirable practice to have the resolution sufficiently broad to cover each agency appointment specifically. No special form is required, but it is suggested that the text of the resolution follow the indenture language as closely as possible to indicate that this is the specific appointment the company covenanted to make. It is also recommended that the resolution contain general language designating the issuer's officials (by title) who are authorized to issue instructions to the agent. Although it is not necessary to name the agents in the securities themselves, it will facilitate subsequent processing if the security contains the name of the bank to which it should be presented for payment, registration of transfer, and so on.

The incumbency certificates should include specimen signatures of the issuer's officers, particularly those who signed any of the bonds or debentures. If facsimile signatures are used, the specimen security suffices for this purpose, but the agent should still have the signatures of the officers authorized to instruct it. If the agent is a bank other than the trustee, it should also have specimens of the signatures of all officers of the trustee that authenticated the securities.

Finally, the agent should obtain such detailed instructions from an authorized official of the obligor as are necessary to enable it to carry out its duties expeditiously. These instructions include the source of funds to pay principal and interest, the disposition to be made of canceled securities, statements and reports to be rendered, and so on. As a practical matter, because the agent wishes to follow a specific routine and usually knows more than does the issuer about what should be done, it is customary for the agent to explain to the issuer the procedure it intends to follow and to request the issuer's confirmation and approval.

SECURITY REGISTRAR

Before the UCC was adopted, there was no statutory requirement that corporate or municipal issuers maintain "books of record." However, for almost all publicly sold debt issues the issuers assumed a contractual obligation to do so in the indenture, pursuant to which the securities were issued and which provided for an office or agency where registrations of transfer and payment could be carried out.

The registrar appointment is important in the modern fully registered issue, and there are many reasons why the trustee should be designated as principal registrar to maintain the record of registered holders and of registrations of transfer. The list of holders is essential for other purposes, such as selection of securities for partial redemption and mailing of notices. Both time and expense are saved if the trustee is made responsible for maintaining this record. Interest and principal payments are usually made to individual holders by check (and by wire to DTC). It is important that this be done by the bank that maintains the record of holders. In any place where registration facilities are required that is not also the location of the trustee, the registrar or co-registrar should also be given the necessary authority to "authenticate" the obligations. This is an agency function and the granting of this authority constitutes an appointment in addition to the registrar function.

Authentication on original issuance should be only by the trustee, as should the authentication of securities in replacement of mutilated, lost, stolen, or destroyed securities. These transactions entail creating additional indebtedness with respect to which the trustee has special fiduciary responsibilities. However, authentication of securities on transfer, exchange, or partial redemption does not involve the same degree of responsibility and, where desirable to avoid unnecessary expense to holders, may properly be done by a responsible institution other than the trustee under appropriate safeguards.

Many existing mortgage indentures are intended as permanent financing media, and because of certain language in the original indentures, there may be questions about whether an authenticating agent can be appointed for additional series of securities to be issued under these indentures. This is an example of the type of inflexibility that should be avoided in drafting indentures. In such indentures, every effort should be made to find a legal resolution, for it is obvious that the rights of holders of existing obligations will not be affected. If these legal questions cannot be resolved, the procedures for obtaining the consent of the requisite percentage of holders should be simplified. A fully registered security means that both the principal and interest are registered in the holder's name. From the holder's standpoint, there are a number of advantages to registration. Negotiability is restricted, and, in the case of theft or loss, the expense of replacement is reduced and the risk of losing the entire investment is almost eliminated. Interest is paid by check, and the chore of detaching and collecting interest coupons every six months is eliminated. In the event the security is called, or the trustee or issuer wish to communicate with the holder, a notice or letter can be mailed directly to the registered holder. The main disadvantage is that the security cannot be disposed of by delivery to a purchaser but must be surrendered to the registrar to effect the registration of transfer.[3]

To effect a registration of transfer, the security must be accompanied by a form of assignment that has been executed by the transferor, assigning the holder's interest in the security in blank or to a specified transferee. The registrar will require that the holder's signature to the assignment be guaranteed. Most major security registrar banks normally require that the guarantee be by a member firm of the New York or American Stock Exchange or other acceptable regional stock exchange, or by another commercial bank or one of its correspondent banks. Other registrars have similar requirements, modified to meet their particular needs and operating policies.

It has always been difficult to maintain current signature cards on the hundreds of banks and member firms of the stock exchanges. In the past, the trustee and transfer agent received each day many cards that needed to be filed immediately and discontinued signature cards pulled from the files. Each signature guarantee was to be checked against the signature cards. It was no longer economical to maintain this archaic system, so in 1994 the "medallion program" replaced the signature cards. The medallion is a registered stamp maintained by banks and brokerage firms and represents an official guarantee of the signature of the registered security owner. Institutions using the medallion initially pay a fee for it. The medallion stamp must be maintained in a dual-controlled environment to safeguard its use only for guaranteeing signatures of known registered security owners.

The registration of both principal and interest requires that a new security or securities be prepared and issued on every transaction, such being usually issuable in any denomination that is a multiple of $1,000 (or in the case of municipal securities, in multiples of $5,000). If the registrar has been appointed as authenticating agent, it will authenticate the new certificates, under advice to the trustee that it has canceled (obligor's signature only) an equal principal amount of securities, including in the certification the serial numbers of the certificates issued and canceled, and will ship the canceled securities to the trustee.[4]

If the registrar is not an authenticating agent, both the old and new certificates must be delivered to the trustee, which will cancel its authentication certificate on the old securities and authenticate the new ones to be delivered. Information on the particular transaction--including name, address, and taxpayer identification number of both the transferor and the transferee; the security numbers canceled and issued; and the principal amount--must be input to the registrar's security holder record file. A transfer or journal sheet is normally prepared reflecting each day's activity for the particular issue. Although most major security registrar banks maintain the permanent record as part of their automated recordkeeping procedures, it may be desirable to produce daily "hard copy" of such transactions, either for research purposes if such is not otherwise readily available or to forward it to the obligor. When more than one registrar is involved, only the principal registrar maintains individual registration records of the holders. All co-registrars must therefore furnish the information (usually a copy of their transfer sheets) to the principal registrar. Almost all municipal debt securities issued before July 1, 1983, were in bearer form and many provided for the registration thereof at the holder's option. Most corporate obligations sold before 1968 were similarly issued. Such registration privilege could be as to principal only or as to both principal and interest. In the case of corporate issues, the privilege had, however, to be set forth specifically in the indenture.

Registration as to principal only means the principal of the security is registered in the holder's name. The bearer interest coupons remain attached and are used for collection of the semi-annual interest in exactly the same manner as if no registration had occurred. Registration of such securities is also accomplished by presenting the security to the registrar accompanied by an executed assignment, with the signature guaranteed in the same manner as a fully registered security. The registrar enters the date and name of the registered holder on the special registration panel on the back of the security, and the registration is authenticated by the signature of an authorized officer of the registrar opposite the name of the holder. A special transfer sheet is usually prepared by the registrar showing the security number and a transfer from "bearer" to the name of the holder. This transfer is posted to a subsidiary record file (or ledger sheet) under the name and address of the holder, which shows the date, number, and principal amount of the security registered as to principal in the holder's name. Any subsequent registration as to the principal of securities of the same issue in that holder's name will also be posted to the particular record file by showing a debit to the transferor and a credit to the transferee. A release of a security registered as to principal is accomplished in the same manner as a transfer, except that the word "bearer" instead of the name of a transferee is entered in the registration box. Full negotiability by delivery is then restored. An assignment in blank by the former registered holder is required to effect such "deregistration." No posting to the trustee's principal record of securities issued file is required in the case of registration as to principal only, or on transfers of such securities, for there is no change in the serial number or principal amount of securities outstanding.

In the early 1990's, DTC created the Fast Automated Securities Transfer program (FAST). Under this program, DTC leaves securities with the transfer agents in the form of a balance certificate registered in DTC's nominee name, Cede & Co. The balances are adjusted daily based on DTC's deposit and withdrawal activities. Securities may be added at the time they are made DTC Eligible or convert already eligible issues which had previously not been included in the FAST Program. Written agreements between the transfer agent and DTC are entered into where the agent agrees to the FAST criteria. In summary, this requires the agent to certify that: 1. all transfer requirements have been met; 2. the balance for each FAST issue has been confirmed via the FAST balance confirmation system; 3. DTC will receive interest or dividend payments based on DTC's confirmed FAST balance; 4. the agent will accept from and return automated information to DTC relating to transfers; and 5. the agent must agree to participate in DTC's direct mail program relating to the mailing of certificates to investors

PAYMENT OF INTEREST

The agent's first obligation is to make certain that requisite funds are obtained before each interest payment date. Many banks follow the practice of billing their principals for all interest payments due. This is an expensive but sometimes necessary step when required interest payments are based on variable rates. (The obligation of the issuer to provide the necessary funds is an absolute one, and their officials should be capable--without reminder--of making funds available on time and in the proper amount.) When deposit with the paying agent is by check, it should be in sufficient time to enable the agent to complete collection of the check and have available funds on the payment date. When the paying agent is willing to accept deposit of immediately available funds on the payment date, extreme care should be exercised in following the usual and customary practice of mailing the interest checks on the business day preceding the payment date. This decision, including the advance mailing of the checks on a staggered basis, should be made only after full consideration of the possible consequences of the obligor's failing to deposit the requisite funds on the payment date.

Although almost all indentures provide for the payment of interest by check (occasionally one does see the use of "drafts" permitted). The use of wire transfers and direct deposit credits through automated clearing house ("ACH") mechanisms is increasing. The Group of Thirty's recommendations to pay all debt service payments to the depositories in same day funds required significant controls of receipt and disbursement of debt service funds. All debt service funds received by DTC by 2:30 p.m. eastern time are paid to its participants as a same day payment. This practice significantly reduces the cost of funds to banks and brokers which often paid their clients on the payable date even though the depository typically did not pay interest and dividends until the day following receipt of funds. The same-day funds payment convention does require coordinated communication with obligors and a closely monitored system of debt service receipts and disbursements. Under qualified indentures all funds deposited for payment of interest must be held in trust, whether or not they are held by the trustee. If the agent is a bank other than the trustee, it must--at the time of accepting its appointment--execute a letter of undertaking to the trustee to hold in trust for the benefit of the security holders all sums deposited with it for the payment of principal or interest on the securities and to give prompt notice to the trustee of default by the obligor in the making of any such payment.

The paying agent's responsibility is complicated by the necessity of complying with the relevant provisions of the Internal Revenue Code and with the regulations of particular taxing jurisdictions. All payments of interest on taxable security issues in excess of ten dollars must be reported to the federal government, and under specific provisions of the Interest and Dividend Tax Compliance Act of 1983, the paying agent may be required to withhold a portion of the payment.[5] For security issues sold before July 18, 1984, it is also necessary to withhold the requisite taxes on all payments to nonresident aliens and to process and file with the federal government the appropriate tax forms.

The requirements of particular state tax laws must also be taken into consideration. For example, any corporation incorporated in Pennsylvania or with a treasurer's office in that state is subject to the Pennsylvania Corporate Loans Tax. Unless the tax is assumed by the corporation, it must be withheld from all payments to Pennsylvania residents. The corporation is entitled to a credit with respect to payments to all non-Pennsylvania residents, but proof of such payments must be supplied. The agent must, therefore, obtain evidence of the residence of each holder to whom payment is made, so that the necessary proof to support the corporate return may be supplied. In the case of bearer securities, this is accomplished through the use of a memorandum certificate of ownership.

Payment of Registered Interest

Interest is usually payable semi-annually, although in recent years a number of variable rate issues have provided for quarterly and monthly payments. Such interest will be due and payable on fixed dates, all accruals of such interest being for the prescribed periods. A transfer of the obligation normally transfers the right to any interest accrued, the purchaser paying this amount as part of the purchase price.

To give the paying agent sufficient time to pay interest on registered security issues, without disrupting the trading of the securities, a procedure was developed in the late 1960s whereby the contract between obligor and holder provides for a record date before the end of the accrual period for determination of holders entitled to the payment.[6] As a result, the transfer books need not be closed at all during this period.

Inasmuch as the basic obligation calls for payment of interest on the interest payment date, and the full six months' interest does not become payable as a debt until such date, the obligation to pay on such date to holders of record as of a preceding date must be set forth clearly and unambiguously in the indenture and on the face of the security.

The standard uniform record date for interest payable on the first day of a calendar month is the close of business on the fifteenth day of the calendar month preceding the date of payment. If interest is payable on the fifteenth, the record date is the close of business on the last day of the preceding calendar month. In the event of a failure to pay on the due date, the established record date is of no effect and the transfer of the security gives to the transferee the holder's rights to the defaulted interest. This outcome should be stated clearly in the indenture and provision should also be made for determination of the persons entitled to payment of such defaulted interest. It is recommended that, upon receipt of notification of intention to pay the defaulted interest on a certain date (including arrangements satisfactory to the trustee for the deposit of the funds), the trustee establishes a special record date, which should be not more than fifteen nor less than ten days before the proposed payment date and not fewer than ten days after receipt of the notice of the proposed payment. Notification of the proposed payment and of the special record date should be mailed to the security holders by the trustee not less than ten days before the special record date.

Interest so payable to "record date" holders of fully registered securities is paid by check issued and mailed to them, at the address shown on the registration records. Payments to DTC or to holders of private placement securities are usually transmitted by wire transfer. If the interest disbursing agent is other than the registrar, the latter will prepare a certified list of registered holders, as of the record date, with the total holdings of each, and deliver it to the disbursing agent. These checks are usually mailed on the business day preceding the interest due date to ensure that in most cases the check will be received by the holder on the date the interest is due.

The total amount to be disbursed should be proved to the trustee's registered security control record to ensure that the registrar's security holder records are in proof with the trustee's control. Each transaction that changes the outstanding principal amount of securities should be posted to the trustee's record of securities issued file. When, however, an issue is outstanding in both bearer and registered form, it is necessary to maintain a subsidiary control of the outstanding fully registered securities. This practice facilitates a quick proof of registered interest disbursements, certifications of registered securities outstanding, and other transactions relating to such securities. This record may be maintained as part of an automated securities transfer system or off-line in a manual ledger record. In the latter case it is maintained by posting from a daily journal covering all registration activity for each day. This journal records the total principal amount of fully registered obligations canceled or discharged or issued during the day for each separate issue on which there was activity. The totals are then posted to the registered securities outstanding control record for each such issue.

Payment of Bearer Interest

Most corporate debt obligations issued before 1968, and almost all state and municipal obligations issued before July 1, 1983, were issued in bearer form. As previously stated, very few bonds in bearer form are still outstanding. But because bearer bonds are still outstanding, it is important and necessary to examine in some detail the means whereby interest is collected by the holders thereof. This is accomplished by attachment to each such obligation of a sheet of bearer coupons, one for each interest payment date to, and including, the date of maturity of the principal obligation. Until they become payable, these coupons are an essential part of the security itself and together with it constitute a single obligation.[7] Once they have matured and become payable, however, they constitute separate and distinct obligations and may be transferred by delivery separate from the security itself. Payment to bearer, even though other than the holder of the security, will discharge the debt.

As noted earlier, interest is usually payable semi-annually, although infrequently provision is made for payment at different intervals. On a $20 million, thirty year security issue consisting of all bearer securities of $5,000 denomination that remain outstanding to maturity without interim sinking fund or redemption payments, 240,000 separate interest obligations will have to be processed. It follows that the function of the coupon paying agent is one of the more important to be performed in servicing the pre-July 1, 1983 obligations of state and municipalities, old corporate security issues, and Eurodollar issues.

Because when due, the coupon becomes a separate obligation, it must incorporate a separate and distinct promise to pay. When the security is subject to prior redemption, all coupons maturing after the first possible redemption date should have this promise qualified by language such as "Unless the security hereinafter mentioned shall have been called for previous redemption and payment of the redemption price thereof duly provided." Each coupon will contain the name of the issuer, the date on which it will become due, the specific amount due thereon, the place of payment, and a statement that it represents interest for a specified period on the security designated by serial number. The coupon will be validated by the signature (usually facsimile) of the treasurer or other authorized official of the issuer. To facilitate identification and processing, the coupons attached to each security should be numbered in consecutive order, the first maturing coupon being number 1, the second number 2, and so on. All coupons maturing on the same date from securities of the same issue will bear the same coupon number.

The holder of a security may detach the coupons and forward them directly to the paying agent and receive a check in payment. Because this check must also be processed, this method of collection will delay receipt of usable funds by the holder, and it is not the method most frequently used. From the agent's viewpoint, it is the most expensive way in which payment has to be made. The normal collection procedure follows the same pattern as is used in processing checks, except that credit is usually not passed to the depositor's account until it is actually collected. Each bank provides special envelopes (generally referred to as *shells*) for its depositors in which coupons may be enclosed and deposited for collection. The holder writes his or her name, address, and taxpayer identification number on the shell, together with a description of the security, the denomination of the coupon, and the total face amount of coupons deposited. The bank of deposit then forwards the shell, together with all shells received from other depositors, to its correspondent bank in the city of collection. The latter accepts it as a deposit from the forwarding bank and assigns a collection number to the total deposit, which may represent many coupon shells for many different issues. After proving each collection, this bank then sorts the shells by issues and paying agents and presents the coupons to the respective paying agents. Most of this processing takes place before the maturity date, and the paying agent accepts coupons for processing about a week before the actual due date. On the due date the paying agent makes payment to the presenting bank for all coupons presented, up to and including such date. On the same date each bank through which the coupon has been processed passes the preestablished credit to its depositor.

When default has been made in payment, or where a particular coupon is mutilated or is otherwise irregular or has been detached from a previously called security, it must be returned through the same channels used in its collection and each depositor's account must be charged back for the amount of the item.

In New York City the major banks, and banks in certain other cities, provide for collection of all coupons through a central clearing house. Each morning all collecting banks transport all their collection items to the clearing house, where they are delivered to the paying banks. For the total deposits and receipts, a net credit or debit is made to the bank's account at the Federal Reserve Bank. The aggregate of return items that have to be charged back is handled in the same manner. This arrangement facilitates the collection process and reduces to a minimum the number of checks that have to be prepared and issued by the agents. Together with the preliminary work performed by the banks in their capacity as collecting agent, it has also minimized the costs to issuers for servicing of their coupons.

The paying agent must examine each separate coupon presented to see that it is a valid obligation, that it is a matured obligation and one the agent is authorized to pay, that the security from which it was detached has not been previously called for redemption, that the coupon has not been canceled, that it is not otherwise mutilated, and that no stop order is on file with respect to the particular coupon. The amount of each separate shell and collection item must also be verified. If everything is found to be in order, the coupons are canceled by perforation. The total number of all coupons for each issue received each day is compared with the total collection items received, and the appropriate account charged for the total payments. If payment is refused for any reason, the coupon is returned uncanceled to the presenting bank (or to the presenter if not a collecting bank) and, if an aggregate credit has been made, against an appropriate charge back. When a clearing house arrangement is utilized, all coupons are usually processed and paid on the same day they are presented to the agent. Any coupons or shells being returned for the reasons indicated above should be returned immediately or, if presented through a clearing house, in the next day's clearing.

Most coupons are payable on the first or fifteenth day of the month, and the few days immediately preceding and following these dates are periods of heavy volume. During the remaining days of the month, the work processed during these periods is audited and verified by personnel other than those who handled the payment. In this operation the coupons are broken down by the maturity date, and the total coupons paid for a designated period (usually monthly) are proved to the total charge made during the period to the coupon account. Because it is necessary for the coupons to be segregated by coupon number (or maturity date), the paying agent will maintain the appropriate breakdown by a subsidiary data record. Where a single obligor has a number of separate issues of securities outstanding, it is entirely appropriate to maintain a single cash account for all issues and to provide the necessary breakdown by issue and maturity by subsidiary records.

A corporate issuer is required under qualified indentures to maintain a list of all information coming into its possession of names and addresses of its security holders annually. If this information is derived from the collection of interest coupons, the agents must maintain it in current form for filing with the trustee. The information is derived from the shells in which the coupons are received.

When two or more banks act as paying agents for a particular issue, the work of all agents must be coordinated, The normal procedure is for one bank (usually the trustee) to be designated the principal agent and for all funds to be deposited with the bank. If the other agents are correspondents of the principal agent, authority is given for charging the account of the principal agent for payments by the co-agents, and the principal agent is responsible to the issuer with respect to all payments made. Once the coupons have been paid, verified, and canceled, and appropriate charge has been made to the coupon paying account, the work of the paying agent is concluded. The problem of making appropriate disposition of the canceled coupons still remains and will be discussed later in this chapter in connection with accounting and destruction procedures.

PAYMENT OF PRINCIPAL

Although all new debt financings are now issued in book-entry only form, and have been for many years, physical debt obligations for older issues are still outstanding. Theoretically, the same principles that govern payment of coupons should apply to payment of the physical certificate securities themselves. But the procedures followed are usually, however, quite different. In the case of securities, the amount involved in the handling of each item is many times greater, and consequently the risk is substantial. Coupons are handled on a volume basis; physical securities, on an individual basis.[8] Whereas the trustee is responsible for proper accounting for both securities and coupons, the latter are usually accounted for by total amount by maturity date, while accounting for principal obligations is done individually, by serial number.

The security payment personnel work from instructions prepared by the account administrator. Although in the case of coupons one set of instructions is normally sufficient for all maturities, it is usually desirable to prepare a separate set of instructions for each separate principal payment. These instructions should contain all essential information so that operations personnel do not have to refer to the indenture or other source material. In the case of a redemption payment, the amount of the premium payable must be shown, as well as the specific serial numbers of the particular securities called.

Because payment for principal obligations is made by check or sometimes by wire transfer, the identity of the individual presenter can be preserved.[9] Each day's work represents a dollar volume, and one of the essential factors in any procedure is maintenance of proper controls. It is desirable to have control maintained separate and apart from the personnel making the actual payment. For each item presented, there is indicated on the automated security log or in the case of a manual processing system, a control ticket containing the name of the presenter, a description of the issue and its CUSIP number,[10] the aggregate face amount of the securities, and the serial numbers thereof. One copy is given to the presenter (in the case of a window item), another is sent to a security control (audit) unit, and the other two copies accompany the securities to the payment desk. Here the securities are examined to determine that they are valid, that they are in good order with no mutilations, and that no stop payment order is on file with respect to the particular securities, and such other checks are made as may be indicated for a particular issue. The amount of the payment is computed and entered on the control ticket. The item is then recorded on the automated system and a check is printed on which the number of the control ticket is entered. The securities are subsequently canceled and the check is returned through the control clerk for delivery against surrender of the receipt or for mailing to the presenter. The control clerk is responsible for seeing that a check is delivered for each control ticket processed. As a separate audit, the system or in the case of a manual system, another person proves the total securities canceled for the day to the total funds disbursed. A copy of the control ticket accompanies each block of canceled securities, and the original, with the number of the check issued entered thereon, is filed for record purposes.

When part of the security issue is called before its stated maturity, the serial numbers of the securities presented must also be examined to ensure that they appear on the list of called securities.

Care must be exercised that payment is made only to the registered holder or that an appropriate assignment is received. Where payment is made to the registered holder, no assignment is necessary. Registered securities must also be delivered to the security registrar for proper discharge from the registration records. In the case of a partial call, most registered securities of large denomination are called in part only. The holder of such an obligation is given a new security for the unredeemed portion. Where there is a separate registrar, a special transfer sheet is prepared showing reduction in the amount of such registered securities. It is important that the principal transfer agent communicate with all co-transfer agents prior to processing a partial call for redemption. All co-transfer agents should be required to submit journals to the principal agent no later than one business day after any transfer. The principal agent should post all activity before processing the call and notify the co-transfer agents that the books will be closed for a specified period.

Because all securities are controlled on the trustee's principal record of securities issued, one copy of the control ticket may be used to reflect the cancellation, reducing the trustee's control of outstanding securities. Since for purposes of the indenture, securities cease to be outstanding on the redemption date when the required funds are deposited in trust, the recommended procedure is for the entire principal amount called to be debited from the trustee's principal control record on the redemption date. A separate subsidiary control record should be established to reflect the actual surrender and payment of the securities, and the cash balance reflected in this record should always prove to the funds in the redemption account.

Exchange Agent

The function of the exchange agent is similar to that of a registrar in that it involves the exchange of securities of an issue for other securities of the same issue provided such is permitted by the terms of the indenture. In actual practice, a separate exchange agent is usually not appointed, the registrar assumes this function. One form of exchange, though very rare today, is that of fully registered securities for the coupon bearer type, or the reverse, for pre-1983 issues when such bearer securities were authorized. Upon receipt of bearer securities with a request for issuance of an equivalent amount in fully registered form, the former will be canceled and a registered security or securities prepared, with the transaction information input to the security holder records file. The canceled bearer securities and the registered piece are delivered to the trustee with a request for authentication of the latter. (If the registrar-exchange agent has been appointed as authenticating agent, it authenticates the registered security, under advice to the trustee that it has canceled an equal principal amount of bearer securities, including in the certification the specific serial numbers of the securities issued and canceled.) On a reverse transaction, involving the issuance of bearer for fully registered securities, the canceled registered piece is delivered to the trustee after discharge, and the appropriate number of bearer securities is requisitioned. After detaching all coupons for which interest has been paid, the trustee (or the authenticating agent) authenticates and delivers the requisite amount of previously unissued bearer obligations. A very small number of issues still follow the practice of having the trustee "hold alive" any bearer securities that have been surrendered for exchange, on the theory that on an exchange back to bearer form, a supply of certificates will be available. Although this does reduce the cost to the issuer in the event additional securities must be printed, it adds substantial liability to the trustee, which must safely control the authenticated bearer securities pending their possible reuse. This is a common practice with municipal securities and systems have been designed with the appropriate controls in place to maintain current inventories of bearer securities deposited to vaults on exchange for registered securities.

Most banks, however, follow the practice of canceling all securities received for exchange, if permitted by the governing document, so that no securities bearing the same serial number can be reissued for any purpose. Where there is likelihood of frequent requests for exchange, a supply of unissued bearer securities can also be lodged with the trustee for this purpose. This is a more popular mode with the few remaining outstanding bearer corporate securities as well as with the Eurobonds.

Where both coupon and registered securities are authorized, special provisions must be made for the interchange of the two forms between the record and payment dates. The coupon for the interest payable on the payment date should be detached from the bearer securities before their presentation for exchange, or delivery in exchange, of an equal amount of registered obligations. The function of the interdenominational exchange agent is important in fully registered issues to permit security holders to ``split" or ``consolidate" the number of pieces they hold. In the case of corporate securities issued in connection with a subscription offer to stockholders, denominations of $500, $100, and even $50 may be authorized. Often these denominations are freely interchangeable, although the more common provision is to permit consolidation into securities of $1,000 denomination or multiple thereof, but no split of $1,000 securities into smaller denominations. The reason for this limitation is the substantial cost of servicing small denomination securities.

CONVERSION AGENT

The use of the convertible corporate type of debt security has varied in popularity during the past thirty years, as changes in economic conditions and the market's receptivity to such "equity kickers" have waxed and waned. In the case of a corporation that is rapidly expanding or whose credit is not considered top tier by investors, such a vehicle provides a means of raising equity capital, usually at considerably less cost than direct equity financing. During a period of rising stock prices, the conversion privilege is a valuable one, and many convertible debentures sell at substantial premiums above the price they would command as straight debt securities. The usual security into which such an obligation is made convertible is the common stock of the issuing company.

The indenture controls the terms and conditions on which the privilege may be exercised, and these terms and conditions should also be set forth in the debenture itself in reasonable detail. The debenture may be made convertible into a fixed number of shares of stock, but the more usual provision is to fix a dollar price at which shares of stock may be purchased by use of the principal of the debenture. This price is subject to adjustment to reflect any change in the ratio of number of shares outstanding (other than through conversion of other debentures of the same issue).[11] Provision may also be made for an arbitrary increase in the conversion price at stated intervals during the life of the debenture, to encourage conversions during the earliest period. A common practice is to set the initial conversion price at a figure somewhat higher than the current market price of the common stock. This offers the advantage of the company's having a less expensive debt security for a period of time, but one it will likely never be called on to pay, except through the issuance of common stock at a price higher than could be obtained by an immediate issue of such stock. To achieve the same purpose it is sometimes provided that the conversion privilege cannot be exercised until a stated time has elapsed after issuance of the debentures.

When the convertible debentures have been issued, the company must authorize and reserve for issuance the maximum number of common shares that could be issued on conversion of the entire debenture issue. This authorization involves all the steps that would have to be taken if a number of shares were being concurrently issued publicly, including the necessary registration under the 33 Act and the listing of such additional shares on any securities exchange on which the stock is listed. The trustee should make certain that all proper steps have been taken.

The function of the conversion agent is to receive any debentures surrendered for conversion, compute the number of shares issuable, requisition such shares from the company's transfer agent, and, upon their receipt, cancel the debentures and deliver the shares to the presenter.

Often a fractional interest is involved, which may be handled in a number of ways. The almost universal practice, however, is to pay the value of the fractional interest in cash using the current market price of the stock to give the holder the equivalent value of the fractional interest. The indenture should set forth clearly the particular method to be followed.

Exercising the conversion right is a privilege to the holder of the debenture, who has the option of deciding when to exercise the privilege. Conversion can frequently be forced by the company, however, by its calling the outstanding debenture issue for redemption. This places a termination date on the conversion privilege and, if conversion is favorable, results in conversion of the entire issue. If the conversion privilege is not favorable, there is seldom reason for a redemption call.

It is desirable to have the conversion privilege continue until the maturity or redemption date of the debentures. Some issues provide for an earlier termination date of convertibility, and invariably substantial losses are sustained by security holders who receive no actual notice or misunderstand the provisions of their security. There is usually no good reason for such earlier termination, for it is to the advantage of neither the company nor its security holders and should be avoided. The trustee should be diligent in endeavoring to change an arbitrary provision. If unsuccessful, the trustee should insist that security holders be informed of their right to minimize their losses. Another problem is the matter of accrued interest to the conversion date. The problem may be handled in a number of ways. Occasionally an adjustment is made as between accrual of interest and accrual of dividends. This is an exceptional provision and is feasible only where the company has a fixed dividend policy with fixed dividend payment dates. The more common provision is to state that no adjustment for accrued interest or dividends will be made. It is up to the holder to time the conversion in such a way as to be of the greatest advantage.

A convertible issue presents special problems where a record date is involved if a debenture is presented for conversion after a record date and before the interest payment date. Rather than suspend the conversion privilege during this period, the person converting should be required, as a condition to conversion, to deposit funds equal to the amount of interest that would otherwise be payable on the interest payment date on the debenture or portion thereof to be converted. These funds are then used to offset the payment that is made to the person in whose name the debenture was registered on the record date. This practice is especially desirable in a situation where the record holder has sold a debenture after the record date to an individual who converts before the interest payment date. As part of the sale, the seller normally delivers a check for the full interest due to the purchaser, conditional on the payment of interest by the obligor, with the exception that the seller will receive this amount back on the interest payment date. The purchaser having received this check, deposits equivalent funds at the time of conversion.

The necessity for requiring a deposit can be illustrated by a hypothetical situation in which, after a record date, dealer A buys twenty-five $1,000 debentures from twenty-five individuals and exchanges them for five $5,000 debentures. Dealer A then sells the $25,000 principal amount to various other dealers, of whom dealer B, receiving $5,000 principal amount, decides to convert before the interest payment date. As the result, the obligor is not required to deposit funds for payment of interest on that $5,000 principal amount. Because the twenty-five individual holders of record are entitled to receive their interest on the payment date, the amount equivalent to interest payable of $5,000 debentures must be obtained from dealer B at the time the debenture is presented for conversion.

In the event that the obligor defaults in the payment of interest on the payment date, the funds so deposited would be repaid to the person effecting the conversion. The provisions in the indenture establishing this condition to conversion must, however, be qualified to the extent that such deposit need not be made if the obligation converted has been called for redemption on a date before the payment date. Since there is no obligation for payment of interest on an interest payment date on securities called for prior redemption, there would be no record date for such payment. One question that may arise is the possibility of receipt from a debenture holder of a check that cannot be collected before mailing of the interest checks has to be made. If this check should prove uncollectible, a loss may result. This can be resolved by withholding delivery of the new securities for a sufficient period to allow for collection. Probably no special indenture language is required, but this problem should be kept in mind.

Note that most convertible debenture issues provide for a sinking fund. It is both customary and proper to provide that the obligor will receive credit against its sinking fund requirement for all debentures converted into the company's stock.

SUBSCRIPTION AGENT

One of the collateral and important functions frequently performed is that of subscription agent in connection with the issuance of convertible debentures. In states where stockholders have preemptive rights, any issuance of stock or securities convertible into stock must first be offered to existing stockholders. Even when no preemptive right exists, such offering to existing stockholders is frequently the most feasible way of completing a successful offering.

The offering is made by issuing subscription warrants to existing stockholders. After the amount of the total offering has been determined, an appropriate ratio to existing shares is determined, and each shareholder is given the right to subscribe to a pro rata portion of the new offering. These rights are often valuable, the measure of value being the difference between the offering price and the market value of the debentures. Warrants are usually issued by the company's stock transfer agent and evidence the right to subscribe to a specified principal amount of debentures. The offer is normally underwritten, the underwriters agreeing to purchase all debentures not subscribed for through the exercise of warrants. Under the underwriting agreement, the life of the warrants is customarily limited to a period of two or three weeks from their date of issue.

The function of the subscription agent is twofold. First, it accepts and processes subscriptions to the debentures. This involves receipt of warrants with checks in payment of the subscribed debentures. When issuable, the debentures are requisitioned from the trustee and delivered to the subscribers.

The second function concerns the purchase and sale of rights. A stockholder who is unwilling to subscribe to the debentures is still entitled to the value of the rights represented by the warrant. Others may wish to exercise only a portion of their warrant and sell the balance of the rights, while some may wish to acquire a larger interest than their warrant entitled them to and therefore need to acquire additional rights. By reason of the large number of small holders, trading of such rights through normal brokerage channels might be very expensive. For the convenience of such holders the subscription agent is permitted to purchase and sell rights. It offsets purchase and sale orders for each day's activity and either purchases or sells the net position in the open market. The average price received on all transactions for the day is used to determine the price at which all purchases are computed. A small commission charge is imposed on the holders for this service

PUT/DEMAND OPTION AGENT

For those issues with a "put" or "demand" option, the paying agent must be prepared to accept the securities against payment, usually at par, to the registered holder. In some issues, the securities are purchased by a remarketing agent rather than the issuer itself. Chapter 4 explained the role of the remarketing agent and the tender agent.

ACCOUNTING AND DESTRUCTION

The purpose of every security indenture is to secure payment of the obligations issued. The proper accounting for all such obligations is one of the trustee's main functions. Provision must also be made for proper disposition of all obligations canceled because of transfer, payment, exchange, or conversion or for other reasons. Although these functions are usually performed by the trustee, they may be performed by the agent, but with full liability accruing to the trustee if such canceled securities are not property controlled and disposed of by the trustee pursuant to its policies and current regulations.

Accounting for Interest Obligations

A fully registered security represents the obligation for both principal and interest. When such a security is surrendered and canceled, the trustee is entitled to assume that all amounts due with respect thereto have been paid or otherwise discharged. It is desirable, however, for the trustee to maintain a more current account of interest payments. When it acts as registrar and interest disbursing agent, its own records will provide requisite evidence of payment of all amounts of registered interest due. When the issuer or another agent disburses registered interest, the trustee should establish an appropriate procedure for ascertaining that all registered interest payments have been made. The most common and practical way to accomplish this is for the trustee to receive and rely on a certification by the disbursing agent of payments made. Whatever the form of the evidence received, it should be sufficient to establish the fact of payment.

Accounting for coupon interest is a different matter. The coupons represent separate and distinct obligations, and satisfactory evidence of their payment or cancellation should be received. A great deal of progress has been made over the years in simplifying the procedure of accounting for interest coupons. In the early days of corporate security issues, a very elaborate procedure was followed. Large coupon ledgers were prepared that included a separate page for each security issued. As the coupons were paid they were carefully pasted in the appropriate page on this ledger sheet, with the date of payment entered. This provided a complete record, but the expense involved was substantial. For almost all corporate issues this practice has been obsolete for many years, although some municipalities still follow it.

A major step forward was achieved when issuers permitted trustees to dispose of canceled coupons by destroying them (usually by cremation). Concern for the environment and restrictions against burning have substituted shredding of securities in place of cremation. Agents and trustees must take the business of destroying securities very seriously to avoid future presentation of securities for payment which were reported as destroyed. At first, an appropriate certification was prepared as evidence of such destruction. The burning was witnessed by both obligor officials and the trustee, but later, the trustee was permitted to perform this task alone. An elaborate exhibit was attached to the destruction certificate that included a description of the issue, the maturity date and amount of the coupons, and the security serial numbers. This costly procedure necessitated that all coupons paid be sorted in numerical order so that they could be listed on the appropriate schedules.

In the late 1940s, a number of trustees began to question the necessity for such an elaborate procedure. Investigation revealed that these detailed schedules were seldom if ever referred to. Such detail was, therefore, unnecessary for proper accounting. As a result of these studies, the accounting and destruction procedure was changed. Now this accounting needs only to be done by total number of coupons and total dollar amount for each coupon maturity date. The necessity for sorting and listing of coupons by security serial number has thus been eliminated, although some banks using computer-generated payment records still follow this practice.

To ensure proper accounting control, most trustees maintain a subsidiary computerized destruction ledger. The total interest due is entered for each interest maturity date. The total registered interest disbursed and the total value of coupons of that maturity shown by each destruction certificate are debited. The resulting balance, if any, shows the amount of coupons outstanding and unpaid.

When paying agents other than the trustee pay coupons, their subsequent shipment to and audit by the trustee involves an expensive and time-consuming arrangement. The trustee and the issuer should therefore authorize the paying agents to complete disposition of the canceled coupons by satisfactorily destroying them. The certificate of such agent may be relied on by the trustee as evidence of such destruction.

Accounting for Principal Obligations

Each security canceled for any reason must be included in an appropriate accounting. The destruction certificates covering principal obligations are similar to those covering coupons, except that the serial numbers of the securities are shown on the certificate or the supporting schedule. There is no reason for identifying and reporting the reason for the cancellation (i.e., transfer, exchange, payment, etc.) except with regard to any remaining inventory of unissued securities.

Registered securities are processed in a different manner than coupon bearer securities. When registered securities are canceled because of transfer or for any reason requiring assignment of the security, destruction is usually deferred for a reasonable period of time, usually one year, and an image or microfilm record is made of the security and the assignment before destruction. When the assignment is received separate from the security, it is usually imaged or microfilmed with the security and destroyed with it, together with any documentation supporting a "legal" transfer (e.g., one involving a corporation or a decedent). It is important that the laws of each particular jurisdiction be consulted when establishing canceled security retention and destruction periods.

LOST, STOLEN, AND DESTROYED SECURITIES

Securities are sometimes stolen or, more frequently, lost or misplaced by the holders. The holder then notifies the trustee (or, in the case of a tax-exempt security, the fiscal agent or registrar) and requests that a stop order be placed against the particular security or coupon. Care should be used in acknowledging any such request, for the trustee may be placed in a position where it cannot comply. Registered securities that have been endorsed and bearer securities and coupons are fully negotiable and as such are valid obligations in the hands of a bona fide purchaser.[12]

The trustee or registrar (or fiscal agent) receiving a stop order should promptly note its records and communicate the information to all agents. In addition, the trustee or agent must promptly furnish such information to the Securities Information Center (SIC), the entity designated by the SEC to receive reports of loss or theft.[13] The SIC maintains a data base of such information in order to respond to inquiries by institutions involved in receiving, holding, or processing securities. Holders sometimes fail to notify the trustee that a lost security has been found, particularly in the case of coupons. Neither the trustee nor any agent should take it upon itself to remove a stop, even if a long period of time has elapsed, unless (1) the missing security has been surrendered to the trustee and is canceled by it, or (2) before the issuance of a replacement (or payment, as later discussed) the holder who requested the stop order notifies the trustee and requests that it be removed.

When a stop order has been filed with the issuer (or trustee or agent) and the security is thereafter presented, the issuer or agent is permitted to discharge its responsibility for such adverse claim[14] in any reasonable manner. It is recommended that the procedure outlined in the UCC always be followed.[15] Notice to the adverse claimant must always be by registered or certified mail, and the person presenting the security must be named. This notice must also grant the option of a court order or the filing of a sufficient indemnity bond.

Most indentures provide for replacement of securities that have been lost, stolen, or destroyed upon the furnishing of satisfactory indemnity. This indemnity is usually a surety bond executed by the holder and a surety company, satisfactory to the obligor issuer and the trustee. Some outstanding security issues have no provision for issuance of replacement certificates, including a number of municipal and other public and quasi-public issues.

Under the UCC, the issuer (and the trustee) must issue a new security in place of the original if the owner (1) so requests before the issuer has notice that the security has been acquired by a bona fide purchaser, (2) files with the issuer a sufficient indemnity bond, and (3) satisfies any other reasonable requirements imposed by the issuer.[16] Two conditions preclude the owner from receiving a replacement security: the failure by the owner to notify the issuer within a reasonable time after the owner has been notified, and registration of a transfer of the original security before the issuer receives notice. If when presented, the original security was properly endorsed, the issuer is protected under this rule and may refuse the demand for a replacement.

After a security has been replaced, if a bona fide purchaser presents the original for registration of transfer or payment, the issuer must register the transfer unless registration would result in an over issuance, in which case the issuer must either purchase and deliver a like security if reasonably available or, if not, pay the amount such purchaser paid for the security with interest from the date of demand. The issuer may recover the replacement security from the buyer to whom it was issued (or anyone taking from such person except another bona fide purchaser) in addition to exercising any rights it may have under the surety bond. Many indentures permit the obligor company to avoid the complications of issuing a replacement security by paying the lost security or coupon if it has, or is about to, become due and if the other conditions related to replacement are complied with. In the case of a convertible debenture, the indenture should specify that the right to convert is not destroyed by paying instead of issuing a new debenture.

MISCELLANEOUS FUNCTIONS

Certain other functions may be required to be performed by the trustee or the company's agents, depending upon the terms of a particular issue. The more significant of such subsidiary functions are outlined next.

Validating Securities and Coupons

When a security is mutilated for any reason, the easiest solution is to cancel it and issue a new security in replacement. Where mutilation relates only to a single coupon, however, it is much simpler to validate such coupon by having an official of the company sign a statement on the back of the coupon to the effect that it is a valid obligation. If this procedure is not feasible, the trustee itself may validate the coupon. The language used should be substantially as follows: "This coupon belongs to Security No.-- and is a valid obligation of the obligor." The security itself should always be examined to ascertain that it is in fact a valid obligation.

Exchanges Under Judicial Reorganization or Recapitalization Plans

An important function is involved in consummating a reorganization or recapitalization plan. The agent is in effect acting for the reorganization proceedings and delivery of the authorized cash and securities.

Because of the complexity and diversity of such plans and arrangements, no effort will be made to describe the procedure in detail. In considering acceptance of an appointment, the agent should ensure that the plan has been validly confirmed by appropriate court order, that the claims and distributions schedule are clear, that proper direction and instructions about its functions have been received and approved by the court, that a definite termination date for the exchange is set, and, most importantly, that the compensation to be paid for its services is sufficient to cover the expense and detail of the work involved.

Agent for Securities Not Issued Under an Indenture

The most important securities of this type are those issued by states, municipalities and authorities. Generally the same services are required as in the case of corporate obligations, with, however, a much greater emphasis on the paying agent and registrar functions. The procedures followed are similar except that the canceled securities are either shipped to the finance officer of the state or municipality, or the agent itself performs the accounting and destruction service customarily performed by the trustee in the case of corporate obligations.

In regard to corporations' direct placement financing, long-term notes are sometimes issued under purchase agreements not requiring the service of a trustee under an indenture. A bank is frequently, however, appointed agent of the obligor company to service such a note issue. It maintains a record of the note holders, makes interest payments, determines allocation of periodic sinking fund installments, acts as exchange agent, and in general performs all the ministerial details that the company itself would otherwise be required to perform.

MUNICIPAL SECURITIES AND THE DEPOSITORY

Certificate Immobilization

The benefits of certificate immobilization and centralization have been understood in the corporate security sector for many years. However, until the enactment of TEFRA[17] legislation, municipal securities issuers possessed little knowledge of fully registered instruments, as bearer securities were the norm. Municipal trades were traditionally settled by physical delivery versus payment (known as *DVP*) at the premises of the purchaser. Anticipating the potential impact of DVP for registered municipal securities trades, the Municipal Securities Rulemaking Board established regulations to automate settlement practices.

One of the rules that affected security registrars required the use of book-entry delivery systems to expedite the settlement process.[18] This required, in part and allowing for specific exceptions, that interdealer transactions be settled by book-entry delivery at DTC. Almost all publicly traded municipal security issues have settled through DTC. When a security obtains eligibility, the underwriter directs the trustee/security registrar to register the securities in DTC's nominee name, Cede & Co. The securities are then delivered to the depository against a trust receipt, generally one business day prior to the closing date. DTC assumes custodial responsibility for the securities by placing the physical securities in its vault. Upon joint notification by the trustee and the underwriter that all conditions precedent to the issuance of the securities have been met (i.e., that the security issue has closed), DTC will credit the appropriate value of the securities to the lead managing underwriter's account and processes book-entry deliveries to the accounts of the syndicate members and other purchasers of the issue.

For older issues allowing the issuance of physical securities, subsequent transfers of ownership may be affected either through book-entry notation on the participant's records or through withdrawal of physical securities from DTC's vault to be reregistered in the name of the purchaser or purchaser's representative, a process referred to as *withdrawal by transfer*. To eliminate the issuance of physical securities, new security issues no longer allow the issuance of certificates. One balance certificate per authorized interest rate is issued in the name of DTC's nominee. This effort has reduced the numbers of interest checks issued by paying agents and has served to speed the payment process. Nevertheless, a significant number of registered interest checks are still issued by transfer agents for securities which were not immobilized.

At the end of each business day, DTC nets all trades for each participant and either collects funds from or pays funds to them, depending on their net position.

Book-Entry-Only Securities

Municipal certificate immobilization through depository settlement gained momentum and quickly expanded to a procedure that had been employed by the U.S. government securities market for many years: book-entry-only issuance

(BEO). This program requires that issuers create a single "global" certificate for each maturity within a specific security issue. The underwriter instructs the security registrar to register the global certificates in DTC's nominee name, the certificates to be held in the depository's vault until final maturity or redemption. Any reduction to the authorized principal amount of securities outstanding, usually the result of a partial call for redemption, will be posted on DTC's records and on the records of the trustee and security registrar. No physical securities change hands until the issue is paid in full at which time the trustee or security registrar cancels and disposes of the global certificates.

The purchaser of BEO securities receives a confirmation of any trade from its broker-dealer or bank. Subsequent activity, such as payments of interest and principal, is reflected on the customer's account record and evidenced by periodic statements furnished by the broker-dealer or bank. Until the securities are sold or otherwise disposed of, the security position will remain on the broker-dealer or bank's participant account record at DTC. Transfers of ownership occur only through book-entry debits and credits to the purchaser's and seller's participant account records.

In this environment the trustee must recognize and meet the challenges presented by the issuance of BEO securities. Obviously, a lost revenue opportunity will impact the profitability of the organization, but of additional importance is the loss of the capability of direct contact with those whom the trustee represents--the security holders.

DTC generally does not release participant records information without the written consent of the issuer. Consequently, the trustee must obtain a blanket authorization from the issuer consenting to the release of information by DTC upon the request of the trustee. In a default situation, the trustee must have the ability to reach security holders in order to obtain direction or consents and to provide critical information in a timely manner.

The need to standardize the processing practices of the trustee and security registrar has increased significantly with the growth of depository-eligible municipal securities. In order for a new security issue to be accepted as eligible by DTC, the trustee or agent is required to execute an operational agreement or representation letter which sets forth, *inter alia*, the required procedures governing delivery of original issuance securities, timeliness of certificate transfers, reporting and notice formats and time frames, methods of transmitting interest and principal payments, and municipal call processing procedures.

It is important that the appointed trustee and security registrar use their best efforts to comply with the terms of the arrangement to ensure the continuing eligibility of the issue for which they act. DTC will generally provide trustees and security registrars with periodic performance reports so that any processing concerns can be identified and resolved in a timely manner.

[1] For an excellent review of the cases and decisions related to these services, see Egon Gutman, *Modern Securities Transfers* (rev. ed) 1989

[2] See SEC Rule 17Ad-1(g), 17 CFR 240.17Ad-1, and question (28) in SEC Interpretative Release 34-17111 (Sept. 2, 1980).

[3] See chapter 2, note 2 *supra*.

[4] It may be more desirable for the registrar to enter into an agreement with the trustee whereby the registrar destroys the canceled certificates and gives the trustee a destruction certificate.

[5] See chapter 13, note 10, *supra*. This withholding, referred to as *backup withholding*, is imposed if a nonexempt payee fails to give the payer an obviously correct taxpayer identification number and, for accounts opened after January 1, 1984, with a statement that the holder is not

subject to backup withholding. Both statements must be certified under penalty of perjury.

[6] The Municipal Securities Rulemaking Board (MSRB), with the concurrence of the SEC and the Government Finance Officers Association, strongly recommended the use of the standard record dates for registered tax-exempt issues, in *Notice Concerning Recommended Standards on Registered Municipal Securities* (May 6, 1983).

[7] It is, however, possible and proper to have the security "stripped" of its coupons with the principal sold at a discount (much like a zero coupon security) and the coupons sold as a separate instrument. In the latter case, the investor receives semiannual payments representing the amortization of investment plus interest on such investment.

[8] Since the mid-1970s, a matured municipal and corporate security clearing system has been used by members of the New York Clearing House, following procedures similar to the daily clearing of coupons.

[9] See chapter 13, note 10, and chapter 17, note 5 *supra*. In addition, payers are required under income tax regulations to report the "gross proceeds" paid to any non-exempt holder from the redemption of both corporate and municipal obligations.

[10] The term *CUSIP* is an acronym for the Committee on Uniform Security Identification Procedures, of the American Bankers Association. Since 1967, a standard alphanumeric numbering system has been used by all segments of the securities industry. The standard consists of nine characters, the first six being the issuer number, the next two being the issue number, and the last being a check digit. The numbers that appear on the face of each stock and security certificate are assigned by the CUSIP Service Bureau of Standard & Poor's Corporation under contract to the American Bankers Association.

[11] For an excellent review of the problems inherent in drafting antidilution provisions, see Tomczak, *Corporate Trust and Commercial Finance Agreements* (1984), sec. 1.45 *et seq*.

[12] Defined in UCC Article 8 as "a purchaser for value in good faith and without notice of any adverse claim."

[13] Rule 17f-1 (17 CRF 240.17f-1, July 1, 1979).

[14] A claim by someone not in possession of the security. It includes a claim that a transfer was or would be wrongful or that a particular person is the owner or has an interest in the security.

[15] UCC sec. 8-403.

[16] Id. sec. 8-405.

[17] See chapter 2, note 7, *supra*.

[18] MSRB Rule G-12(f)(11), effective Feb. 1, 1985.

EIGHTEEN

LEGISLATION, REGULATION AND RISK MANAGEMENT

THE TRUST INDENTURE ACT OF 1939

The idea of regulation--particularly by the federal government--is a fixed and accepted principle in everyday business life and is assuming greater significance each year. Even so, there are still wide differences of opinion about the proper scope and purpose of such regulation and the limits to which it may properly be extended. In certain areas, regulation undoubtedly is important, but it should normally be limited to the establishment of minimum standards or modes of conduct deemed essential to the public interest to which all engaged in the particular activity are required to adhere. The value of regulation is directly proportional to the uniformity of standards that exist, or are capable of existing, in the particular activity.

The scope and value of government regulation are necessarily limited. That is, trust indentures do not in themselves constitute a "business"; they are simply the instruments by which all types of businesses secure financing, and each type of financing produces its own type of indenture.

The trust indenture was developed with few restrictions imposed by governmental authorities. Legislation concerning the sale or distribution of securities was initially limited to the blue-sky laws enacted by various states that focused on fraudulent devices in the sale of securities.

Following the financial collapse of the 1930s, defaults under indentures became numerous, and many people's savings were depleted or, in some cases, wiped out. The concurrence of the drop in security values with the Great Depression brought the whole security structure to public attention. The result was the enactment by Congress of a series of security acts designed to protect investors.

The first legislation was the Securities Act of 1933 (33 Act). sometimes called the "truth in securities" act. With certain exceptions, this act requires filing with the Securities and Exchange Commission (SEC) a registration statement covering each public issue of securities, and the use of a prospectus in connection with their sale and distribution. Stringent penalties are imposed for misrepresentations or misleading statements in either of these documents. The act covers both stock and bonds offered for sale in interstate commerce and through the mail. The 33 Act has two basic objectives: it requires that investors receive financial and other significant information concerning securities offered for public sale, and it prohibits deceit, misrepresentations, and other fraud in the sale of securities. Violations of the 33 Act can result in both civil and criminal liability, The act gives purchasers the right to claim damages from the issuer, the principal officers signing the registration statement, the directors, the accountants, the engineers, and others responsible for the material in the registration statement, as well as the underwriters connected with the issue, if the prospectus contains an untrue statement of a material fact or omits a material fact. A material fact is one that an investor would deem to be important to making a decision whether to invest in a company.

The Securities Exchange Act of 1934 (34 Act)[1] was designed to regulate national securities exchanges, the listing of securities thereon, and the purchase and sale of securities through the facilities of such exchanges. Section 4 of this act also created the SEC to administer both this and the 33 Act to replace the Federal Trade Commission as the primary regulator of the securities industry. The SEC was empowered with broad authority over all aspects of the securities industry, including power to register, regulate, and oversee brokerage firms, transfer agents, and clearing agencies, as well as the New York Stock Exchange and the other exchanges and, under Section 15A, known as the Maloney Act of 1938, the National Association of Securities Dealers, Inc., all of which must ensure market integrity and investor protection. In 1975, all municipal securities brokers and dealers were required to register with the SEC. The SEC does not judge the quality of a company or its securities, only the truthfulness of its documents. The 34 Act also gave the Federal Reserve Board the power to regulate and control margin trading, the practice of using credit to purchase stock. The Federal Reserve Board fixes the margin requirements, that is, the percentage of cash required to be paid by an investor, and the SEC has the responsibility to enforce them. Other amendments and additional legislation have continually broadened the scope of the SEC's authority. Today, it also regulates tender offers, proxy solicitations, investment companies, investment advisers, and transfer agents. The SEC also monitors corporate acquisition and merger activity.

Section 211 of the 34 Act directed the SEC to "make a study and investigation of the work, activities, personnel, and functions of protective and reorganization committees in connection with the reorganization, readjustment, rehabilitation, liquidation, or consolidation of persons and properties and to report the result of its studies and investigations and its recommendations to the Congress." As a part of this study, the commission included a report on the activities of trustees under indentures.

Because of this report, the so-called Barkley bill was introduced in the Senate in 1937 and was referred to a subcommittee of the Committee on Banking and Currency. Although the measure was favorably reported by the committee, the Senate did not vote on it during that session. A similar bill was introduced in the House of Representatives in 1938 and in both the House and the Senate in 1939. The latter bill was enacted by Congress as the Trust Indenture Act of 1939(TIA) and became effective on February 3, 1940.

The TIA was the first attempt by the federal government to regulate the indentures under which securities are issued. In its report the SEC recommended extremely stringent provisions, including continuous supervisory administration by it, and the initial bill introduced embodied these provisions. The legislation enacted was worked out by the SEC and a special committee of the American Bankers Association after extended hearings before committees of the House and Senate. The final version of the TIA differed substantially from the bill originally recommended and did not alter the basic concept of the trust indenture as a special financing contract among the parties.

The TIA was enacted as Title III to the 33 Act, and its administrative provisions were drafted to dovetail with the SEC's administration of the 33 Act. In general, it required that all indentures, with specified exceptions, be submitted to the SEC for "qualification" along with the issuer's registration statement under the 33 Act.[2] The actual "regulation" provided by the TIA consisted solely of the qualification of the indenture. Once the indenture was qualified, the SEC, with one minor exception, had no further jurisdiction over the indenture or over the obligor, the trustee, or the security holders. The essential purpose of the 33 Act and the qualification of indentures thereunder, was to ensure that every indenture contained the minimum standards imposed by the 33 Act and conformed to the requirements of the TIA.

In general, the legislation accomplished three basic purposes: (1) the establishment of certain minimum standards with respect to specified acts and duties of the obligor and trustee to which all indentures must conform (accomplished by requiring the inclusion, or incorporation by reference, in each qualified indenture, of specified provisions that became an essential part of the contract); (2) to include minimum standards of responsibility and accountability for trustees under indentures and to eliminate the broad exculpatory provisions formerly included; and (3) to eliminate any conflicting relationships between the trustee and the obligor and between the trustee and underwriters for the obligor.

Although the original TIA did not eliminate defaults or losses to investors, it did not prove to be the burden that many trust companies had feared. The TIA went into effect in 1940 and became accepted as part of the normal routine of indenture administration. Whereas the prescribed provisions were required only in indentures qualified under the TIA, most of them came to be accepted as reasonable standards for all indenture administration for corporate as well as municipal debt securities and came to be included in practically all indentures, whether or not qualification was required.

Before the original TIA was enacted, all rights under the indenture contract were enforced by the common law of contracts and fiduciary obligations with appropriate remedies for breach of the contract available in state courts. The legislative history of the 33 Act itself suggested that Congress intended that this approach be continued, instead of having the TIA be a matter of federal law, enforceable in federal courts.[3] In 1975, however, a federal district court in *Morris v. Cantor*[4] held that the TIA created substantive liabilities for violations of the provisions of qualified indentures and that indenture security holders could enforce such liabilities as a matter of federal law in a federal court.[5] The judge concluded that the TIA "must be viewed as an indirect method of imposing nationally uniform and clearly defined obligations upon those associated with the issuance of corporate debt," and held that the act "created liability" as though it had directly mandated the same actions of trustees and issuers, and consequently, conferred jurisdiction upon district courts over lawsuits to enforce that liability.[6] Thus the existence of a private right of action was held to follow.

THE TRUST INDENTURE REFORM ACT OF 1990

The first comprehensive revision of the TIA became effective November 15, 1990. Its principal purpose was to modernize the fifty-year-old TIA. As stated in the Senate committee report accompanying the reform bill in 1989:[7]

"During this period, however, the public market for debt securities has undergone significant changes. Innovations in the forms of debt instruments have produced securities, such as collateralized mortgage obligations, which were not contemplated in 1939. Technological developments and regulatory changes have resulted in new distribution methods including shelf offerings, direct placements and "dutch auctions." In addition, public securities markets have been profoundly changed by the increasing internationalization of the securities markets. Thus, current market practices conflict with many of the assumptions underlying the Act, which were based on financial customs prevailing in 1939. . . . Enactment of Title IV would conform the Act to the present realities of the market and make it adaptable to future developments, while easing the administration of the Act."[8]

The following are the most significant features of the TIRA, discussed in detail in other chapters:

> 1. The trustee's resignation for a conflict of interest is postponed until there is a default under the indenture. Except in certain limited instances, a creditor relationship with the obligor has been added as a conflicting interest.[9] There is, however, one conflict that is operative at all times; that is the absolute

prohibition that the obligor and its affiliates cannot serve as trustee for its own securities.[10] To obviate the need to resign as the result of a "technical" default, the trustee's resignation is automatically stayed, except in the case of a payment default, pending its application to the SEC that such default may be soon cured or that its continuing on as trustee will not be inconsistent with the interests of the bondholders.

2. The elimination of the need to set out all the provisions of TIA sections 310 through 317 in the indenture. The TIRA now mandates such provisions as a matter of federal law, with the optional provisions now deemed to be included unless they are expressly excluded.

3. The trustee's "annual" report need only be prepared and sent out to the security holders if there has been: (a) any change to its eligibility and qualifications under section 310(b); (b) the creation of or any material change in the relationships specified in section 310(b) (1) through (10); (c) any change in any loans owed by the obligor to it or in any property or funds in its possession; or (d) the happening of any of the transactions spelled out in section 313(a) (3), (6), (7), or (8).[11]

4. The obligor is required to give the trustee an annual no-default certificate, a requirement which already exists in most corporate indentures. The major difference is that the TIRA requires that it be signed by the obligor's principal executive officer, principal financial officer, or principal accounting officer.[12]

5. The authority for, but not the requirement of, the obligor to establish a record date for determining those holders entitled to vote on or consent to any

change in the indenture.[13]

6. The appointment of any successor trustee becomes effective only upon the appointment of and acceptance by a successor. This provision, which is found in many indentures to prevent the orphaning of trusts, will apply in all situations, including the voluntary resignation of the trustee in anticipation of an obligor's default.[14]

7. The so-called clawback period has been shortened--from four to three months preceding the filing of a proceeding under the Bankruptcy Reform Act of 1978--during which any payments made to the trustee bank must be shared with the security holders. This change merely conforms the requirement to the preferential claim period in the Bankruptcy Act.[15]

8. The TIRA provisions apply to all outstanding indentures and supersede any inconsistent provision of any outstanding indenture. The only exception to the latter would be the *optional* provisions not contained in pre-November 15, 1990 indentures.

9. Indentures can now be qualified with a trustee to be appointed after the registration statement is effective (under a Rule 415 shelf registration filing), provided that the issuer files an application simultaneously with the trustee's statement of eligibility. The application will be effective automatically after ten days, unless the SEC issues an order finding the trustee ineligible.[16]

10. A foreign bank can, under certain circumstances, act as a trustee.[17]

11. The SEC has sweeping and open-ended exemptive authority to act by rule, regulation, or order to exempt any person, indenture, security, or transaction from any one or more of the provisions of

the Act, if such is necessary or appropriate in the public interest.[18]

12. Criminal sanctions for the violation of the TIA's provisions, which together with the SEC's new enforcement powers[19] and the retroactive effect of the TIRA, can be used against an issuer or trustee that fails to perform any of the specified duties. Although this may cause some concern to corporate trustees, also note that TIA section 309(e), which was not affected by the TIRA, provides that the SEC is not empowered to conduct an investigation for the purpose of determining compliance with its provisions or to enforce such provisions. It is fairly obvious however, that both issuers and trustees should ensure that they have timely and comprehensive procedures in place to avoid any failure to comply with any of the provisions of this federal law.

To maintain some historical perspective with regard to this legislation, it is interesting to note that some of the concepts embodied in the TIRA had their origins in the proposed Federal Securities Code, a project begun in 1972 by the American Law Institute to review and codify the laws relating to securities distribution and markets, investment advisers, trust indentures, investment companies, and utility holding companies.[20] The code included provisions that the duties and responsibilities of trustees and others be interpreted, approved, and enforced exclusively as a matter of federal law, that certain enumerated provisions would be required to be included in every qualified indenture (e.g., notice of "payment" default), and the expansion of the SEC's enforcement authority to a level comparable with that provided in other areas of securities law. The final official draft of the code, which was completed and approved by the American Law Institute in 1978, received the support of the

SEC, but legislation to enact it was never introduced in Congress.

THE UNIFORM COMMERCIAL CODE

Although the UCC deals with all facets of commercial practice, Articles 8 and 9 are of particular importance in the corporate trust field. Most Code provisions have been adopted in 49 states, as well as the District of Columbia and the Virgin Islands. Louisiana, which adopted only Articles 1, 3, 4, 5, 7 and 8, adopted a version of the Revised Article 9 in 2001.

Article 2A deals with leases, ranging from consumer rental of automobiles to commercial leases (to the extent not preempted by federal law) of equipment such as aircraft and industrial machinery. This article is significant to banks acting as fiduciaries in financing of leased equipment.

Article 4A deals primarily with the wholesale wire transfer of funds between businesses of financial institutions. Application of this Article is restricted to "credit transfers", that is, transfers where the instruction to pay is given by the institution making the payment. Not all states have adopted Article 4A. While the Article is significant in many areas of a bank, it has special significance for corporate securities services areas engaged in wire transfer of funds. Understanding wire transfer procedures and making wire transfer payments in accordance with bank security and other procedures is essential to protecting banks from claims arising under UCC 4A.

Article 5 deals with letters of credit and sets rules governing these instruments. This article, among other things, establishes formalities that must be met in creating a binding letter of credit, in presenting it, in honoring it or rejecting it, and in exercising remedies for improper dishonor or repudiation. Letters of credit often play an important part in enhancing the credit of debt financings and are held by a trustee which also is responsible for presenting them and reissuing them under certain circumstances. Article 8 deals with investment securities and conforms or establishes certain basic principles:

>1. It makes all investment securities negotiable. This makes possible increased flexibility in the form of these instruments without fear of creating problems of negotiability.
>
>2. It broadens the application of the rules relating to fiduciary transfers, placing responsibility on the fiduciary rather than the transfer agent, and in effect penalizing the transfer agent that requires excessive documentation.
>
>3. It defines the responsibilities of an authenticating trustee, transfer agent, and registrar.
>
>4. It imposes direct and independent responsibility and liability on the transfer agent or registrar for their acts. It is no defense to show that such action was strictly in accordance with a principal's direction.
>
>5. It establishes guides for issuers and transfer agents in dealing with adverse claims.

Under the 1977 amendments to Article 8, provision was made for the use of uncertificated securities, i.e., a share, participation, or other interest in property or an enterprise of the issuer or an obligation of the issuer that was not represented by an instrument, and whose transfer was registered on the issuer's books without a certificate being issued.

In 1994, the revised Article 8 was approved by the American Law Institute and the National Conference of Commissioners on Uniform State Laws. The revision establishes rules concerning the system through which securities are held. It specifies the mechanisms by which ownership and other interests in securities are recorded and changed, and some of the rights and duties of the parties who participate in the securities holding system. Revised Article 8 deals with "direct" versus "indirect" holding systems. It minimizes the "certificated versus uncertificated" distinction reflected in the old Article 8. The most significant distinction is whether one has a "direct" or an "indirect" relationship with the issuer, as when the investment is held through one or more intermediaries. In addition, the revision specifies that the interest of the ultimate beneficial owner will not constitute a direct property interest in the asset. A new term was established for this interest, namely *securities entitlement*, which is the holder's package of rights and interests against a securities intermediary and its property.

Article 9, which was revised effective July 1, 2001, deals with secured transactions and its impact on commercial transactions is probably more extensive than that of any other UCC article. Unlike Article 8, which deals specifically with investment securities, Revised Article 9 was not drafted with corporate indentures primarily in mind. It is nevertheless important to this area since it establishes uniform rules relating to all security transactions involving personal property, regardless of the form of the particular transaction or the security documents. The present trend toward more special-purpose secured financing, where equipment leases, receivables, other debt obligations, and the like constitute the principal security, makes an understanding of the basic purposes and principles of the article particularly desirable. Personal property or fixtures include goods, documents, instruments, general intangibles, chattel paper, accounts (or contract rights), and any sale of accounts (or contract rights) or chattel paper.

Revised Article 9 changed the rules where to file a financing statement. It is now the state of incorporation of the obligor or debtor, not the location of the personal property or fixtures. Also, the debtor does not have to sign the financing statement.[21] In addition to providing a single body of law for security transactions affecting personal property, the UCC made significant changes or clarifications in four important areas:

1. It provides statutory authority and rules for accounts receivable financing.

2. It specifically authorizes and makes effective both arrangements for subjecting after-acquired property to a security agreement, and arrangements for the making of future advances under the agreement without the necessity of preparing, signing, and recording or filing of supplemental agreements. This greatly facilitates security arrangements involving property that is constantly being disposed of and replaced, such as inventory.

3. It permits the debtor to mortgage its inventory, stock-in-trade, or similar property and continue to operate the business in a normal manner and in accordance with the understanding and agreement of the parties, without the necessity of cumbersome provisions for the flow of proceeds.

4. It recognizes and provides for the special status of the purchase money security interest.

Most corporate mortgages secure obligations that will be outstanding for many years. Some railroad bonds have maturities extending for a hundred years or more, and many corporate mortgages, particularly those of public utilities and railroads, are open-end indentures, designed to serve as permanent financing media. As security, the obligor customarily mortgages all land, plants, equipment, machinery, fixtures, franchises, and all other items of property, real, personal or mixed, then owned or thereafter acquired, which generally constitute its fixed plant and property account, permanent investments, and other classes of property exclusive of cash, receivables, merchandise, and the like. Although in most normal commercial financing arrangements, the intrinsic value of the collateral is readily measurable and adequate to secure the loan, the real security underlying a corporate mortgage is the "going concern" value of the business itself rather than the special value of the individual items of property. The importance of the security interest is the priority claim against the capital assets of the business that are necessary to its continuance as a going concern. Because the specific items of property are constantly being replaced or otherwise changing, the effectiveness of the after-acquired property clause is of paramount importance.

Although no further action is required to continue the perfected status of the security interest in personal property covered by a corporate mortgage of real and personal property recorded before the effective date of the UCC, it is not clear what action, if any, should be taken with respect to personal property acquired after the effective date. If a supplemental mortgage is executed and filed, or if there is additional financing under the mortgage, the requisite financing statement should be filed in the state's Department of State.

If the obligor has outstanding more than one mortgage covering its property, and there is additional financing under a junior or refunding mortgage, financing statements under all mortgages have proper order of priority because of the "first to file" rule.

When partial releases of personal property are executed under a corporate mortgage, it would seem unnecessary to make any filing with respect to such partial release unless it involves the release of all such property in the jurisdiction. If necessary to protect the purchaser of the property released, execution of the release on the bill of sale should be all that is required.

THE BANKRUPTCY CODE

In 1938, the Chandler Act, which amended the Bankruptcy Act of 1898, was enacted. The act has been subsequently amended, once by the Bankruptcy Reform Act of 1975, again by the Bankruptcy Amendments and Federal Fiduciary Act of 1984, and most recently by the Bankruptcy Abuse Prevention and Consumer Protection Act of 2005. The Code's provisions are known as Chapter 7, which govern corporate liquidations; Chapter 9, which govern municipal reorganizations; Chapter 11, which govern corporate reorganizations; Chapter 13, which govern personal bankruptcies with a plan of repayment after either three or five years; and the new Chapter 15, which govern international or Cross-Border insolvency cases.

INVESTMENT COMPANY ACT OF 1940

Investment companies are financial institutions that invest the funds of a large number of individual investors in a substantial portfolio of securities and thus obtain economies of scale that might not be available to the individual through direct investment in securities of his or her choosing. The act regulates the organization of companies that engage primarily in investing, reinvesting, and trading in securities and whose own securities are offered to the investing public. The act is designed to minimize conflicts of interest that arise in these complex operations. Under the act, the investment companies must disclose their financial condition and investment objectives and policies to investors when stock is initially sold to them and on a regular basis thereafter. The disclosure of information about the fund and its investment objectives and investment company structure and operations is the primary focus of the act.

The act's major provisions require that a registration statement must be filed with the SEC explaining the company's background, mode of operation, and intended investment policy. Closed-end companies may issue funded debt or incur a bank loan only if it is covered three times by assets; preferred stock must be covered twice. Closed-end companies may issue only one class of bonds and one class of preferred. Open-end companies formed after 1940 may not issue senior securities, and any bank loans must be covered three times by assets. Open-end companies must issue both semi-annual and annual reports to investors. All investment company securities are subject to registration under the 33 Act. The SEC closely oversees all sales promotion literature, and standards of conduct regarding, among other things, self trading, affiliation of directors, and custodianship of assets.

INVESTMENT ADVISERS ACT OF 1940

The SEC found that investment advisers were of national concern in that, among other things, their analyses and reports were distributed by use of the mails (i.e., by means of interstate commerce) and related to the purchase and sale of securities traded on national securities exchanges and in interstate over-the-counter markets. The securities analyzed by investment advisers were issued by companies engaged in business in interstate commerce and included securities issued by national banks and members of the Federal Reserve System.

The act, with certain exceptions, requires that firms or sole practitioners compensated for advising others about securities investments must register with the SEC and conform to regulations designed to protect investors. All professional investment advisers are required to provide the SEC with information concerning their fees, organization, and operation; their education and qualifications; the nature and scope of their authority over clients' funds; and other details, as required by Section 3(a)(37) of the 34 Act. They must establish, maintain, and enforce written policies and procedures designed to prevent the misuse of material, nonpublic information (a violation of the act and the 34 Act). It is unlawful for any investment adviser to employ any device, scheme, or artifice to defraud or deceive any client or prospective client. In 1996, an amendment was passed that established $25 million under management as a threshold for registering with the SEC. Advisers who handle accounts aggregating less than that amount do not have to register. Also, as a result of the 1996 amendment, advisers to hedge funds must register.

Not included in the definition of "investment adviser" are a bank or any holding company that is not an investment company (that is, it serves only as an investment adviser to registered investment companies); any lawyer, accountant, engineer, or teacher whose performance of such services is solely incidental to the practice of his or her profession; any broker or dealer whose performance of such services is solely incidental to the conduct of his or her business as a broker or dealer and who receives no special compensation; the publisher of any bona fide newspaper, news magazine or business or financial publication; and any person whose advice relates only to securities issued or guaranteed by the United States.

GRAMM-LEACH-BLILEY ACT OF 1999

With the passage of the Gramm-Leach-Bliley Act, banks surrendered their blanket exemption from having to register with the SEC as broker/dealers and agreed to 13 specific activity-focused exceptions from registration in exchange for the right to engage in more activities, such as merchant banking.

The exception dealing with trust and fiduciary activities has been the most controversial. The SEC in June 2004 voted to propose a new rule that would allow banks to keep, if not all, then most of, their corporate trust services in-house rather than being conducted in a separate broker/dealer affiliate, part of the statutory "push-out" provisions. However, this provision was heavily debated.

On September 19, 2007, the SEC voted to adopt Regulation R, which was proposed jointly with the Board of Governors of the Federal Reserve System in December 2006.

The Trust Exception limits the types of compensation that a bank may receive for effecting securities transactions in its trust and fiduciary capacity to a specified list of fees. A bank will meet the "chiefly compensated" requirement if, on an account-by-account basis, using a two-year rolling average comparison, the bank's "relationship compensation" is greater than 50 percent of its entire compensation from an account or, in the alternative, on a bank-wide basis the bank's relationship compensation is more than 70 percent of its entire compensation.

The types of fees that are counted toward relationship compensation is much broader under Regulation R than those proposed in recent previous releases by the SEC and which caused the corporate trust industry much concern and opposition. Under previous SEC proposals, 12b-1 fees, fees returned to a trustee for making certain types of permitted investments, would be counted as transaction fees that would be not includable in relationship compensation. Under Regulation R, 12b-1 fees are part of relationship compensation. The result is that few, if any, corporate trust functions will now fall under any of the "push-out" provisions.

USA PATRIOT ACT OF 2001

The Uniting and Strengthening America by Providing Appropriate Tools Required to Intercept and Obstruct Terrorism Act, (the PATRIOT Act) was the immediate result of the tragic September 11, 2001 terrorist acts on the United States. The act was intended to deter and punish terrorist acts in the United States and around the world and to enhance law enforcement investigatory tools, among other purposes.

Foreign money laundering is covered by Title III of the act and represents the most significant anti-money laundering legislation since money laundering was first made a crime in 1986 with the passage of the Bank Secrecy Act. The act requires securities brokers, dealers, commodity merchants, advisers and pool operators to file suspicious activity reports (SARs) with the Financial Crimes Enforcement Network (FinCEN) of the Department of the Treasury.

The act has been attacked by several groups as unconstitutional because some of its provisions are thought to infringe on an individual's civil liberties. Many of the act's provisions were to sunset beginning December 31, 2005. After much debate, on March 2, 2006, a "compromise bill" was passed by Congress leaving the act basically intact.

SARBANES-OXLEY ACT OF 2002

The Sarbanes-Oxley Act was passed to provide investors with accurate and timely disclosure of financial and other important data of public companies and to ensure that audits of these companies are performed by independent accounting firms and according to accepted auditing standards.

The act was passed in response to abuses and scandals uncovered after the Chapter 11 bankruptcy filings of Enron Corp., WorldCom Inc., Adelphia Communication Corp., and others. The SEC was given authority to establish rules and regulations in furtherance of the act.

The act provided for the creation of the Public Company Accounting Oversight Board to oversee the auditing of public companies that are subject to the securities statutes. The goal was to ensure that these audits are informative, accurate, and independent of influence from the company being audited. The act requires public accounting firms to register with the Board and makes it unlawful for a registered public accounting firm to provide certain non-audit services to a company while auditing it. Further, the lead auditor or coordinating partner and the reviewing partner of the auditing firm must rotate off of the audit every five years. Also, the chief executive officer, controller, chief financial officer, or any person in an equivalent position in the company being audited cannot have been employed by that company's audit firm during the one-year preceding the audit.

The act provides for enhanced financial disclosures and accelerated the filing deadlines with the SEC. It also required the CEO and the CFO to certify that the financial statements are accurate and complete and that the company has established audit committees and internal controls.[22]

ENERGY POLICY ACT OF 2005

In August 2005, Congress enacted the Energy Policy Act which repealed the Public Utility Holding Company Act of 1935 (35 Act) effective February 8, 2006 and transferred certain authority to the Federal Energy Regulatory Commission (FERC). FERC was given broad authority and access to the books and records of utility holding companies. It enacted the Public Utility Holding Company Act of 2005. This act does not impose any of the substantive restrictions that effectively barred many entities from ownership of public utilities.

With the repeal of the 35 Act, the SEC no longer has oversight authority for electric and gas holding companies which included oversight over mergers and acquisitions. The repeal was demanded because proponents argued the that ownership restrictions and SEC filing requirements were unduly burdensome and effectively barred investment in the utility industry for many new investors who could bring new ideas and vitality to the industry.[23]

SECURITIES PROCESSING REGULATIONS

Banks serve as major processors of securities and are regulated by three regulatory bodies. The Board of Governors of the Federal Reserve System is responsible for regulating state chartered banks which are members of the Federal Reserve System. The Office of the Comptroller of the Currency, a unit of the U. S. Treasury Department, is responsible for the regulation of nationally chartered banks and the Federal Deposit Insurance Corporation regulates banks which are not members of the Federal Reserve System. Each of these regulatory bodies supervises and enforces banking laws and regulations through regular examinations of their assigned banks.

Partially as a result of the intense criticism of the securities processing industry arising out of the heavy volume in securities trading during 1968-1970, a number of studies by Congressional committees were made to determine the nature and extent of any additional legislation that would improve the clearance and settlement of securities transactions.[24] The most significant result was the enactment of the Securities Acts Amendments of 1975, sometimes called the National Exchange Market System Act[25] The main thrust of this legislation was to authorize the establishment of "a national system for the clearance and settlement of securities transactions and the safeguarding of securities and funds related thereto."[26] To implement this objective, the 34 Act was amended by adding section 17A[27] to provide for the federal regulation of clearing agencies and transfer agents. The SEC and the federal bank regulatory authorities were given the authority to adopt rules and regulations governing the conduct of transfer agents and to enforce compliance.[28]

Pursuant to its authority, the SEC has promulgated rules implementing (1) the registration of transfer agents;[29] (2) requirements for the almost universal fingerprinting of all persons engaged in the sale of securities, those who have access to the handling or processing of securities, monies, or books and records relating thereto, and those who have direct supervisory responsibility over persons engaged in such activities;[30] (3) the promulgation of minimum performance standards and recordkeeping requirements for all registered transfer agents, including transfer turnaround requirements;[31] (4) the establishment of a reporting and inquiry system for all lost, stolen, missing, or counterfeit securities, the prime objective of which is to prevent the misuse or fraudulent use of such securities particularly as it relates to collateralizing loans;[32] (5) regulations governing the maintenance of accurate security holder files and safeguarding of funds and securities;[33] (6) the requirement that any registered transfer agent acting as a depositary in the case of a tender offer (or as an exchange agent in the case of an exchange offer) must establish special designated accounts with DTC to permit securities to move to and from the tender/exchange agent through a book entry mechanism;[34] (7) the timely mailing of transfer agent journals by a co-transfer agent to the recordkeeping transfer agent and a maximum time period in which to respond to dividend and interest inquiries;[35] (8) a requirement for the filing of an annual report on form TA-2;[36] (9) the establishment of structure for signature guaranty programs;[37] (10) the prior notification by transfer agents to a qualified registered securities depository (e.g. DTC) of the assumption or termination of services on behalf of an issuer or change of a transfer agent's name or address;[38] (11) requiring transfer agents to conduct searches in an effort to locate lost security holders, and to maintain written procedures to effect compliance;[39] and (12) requiring transfer agents to file information on lost security holders with the SEC on amended form TA-2.[40]

Each year, as of December 31, the trustee is required to report the type and the volume of corporate trust and agency business it has on the Annual Report of Trust Assets - Form FFIEC 001, Schedule C - Corporate Trust. As new concerns and problems appear, additional regulations will be promulgated--unless the securities industry itself is able to resolve these to the satisfaction of the federal regulatory agencies.

The Municipal Securities Rulemaking Board was also created to regulate brokers, dealers, and banks dealing in municipal securities, with rules subject to SEC approval and enforcement shared by the National Association of Securities Dealers and bank regulatory agencies.[41]

RISK MANAGEMENT

During the past twenty years increasing numbers of corporate trustees have placed greater emphasis on managing the potential risks inherent in the business. Risk management works best when it is an established unit within the bank. The unit will typically report to the senior officer in charge of the fiduciary lines of business. In some banks, the fiduciary risk manager may report directly to the chief credit officer or the chief executive officer of the bank.

The Office of the Comptroller of the Currency revised Regulation 9 ("Reg 9"), dated January 2, 1997, which provides the basic regulations for managing trust business lines. Not only does Reg 9 establish the need for policies, account pre-acceptance and post acceptance reviews; it also sets forth the requirements for audits, recordkeeping, control of assets and establishes the need for a fiduciary audit committee, to name just a few of its purposes. Corporate trustees often review Section 9.6(c) - Annual Review and argue it is not applicable to corporate trusts. Although this section requires an annual account review at least once every calendar year, it specifically limits the annual review to accounts for which the bank has investment discretion. It can be argued that typically corporate trustees do not have discretion over investments since they are directed by the obligor. A good management tool is to mandate an annual account review of all trustee appointments. The review allows a structured opportunity for account officers to verify that all governing document requirements are being satisfied.

Reg 9, along with the other rules and regulations noted earlier, establish the need for a structured risk management program. But risk management should not be confused with the function of the internal auditor, who satisfies Reg 9 by completing an annual internal audit. Risk management officers should be an integral part of running a business. Although business line managers may find it difficult to accept the role of the risk management officer as an infringement into the business line management process, it is through the specialized focus of the risk manager that business decisions can be improved. The business line manager's job is to focus on the revenues to be derived from new business to achieve financial goals. Consequently, he or she cannot possibly fully absorb the regulations and also be responsible for personnel, revenue growth and new product delivery. Through the use of risk management, therefore, a continuing awareness of potential operational challenges, costs, policies, procedures and regulations can improve the quality of internal audits and regulatory examinations. This in turn creates sound business practices.

Some banks also employ the use of a peer group review to improve daily operations. Typically, the department manager selects a sample of accounts to be reviewed for compliance with the governing document(s), policies, procedures and regulations. The reviewing parties should be administrators who are not assigned to the accounts. The peer review helps identify systemic and isolated issues within the department. As automated compliance systems and imaging have become popular, it has become feasible for the department manager to conduct, by means of desktop technology, the peer review by random-sampling compliance items and completion of automated ticklers.

Managing within the governing regulations and managing risk are considered by some managers as time consuming and overpowering. The art of running the business, however, is to establish a leadership role by recognizing the need for regulatory compliance while not sacrificing client service and product development.

---

[1] Codified in scattered sections of 15 U.S.C. sec. 77 and 78 (1976).

[2] TIA, sec. 305(b). See section 304 for securities exempted from the act.

[3] See Dropkin, "Implied Civil Liability Under the Trust Indenture Act: Trends and Prospects," 52 *Tul. L. Rev.* 299, 322-24 (1978).

[4] 390 F. Supp. 817 (S.D.N.Y. 1975).

[5] This result was recognized as a possibility in a footnote of Caplin v. Marine Midland Grace Trust Co., 406 U.S. 416, 426n.17 (1971).

[6] 390 F.Supp. at 822.

[7] Report 101-155, Senate Comm. on Banking, Housing & Urban Affairs (Oct. 2, 1989).

[8] Id. at 29.

[9] TIA, sec. 310(b).

[10] Id. sec. 310(a)(5).

[11] Id. sec. 313(a). See also chapter 13, note 4, *supra*

[12] Id. sec. 314(a)(4).

[13] Id. sec. 316(c).

[14] Id. sec. 310(b), last sentence.

[15] Id. sec. 311.

[16] Id. sec. 305(b)(2).

[17] Id. sec. 310(a)(1).

[18] Id. sec. 304(d).

[19] See Securities Enforcement Remedies and Penny Stock Act of 1990, P.L. 101-249.

[20] See generally, Richard Stark "The Trust Indenture Act of 1939 in the Proposed Federal Securities Code", 32 *Vand. L. Rev.* 527 (Mar. 1979); SEC Release No. 33-6242 (20 SEC Docket No. 19 at 1483, Sept. 18, 1980).

[21] *The New Article 9, Uniform Commercial Code*, Second Edition, American Bar Association, Corinne Cooper, Editor, May, 2000.

[22] American Bankers Association, On-Line Training Course, *A Survey of Corporate Securities Services*, Part A, 2005, Romano I. Peluso.

[23] CRS Report for Congress, *The Repeal of the Public Utility Holding Company Act of 1935 (PUHCA) and Its Impact on Electric and Gas Utilities*, November 20, 2006, Adam Vann

[24] In particular, U.S Senate, Committee on Banking, Housing and Urban Affairs, R*eport of the Subcommittee on Securities,* 92d Cong., 2d sess. (1972); U.S. House Committee on Interstate and Foreign Commerce, *Report of the Subcommittee on Commerce and Finance,* 92d Cong., 2d sess. (1972).

[25] Pub. L. No. 94-29 (June 5, 1975).

[26] Id. sec. 2.

[27] Id. sec. 15.

[28] Securities Exchange Act of 1934, sec. 17A(d).

[29] Rule 17-2-1 (17 CFR 240.17-2-1, Oct. 22, 1975).

[30] Rule 17f-2 (17 CFR 240.17f-2, Mar.16, 1976).

[31] Rules 17Ad-1/7 (17 CFR 240.17Ad-1 to 7, June 16, 1977).

[32] Rule 17f-1 (17 CFR 240.17f-1, July 1, 1979).

[33] Rules 17Ad-9/13 (17 CFR 240.17 Ad-9 to 13, June 21, 1983).

[34] Rule 17Ad-14 (17 CFR 240.17Ad-14, Jan. 19, 1984).

[35] Rule 17A-10 (17 CFR 240.17Ad-10, Apr. 1, 1986).

[36] Rule 17Ac2-2 (17 CFR 240.17Ac2-2, May 5, 1986).

[37] Rule 17Ad-15 (17 CFR 240. 17Ad-16, Jan. 6, 1992)

[38] Rule 17Ad-16 (17 CFR 240.17Ad-16, Feb. 1, 1995)

[39] Rule 17Ad-17 (17 CFR 240.17Ad-17, Oct. 1, 1997)

[40] Rule 17a-24 (17 CFR 240.17a-24. Oct. 1, 1997

[41] The Internet, www.msrb.org - *About the MSRB*

II

MANAGEMENT

Management is tasks. Management is a discipline. But management is also people. Every achievement of management is the achievement of a manager. Every failure is a failure of a manager. People manage rather than ``forces'' or ``facts.'' The vision, dedication, and integrity of managers determine whether there is management or mismanagement.

Peter F. Drucker, *Management*

What we need today, perhaps, is not new theory, concept or framework but people who can think strategically.

Kenichi Ohmae

INTRODUCTION

During our years of involvement in the corporate trust industry, we have observed that bank trustees continue to hire with the same motivations as when we started in this business. The corporate trust industry provides technical training, often on a transactional basis, to get the corporate trust administrator or management trainee productive in the job as early as possible. The only difference in today's management environment is the required competitive efficiencies of the business demand fewer staff to do the work. While transactional training will get the job done, it does not provide opportunities for new employees to develop an understanding of the relationship of their job and its responsibilities to the overall corporate trust function and the business plan that drives it. A planned training program that links the organization's strategy and business plans to individual job requirements and accountabilities will allow individuals to reach their personal goals while improving the potential for achieving the business plan.

The human side of the enterprise includes managerial issues and concerns related to the components of the business, i.e. strategy, planning, philosophy, process, organization of the work, training and development, performance evaluation and advancement opportunities. Our experience during our years of teaching and working in the industry is that little attention has been paid to these issues and concerns in developing the corporate trust professional, as these issues are viewed to be the role of senior management. Management is a skill and responsibility that must be learned and experienced at all levels, starting with the taking of responsibility for managing oneself.

The ensuing chapters are not designed to teach the profession of management. The chapters are brief and represent a framework within which corporate trust professionals can begin to appreciate and understand the complexities and dynamics of a professional environment.

Management is an interactive process, requiring trust, cooperation and understanding between managers and subordinates. Effective management operates on three levels: manager to subordinate ("managing downward"), subordinate to manager ("managing upward"), and manager to manager and subordinate to subordinate ("managing laterally").

The structure and size of each organization will affect the implementation, ideas and guidelines in the following chapters. The assumptions and premises should not be affected by the numbers of people or levels of management. The level of interest and inclination of the managers, who are in a position to influence the desired outcome, will be the key factor in training and developing the corporate trust professional.

Numerous articles and books are available on the views and philosophies of management, however managers (and those who would like to be one) should find the concepts, principles and approaches helpful in the following books: *The Concept of Corporate Strategy* provides a useful discussion on the formulation of corporate strategy and implementation[1]; *The Transformation of Management* covers the four great questions facing all managers at all levels in all type organizations: Mission (what are we trying to accomplish?), Competition (how do we gain a competitive edge?), Performance (how do we deliver the results?), and Change (how do we cope with change?)[2]; *Coaching For Improved Performance* is a practical approach to dealing with the obstacles to work performance and the means to counsel employees in overcoming the obstacles[3]; *Becoming A Manger* is a compliment to the other works in identifying

435

the skills necessary to transition from star performer to competent manager.[4]

[1] Kenneth R. Andrews. 1987. Homewood, IL: Richard D. Irwin, Inc.
[2] Mike Davidson. 1996. Boston: Butterworth-Heinemann
[3] F. F. Fournes. 1978 New York. Van Nostrand Reinhold
[4] Linda A. Hill. 1992. Boston. Harvard Business School Press

NINETEEN

STRATEGIC AND TACTICAL PLANNING

When examining the management aspects of the corporate trust function, it is necessary to take a view of the function as being a separate business or product line within a larger financial services institution. For any business to survive and succeed, it must be driven by a strategy that clearly defines its purposes or goals to keep the business moving in a deliberately chosen direction. The structure of the organization must support the chosen strategy. No student of management or of organization development would, however, suggest that strategy is a static, immovable force. It and the structure must be adaptable to change; it must be flexible enough to permit the organization to modify its approach, and even to dramatically change direction as the needs of its market, and of the environment in which it operates, change. The consolidation of banks during the past twenty years has tested the flexibility of many corporate trust strategic plans as well as the resiliency of corporate trust professionals. For those banking companies and their staffs not involved with consolidations, strategic planning has emerged as a heightened focus to compete effectively in the consolidating businesses.

Corporate strategy has been defined as

> the pattern of decisions in a company that determines and reveals its objectives, purposes, goals, produces the principal policies and plans for achieving those goals, and defines the range of business the company is to pursue, the kind of economic and human organization it is or intends to be, and the nature of the economic and noneconomic contribution it intends to make to its shareholders, employees, customers, and communities.[1]

Another excellent definition was written by Alfred D. Chandler in *Strategy and Structure* in which he postulated that is "the determination of the basic long-term goals and objectives of an enterprise and the adoption of courses of action and allocation of resources necessary for carrying out these goals."[2]

An organization's strategic business plan is based on its articulated strategy as expressed in terms of long-range direction, purpose, and corporate culture. One of the best known and most widely read authors on management is Peter Drucker. In his landmark study of the subject he observed:

> 1. It is not a bag of tricks, a bundle of techniques. It is analytical thinking and commitment of resources to action. . . . 2. Strategy planning is not forecasting. It is not masterminding the future. . . . 3. Strategic planning does not deal with future decisions. It deals with the futurity of present decisions. . . . 4. Strategic planning is not an attempt to eliminate risk. It is not even an attempt to minimize risk. . .
>
> . . . Strategy . . . answers the questions. What is our business, what should it be, what will it be. . . . It thereby determines what the key activities are in a given business or service institution. Effective structure is the design that makes these key activities capable of functioning and of performance.[3]

Strategy is thus the driving force from which all else in the organization flows and is the means to direct the organization in the pursuit of its mission, the components of which are discussed next.

The strategic plan for the corporate trust business must flow from both the strategy and the strategic plan of its parent institution. Because the corporate trust function is not a fully independent entity, its strategy and planning process are guided by the institution's direction and demands, its guidelines, and its policies. Within any such parameters, however, corporate trust managers are responsible for developing its culture, plans, objectives, and supporting structure. The corporate trust manager, together with the members of the corporate trust organization, must drive the business within the context of its business plan. Axiomatic is the policy that "those who *implement* the plans must *make* the plans.[4]

THE NEEDS ANALYSIS

Before developing a strategic business plan it is necessary to establish a process whereby each of the essential elements leads into and influences the others. Figure 1 depicts this process flow and the interrelationships of the strategic and tactical business plans. This process contains an issues and needs analysis covering an "environmental scan" of the corporate trust and securities processing business, the present and projected economic capital financing environment, the nature and extent of the competition for corporate trust appointments, the strategic posture of the institution, and the present state of the corporate trust function.

The *critical issues analysis* is simply an understanding and evaluation of those conditions under which the corporate trust function is operating and can expect to operate during the next three years.

The framework for such an analysis should focus on three levels:

    1. *The industry.* (a) How has technology changed trustee and securities servicing business? (b) What legislation and regulation is impacting the development, production, and delivery of the services? (c) How have judicial decisions affected the evolving role of the indenture trustee? (d) How are economic conditions and changes in the capital markets, including types of financing vehicles, being handled? (e) What is the competition for obtaining profitable appointments? (f) What has been the

impact of changing demands and expectations of the clients and the security holders?

2. *The bank.* (a) Does the bank's strategy enhance or detract from the corporate trust business? (b) Will the bank's response to changes in limitations on or expansion of the permitted scope of its activities help or hinder the function? (c) Does the bank's management actively support or simply tolerate corporate trust activities? (d) What demands does the bank's senior management place on the corporate trust function as a profitable business line? (e) Do other areas of the bank provide product and market development support? (f) Does the bank provide resources to support and expand the function? (g) Have the risk factors increased to the point where losses or potential losses outweigh the return generated?

3. *The corporate trust function.* (a) What has been the financial impact resulting from technological changes in the industry, from a changing and volatile economic environment, from increased government regulation and intervention, from increasing competition, and from greater demands by clients and security holders? (b) At what stage is the function in its organizational development, including managerial and technical/professional staffing; personnel training, development, and evaluation; and meeting the needs and demands of a changing work force? (c) What is the underlying basis for the development of new business, i.e., the corporate trust's marketing responsibilities, and to what extent is it dependent upon the sales solicitation efforts of noncorporate trust people? How are internal sales managed? How are new services created or existing services modified? What has been the impact on the marketing and sales efforts resulting from the banks

relationships with its corporate and municipal clients? (d) How does the existing technology support the function? What are the major shortcomings or deficiencies of the processing and information systems? How much support can be expected from the institution's systems development staff? What major changes are needed, or enhancements to the existing systems, to remain price and market competitive? What effect will the greater use of microcomputers and remote processing have on the delivery and cost of agency services?

When these questions have been answered, the next step is a *critical needs analysis*. In this instance, the issues identified earlier and responses to them can be divided into two categories, those having a longer range impact, which should be addressed over a three to five years, and those that must be addressed within one to two years. In each time category, the critical needs can be grouped as follows:

Financial Management

Marketing Development

Technological Development

Organizational Development

Organizational Structure

In this part of the planning process, we identify those issues and needs essential to both the strategic and annual business plans.

THE STRATEGIC PLAN (See Fig. 1 at page 448)

As discussed earlier, the components of the plan will be an evaluation of the present state of the business (what are we doing?), an understanding of what the business will be like (what will we be doing?), and a posture reflecting the direction in which the business should go (what do we want to be doing?).

In addition to identifying critical issues and needs, we must examine the various services offered and the markets for them by matrixing the various trustee and agency services against the several target markets, indicating for each: (1) whether the service/market exists [E], is planned [P] or is possible[?]; (2) the attractiveness of the service/market on a scale of five down to zero, in terms of profitable business and opportunity to increase volume and/or market share; and (3) the perceived competition for the service/market on a scale of five to zero.

The matrix for the Paying Agent service might look like this:

Service	Corporations	Governments	Banks
Paying Agent	E-5-4	E-4-5	P-3-5

A further refinement of this matrix would include an analysis of the financial components affecting each service/market in regard to (1) the relative significance of both fixed and variable costs (high-medium-low); and (2) the relative significance of the profit margins (high-medium-low) for both incremental and fully absorbed costs.[5] Thus, our paying agent example might look like this:

	Cost	Profit
	Fixed/Variable	Incr./Fully Abs.
Corporations	M/M	H/M
Governments	M/H	H/M

Too often when fully absorbed costs are calculated and reviewed, fees or balances which are credited to other units within the bank are omitted. Letter-of-credit fees and government securities trading fees are examples. Demand deposit balances, generated by corporate trust transactions, should also be taken into consideration when evaluating profit margins.

When reviewing the terminating or maturing accounts and potential new corporate trust business, an analysis should be completed for each of the major service/market categories: trustee for debt issues of corporations, governments, and other banks; bond registrar for corporate and government debt issues; transfer agent (and registrar) for corporate equity issues; and paying agent for corporations and governments. For each of these components, an analysis can be made of: (1) the historical size and direction of the market and the environmental factors influencing the numbers and the direction (e.g., unsecured versus secured debt, straight versus convertible, fixed rate versus floating rate); (2) the nature and extent of the existing and projected competition for such appointments and of the perceived strengths and weaknesses of the most significant competitors; and (3) the major existing and projected strengths and weaknesses of the corporate trust function in providing such services against the competition.

These analyses establish realistic parameters and opportunities for the business. The analyses may also result in a decision by senior management, not to grow the business, but either to let it run down or simply sell it off. (This obviously is the risk inherent in fully understanding the dynamics, components, and profit potential in any business line!)

Assuming that the signs are favorable, and the risk/reward analysis is positive, the next step is to decide on a *strategic overview and posture*, including a statement of the function's key objective or mission; a delineation of the services to be offered to the particular identified markets; the strategic theme reflecting what level of emphasis will be placed on particular services and markets; the business objectives in terms of market share, profit margins, year over year profit dollar growth, return on expense investment, or any other determinant or standard the institution establishes for its business lines.

Although it is not intended to be a definitive statement of the overall mission or goal of the corporate trust function, it is evident that this overview should include making a contribution to the bank's growth and profitability by providing professional corporate trust services to its clients on a cost-effective and profitable basis.

When the strategic overview has been completed, it should be translated into the strategy to be applied to the continuation of existing services and markets, the enhancement of such services and the broadening (or narrowing) of the target markets of each, and the planned development and delivery of new services to the same or different prospective markets. Inherent in this part of the strategic business plan is the consideration and projection of resources needed to accomplish the plan. The resource needs can be divided into staff (number, type, mix), space (how much and where), and furniture and equipment, including technological support. The use of personal computers, integrated cellular telephones, BlackBerrys, the availability of sophisticated software programs and the Internet make technological support and research efforts less onerous when developing new services. Also to be considered is the projected organization structure necessary to support the plan and the interdependence of other units involved in developing, producing, implementing, and delivering the various services.

The final part of the strategic business plan is alternative and contingency planning. Because the previous parts of the plan were based on certain assumptions, which might not prove to be accurate or viable, we must consider alternative strategies. The areas of the strategic plan most susceptible to uncertainty are economic environment, legal and regulatory restrictions, competition, automation technology, and availability of trained staff.

THE ANNUAL BUSINESS PLAN

Each institution must establish a framework and process for its annual planning cycle, as well as the type and details of the plan itself. The plan's several separate but interrelated subplan components include a marketing plan, an activity/volume plan, an automation technology plan, a human resources plan, and, certainly, a financial plan.

The marketing plan includes not only the "how, when and where" but also the projected results. The marketing plan constitutes the sales objectives that are believed to be viable and realistic based upon market analysis and experience.

The activity/volume plan is simply a projection of the extent to which the existing and planned book of business will result in certain types of projected activity and the volume of each. These projections take into consideration the number of projected new trusteeships, the projected volume of certificates to be issued and canceled by the transfer agent and the number of trustee and agent appointments scheduled to mature or terminate. Data are essential to evaluating and assessing the needs for resource support, and to development of the income and expense plan. The corporate trust manager who insists on one system which can process the work, provide the required administrative ticklers and reports and also create the necessary management reports from one data base, will produce a more accurate analysis when developing the strategic and business plans.

The automation technology plan addresses the needs of the business in being able to efficiently and effectively deliver its services. The plan should specify the needs for system maintenance and software enhancement, hardware, and of course, the costs of completing the cost/benefit analysis.

The human resource plan will focus on the personnel needs of the function and its staff, including an assessment of the current staff, i.e., its adequacy in terms of numbers and expertise, training and development, and an appropriate compensation program. This plan also translates these needs into organizational objectives, as well as personal improvement objectives for the staff members. In the following chapters, we describe main elements of organization and structure and the establishment of training and development programs and an evaluation process.

The final part of an annual business plan addresses the function's financial objectives. It covers the expected income from each of the major services provided and is usually quantified on a quarterly basis. The expense side is the allocation and use of all resources required to meet the income objectives. In almost every institution this requires a detailed analysis of the fixed (e.g., space) and variable (e.g., overtime) costs of the business. Some of these expenses are charged directly to the function as a profit center, whereas others (e.g., corporate overhead) go through the institution's cost allocation systems.

The biggest expense, usually running between 60 and 70 percent of the total, relates to people, and therefore receives the most attention from managers as they seek to achieve increased productivity. The technology plan has absorbed some of the expense formerly applied to personnel. Some companies have been able to achieve these efficiencies while fixing the cost of production through automation. (Because of the impact of training, development, and performance planning achieving higher levels of productivity, chapters 21 and 22 address these topics separately.)

Finally, it is necessary to understand that the organization's structure must flow out of both the nature of the business itself and the strategy that drives the business. Peter Drucker put it this way: "Organization is not mechanical. It is not 'assembly.' It cannot be prefabricated! Organization is organic and unique to each individual business or institution.

For we now know that structure to be effective and sound must follow strategy.[6]

---

[1] Kenneth R. Andrews, *The Concept of Corporate Strategy*, 13 (1987).

[2] Alfred D. Chandler, *Strategy and Structure*, 13 (1962)..

[3] Peter Drucker, *Management*, 123, 523 (1974).

[4] Texas Instrument's Patrick Haggerty quoted in Tom Peters and Robert Waterman, *In Search of Excellence*, 31 (1982).

[5] Incremental profit is the gross income minus fixed expense and corporate overhead that is allocated to the function. Fully absorbed profit (sometimes referred to as NIBT, net income before tax) is gross income minus the total of all expense (variable, fixed, direct, indirect, or allocated) attributable to being in the particular business.

[6] Drucker, *Management*, 523.

FIGURE 1
Planning Process Flow

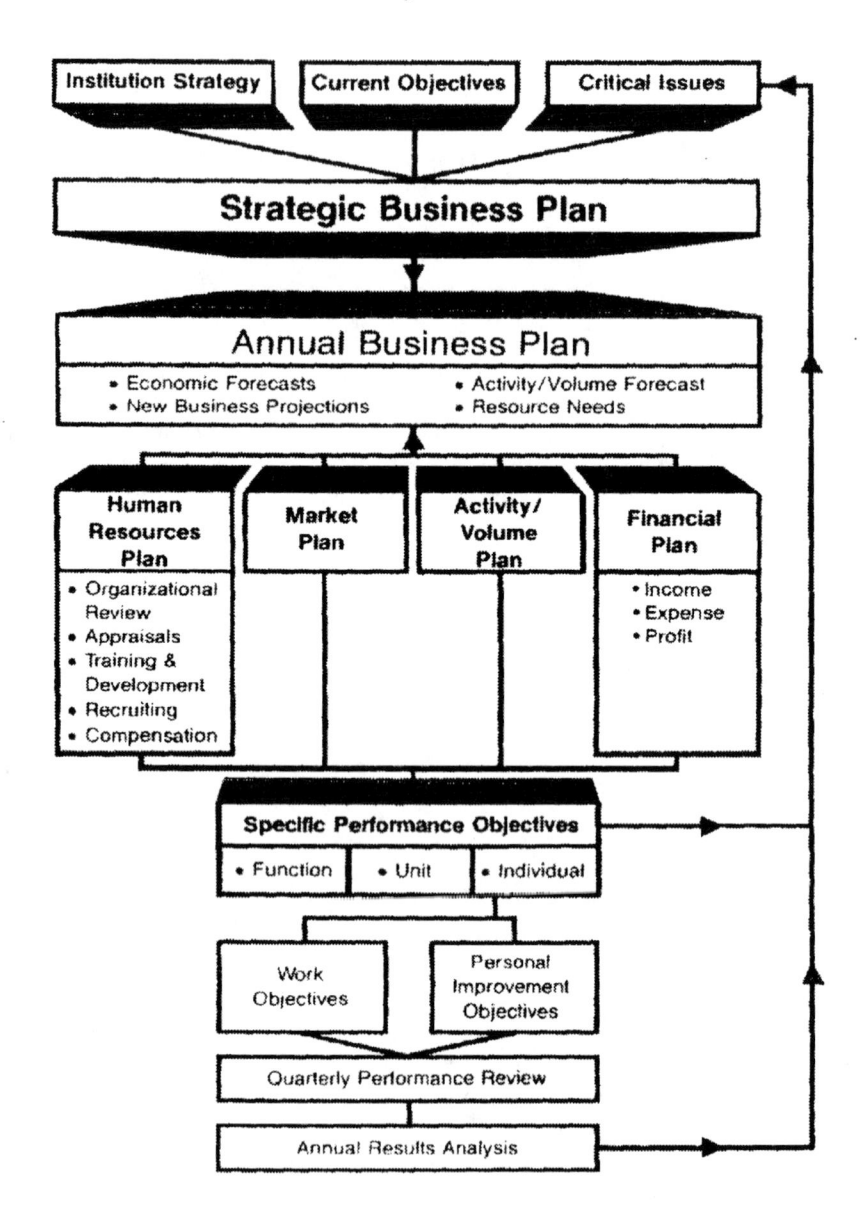

TWENTY

ORGANIZATION AND STRUCTURE

Now that we have discussed what drives the business and the planning process, we shall look at the organizational entity and how the components fit together in the overall strategy.

In practice, the reporting relationships and interdependencies of the activities performed are determined (and even governed) by the senior managers who make the decisions. The very size of the organization and its geographic locations directly influence both the organizational makeup and the structure of the function.

In its basic application, "organization" should not be thought of as a chart containing a series of boxes connected by solid and dotted lines to reflect reporting relationships. (Such a chart is, of course, useful in larger organizations to help keep track of who reports to whom in what work unit.) Rather, an organization is simply the arrangement and relationship of the work done by people. It reflects the results of deciding what products or services are to be offered for sale; which type of work units are needed to generate, produce, and deliver the product or service; how the work units will receive input and how they will deliver output; and how they will work together to achieve a profitable result. Structure, then, is both the design of the organization and the design of the processes to make the organization effective in the areas of communication, reporting relationships, interdependencies among units, technology and assignment of accountability. It is management's conclusion about how best to create and maintain the necessary work units and their relationship to each other, at a particular time.

When discussing organization and structure, we assumed

that the function includes the following key business activities: administration of trust indentures and other debt financing instruments and agreements, as well as agency servicing agreements; operational servicing and processing of debt and equity securities, maintenance of related records and data files; and marketing of both trustee and agency services to existing and prospective clients. This arrangement is often referred to as *product divisionalization*, that is, in most banks, the corporate trust function as an integrated business line or product center is a relatively self-contained business unit in most banks.

Some organizations do have separate divisional lines with corporate trust operating functions reporting separately from the administrative division. When the administration and operations are separate, the organization should be maintained with a "boldface" dotted line on the organization chart. Service agreements between both divisions should be considered to establish the quality and delivery standards each division expects of the other. Typically the only unit not reporting to the corporate trust manager, either directly or by a dotted line, is the unit which processes the cash and asset transactions and client asset statements. Each of the key business activities interfaces with the others--the natural order of the work flows between and among them. The output of one becomes the input of another.

The final product, or output of the function, is the result of the efforts, and value added, of each and all of the work units in the process. As an integrated function, it is responsible and accountable for the expenses it incurs (including the overhead of simply being part of a larger organization) and the income it produces, resulting in a profit contribution to the bank.

In many banks where all the work units are not under "corporate trust management," an effort is made through the practice of *transfer pricing* to charge the income-producing center with the expense of the work performed by any noncorporate trust work units. This approach works only if the rates to be charged are negotiated in advance; the activity volume is accurately captured; the resultant expense is monitored and evaluated on a regular basis; and it is, in fact, a cost-effective means of producing and delivering the services.

But too often, in a transfer-pricing structure, the corporate trust account is assumed to carry the same volume and level of cost as other trust accounts in the trust organization. Likewise, the balance credits earned from corporate trust deposits are also not considered in the equation of revenue and cost. Corporate trust managers can thus immediately improve their cost structures with the appropriate analysis.

Transfer pricing does not address the real-people issues of full product ownership or the developmental options of the employees or the managers (these are examined in chapter 21).

In the corporate trust organization, it is generally agreed that a "functional" structure best achieves the overall business goals indicated earlier. The integrated functional structure provides the greatest number of options for the most effective management of the people and the work involved. The classic problem of "we versus them" is greatly mitigated when all parts of the business line operate in a common environment under a management team that is responsible for the entire corporate trust function. On such a basis, the structure of the line units then is:

FUNCTION HEAD

Marketing	Administration	Operations
Product Development	Trustee	Securities Processing
Research	Agency	Funds and Payments
Sales		Records

with such staff support units as are necessary.

(In some very large corporate trust banks the product divisionalization is carried even further, so that separate product centers are established--each having marketing, administration and operations responsibilities--all within the overall corporate trust function.)

This arrangement, reflecting the major responsibilities of the business and the resulting interdependencies and accountabilities, is not, however, universal among the corporate trust banks. In fact, in some banks, each of the three main components is in a separate department--the only common manager being the bank's president! In those banks corporate trust is usually defined as, and limited to, the administration activity. However, even in this instance, attention to the organization and structure of the unit is critical.

Even under this optimal structure the function is not a completely stand-alone business, that is, fully integrated both horizontally and vertically. It still requires the support of other line and staff organizations within the bank, including wire transfer, check reconcilement, government securities trading, personnel, auditing and commercial banking units for marketing support.

Having looked at the corporate trust function as a whole, we will now exam each of the three main components.

MARKETING

New business is the lifeblood of the function; there must be continuous infusions of new business appointments. Without the continued inflow, the organization will simply not survive, as fixed expenses will continue to mount to the point at which the function cannot produce income to cover both the variable expenses and the overhead. In addition, no successful institution can offer a service indefinitely if the profits levels do not justify the investment in space, equipment, and people. Today, most successful banking organizations also demand that the business line evidence a year-over-year growth in its profit contribution. Nevertheless, some banks still view the function as an accommodation service--something it must offer to be perceived as a full-service financial provider--even though it does not contribute to the bank's net earnings. The evidence of corporate trust divestitures during the past two decades suggests the "accommodation service" view for most banking services and products cannot be sustained.

The marketing of corporate trust services, like most other non-asset-based banking functions, must be done on two different levels. First, corporate trust services must be marketed to the commercial banking officers who form the first line of salespeople in generating corporate trust appointments. Second corporate trust personnel must directly market to corporate and municipal issuers. In the first instance, the banking officers become the eyes and ears of the corporate trust selling effort, as they are usually in the best position to determine whether their clients will need corporate trust services because of their more frequent calls on clients. Unfortunately, they are also called upon to do the same for all (or most) of the other services being offered by the bank--and it must be recognized that corporate trust appointments may not be uppermost in their minds in seeking additional relationships with the client. A variety of incentives have been used by corporate trust managers to keep their products at the top of the list of commercial bankers. This effort often results in other product managers presenting a similar incentive effort. Banking officers like to sell products and enhance the products offered to their clients. Although few of us will reject a monetary incentive, timely, accurate and responsive quality service, is what banking officers will see as the real incentives.

It is for this reason that banking officers must be made aware of the corporate trust services offered, be comfortable in seeking such business, and know whom to call for technical sales help or to whom to refer a potential appointment. A great deal of the corporate trust marketing effort is organized to ensure that these matters are addressed to as many commercial banking officers as possible. One easy way to accomplish this is to "take a banker to lunch" and review the potentially profitable opportunities for the bank (thus enhancing that particular banking officer's value to the bank as well). Although the news of quality service and experienced staff will spread quickly among the banking officers, the news of poor quality work spreads even faster. It is not always possible to accomplish the desired marketing objectives by relying solely on others to do the sales work. In those instances where the corporate trust function has the only relationship, or where a technical sales call for a particular transaction would be more directly productive, this should be done by a knowledgeable corporate trust officer.

In either case, however, the responsibility for product development (i.e., what new or modified service to what market segment) and basic research must be assumed by those people who have the greatest knowledge of the nuances of the service and the capabilities of the function. Whether or not the marketing activity is specifically within the corporate trust structure, the expertise and knowledge required does not change. The requirement to fully understand the nature and workings of corporate trust activities and the function's ability to deliver the services with a resultant profit is essential to successfully accomplish any marketing objectives

ADMINISTRATION

Once the appointment has been obtained, it must be administered in a professional manner, consistent with the particular duties and responsibilities of the appointment and with knowledge of the potential liabilities involved. The organization and structure of the administration function is to provide for one or more account officers and/or administrators (or teams of such) who are accountable for discharging the bank's duties and responsibilities under the particular appointment documents. This can run the gamut from a one-person unit to a structure that uses many people organized into discrete work units or teams.

In the latter case, the people are organized in one of two ways, by allocating the work (1) on a functional or product basis, with a separate team handling each different type or appointment (e.g., being responsible only for municipal housing issues) or just one aspect of the work involved in all accounts (e.g., giving comments on indentures or handling the various sinking funds) or (2) on a divisional basis where each team is fully responsible for all aspects of a diverse set of trustee and agency appointments. In practice few corporate trust functions are organized purely on a functional or divisional basis but somewhere on the spectrum between them. In the smaller banks, the tendency is toward the divisional structure, in which a few account officers and administrators do everything. In the larger banks, which probably have a very heavy volume of diverse appointments, more specialization tends to be the case, the result being a structure more reflective of a functional or product approach.

OPERATIONS

In almost every organization, the operations function was not created anew but grew piecemeal with a structure that responded to the type and volume of appointments over a period of years. The advent of the all fully registered corporate bond issues in the late 1960s, the proliferation of tax-exempt issues and creative financing vehicles, the increased numbers of smaller companies selling debt and equity securities, and the widespread use of computerized systems have all had a significant impact on the organization of the function and its structure. The use of personal computers and of software which can extract required data from one central system and download it to operational and administrative workstations has improved the productivity, and quality of corporate trust product delivery systems.

It is not possible to define a precise model, given the great diversity of activities that may be performed within the operations function. Even so, we can describe generally the basic areas of activity that are usually found in a corporate trust operations organization. These include (1) processing securities, (2) receiving and disbursing debt service funds, (3) maintaining records and data files and (4) fee billing.

With respect to securities processing, the organization of work performed follows from the logical flow of the work required. This normally follows a pattern that includes:

1. Receipt of the securities
2. Examination of the securities
3. Input of data to debit and credit security holder accounts
4. Cancellation of the incoming securities
5. Issuance of new securities and/or payment

vehicles

6. Delivery of new securities and/or payments

Each of these activities is part of both the receipt of work and the output of work--in effect each of the parts must be organizationally structured to achieve the maximum efficiencies.

Securities may be received either through a collection or clearing system, which generally is a bulk shipment of securities for the agent to process, or directly from an individual security holder (or broker) by mail or in person. The next step is examining each security to ensure, among other requirements, that it is in appropriate form for the action requested to be effected, that is, registration of transfer, exchange, payment, and so forth. Assuming that the item is not defective and the action requested can be effected, it then goes to operations personnel who make the necessary changes in the security holder file.

When registering a transfer, the appropriate debit is posted to the transferor's account with an offsetting credit to the transferee's account, or in the case of a new account, the posting of new account information. At the same time, systems are activated to produce new certificates in the name of the transferee. If the transaction is a redemption or maturity, the offsetting credit to the account debited is the production of a check or other payment vehicle. For a convertible issue, the offset to the cancellation of the surrendered certificates is the production (or requisition from the stock transfer agent) of the appropriate number of full shares of stock. The incoming securities are then canceled and ultimately disposed of, the new certificates (or payment checks) being sent back to the person surrendering the securities. This may include their direct mailing, their return over the window or back through the particular collection or clearing system, thereby completing the full cycle of the processing function.

The second major operational activity involves the receipt and disbursement of funds. In almost every corporate trust organization, specific people are designated to follow for, and book in, the required debt service funds or dividends. Because the role of paying or disbursement agent is really that of a conduit, the other side of this activity involves the calculation of the funds required to be disbursed and the actual disbursement thereof. These typically include payments of interest on registered bonds and dividends on stock, payments of interest against surrender of bearer coupons, payments of principal on account of a partial redemption or upon the maturity of an issue. The activity is not performed in isolation but requires coordination between and among the account administrator and the operational units involved in the processing of the underlying securities.

The third major area of activity is maintaining the records. Whereas much of the information required to be maintained is an integral part of the securities processing and payment functions, other records must be kept, whether they are to establish appropriate audit trails, meet SEC reporting requirements, provide for accurate cash controls, perform the billing function, or simply to provide management information on levels of activity and volume. In addition, it is important that every operations officer pay attention to all proof and control activities within the function, including the daily reconcilement of all individual cash and securities transactions to the unit's control records. Maintaining records is the functional need that must be integrated into the organization, rather than the identification of which people or units do what work.

The fourth function is the fee billing unit, which calculates all transaction and administrative fees and bills the corporate trust clients. Too often this unit is isolated from the corporate trust operations function. The fee billing unit can also be responsible for billing all clients for debt service. To provide billing integrity and efficiency, the corporate trust operations system should be the source of all billing data. A sound billing system will produce automated bills, send reminder notices for past due bills, maintain records for reimbursable expenses and appropriately age outstanding bills in accordance with the bank's general policy on fee and expense recovery.

In most institutions, this operational work is structured along functional lines under the management of an experienced officer. Ideally, this person is a people manager, capable of dealing with complex automation needs, processing procedures, and techniques, all in a fast-paced and action-oriented environment.

We now turn to the training and development needs of the staff that implements the business plan.

TWENTY ONE

TRAINING AND DEVELOPMENT

Perhaps the most important part of a manager's job is establishing and maintaining an environment in which people are encouraged and helped to develop and improve their knowledge and skills. Too often, training and development receives its greatest emphasis in the business plan phase of the annual budget process and later are de-emphasized as management demands adjustments in the expense portion of the business plan. It is generally agreed that to accomplish the desired results any developmental effort should be on a building-block basis. The cumulative effect of such an approach is that the individual becomes increasingly more knowledgeable and skillful (i.e., productive) in his or her existing position and demonstrates potential for increased levels and/or scope of responsibility. The end result is motivated persons with increased value to themselves, and more value to the organization. This in turn gives both the individual and the organization more options for the type and nature of their future responsibilities and the position in the organization at which they work.[1]

One primary concern of every manager is to control risk. A comprehensive training program can help to manage risk through well trained people. Whether an in-house training program is developed or external training resources are used, well trained people tend to be more motivated with less resultant performance risk.

The starting point for any manager is to do a manpower audit. Simply put, it evaluates the degree and breadth of knowledge and skill of the existing staff against the needs of the organization as determined by its strategic and tactical business plans (as discussed in chapter 19). Included in the analysis must be what numbers of people and what mix (specialists, generalists) are necessary, what the projected personnel turnover is, and what the personnel vulnerabilities are. This is in effect a personnel needs analysis that highlights the particular recruiting, staffing, training, and development needs of the organization. The exercise of a manpower audit will also produce the names of personnel with the most and least potential. Management must decide if those personnel with the least potential can grow into high potential staff through training and development efforts. When working with people, too often managers devote eighty percent of their time to those staff members with the least potential and only twenty percent of their time to the personnel who have the potential to implement the strategic plan and achieve the business plan.

As discussed earlier, the increasingly complex nature of the corporate trust business has led to more specialization of work by administrators and account officers, particularly in the larger organizations. It is evident that, carried too far, it may over a longer period of time be counterproductive to the development of a well-rounded professional administrative staff. A great deal of learning experience may be sacrificed under the guise of efficiency. In such situations, individual training and development needs must be factored into a comprehensive training program to ensure that diverse learning opportunities are made available.

The major drawback resulting from training only specialists can, of course, be overcome through appropriate job rotation, provided it is in fact accomplished through a defined plan. The timing of rotational moves and attention to structured training experiences require careful follow-up by the manager for it to be effective. It seems evident, however, that any particular corporate trust organization is significantly better served and the individual is better equipped for greater responsibilities if he/she is not limited to a functionally driven set of accounts or work responsibilities but rather is thoroughly trained and experienced in all facets of administering debt and equity accounts, covering as wide a range of diverse types of appointments as is possible.

Before developing any type of comprehensive training program, it is essential to define the job, including its objectives, accountabilities, and the requisite knowledge and skill competencies. The competencies would be those related to technical, managerial (including self-management), and interpersonal factors. Incorporated in such a job description or position profile would be the essential elements of an account administrator's or officer's job as follows:

Key Objective:

To contribute to the growth and profitability of the bank by providing expert innovative trust and agency services for issuers and holders of corporate, state, and municipal securities and by meeting the changing demand of the economy and of the banking and securities industry.

Primary Accountability:

To represent the bank in all facets of corporate trust administration, including the review, negotiation, execution, and delivery of indentures and other financing agreements; the establishment and implementation of procedures relative to the administration of such agreements; the enforcement of the provisions of such agreements in accordance with the Trust Indenture Act and other securities laws and regulations, with emphasis on the rights of security holders and the risks and liabilities of the bank related thereto.

Reporting Relationships:

Reports to an administration manager (for officers). Has responsibility for supervising and training account administrators.

Interface Relationships:

Interfaces with operations units, commercial banking officers, existing customers, correspondent banks, investment bankers, law firms, and underwriters.

Accountabilities: *(level determined by training and experience)*

Account Acceptance Performance:

(1) Reviews, negotiates, and renders comments on new indentures and other financing instruments so that they meet the requirements for acceptance by the bank; (2) evaluates bank's duties, responsibilities, and potential liabilities; (3) handles all matters related to the closing, including the review of required documents, preparation of internal records, and instructions to operations units; and (4) develops and/or negotiates fees and pricing matters with client.

Account Administration Performance:

Completes the following administrative transactions, as applicable, in a timely and effective manner: (1) establishment, maintenance, and use of internal records, files, and instructions; (2) review of certificates and opinions; (3) analysis of financial statements; (4) receipt and movement of funds and collateral; (5) preparation of annual trustee's reports; (6) processing of sinking funds and redemptions; (7) investment of trust funds and valuations; (8) processing of releases and withdrawals; (9) processing satisfactions, resignations, change of corporate name and consents, and waivers; (10) arranging security holder meetings; (11) processing successor trusteeships; (12) processing mergers and acquisitions; prepares annual account reviews and participates in peer account, policy and procedure reviews.

Planning Performance

Develops specific objectives for annual performance, including: (1) recommendations in modification of policies, procedures, and methods to improve administration services; (2) planning and establishing priorities in workflow and organization; and (3) participates in revenue generating and expense reduction planning.

Human Resource Performance (for account officers)

1) Supervises the daily work flow of administrators and reviews all required documents; (2) provides training and development consistent with work standards and the training guidelines for administrators; and (3) conducts appraisals of non-official staff and provides appropriate assistance to administration management.

Marketing Performance

(1) Promotes relationships with current customer base and other contacts; (2) contributes to the planning process by assisting in the identification of new prospects; (3) evaluates prospective new business in conjunction with administration management; and (4) participates in new product development and sales material production.

Knowledge Competencies:

(1) Principles of and developments in corporate and municipal finance; (2) federal and state securities statutes, particularly TIA and applicable provisions of the UCC; (3) federal and state securities regulations, particularly those of the Federal Reserve Board and SEC; (4) structure and content of basic documents, including bond mortgage, debenture indenture, private placement agreement, agency agreements for debt and equity, leverage lease documentation, commercial paper documentation, depository and escrow agreements; (5) applicable bank and administration policies and procedures; (6) trends and developments in corporate trust industry, including applicable court decisions, securities processing procedures and tax requirements; (7) administration's technical, managerial, and human resource planning process; (8) investment banking and underwriting functions; and (9) industry rules and practices, particularly those from the New York Stock Exchange (NYSE) and the Municipal Securities Rulemaking Board (MSRB).

Skill Competencies:

(1) Effectively negotiates trust and agency agreement provisions and related fees to meet organization's standards; (2) administers trust and agency accounts in accordance with legal and bank policies and standards; (3) makes investments as directed by obligor/principal by completing appropriate instructions and accurately calculating discounts, interest, etc; (4) effectively and within specified guidelines manages default situations and bankruptcies; (5) provides operations units with timely and accurate instructions for processing for all account transactions; (6) effectively prepares, maintains, and utilizes internal administration records and files; (7) does appropriate research and develops timely response to

customer inquiry on transactional project; and (8) carefully analyzes current and potential problems and makes sound recommendations/decisions based upon such analysis.

Managerial Competencies:

Planning

(1) Understands objective-setting process and establishes meaningful and realistic performance objectives with supporting action steps; (2) effectively ranks current and projected work responsibilities and assignments by priorities; and (3) assesses consequences of current and planned programs and work assignments.

Leading

(1) Effectively and efficiently trains and develops subordinates; (2) motivates subordinates to reach high standards of quality and to stretch own performance expectations; (3) develops and leads a transactional team or task force project; and (4) willingly delegates work and responsibility, including scheduling of work for maximum efficiency.

Organizing.

(1) Manages own time, including scheduling and prioritizing of work to be done; (2) handles multiple assignments regularly and completes them in a thorough, timely manner; and (3) recognizes and uses staff support resources as needed.

Controlling

(1) Effectively monitors and controls work in progress; (2) implements administration performance standards and takes corrective action when necessary; and (3) effectively monitors and conserves allocated expense dollars and other resources.

Interpersonal Competencies:

(1) Performance results--desires to excel and perform above standards; (2) customer contact--establishes and maintains working relationships to assure responsiveness to customer concerns and inquiries; (3) problem solving--works with others in developing relevant information, reaching best solution scenario and implementing decision reached; (4) influence management--accomplishes desired results through others over whom there is no direct control, including desirable changes in methods and procedures; (5) communicating--achieves clear understanding through effective oral and written communication, on a timely basis, with subordinates, peers, superiors, customers, and bondholders; (6) sensitivity--recognizes the needs, feelings, and expectations of others and manages the relationships to assure productive results; (7) professional image--presents a positive professional image, including oral and written communication and personal appearance, to customers and contacts.

In conjunction with the use of the position profile, it makes a great deal of sense to have in place also a fairly detailed articulation of the expected standards of performance for the position.

This guideline enables managers to determine, monitor, and evaluate what the expected results or outcome of the training program. It also provides the individual administrator and officer with full understanding of the expected standards of performance upon which he/she will be reviewed and appraised (as discussed in chapter 22).

The organization determines these standards according to the work to be done, the relationship among the people in the process, the organization's policies and procedures, and the level of service quality that the organization desires to provide its clients.

When a position's accountabilities and requirements have been defined through the position profile and performance standards, the development of a training program simply flows from a logical analysis of how and when the particular components need to be addressed. The program itself should be comprehensive in its approach and detailed in its implementation. The program's individual components depend, of course, on the results of the needs analysis from the perspective of the particular corporate trust organization and the needs of the individual. It might be useful at first to retain a consultant, experienced in designing and developing performance-based training programs. The nature and extent of the administrator's educational background, his/her previous jobs, and familiarity with the subject matter, will permit the manager to tailor the comprehensive program to the identified needs of the particular person (being in effect an "individual educational prescription").

Besides training in the technical aspects of the position, the administrator may need additional instruction and/or coaching on such seemingly basic requirements as the ability to write good business letters and memoranda, skillful verbal communication, and an understanding of basic economics, finance, and accounting.

ELEMENTS OF A SUCCESSFUL TRAINING AND DEVELOPMENT PROGRAM

For a training program to be successful, management must demonstrate its commitment to it, starting with the senior business manager who must make training a priority objective, for both the business and for each individual in the organization. Management should include training as part of regular staff meetings and also attend training sessions where possible. Effective training is not a one-shot occurrence, but an ongoing process that builds on itself. Management's continuing involvement reinforces the importance of training as a cultural imperative within the organization.

The development of a carefully considered training program is essential to achieve senior management "buy- in", as well as its acceptance by the people involved. Elements of the plan include: efficiency gains anticipated, expense reductions, error reductions, improved management control, better audits, increased sales and improved customer service.

When possible, numbers should be used to support the plan results. The training program should also be designed to support the strategic objectives of the business unit, and produce the greatest overall benefit for the expense incurred.

KEY FEATURES OF A COMPREHENSIVE TRAINING AND DEVELOPMENT PROGRAM

There are a number of ways to provide developmental training to corporate trust staff. Some organizations rely exclusively on outside conferences, workshops and schools. Others rely on in-house training delivered by either their own staff using external consultants and teachers. A third approach would be a combination of internal and external resources and uses as wide a variety as possible of the ways and means to achieve the desired results. The training should also take place over a period of time during which it is reasonable to expect the desired knowledge and skill competencies to be acquired and effectively implemented.

The components of the program could include technical classes on specific core administrative and operational topics; broader classes covering sales training, investments, document review and other advanced level topics including defaults and litigation; the bank (or division's) policies and procedures; industry updates on current events and trends; use of an administrator's "handbook" containing relevant policies, procedures, and guidelines; availability of a library of appropriate books, articles, judicial decisions, statutes, and regulations; orientation tours to other areas of the bank with which the corporate trust function interfaces; and attendance at industry-sponsored schools, seminars, and conferences.

The list of specific topics will grow quickly if input from the staff is solicited. To do that, a training coordinator should be designated to obtain feedback from all levels within the organization. Priorities can then be set to focus the developmental training on the most critical needs of the organization. A most important factor is to ensure that the coverage of any training program be flexible, and be tailored to the needs of the particular group of participants involved.

Once the program courses and content is selected and prioritized, deciding how the material will be presented and by whom is the next step. In many institutions, there are individuals who can make presentations in a specific area in which they have developed expertise. For most institutions however, it will be necessary to supplement such in-house expertise with that from external consultants and industry experts.

Any and all of these teaching vehicles or resources should be combined with the essential element of on-the-job training (OJT). In fact, it is usually much better to use an actual transactional experience with appropriate reading and coaching, on the assumption that during the OJT the manager has clear standards and objectives against which to train. It is essential that the overall training program provide (and hold the manager accountable for) extensive coaching and counseling on the application and use of knowledge and skills required of the position. "Coaching goes far beyond the short-term need to help someone learn the mechanics of preparing a budget and setting a proposal up. It is the principal means through which people learn what makes the organization tick, what it stands for, and how they can contribute to it over time."[2] As noted earlier, a comprehensive training and development program must focus on both the content and timing of the subject matter to be covered. Its implementation must be clearly tailored to the individual, as determined by his/her previous experiences, identified needs, and demonstrated abilities.

The program will grow as the years go by provided there is a commitment to providing developmental training on an ongoing and consistent basis.

Training is the right of every employee. It provides added skills and knowledge that are essential for an individual to grow and develop professionally. Good people will not stay, if they are not challenged and growing. Consistent, well-delivered training in a variety of topics is the key to motivating people to invest their future in the corporate trust business. It will continue to be the most important competitive advantage of the successful corporate trust provider.

The results of any training initiative should be measured with a data base created to keep track of the training provided, who attended, the expense involved, and most importantly, the benefits achieved. Measuring the results also supports any initiative to obtain additional resources for expanded professional development.

It is also evident that training will be a much more visible part of future audit and regulatory examinations; be included in customers' "requests for proposals"; and be considered by rating agencies and bond issuers seeking a professional level of expertise in a trustee. The successful corporate trust provider must demonstrate an ongoing effort to improve the professionalism and technical competence of its staff.

[1] The Certified Corporate Trust Specialist designation offered by the Institute of Certified Bankers is intended to "hallmark" the industry's most experienced professionals. This program should also encourage other corporate trust practitioners to increase their level of competence and technical knowledge through a program of continuing education and development.

[2] Tom Peters and Nancy Austin, *A Passion for Excellence*, 1985. New York. Random House

TWENTY TWO

PERFORMANCE PLANNING, EVALUATION AND CAREER DEVELOPMENT

The effectiveness of any business rests not only on the design of the structure and the skills of the people but also on how the system combines these elements and develops a process that motivates and rewards people to reach the desired goals.

Twenty years ago, motivating and rewarding people usually meant giving them additional responsibility, recognized on the organization chart as "upward mobility". No longer does promotion always mean upward recognition.

Because management positions today are filled with managers who may have ten to twenty years until retirement and because technology and banking consolidations continue to find efficiencies in the business, managers must convince their staffs that professional growth may be lateral expansion of knowledge and responsibility. Managers must work with their personnel staffs to develop the mindset that lateral professional growth can also earn the compensation rewards expected with increased responsibility. Although these rewards may not be in the form of merit increases, incentive pools to allow reward lateral growth and special pools to reward one time special performance efforts, must be available to foster the lateral professional growth mindset.

The discussion in the preceding chapters set the stage for our consideration of the interplay among structure, process, and people, particularly how an individual's performance, skills, and productivity can be effectively managed.[1]

Such a system, whether highly formalized or not, is derived from the business plan and the concomitant objective-setting process--a plan for what people are required to do. Using regular feedback, the organization can then determine how effectively the structure, process, and people interact to meet the organization's business strategy.

This system is universally referred to as the *employee evaluation* or *appraisal procedure*. Performance appraisal is simply the process of identifying, measuring, and developing people. A well-defined process not only evaluates current performance but also includes mechanisms to reinforce strengths and correct problems for the benefit of future performance. It should also be designed to identify high potential individuals who can be groomed for future advancement and responsibility.

The preceding chapter cited the need to identify knowledge and skills that people must possess to perform their jobs as corporate trust administrators or account officers. But the position profile alone does not convey the dynamic perspective of the job. Rather, it requires a concerted effort by both the manager and employee to understand the job required, the priorities necessary to meet tactical objectives, and the concerns of the individual for defining his or her career aspirations.

Managers and their subordinates can interact only in an environment in which the managerial philosophy and the recognition of an individual's development process are fully supportive. It is not an easy task, and yet without it, there exists no applied management of people, either in their personal development or in the providing of assistance required to enable them to effectively contribute to the desired objectives of the organization. Real people management produces a climate of trust and confidence and consequently, greater receptivity to the feedback required for continued growth.

The process of identifying job skills, training employees, and developing programs provides not only the initial understanding of the job but also the definition and communication of job-relevant behavior, competencies, and skills as reflected in the business plan. Once the organization's strategic business plan has been developed and communicated, specific annual objectives can be established. Flowing from the specific objectives statement is an identification of the tasks needed to be done. Such planning permits congruency between organization needs and individual expectations.

Planning enables us to make the most effective and economical use of manpower, equipment, facilities and money. If we identify in advance our needs for people, we can develop individuals inside an organization so that they will be ready when the opportunity for promotion appears. Planning allows subordinates to know what is required of them and to give them an opportunity to participate in the decisions that are made.

Planning in this respect is analyzing the needs of the organization and matching them to the strengths, talents, and expertise of its employees. Using a needs analysis approach, a manager identifies the specific areas in which each subordinate lacks the required knowledge and skill competencies for the job and/or does not meet the expected standards of performance. In addition such analysis should focus on the developmental opportunities that the particular administrator, supervisor, or officer needs to provide for his or her growth in the organization, including individual coaching; participation in special projects outside the individual's routine work assignments; involvement in task forces, especially those involving interaction with professionals outside the individual's own work unit; and job rotation. These are examples of lateral career growth opportunities within the individual's own organization.

A corollary to this analysis is the identification of the individuals who are evaluated as being in either the top 10 percent or the bottom 10 percent in terms of their performance and potential for advancement. This analysis is best done when the employees' competencies, performance standards, and performance results expected in a particular position are in writing. The competencies should reflect the differing expectations as dictated by level within a job family. For example, distinctions need to be made between an administrator and an account officer. This also communicates the performance expectations for the next higher level position. The manager assesses and matches these expectations against the strengths and weaknesses of his or her subordinate to find areas for development. This cannot be a unilateral effort but rather the result of understanding and agreement between the manager and subordinate.

In this analysis, both the manager and the subordinate review (1) the position profile reflecting expected performance accountabilities, technical knowledge, and skill competencies, relevant managerial competencies, and interpersonal factors; (2) the specific objectives previously established; (3) the performance standards for the position's various activities and duties; (4) the reasons that expected work results or objectives were not accomplished or not accomplished on a timely basis; and (5) what obstacles are present preventing the expected growth and development of the individual. In essence, these are also the major points of review during an appraisal meeting, a subject discussed later in this chapter.

Because this process of performance review, identification of deficiencies and opportunities, establishment of personal improvement and work objectives, and implementation of training and development efforts constitutes a complete system circle, it is in effect a continuous cycle of planning, implementation, and review. In this regard, it is quite similar to the planning process described in chapter 19.

Now that the needs analysis has been completed and the specific areas in which the individual is deficient--or in which learning and experience opportunities would enhance the individual's development and advancement--have been identified, the next logical step would be the negotiation, understanding, and the agreement between manager and subordinate about the desired results of the training effort. This objective-setting process is also effectively used in establishing the expected results of designated performance responsibilities and activities. In approaching this effort, the individual and his or her manager must know where they are going before they can expect to get there. The more clearly the end result or outcome sought, the easier it is to determine the best route, the best timing, and the best method of achieving it.

Often this process becomes so detailed and time-consuming that the participants rebel against it. They continue, however, to go through the motions (because it is expected) but produce nothing more than the same objectives year after year, or others that neither stretch the individual's talents and abilities nor provide for innovative or creative actions designed to resolve existing deficiencies or meet changing performance expectations.

In this connection, the following guidelines should be helpful in highlighting some commonly encountered difficulties:

>1. Objectives should focus only on the position's most significant aspects and the individual's major developmental needs within the context of a year's period.
>
>2. The number of objectives should be manageable, even as few as one or two, but certainly not more than five or six.
>
>3. Each objective should be articulated so that the result or outcome is verifiable at the end of a given period. The manager and the subordinate must be

able to evaluate whether the objective was achieved or to what degree it was accomplished. This does not mean that all objectives, and especially those related to personal development and improvement, must or can necessarily be quantified.

4. To the extent that the result sought to be accomplished can be quantified, it should be in terms of quantity, quality, time, or cost.

5. The objectives should be challenging, yet reasonable, and should require stretch effort for their accomplishment. Writing a "maintenance" objective reflecting no change from existing performance is simply a waste of time and effort.

6. The manager and subordinate should agree on the priorities of each objective.

7. The objectives should be stated in writing and should include the results to be accomplished, the standards or means of validating the results, the action plan or program steps necessary to meet the objective, the expected timing or schedule for each action step, and, if applicable, the cost incident to the performance of each action step.

8. The manager should ensure that the objectives are consistent with the organization's business plan and that they, at the same time, will meet the deficiencies and opportunities identified in the needs analysis.

In essence, an objective is simply an important end result that adds value to the individual and to the organization. Without an orderly and integrated development and implementation of the objective, the necessary congruence between the organization's business plan and its goals and the developmental needs of the individual may not be realized.[2] The establishment of objectives, whether directly work results-related or in the nature of a personal development need, must also include regular feedback. Employees must have an opportunity for two-way communication to discuss and review the progress they are making (or not making) in achieving the desired results. "Each individual needs to get accurate information about the difference between what he is trying to do and how well he is doing it. He needs to be able to use this information to correct or change his actions. Then, basically, he is steering himself."[3]

Although almost every manager would insist that he or she provides feedback to subordinates, it is usually on a transactional basis--the "one-minute praise" or, more likely the "one-minute chewing out." Instant evaluation of and comment on a subordinate's performance is, of course, important, desirable, and necessary, but it should not take the place of an organized, scheduled, and reasonably detailed review of an individual's overall performance results during a given period.

Basic questions that need to be answered during such a review are (1) Does the subordinate know what is supposed to be accomplished? (2) Are there obstacles beyond his or her control? (3) Does the subordinate know how to do his or her job? (4) Could the subordinate do the job if he or she possessed additional knowledge and skill competencies? (5) What support should the manager provide? and (6) Is the expected performance result or objective still viable and necessary?[4]

This review should not take place only once a year, during an annual performance appraisal meeting. Rather, the subordinate's performance and developmental efforts requires a more frequent mechanism. In many organizations the manager establishes a quarterly performance review (QPR) that provides an opportunity for the necessary two-way communications regarding subordinate's overall work performance, developmental results, identification of further needs, and review of the next quarter's action steps and expected results. Because external factors, including volume of work, external situations, and even a change in business plans may impact the individual's performance and objectives accomplishment, the QPR is a timely way to make adjustments and changes in direction, priority, and timing of the previously agreed-to expected performance results and objectives.

QPR can be a very effective means of providing the manager with an opportunity to discuss the subordinate's performance and to further reinforce his or her commitment to support that subordinate's training and development process. If, in fact, performance is not up to standards or expectations, this also provides a vehicle for getting agreement that specific problems do exist, for discussing alternative solutions, for mutually agreeing on actions to be taken to resolve the problem, and for reaching an understanding that there will be further follow-up to ensure that the agreed-upon action has been taken.

To be effective, the QPR should not be a spur-of-the-moment meeting. It should be held in a private, quiet area with sufficient time scheduled for a relaxed discussion. The manager should focus on specific performance results, with necessary supporting "data" or observations of behavior, and not on inferences or evaluations of behavior. When reviewing the accomplishment of objectives, the manager should review the progress that the individual is making in completing (or not completing) the appropriate action steps. Discussion should also be held on the results of any specific training and development programs that occurred during the preceding quarter. This meeting also permits both manager and subordinate to reevaluate the next quarter's expected performance results and to make any necessary modifications. In all of this, it should be evident that the QPR itself is an integral part of an overall developmental process.

At the completion of a business cycle, normally a year, a complete review of the subordinate's performance will take place. This annual appraisal should involve a review of all objectives, and of factors that contributed to the subordinate's meeting or not meeting the agreed upon expectations. The appraisal should include the evaluation of the subordinate's technical work performance, general performance factors, knowledge and skill competencies, completion of objectives, and a developmental plan for the ensuing year.

The annual appraisal process consists of three interrelated parts: (1) the completion of an appraisal document by the manager and the completion of the same form by the subordinate; (2) an appraisal meeting, similar to a QPR, in which the manager reviews both documents with the subordinate, focusing on the major differences between the evaluation and the self-assessment, as well as the demonstrated strengths and weaknesses of the subordinate; and (3) establishment of a developmental plan for the ensuing year, based on an understanding of and agreement regarding the needs of the subordinate and the organization.

Although the form of any appraisal document varies widely from institution to institution, and even within an institution, the essential elements (or competencies) of the position, the necessary knowledge and skill competencies, the expected standards of performance, and the accomplishment of agreed-upon objectives are included.

---

[1] Although chapter 21 covered account administrators and officers, most of the discussion in this chapter is equally applicable to operations supervisors and officers.

[2] For additional discussion on this topic see Drucker, *Management*, ch. 34 ("Management by Objectives and Self-Control")

[3] Gordon Lippitt, *Organization Renewal*, 78 (1969).

[4] See Ferdinand F. Fournies, *Coaching for Improved Work Performance*, 107-133 (1978)

TWENTY THREE

ACQUISITIONS AND DIVESTITURES

Authors' Note: Although this topic is mainly of interest to senior corporate trust managers, it also is important that professionals in the business line understand the factors that enter into such decisions. In addition, knowledge of the extensive implementation process that results from such a decision will enable the corporate trust professional to add value to such process.

Understanding the factors and considerations in the decision to purchase or sell a corporate trust business, and its implementation, has become vitally important. The past fifteen years have witnessed a major consolidation in the corporate trust industry, at levels never seen before. Much of this results from either the purchase of one institution by another, or the merger of two institutions to form a new banking institution. In addition, perhaps 40% of the remaining consolidations result from the sale of the corporate trust function to another bank.

It is expected that the era of consolidations in the entire securities and information processing industry, including corporate trust, will continue as banks, which now prefer to be known as financial service organizations ("FSO"), drive to realign themselves for the 21st century. The result will be a small group of FSOs that are global players involved in all aspects of providing securities and information processing services to both institutional and retail clients in many countries. Other FSOs will offer tailored services in a specific geographic market or will deliver specialized services. The latter will not devote substantial resources to development of products, but will be basically distribution vehicles. They can be expected to form strategic alliances with major FSOs for product research and development, support and perhaps even capitalization. Their strength will lie in delivering personalized and/or specialized services to a selected group of buyers, in a regional or local market

In this changing environment for trust and information processing services, FSOs will evaluate their business to determine if they should expand the business, or divest it. Among the questions asked, will be: What is the FSO's strategic direction and how will it allocate its resources? If it includes these types of services, then the issue is whether it can dramatically grow the corporate trust function through new and repeat business from existing customers, or only through acquisitions.

Management will question current and projected revenue components, its expense profile (both direct and indirect) and its profitability in terms of return on equity, and its efficiency index (which is the reciprocal of its profit margin). In addition to determining the need for additional technology resources, this evaluation will include the FSO's current corporate trust market share position versus its current and projected competition in regard to the products offered, and the markets served. Executive management's decision will be based on an understanding of the dynamics of the business, a careful evaluation of the potential revenues, and the relevant direct, indirect and allocated expenses. For many FSOs the quality and extent of ongoing relationships with its customers also will be an important factor in the evaluation.

If a decision is made to grow the business through acquisition, then two scenarios must be considered: (1) the purchase of an "in-market" corporate trust organization, capable of being merged into the existing organization structure; and/or (2) the purchase of such an organization outside the FSO's current geographical area. This is commonly referred to as a *strategic positioning move*, designed to establish an instant regional presence.

In the first scenario, the FSO buys an existing book of business and a known revenue stream. It is not likely to result in the significant hiring of additional staff, unless there is a major increase in number or accounts and activity volume. Rather, this move is designed to enlarge the revenue stream while spreading the expense over a larger account base. It may also have the effect (real or client perceived) of denying a competitor from entry into the FSO's regional area.

In the latter case, even though the operations activities will be consolidated into the FSO's existing processing facilities, it is likely that the FSO will maintain the seller's administration facility, particularly if local presence is necessary for it to maintain and expand the business. By expanding its franchise into a new geographical area, the acquiring institution will be able to leverage its existing product line, and its sales and marketing efforts.

Management's decision to sell its corporate trust business may be driven by current economic considerations, such as an unacceptable profit margin, a lower than acceptable return on equity, or simply an insufficient revenue stream even with an acceptable profit margin. Longer range considerations will include the necessity to invest in technology without perceived significant payback, no real growth potential without major acquisitions, or simply a decision that the use of the FSO's resources will yield greater benefits from other lines of business. In attempting to reach an "unbiased" decision of whether to grow or sell the business, management will need to evaluate the desirability of retaining a financial advisor or management consultant.

THE PLANNING AND PROCESS OF BUYING

Once the strategic decision has been made to grow through acquisition, management should develop a list of potential targets which meet its pre-determined standards for credit quality, fiduciary and operations controls, and payback and profitability levels. In practice, most acquisitions have been, and will probably continue to be, opportunistic and reactive to a book of business being put up for sale.

If the seller has decided on a "private sale", it will approach the potential acquirer on an informal basis (after the latter has signed a confidentiality agreement) to evaluate whether there is a real level of interest. If however, the seller has decided to open it up to competitive bidding, it will contact those institutions which it believes would be interested. Either way, it is also possible that the seller may retain an advisor or third party intermediary to assist in this process.

After signing a confidentiality agreement, potential buyers will receive an "offering memorandum" (described later in the chapter). Following an evaluation of this information, a potential buyer will determine whether it is sufficiently interested to submit a non-binding indication of interest. This is not a formal bid, but rather enables the seller to determine if that prospective buyer's level of interest i.e. price and conditions, warrants further consideration.

Whether the transaction is a private sale, or a bidding situation, the prospective buyer will submit its due diligence questionnaire to the seller. This document is an extensive series of questions designed to supplement the information in the offering memorandum, and elicit full disclosure of the book of business, including its products, markets, controls, and systems. In addition, detailed activity levels and volumes will be requested, as well the components of the business's revenue stream and direct expense data. Very often, the potential buyer will request biographical data on the seller's senior officers, as well as its organization and staffing levels. This information will give an indication of the potential staffing levels which the buyer may need. A potential buyer also reviews personnel expense.

The next stage in the process is for the potential buyer to conduct its due diligence review. This is a critical part of its evaluation effort as it enables the buyer to visit the seller's facility and to examine samples of actual account files, audit reports, policy and procedure manuals, minutes of the corporate trust committee, and to review the status of all defaulted accounts and pending litigation. In addition, the potential buyer will visit the operations area, including its records rooms and certificate inventory vault, its security holder relations section, and its processing sections. In addition, it will want to review the seller's systems capabilities as well as the hardware configuration. From the buyer's perspective, the more it can see, and the more information it has, the more informed its bid will be and the less likely there will be unpleasant surprises later on.

The buyer must prepare carefully for this review, including plans to visit the seller's corporate trust facilities if other than at the main office. A specific action plan must be developed for designated employees to review specific areas, including a representative sample of different type accounts, acceptance criteria, regulatory and audit reports, defaulted accounts and litigation. In addition, documents evidencing acceptance criteria, covenant compliance (i.e. the tickers), fee processing, collateral processing, funds movement and investments, securities processing and escheatment should be carefully examined. Checklists are recommended for help in later evaluating what was seen during the due diligence review.

The last step for the buyer is to put together a carefully worded bid, that includes the total price to be paid for the business, and whether it is all cash, or cash and other value. The timing of the payment is also spelled out; normally most of the purchase price is paid at the sale closing, with an additional payment made some months later depending on the retention of the accounts and associated revenue stream. The buyer may not wish to purchase accounts which it perceives carry extraordinary liability or did not fit its business profile, without special indemnification. In any event, the names of such accounts should be disclosed prior to closing the sale. In addition, the bid may contain some commitment with regard to the retention of the staff and, if applicable, the maintenance of facilities in selected locations. The document may also comment how the buyer plans to make the transition and conversion of accounts. This is a critical document for the buyer, as it is its formal offer to buy the business with any conditions being spelled out.

THE PLANNING AND PROCESS OF SELLING

If a decision is made to sell the business, a thorough set of plans must be developed so that the process results in the highest price possible being paid for the business, with the least interruption to the clients in the administration of the accounts, and the highest possible retention of both staff and clients.

At the outset, management must collect all the necessary data to be included in an offering memorandum. It is this initial document which is used to educate the prospective buyer with the basic information about the book of business. A typical book will contain the following sections:

> 1. An *executive summary*, containing an overview of the business, key investment considerations and the seller's reasons for selling the business.

2. A *business description*, including: an organization overview; the administrative/sales organization; administrative systems; operations organization and operational systems.

3. A *book of business* with, account data by office location, capacity and product type; maturity schedule projections; new business and account termination history for reasons other than redemption or maturity.

4. The *operational performance*, covering processing capability and volumes by selected categories; and processing quality.

5. The *financial performance* covering, three years of revenue, expense, and operating contribution; average daily cash and demand deposit account balances; and, as appropriate, fees and other revenue by location and product.

Collecting these data can be difficult if they are not readily available. All the available data should be presented in a clear, concise and easily understandable format. The seller should view this document as a marketing piece, perhaps the most important one it will produce, for it can result in either exciting a prospective buyer, or conversely, dampening its enthusiasm for the business, all of which will be reflected in the subsequent bid.

Another critical component of the sale process is developing an extensive internal and external communications plan. This document must be carefully tailored to the FSO's organization, and to the hierarchy of the corporate trust department's clients. Both components must address: the initial announcement of the decision to sell, the announcement of the winning bidder, and the announcement of the closing date for the sale (i.e. the date of the business' legal transfer).

The internal component should carefully orchestrate both the timing and delivery mechanism of each of the three announcements. It is usual to brief the directors and executive management of the FSO just prior to each of the announcements being made to the corporate trust staff. It is desirable to make these announcements to the corporate trust staff in a group meeting. If there are staff members in other locations, they can be tied in by using, as appropriate, video or telephone conferencing facilities. Afterward, a general announcement is usually distributed to the rest of the FSO's business and support units.

The plan for making the external announcement should take into account the necessity of making personal calls on key clients, and either personal calls on or telephone calls to other clients and financial intermediaries. Coordination with the commercial bankers for joint relationships is important. The value of personal visits by the account officers/administrators on their key accounts should not be underestimated. Experience has shown that such contacts are one of the most important factors in retaining the client's business. In addition, a written press announcement should also be prepared for the news media, with all inquiries from the media being directed to a designated spokesperson.

A plan should be drawn up with the personnel department to provide special support for the staff, and to encourage them to remain, at least until the closing date. To encourage them, the FSO may implement a cash retention award, distributing a bonus based on the value of the accounts transferred at the closing or the price paid for the business, and offering an enhanced severance program for those employees who are either not offered jobs within the FSO or are not hired by the buyer.

Before scheduling the due diligence reviews, the accounts should be "scrubbed". That is, all open account compliance items should be reviewed and resolved, the account files and documents should be reviewed, any out-of-proof conditions or open audit items should be resolved. This process should also help in the review of a sample group of accounts by the potential buyers. During the due diligence reviews, the seller should ensure that all the necessary documents and files are made available to the prospective buyers. To avoid any unnecessary interruptions to the staff, it is highly recommended that all such files and documents be assembled in a separate room away from the area where the seller's staff is located. One or two senior officers from the seller's management team should always be present and available to answer any questions and to assist the buyers in obtaining necessary data. It is also recommended that the potential buyers do not have any access to either the seller's working area, or to the members of the staff except through identified senior contacts.

Following the completion of the due diligence reviews, each prospective buyer will submit a binding bid to the seller, as discussed earlier. Seller's management will review all the bids and evaluate both the financial component, (i.e. the total price offered and the timing of the payments), and the non-financial considerations, such as the retention of existing staff, the transition/conversion process, and their perception of client retention. Although the price is clearly the most important factor, seller's management must be "comfortable with the deal".

Once an offer is accepted, then the arduous task of negotiating a definitive purchase contract begins. To facilitate the negotiations, the seller may require a bidder to submit a proposed purchase contract with its bid. In addition, there will need to be executed a servicing agreement to cover the transition period between the closing date and the date when the accounts are legally transferred. Although the systems can be converted, and the handover of the account files and documents can occur at or just prior to the closing, the legal transfer of the accounts may take in excess of a year to complete. Most states have no legal mechanism to automatically transfer the accounts as a matter of law. Some indentures or agreements, however, do provide for the automatic succession of the trustee appointment if the trustee consolidates with, merges or converts into, or transfers all or substantially all of its corporate trust business to another FSO. Agency agreements and an overwhelming majority of trust agreements require that a tripartite agreement be executed to effect the transfer. This tripartite agreement is signed by the principal (in the case of an agency relationship) or the obligor (in the case of a trust agreement), and by both the resigning agent or trustee and the successor agent or trustee.

Often overlooked by FSOs considering a divestiture of their corporate trust business is the need to maintain a small staff of professionals for at least a year (and often longer than that) following the closing. The post-sale professional staff will provide oversight and maintain control over the FSOs potential liability, while assisting the buyer to become familiar with its new book of business. In addition to executing tripartite agreements over many months, there will be a significant number of questions from the buyer's staff with regard to pre-closing data, records and documents which may not have transferred. Obligors will continue to call for several months as will financial intermediaries and brokers. No matter how many notices have been sent to the security holders, there will be a constant and ongoing stream of calls coming in, likely to last for at least twelve months.

III

REFERENCE MATERIAL

THE TRUST INDENTURE ACT OF 1939
AS AMENDED BY
THE TRUST INDENTURE REFORM ACT OF 1990

CONTENTS

SECTION

301	Short Title	494
302	Necessity for Regulation	494
303	Definitions	496
304	Exempted Securities and Transactions	499
305	Securities Required to Be Registered Under Securities Act	502
306	Securities Not Registered Under Securities Act	505
307	Qualification of Indentures Covering Securities Not Required to Be Registered	506
308	Integration of Procedure with Securities Act and Other Acts	507
309	Effective Time of Qualification	508
310	Eligibility and Disqualification of Trustee	509
311	Preferential Collection of Claims Against Obligor	518
312	Bondholders' Lists	523
313	Reports by Indenture Trustee	525
314	Reports by Obligor; Evidence of Compliance With Indenture Provisions	527
315	Duties and Responsibility of the Trustee	533
316	Directions and Waivers by Bondholders; Prohibition of Impairment of Holder's Right To Payment	536
317	Special Powers of Trustee; Duties of Paying Agents	537
318	Effect of Prescribed Indenture Provisions	53
319	Rules, Regulations, and Orders	539
320	Hearings by Commission	540

321	Special Powers of Commission	540
322	Court Review of Orders; Jurisdiction of Offenses and Suits	542
323	Liability for Misleading Statements	543
324	Unlawful Representations	544
325	Penalties	544
326	Effect on Existing Law	545
327	Contrary Stipulations Void	545
328	Separability of Provisions	545

Sec. 301   Short Title

This subchapter may be cited as the "Trust Indenture Act of 1939."

Sec. 302   Necessity for Regulation

(a) Upon the basis of facts disclosed by the reports of the Securities and Exchange Commission made to the Congress pursuant to section 211 of the Securities Exchange Act of 1934 and otherwise disclosed and ascertained, it is hereby declared that the national public interest and the interest of investors in notes, bonds, debentures, evidences of indebtedness, and certificates of interest or participation therein, which are offered to the public, are adversely affected--

>(1) when the obligor fails to provide a trustee to protect and enforce the rights and to represent the interests of such investors, notwithstanding the fact that (A) individual action by such investors for the purpose of protecting and enforcing their rights is rendered impracticable by reason of the disproportionate expense of taking such action, and (B) concerted action by such investors in their common interest through representatives of their own selection is impeded by reason of the wide dispersion of such investors through many States, and by reason of the fact that information as to the names and addresses of such investors generally is not available to such investors;

(2) when the trustee does not have adequate rights and powers, or adequate duties and responsibilities, in connection with matters relating to the protection and enforcement of the rights of such investors; when, notwithstanding the obstacles to concerted action by such investors, and the general and reasonable assumption by such investors that the trustee is under an affirmative duty to take action for the protection and enforcement of their rights, trust indentures (A) generally provide that the trustee shall be under no duty to take any such action, even in the event of default, unless it receives notice of default, demand for action, and indemnity, from the holders of substantial percentages of the securities outstanding thereunder, and (B) generally relieve the trustee from liability even for its own negligent action or failure to act;

(3) when the trustee does not have resources commensurate with its responsibilities, or has any relationship to or connection with the obligor or any underwriter of any securities of the obligor, or holds, beneficially or otherwise, any interest in the obligor or any such underwriter, which relationship, connection, or interest involves a material conflict with the interest of such investors;

(4) when the obligor is not obligated to furnish to the trustee under the indenture and to such investors adequate current information as to its financial condition, and as to the performance of its obligations with respect to the securities outstanding under such indenture; or when the communication of such information to such investors is impeded by the fact that information as to the names and addresses of such investors generally is not available to the trustee and to such investors;

(5) when the indenture contains provisions which are misleading or deceptive, or when full and fair disclosure is not made to prospective investors of the effect of important indenture provisions; or

(6) when, by reason of the fact that trust indentures are commonly prepared by the obligor or underwriter in advance of the public offering of the securities to be issued thereunder, such investors are unable to participate in the preparation thereof, and, by reason of their lack of understanding of the situation, such investor would in any event be unable to procure the correction of the defects enumerated in this subsection.

(b) Practices of the character above enumerated have existed to such an extent that, unless regulated, the public offering of notes, bonds, debentures, evidences of indebtedness, and certificates of interest or participation therein, by the use of means and instruments of transportation and communication in interstate commerce and of the mails, is injurious to the capital markets, to investors, and to the general public; and it is hereby declared to be the policy of this subchapter, in accordance with which policy all the provisions of this subchapter shall be interpreted, to meet the problems and eliminate the practices, enumerated in this section, connected with such public offerings.

Sec. 303   Definitions

When used in this subchapter, unless the context otherwise requires--

>(1) Any term defined in section 2 of the Securities Act of 1933 and not otherwise defined in this section shall have the meaning assigned to such term in such section 2.

>(2) The terms "sale," "sell," "offer to sell," "offer for sale," and "offer" shall include all transactions included in such terms as provided in paragraph (3) of section 2 of the Securities Act of 1933, except that an offer or sale of a certificate of interest or participation shall be deemed an offer or sale of the security or securities in which such certificate evidences an interest or participation if and only if such certificate gives the holder thereof the right to convert the same into such security or securities.

>(3) The term "prospectus" shall have the meaning assigned to such term in paragraph (10) of section 2 of the Securities Act of 1933, except that in the case of securities which are not registered under the Securities Act of 1933, such term shall not include any communication (A) if it is proved that prior to or at the same time with such communication a written statement if any required by section 306 was sent or given to the persons to whom the communication was made, or (B) if such communication states from whom such statement may be obtained (if such statement is required by rules or regulations under paragraphs (1) or (2) of subsection (b) of section 306)

and, in addition, does no more than identify the security, state the price thereof, state by whom orders will be executed and contain such other information as the Commission, by rules or regulations deemed necessary or appropriate in the public interest or for the protection of investors, and subject to such terms and conditions as may be prescribed therein, may permit.

(4) The term "underwriter" means any person who has purchased from an issuer with a view to, or offers or sells for an issuer in connection with, the distribution of any security, or participates or has a direct or indirect participation in any such undertaking, or participates or has a participation in the direct or indirect underwriting of any such undertaking; but such term shall not include a person whose interest is limited to a commission from an underwriter or dealer not in excess of the usual and customary distributors' or sellers' commission.

(5) The term "director" means any director of a corporation or any individual performing similar functions with respect to any organization whether incorporated or unincorporated.

(6) The term "executive officer" means the president, every vice president, every trust officer, the cashier, the secretary, and the treasurer of a corporation, and any individual customarily performing similar functions with respect to any organization whether incorporated or unincorporated, but shall not include the chairman of the board of directors.

(7) The term "indenture" means any mortgage, deed of trust, trust or other indenture, or similar instrument or agreement (including any supplement or amendment to any of the foregoing), under which securities are outstanding or are to be issued, whether or not any property, real or personal, is, or is to be, pledged, mortgaged, assigned, or conveyed thereunder.

(8) The term "application" or "application for qualification" means the application provided for in section 305 or section 307 and includes any amendment thereto and any report, document, or memorandum accompanying such application or incorporated therein by reference.

(9) The term "indenture to be qualified" means (A) the indenture under which there has been or is to be issued a security in respect of which a particular registration statement has been filed, or (B) the indenture in respect of which a particular application has been filed.

(10) The term "indenture trustee" means each trustee under the indenture to be qualified, and each successor trustee.

(11) The term "indenture security" means any security issued or issuable under the indenture to be qualified.

(12) The term "obligor," when used with respect to any such indenture security, means every person (including a guarantor) who is liable thereon, and, if such security is a certificate of interest or participation, such term means also every person (including a guarantor) who is liable upon the security or securities in which such certificate evidences an interest or participation; but such terms shall not include the trustee under an indenture under which certificates of interest or participation, equipment trust certificates, or like securities are outstanding.

(13) The term "paying agent," when used with respect to any such indenture security, means any person authorized by an obligor therein (A) to pay the principal of or interest on such security on behalf of such obligor, or (B) if such security is a certificate of interest or participation, equipment trust certificate, or like security, to make such payment on behalf of the trustee.

(14) The term "State" means any State of the United States.

(15) The term "Commission" means the Securities and Exchange Commission.

(16) The term "voting security" means any security presently entitling the owner or holder thereof to vote in the direction or management of the affairs of a person, or any security issued under or pursuant to any trust, agreement, or arrangement whereby a trustee or trustees or agent or agents for the owner or holder of such security are presently entitled to vote in the direction or management of the affairs of a person; and a specified percentage of the voting securities of a person means such amount of the outstanding voting securities of such person as entitles the holder or holders thereof to cast such specified percentage of the aggregate votes which the holders of all the outstanding voting securities of such person are entitled to cast in the direction or management of the affairs of such person.

(17) The terms "Securities Act of 1933," "Securities Exchange Act of 1934," and "Public Utility Holding Company Act of 1935" shall be deemed to refer, to or after August 3, 1939.

(18) The term "Bankruptcy Act" means the Bankruptcy Act or Title 11.

Sec. 304 Exempted Securities and Transactions

(a) The provisions of this subchapter shall not apply to any of the following securities:

(1) any security other than (A) a note, bond, debenture, or evidence of indebtedness, whether or not secured, or (B) a certificate of interest or participation in any such note, bond, debenture, or evidence of indebtedness, or (C) a temporary certificate for, or guarantee of, any such note, bond, debenture, evidence of indebtedness, or certificate;

(2) any certificate of interest or participation in two or more securities having substantially different rights and privileges, or a temporary certificate for any such certificate.

(3) left blank

(4) (A) any security exempted from the provisions of the Securities Act of 1933, by paragraphs (2) to (8), or (11) of subsection 3(a) thereof; (B) any security exempted from the provisions of the Securities Act of 1933, as amended, by paragraph (2) of subsection 3(a) thereof, as amended by section 401 of the Employment Security Amendments of 1970;

(5) any security issued under a mortgage indenture as to which a contract of insurance under the National Housing Act is in effect; and any such security shall be deemed to be exempt from the provisions of the Securities Act of 1933 to the same extent as though such security were specifically enumerated in section 3(a)(2) of such Act;

(6) any note, bond, debenture, or evidence of indebtedness issued or guaranteed by a foreign government or by a subdivision, department, municipality, agency, or instrumentality thereof;

(7) any guarantee of any security which is exempted by this subsection;

(8) any security which has been or is to be issued otherwise than under an indenture, but this exemption shall not be applied within a period of twelve consecutive months to an aggregate principal amount of securities of the same issuer greater than the figure stated in section 3(b) of the Securities Act of 1933

limiting exemptions thereunder, or such lesser amount as the Commission may establish by its rules and regulations;

(9) any security which has been or is to be issued under an indenture which limits the aggregate principal amount of securities at any time outstanding thereunder to $10,000,000, or such lesser amount as the Commission may establish by its rules and regulations, but this exemption shall not be applied within a period of thirty-six consecutive months to more than $10,000,000 aggregate principal amount of securities of the same issuer, or such lesser amount as the Commission may establish by its rules and regulations; or

(10) any security issued under a mortgage or trust deed indenture as to which a contract of insurance under title XI of the National Housing Act is in effect; and any such security shall be deemed to be exempt from the provisions of the Securities Act of 1933 to the same extent as though such security were specifically enumerated in section 3(a)(2), as amended, of the Securities Act of 1933.

In computing the aggregate principal amount of securities to which the exemptions provided by paragraphs (8) and (9) of this subsection may be applied, securities to which the provisions of sections 305 and 306 would not have applied, irrespective of the provisions of those paragraphs, shall be disregarded.

(b) The provisions of sections 305 and 306 shall not apply (1) to any of the transactions exempted from the provisions of section 5 of the Securities Act of 1933 by section 4 thereof or (2) to any transaction which would be so exempted but for the last sentence of paragraph (11) of section 2 of such Act.

(c) The Commission shall, on application by the issuer and after opportunity for hearing thereon, by order exempt from any one or more provisions of this subchapter any security issued or proposed to be issued under any indenture under which, at the time such application is filed, securities referred to in paragraph (3) of subsection (a) of this section are outstanding or on January 1, 1959, such securities were outstanding, if and to the extent that the Commission finds that compliance with such provision or provisions, through the execution of a supplemental indenture or otherwise--

> (1) would require, by reason of the provisions of such indenture, or the provisions of any other indenture or agreement made prior to August 3, 1939, or the provisions of any applicable law, the consent of the holders of securities outstanding under any such indenture or agreement; or
>
> (2) would impose an undue burden on this issuer, having due regard to the public interest and the interests of investors.

(d) The Commission may, by rules or regulations upon its own motion, or by order on application by an interested person, exempt conditionally or unconditionally any person, registration statement, indenture, security or transaction, or any class or classes of persons, registration statements, indentures, securities, or transactions, from any one or more of the provisions of this title, if and to the extent that such exemption is necessary or appropriate in the public interest and consistent with the protection of investors and the purposes fairly intended by this title. The Commission shall by rules and regulations determine the procedures under which an exemption under this subsection shall be granted, and may, in its sole discretion, decline to entertain any application for an order of exemption under this subsection.

(e) The Commission may from time to time by its rules and regulations, and subject to such terms and conditions as may be prescribed herein, add to the securities exempted as provided in this section any class of securities issued by a small business investment company under the Small Business Investment Act of 1958 if it finds, having regard to the purposes of that Act, that the enforcement of this subchapter with respect to such securities is not necessary in the public interest and for the protection of investors.

Sec. 305 Securities Required to Be Registered Under Securities Act

(a) Subject to the provisions of section 304, a registration statement relating to a security shall include the following information and documents, as though such inclusion were required by the provisions of section 7 of the Securities Act of 1933--

> (1) such information and documents as the Commission may by rules and regulations prescribe in order to enable the Commission to determine whether any person designated to act as trustee under the indenture under which such security has been or is to be issued is eligible to act as such under subsection (a) of section 310; and

> (2) an analysis of any provisions of such indenture with respect to (A) the definition of what shall constitute a default under such indenture, and the withholding of notice to the indenture security holders of any such default, (B) the authentication and delivery of the indenture securities and the application of the proceeds thereof, (C) the release or the release and substitution of any property subject to the lien of the indenture, (D) the satisfaction and discharge of the indenture, and (E) the evidence required to be furnished by the obligor upon the indenture securities to the trustee as to compliance with the conditions and covenants provided for in such indenture.

The information and documents required by paragraph (1) of this subsection with respect to the person designated to act as indenture trustee shall be contained in a separate part of such registration statement, which part shall be signed by such person. Such part of the registration statement shall be deemed to be a document filed pursuant to this subchapter, and the provisions of sections 11, 12, 17, and 24 of the Securities Act of 1933 shall not apply to statements therein or omissions therefrom.

(b) (1) Except as may be permitted by paragraph (2) of this subsection, the Commission shall issue an order prior to the effective date of registration refusing to permit such a registration statement to be come effective, if it finds that--

(A) the security to which such registration statement relates has not been or is not to be issued under an indenture; or

(B) any person designated as trustee under such indenture is not eligible to act as such under subsection (a) of section 310; but no such order shall be issued except after notice and opportunity for hearing within the periods and in the manner required with respect to refusal orders pursuant to section 8(b) of the Securities Act of 1933. If and when the Commission deems that the objections on which such order was based have been met, the Commission shall enter an order rescinding such refusal order, and the registration shall become effective at the time provided in section 8(a) of the Securities Act of 1933, or upon the date of such rescission, whichever shall be the later.

(2) In the case of securities registered under the Securities Act of 1933, which securities are eligible to be issued, offered, or sold on a delayed basis by or on behalf of the registrant, the Commission shall not be required to issue an order pursuant to paragraph (1) of subsection (b) of section 305 for failure to designate a trustee eligible to act under subsection (a) of section 310 if, in accordance with such rules and regulations as may be prescribed by the Commission, the issuer of such securities files an application for the purpose of determining such trustee's eligibility under subsection (a) of section 310. The Commission shall issue an order prior to the effective date of such application refusing to permit the application to become effective, if it finds that any person designated as trustee under such indenture is not eligible to act as such under subsection (a) of section 310, but no order shall be issued except after notice and opportunity for hearing within the periods and in the manner required with respect to refusal orders pursuant to section 8(b) of the Securities Act of 1933. If after notice and opportunity for hearing the Commission issues an order under this provision, the obligor shall within 5 calendar days appoint a trustee meeting the requirements of subsection (a) of section 310. No such appointment shall be effective and such refusal order shall not be rescinded by the Commission

until a person eligible to act as trustee under subsection (a) of section 310 has been appointed. If no order is issued, an application filed pursuant to this paragraph shall be effective the tenth day after filing thereof or such earlier date as the Commission may determine, having due regard to the adequacy of information provided therein, the public interest, and the protection of investors.

(c) A prospectus relating to any such security shall include to the extent the Commission may prescribe by rules and regulations as necessary and appropriate in the public interest or for the protection of investors, as though such inclusion were required by section 10 of the Securities Act of 1933, a written statement containing the analysis set forth in the registration statement, of any indenture provisions with respect to the matters specified in paragraph (2) of subsection (a) of this section, together with a supplementary analysis, prepared by the Commission, of such provisions and of the effect thereof, if, in the opinion of the Commission, the inclusion of such supplementary analysis is necessary or appropriate in the public interest or for the protection of investors, and the Commission so declares by order after notice and, if demanded by the issuer, opportunity for hearing thereon. Such order shall be entered prior to the effective date of registration, except that if opportunity for hearing thereon is demanded by the issuer such order shall be entered within a reasonable time after such opportunity for hearing.

(d) The provisions of sections 11, 12, 17, and 24 of the Securities Act of 1933, and the provisions of sections 323 and 325, shall not apply to statements in or omissions from any analysis required under the provisions of this section or sections 306 or 307 of this title.

Sec. 306 Securities Not Registered Under Securities Act

(a) In the case of any security which is not registered under the Securities Act of 1933 and to which this subsection is applicable notwithstanding the provisions of section 304, unless such security has been or is to be issued under an indenture and an application for qualification is effective as to such indenture, it shall be unlawful for any person, directly or indirectly--

> (1) to make use of any means or instruments of transportation or communication in interstate commerce or of the mails to sell such security through the use or medium of any prospectus or otherwise; or

> (2) to carry or cause to be carried through the mails or in interstate commerce, by any means or instruments of transportation, any such security for the purpose of sale or for delivery after sale:

(b) In the case of any security which is not registered under the Securities Act of 1933, but which has been or is to be issued under an indenture as to which an application for qualification is effective, it shall be unlawful for any person, directly or indirectly--

> (1) to make use of any means or instruments of transportation or communication in interstate commerce or of the mails to carry or transmit any prospectus relating to any such security, unless such prospectus, to the extent the Commission may prescribe by rules and regulations as necessary and appropriate in the public interest or for the protection of investors, includes or is accompanied by a written statement that contains the information specified in subsection (c) of section 305; or

> (2) to carry or to cause to be carried through the mails or in interstate commerce any such security for the purpose of sale or for delivery after sale, unless, to the extent the Commission may prescribe by rules and regulations as necessary or appropriate in the public interest or for the protection of investors, accompanied or preceded by a written statement that contains the information specified in subsection (c) of section 305.

(c) It shall be unlawful for any person, directly or indirectly, to make use of any means or instruments of transportation or communication in interstate commerce or of the mails to offer to sell through the use or medium of any prospectus or otherwise any security which is not registered under the Securities Act of 1933 and to which this subsection is applicable notwithstanding the provisions of section 304, unless such security has been or is to be issued under an indenture and an application for qualification has been filed as to such indenture, or while the application is the subject of a refusal order or stop order or (prior to qualification) any public proceeding or examination under section 307(c).

Sec. 307 Qualification of Indentures Covering Securities Not Required to Be Registered

(a) In the case of any security which is not required to be registered under the Securities Act of 1933 and to which subsection (a) of section 306 is applicable notwithstanding the provisions of section 304, an application for qualification of the indenture under which such security has been or is to be issued shall be filed with the Commission by the issuer of such security. Each such application shall be in such form, and shall be signed in such manner, as the Commission may by rules and regulations prescribe as necessary or appropriate in the public interest or for the protection of investors. Each such application shall include the information and documents required by subsection (a) of section 305. The information and documents required by paragraph (1) of such subsection with respect to the person designated to act as indenture trustee shall be contained in a separate part of such application, which part shall be signed by such person. Each such application shall also include such of the other information and documents which would be required to be filed in order to register such indenture security under the Securities Act of 1933 as the Commission may by rules and regulations prescribe as necessary or appropriate in the public interest or for the protection of investors. An application may be withdrawn by the applicant at any time prior to the effective date thereof. Subject to the provisions of section 321, the information and documents contained in or filed with any application shall be made available to the public under such regulations as the Commission may prescribe, and copies thereof, photostatic or otherwise, shall be furnished to every applicant therefor at such reasonable charge as the Commission may prescribe.

(b) The filing with the Commission of an application, or of an amendment to an application, shall be deemed to have taken place upon the receipt thereof by the Commission, but, in the case of an application, only if it is accompanied or preceded by payment to the Commission of a filing fee in the amount of $100, such payment to be made in cash or by United States postal money order or certified or bank check, or in such other medium of payment as the Commission may authorize by rule and regulation.

(c) The provisions of section 8 of the Securities Act of 1933 and the provisions of subsection (b) of section 305 shall apply with respect to every such application, as though such application were a registration statement filed pursuant to the provisions of the Securities Act of 1933.

Sec. 308 Integration of Procedure with Securities Act and Other Acts

(a) The Commission, by such rules and regulations or orders as it deems necessary or appropriate in the public interest or for the protection of investors, shall authorize the filing of any information or documents required to be filed with the Commission under this subchapter, or under the Securities Act of 1933, the Securities Exchange Act of 1934, or the Public Utility Holding Company Act of 1935, by incorporating by reference any information or documents on file with the Commission under this subchapter or under any such Act.

(b) The Commission, by such rules and regulations or orders as it deems necessary or appropriate in the public interest or for the protection of investors, shall provide for the consolidation of applications, reports, and proceedings under this subchapter with registration statements, applications, reports, and proceedings under the Securities Act of 1933, the Securities Exchange Act of 1934, or the Public Utility Holding Company Act of 1935.

Sec. 309   Effective Time of Qualification

(a) The indenture under which a security has been or is to be issued shall be deemed to have been qualified under this subchapter--

> (1) when registration becomes effective as to such security; or
>
> (2) when an application for the qualification of such indenture becomes effective, pursuant to section 307.

(b) After qualification has become effective as to the indenture under which a security has been or is to be issued, no stop order shall be issued pursuant to section 8(d) of the Securities Act 1933, suspending the effectiveness of the registration statement relating to such security or of the application for qualification of such indenture, except on one or more of the grounds specified in section 8 of the Securities Act of 1933, or the failure of the issuer to file an application as provided for by section 305(b)(2).

(c) The making, amendment, or rescission of a rule, regulation, or order under the provisions of this subchapter (except to the extent authorized by subsection (a) of section 314 with respect to rules and regulations prescribed pursuant to such subsection) shall not affect the qualification, form, or interpretation of any indenture as to which qualification became effective prior to the making, amendment, or rescission of such rule, regulation, or order.

(d) No trustee under an indenture which has been qualified under this subchapter shall be subject to any liability because of any failure of such indenture to comply with any of the provisions of this subchapter, or any rule, regulation, or order thereunder.

(e) Nothing in this subchapter shall be construed as empowering the Commission to conduct an investigation or other proceeding for the purpose of determining whether the provisions of an indenture which has been qualified under this subchapter are being complied with, or to enforce such provisions.

Sec. 310 Eligibility and Disqualification of Trustee

(a) (1) There shall at all times be one or more trustees under every indenture qualified or to be qualified pursuant to this title, at least one of whom shall at all times be a corporation organized and doing business under the laws of the United States or of any State or Territory or of the District of Columbia or a corporation or other person permitted to act as trustee by the Commission (referred to in this subchapter as the institutional trustee), which (A) is authorized under such laws to exercise corporate trust powers, and (B) is subject to supervision or examination by Federal, State, Territorial, or District of Columbia authority. The Commission may, pursuant to such rules and regulations as it may prescribe, or by order on application, permit a corporation or other person organized and doing business under the laws of a foreign government to act as sole trustee under an indenture qualified or to be qualified pursuant to this title, if such corporation or other person (i) is authorized under such laws to exercise corporate trust powers, and (ii) is subject to supervision or examination by authority of such foreign government or a political subdivision thereof substantially equivalent to supervision or examination applicable to United States institutional trustees. In prescribing such rules and regulation or making such order, the Commission shall consider whether under such laws, a United States institutional trustee is eligible to act as sole trustee under an indenture relating to securities sold within the jurisdiction of such foreign government.

(2) Such institution shall have at all times a combined capital and surplus of a specified minimum amount, which shall not be less than $150,000. If such institutional trustee publishes reports of condition at least annually, pursuant to law or to the requirements of said supervising or examining authority, the indenture may provide that, for the purposes of this paragraph, the combined capital and surplus of such trustee shall be deemed to be its combined capital and surplus as set forth in its most recent report of condition so published.

(3) If the indenture to be qualified requires or permits the appointment of one or more co-trustees in addition to such institutional trustee, the rights, powers, duties, and obligations conferred or imposed upon the trustees or any of them shall be conferred or imposed upon and exercised or performed by such institutional trustee, or such institutional trustee and such co-trustees jointly, except to the extent that under any law of any jurisdiction in which any particular act or acts are to be performed, such institutional trustee shall be incompetent or unqualified to perform such act or acts, in which event such rights, powers, duties, and obligations shall be exercised and performed by such co-trustees.

(4) In the case of certificates of interest or participation, the indenture trustee or trustees shall have the legal power to exercise all of the rights, powers, and privileges of a holder of the security or securities in which such certificates evidence an interest or participation.

(5) No obligor upon the indenture securities or person directly or indirectly controlling, controlled by, or

under common control with such obligor shall serve as trustee upon such indenture securities.

(b) If any indenture trustee has or shall acquire any conflicting interest as hereinafter defined--

> (i) then, within 90 days after ascertaining that it has such conflicting interest, and if the default (as defined in the next sentence) to which such conflicting interest relates has not been cured or duly waived or otherwise eliminated before the end of such 90-day period, such trustee shall either eliminate such conflicting interest or, except as otherwise provided below in this subsection, resign, and the obligor upon the indenture securities shall take prompt steps to have a successor appointed in the manner provided in the indenture;
>
> (ii) in the event that such trustee shall fail to comply with the provisions of clause (i) of this subsection, such trustee shall, within 10 days after the expiration of such 90-day period, transmit notice of such failure to the indenture security holders in the manner and to the extent provided in subsection (c) of section 313; and
>
> (iii) subject to the provisions of subsection (e) of section 315, unless such trustee's duty to resign is stayed as provided below in this subsection, any security holder who has been a bona fide holder of indenture securities for at least six months may, on behalf of himself and all others similarly situated, petition any court of competent jurisdiction for the removal of such trustee, and the appointment of a successor, if such trustee fails, after written request thereof by such holder to comply with the provisions of clause (i) of this subsection.

For the purposes of this subsection, an indenture trustee shall be deemed to have a conflicting interest if the indenture securities are in default (as such term is defined in such indenture, but exclusive of any period of grace or requirement of notice) and--

(1) such trustee is trustee under another indenture under which any other securities, or certificates of interest or participation in any other securities, of an obligor upon the indenture securities are outstanding or is trustee for more than one outstanding series of securities, as hereafter defined, under a single indenture of an obligor, unless—

(A) the indenture securities are collateral trust notes under which the only collateral consists of securities issued under such other indenture

(B) such other indenture is a collateral trust indenture under which the only collateral consists of indenture securities, or

(C) such obligor has no substantial unmortgaged assets and is engaged primarily in the business of owning, or of owning and developing and/or operating, real estate, and the indenture to be qualified and such other indenture are secured by wholly separate and distinct parcels of real estate:

Provided, That the indenture to be qualified shall automatically be deemed (unless it is expressly provided therein that such provision is excluded) to contain a provision excluding from the operation of this paragraph other series under such indenture, and any other indenture or indentures under which other securities, or certificates of interest or participation in other securities, of such an obligor are outstanding, if—

(i) the indenture to be qualified and any such other indenture or indentures (and all series of securities issuable thereunder) are wholly unsecured and rank equally, and such other indenture or indentures (and such series) are specifically described in the indenture to be qualified or are thereafter qualified under this title, unless the Commission shall have found and declared by order pursuant to subsection (b) of section 305 or subsection (c) of section 307 that differences exist between the provisions of the indenture (or such series) to be qualified and the provisions of such other indenture or indentures (or such series) which are so likely to involve a material conflict of interest as to make it necessary in the public interest or for the protection of investors to disqualify such trustee from acting as such under one of such indentures, or

(ii) the issuer shall have sustained the burden of proving, on application to the Commission and after opportunity for hearing thereon, that trusteeship under the indenture to be qualified and such other indenture or under more than one outstanding series under a single indenture is not so likely to involve a material conflict of interest as to make it necessary in the public interest or for the protection of investors to disqualify such trustee from acting as such under one of such indentures or with respect to such series;

(2) such trustee or any of its directors or executive officers is an underwriter for an obligor upon the indenture securities;

(3) such trustee directly or indirectly controls or is directly or indirectly controlled by or is under direct or indirect common control with an underwriter for an obligor upon the indenture securities;

(4) such trustee or any of its directors or executive officers is a director, officer, partner, employee, appointee, or representative of an obligor upon the indenture securities, or of an underwriter (other than the trustee itself) for such an obligor who is currently engaged in the business of underwriting, except that—

> (A) one individual may be a director and/or an executive officer of the trustee and a director and/or an executive officer of such obligor, but may not be at the same time an executive officer of both the trustee and of such obligor,
>
> (B) if and so long as the number of directors of the trustee in office is more than nine, one additional individual may be a director and/or an executive officer of the trustee and a director of such obligor, and
>
> (C) such trustee may be designated by any such obligor or by any underwriter for any such obligor, to act in the capacity of transfer agent, registrar, custodian, paying agent, fiscal agent, escrow agent, or depositary, or in any other similar capacity, or, subject to the provisions of paragraph (1) of this subsection, to act as trustee, whether under an indenture or otherwise;

(5) 10 per centum or more of the voting securities of such trustee is beneficially owned either by an obligor upon the indenture securities or by any director, partner or executive officer thereof, or 20 per centum or more of such voting securities is beneficially owned, collectively by any two or more of such persons; or 10 per centum or more of the voting securities of such trustee is beneficially owned either by an underwriter for any such obligor or by any

director, partner, or executive officer thereof, or is beneficially owned, collectively, by any two or more such persons;

(6) such trustee is the beneficial owner of, or holds as collateral security for an obligation which is in default as hereinafter defined—

(A) 5 per centum or more of the voting securities, or 10 per centum or more of any other class of security, of an obligor upon the indenture securities, not including indenture securities and securities issued under any other indenture under which such trustee is also trustee, or

(B) 10 per centum or more of any class of security of an underwriter for any such obligor;

(7) such trustee is the beneficial owner of, or holds as collateral security for an obligation which is in default as hereinafter defined, 5 per centum or more of the voting securities of any person who, to the knowledge of the trustee, owns 10 per centum or more of the voting securities of, or controls directly or indirectly or is under direct or indirect common control with, an obligor upon the indenture securities;

(8) such trustee is the beneficial owner of, or holds as collateral security for an obligation which is in default as hereinafter defined, 10 per centum or more of any class of security of any person who, to the knowledge of the trustee, owns 50 per centum or more of the voting securities of an obligor upon the indenture securities;

(9) such trustee owns, on the date of default upon the indenture securities (as such term is defined in such indenture by exclusive of any period of grace or requirement of notice) or any anniversary of such default while such default upon the indenture securities remains outstanding, in the capacity of executor, administrator, testamentary or inter vivos trustee, guardian, committee or conservator, or in any

other similar capacity, an aggregate of 25 per centum or more of the voting securities, or of any class of security, of any person, the beneficial ownership of a specified percentage of which would have constituted a conflicting interest under paragraph (6), (7), or (8) of this subsection. As to any such securities of which the indenture trustee acquired ownership through becoming executor, administrator or testamentary trustee of an estate which include them, the provisions of the preceding sentence shall not apply for a period of not more than 2 years from the date of such acquisition, to the extent that such securities included in such estate do not exceed 25 per centum of such voting securities or 25 per centum of any such class of security. Promptly after the dates of any such default upon the indenture securities and annually in each succeeding year that the indenture securities remain in default the trustee shall make a check of its holding of such securities in any of the above-mentioned capacities as of such dates. If the obligor upon the indenture securities fails to make payment in full of principal or interest under such indenture when and as the same becomes due and payable, and such failure continues for 30 days thereafter, the trustee shall make a prompt check of its holdings of such securities in any of the above-mentioned capacities as of the date of the expiration of such 30-day period, and after such date, notwithstanding the foregoing provisions of this paragraph, all such securities so held by the trustee, with sole or joint control over such securities vested in it, shall be considered as though beneficially owned by such trustee, for the purposes of paragraphs (6), (7), and (8) of this subsection; or

(10) except under the circumstances described in paragraphs (1), (3), (4), (5) or (6) of section 311(b) of this title, the trustee shall be or shall become a creditor of the obligor.

For purposes of paragraph (1) of this subsection, and of section 316(a) of this title, the term "series of securities" or "series" means a series, class or group of securities issuable under an indenture pursuant to whose terms holders of one such series may vote to direct the indenture trustee, or otherwise take action pursuant to a vote of such holders, separately from holders of another such series: Provided, That "series of securities" or "series" shall not include any series of securities issuable under an indenture if all such series rank equally and are wholly unsecured.

The specification of percentages in paragraphs (5) to (9), inclusive, of this subsection shall not be construed as indicating that the ownership of such percentages of the securities of a person is or is not necessary or sufficient to constitute direct or indirect control for the purposes of paragraph (3) or (7) of this subsection.

For purposes of paragraphs (6), (7), (8), and (9) of this subsection--

> (A) the terms "security" and "securities" shall include only such securities as are generally known as corporate securities, but shall not include any note or other evidence of indebtedness issued to evidence an obligation to repay moneys lent to a person by one or more banks, trust companies, or banking firms, or any certificate of interest or participation in any such note or evidence of indebtedness;

> (B) an obligation shall be deemed to be in default when a default in payment of principal shall have continued for thirty days or more, and shall not have been cured; and

> (C) the indenture trustee shall not be deemed the owner or holder of (i) any security which it holds as collateral security (as trustee or otherwise) for any obligation which is not in default as above defined, or (ii) any security which it holds as collateral security under the indenture to be qualified, irrespective of any default thereunder, or (iii) any security which it holds as agent for collection, or as custodian, escrow agent or depositary, or in any similar representative capacity.

For the purposes of this subsection, the term underwriter" when used with reference to an obligor upon the indenture securities means every person who, within one year prior to the time as of which the determination is made, was an underwriter of any security of such obligor outstanding at the time of the determination. Except is the case of a default in the payment of the principal of or interest on any indenture security, or in the payment of any sinking or purchase fund installment, the indenture trustee shall not be required to resign as provided by this subsection if such trustee shall have sustained the burden of proving, on application to the Commission and after opportunity for hearing thereon, that--

> (i) the default under the indenture may be cured or waived during a reasonable period and under the procedures described in such application, and

> (ii) a stay of the trustee's duty to resign will not be inconsistent with the interests of holders of the indenture securities. The filing of such an application shall automatically stay the performance of the duty to resign until the Commission orders otherwise.

Any resignation of an indenture trustee shall become effective only upon the appointment of a successor trustee and such successor's acceptance of such an appointment.

(c) The Public Utility Holding Company Act of 1935 shall not be held to establish or authorize the establishment of any standards regarding the eligibility and qualifications of any trustee or prospective trustee under an indenture to be qualified under this subchapter, or regarding the provisions to be included in any such indenture with respect to the eligibility and qualifications of the trustee thereunder, other than those established by the provisions of this section.

Sec. 311 Preferential Collection of Claims Against Obligor

(a) Subject to the provisions of subsection (b) of this section, if the indenture trustee shall be, or shall become, a creditor, directly or indirectly, secured or unsecured, of an obligor upon the indenture securities, within three months prior to a default as defined in the last paragraph of this subsection, or subsequent to such a default, then, unless and until such default shall be cured, such trustee shall set apart and hold in a special account for the benefit of the trustee individually and the indenture security holders--

> (1) an amount equal to any and all reductions in the amount due and owing upon any claim as such creditor in respect of principal or interest, effected after the beginning of such three months' period and valid as against such obligor and its other creditors, except any such reduction resulting from the receipt or disposition of any property described in paragraph (2) of this subsection, or from the exercise of any right of setoff which the trustee could have exercised if a petition in bankruptcy had been filed by or against such obligor upon the date of such default; and

> (2) all property received in respect of any claims such creditor, either as security therefor, or in satisfaction or composition thereof, or otherwise, after the beginning of such three months' period, or an amount equal to the proceeds of any such property, if disposed of, subject, however, to the rights, if any, of such obligor and its other creditors in such property or such proceeds.

Nothing herein contained shall affect the right of the indenture trustee--

> (A) to retain for its own account (i) payments made on account of any such claim by any person (other than such obligor) who is liable thereon, and (ii) the proceeds of the bona fide sale of any such claim by the trustee to a third person, and (iii) distributions made in cash, securities, or other property in respect of claims filed against such obligor in bankruptcy or receivership or in proceedings for reorganization pursuant to the Bankruptcy Act or applicable State law;

(B) to realize, for its own account, upon any property held by it as security for any such claim, if such property was so held prior to the beginning of such three months' period;

(C) to realize, for its own account, but only to the extent of the claim hereinafter mentioned, upon any property held by it as security for any such claim, if such claim was created after the beginning of such three months' period and such property was received as security therefor simultaneously with the creation thereof, and if the trustee shall sustain the burden of proving that at the time such property was so received the trustee had no reasonable cause to believe that a default as defined in the last paragraph of this subsection would occur within three months; or

(D) to receive payment on any claim referred to in paragraph (B) or (C) of this subsection, against the release of any property held as security for such claim as provided in said paragraph (B) or (C), as the case may be, to the extent of the fair value of such property.

For the purposes of paragraphs (B), (C), and (D) of this subsection, property substituted after the beginning of such three months' period for property held as security at the time of such substitution shall, to the extent of the fair value of the property released, have the same status as the property released, and, to the extent that any claim referred to in any of such paragraphs is created in renewal of or in substitution for or for the purpose of repaying or refunding any preexisting claim of the indenture trustee as such creditor, such claim shall have the same status as such preexisting claim.

If the trustee shall be required to account, the funds and property held in such special account and the proceeds thereof shall be apportioned between the trustee and the indenture security holders in such manner that the trustee and the indenture security holders realize, as a result of payments from such special account and payments of dividends on claims filed against such obligor in bankruptcy or receivership or in proceedings for reorganization pursuant to the Bankruptcy Act or applicable State law, the same percentage of their respective claims, figured before crediting to the claim of the trustee anything on account of the receipt by it from such obligor of the funds and property in such special account and before crediting to the respective claims of the trustee and the indenture security holders dividends on claims filed against such obligor in bankruptcy or receivership or in proceedings for reorganization pursuant to the Bankruptcy Act or applicable State law, but after crediting thereon receipts on account of the indebtedness represented by their respective claims from all sources other than from such dividends and from the funds and property so held in such special account. As used in this paragraph, with respect to any claim, the term "dividends" shall include any distribution with respect to such claim, in bankruptcy or receivership or in proceedings for reorganization pursuant to the Bankruptcy Act or applicable State law, whether such distribution is made in cash, securities, or other property, but shall not include any such distribution with respect to the secured portion, if any, of such claim. The court in which such bankruptcy, receivership, or proceedings for reorganization is pending shall have jurisdiction (i) to apportion between the indenture trustee and the indenture security holders, in accordance with the provisions of this paragraph, the funds and property held in such special account and the proceeds thereof, or (ii) in lieu of such apportionment, in whole or in part, to give to the provisions of this paragraph due consideration in determining the fairness of the distributions to be made to the indenture trustee and the indenture security holders with respect to their respective claims, in which event it shall not be necessary to liquidate or to appraise the value of any securities or other property held in such special account or as security for any such claim, or to make a specific allocation of such distributions as between the secured and unsecured portions of such claims, or otherwise to apply the provisions of this paragraph as a mathematical formula.

Any indenture trustee who has resigned or been removed after the beginning of such three months' period shall be subject to the provisions of this subsection as though such resignation or removal had not occurred. Any indenture trustee who has resigned or been removed prior the beginning of such three months' period shall be subject to the provisions of this subsection if and only if the following conditions exist--

> (i) the receipt of property or reduction of claim which would have given rise to the obligation to account, if such indenture trustee had continued as trustee, occurred after the beginning of such three months' period; and (ii) such receipt of property or reduction of claim occurred within three months after such resignation or removal.

As used in this subsection, the term "default" means any failure to make payment in full of principal or interest, when and as the same becomes due and payable, under any indenture which has been qualified under this subchapter, and under which the indenture trustee is trustee and the person of whom the indenture trustee is directly or indirectly a creditor is an obligor; and the term "indenture security holder" means all holders of securities outstanding under any such indenture under which any such default exists.

In any case commenced under the Bankruptcy Act of July 1, 1898, or any amendment thereto enacted prior to November 6, 1978, all references to periods of three months shall be deemed to be references to periods of four months.

(b) The indenture to be qualified shall automatically be deemed (unless it is expressly provided therein that any such provision is excluded) to contain provisions excluding from the operation of subsection (a) of this section a creditor relationship arising from--

> (1) the ownership or acquisition of securities issued under any indenture, or any security or securities having a maturity of one year or more at the time of acquisition by the indenture trustee;
>
> (2) advances authorized by a receivership or bankruptcy court

of competent jurisdiction, or by the indenture, for the purpose of preserving the property subject to the lien of the indenture or of discharging tax liens or other prior liens or encumbrances on the trust estate, if notice of such advance and of the circumstances surrounding the making thereof is given to the indenture security holders, at the time and in the manner provided in the indenture;

(3) disbursements made in the ordinary course of business in the capacity of trustee under an indenture, transfer agent, registrar, custodian, paying agent, fiscal agent or depositary, or other similar capacity;

(4) an indebtedness created as a result of services rendered or premises rented; or an indebtedness created as a result of goods or securities sold in a cash transaction as defined in the indenture;

(5) the ownership of stock or of other securities of a corporation organized under the provisions of section 25(a) of the Federal Reserve Act, as amended, which is directly or indirectly a creditor of an obligor upon the indenture securities; or

(6) the acquisition, ownership, acceptance, or negotiation of any drafts, bills of exchange, acceptances, or obligations which fall within the classification of self-liquidating paper as defined in the indenture.

(c) In the exercise by the Commission of any jurisdiction under the Public Utility Holding Company Act of 1935 regarding the issue or sale, by any registered holding company or a subsidiary company thereof, of any security of such issuer or seller or of any other company to a person which is trustee under an indenture or indentures of such issuer or seller or other company, or of a subsidiary or associate company or affiliate of such issuer or seller or other company (whether or not such indenture or indentures are qualified or to be qualified under this subchapter), the fact that such trustee will thereby become a creditor, directly or indirectly, of any of the foregoing shall not constitute a ground for the Commission taking adverse action with respect to any application or declaration, or limiting the scope of any rule or regulation which would otherwise permit such transaction to take effect; but in any case in which such trustee is trustee under an indenture of the company of which it will thereby become a creditor, or of any subsidiary company thereof, this subsection shall not prevent the Commission from requiring (if such requirement would be authorized under the provisions of the Public Utility Holding Company Act of 1935) that such trustee, as such, shall effectively and irrevocably agree in writing, for the benefit of the holders from time to time of the securities from time to time outstanding under such indenture, to be bound by the provisions of this section, subsection (c) of section 315, and, in case of default (as such term is defined in such indenture), subsection (d) of section 315, as fully as though such provisions were included in such indenture. For the purposes of this subsection the terms "registered holding company," "subsidiary company," "associate company," and "affiliate" shall have the respective meanings assigned to such terms in section 2(a) of the Public Utility Holding Company Act of 1935.

Sec. 312 Bondholders' Lists

(a) Each obligor upon the indenture securities shall furnish or cause to be furnished to the institutional trustee thereunder at stated intervals of not more than six months, and at such other times as such trustee may request in writing, all information in the possession or control of such obligor, or of any of its paying agents, as to the names and addresses of the indenture security holders, and requiring such trustee to preserve, in as current a form as is reasonably practicable, all such information so furnished to it or received by it in the capacity of paying agent.

(b) Within five business days after the receipt by the institutional trustee of a written application by any three or more indenture security holders stating that the applicants desire to communicate with other indenture security holders with respect to their rights under such indenture or under the indenture securities, and accompanied by a copy of the form of proxy or other communication which such applicants propose to transmit, and by reasonable proof that each such applicant has owned an indenture security for a period of at least six months preceding the date of such application, such institutional trustee shall, at its election, either--

>(1) afford to such applicants access to all information so furnished to or received by such trustee; or
>
>(2) inform such applicants as to the approximate number of indenture security holders according to the most recent information so furnished to or received by such trustee, and as to the approximate cost of mailing to such indenture security holders the form of proxy or other communication, if any, specified in such application.

If such trustee shall elect not to afford to such applicants access to such information, such trustee shall, upon the written request of such applicants, mail to all such indenture security holders copies of the form of proxy or other communication which is specified in such request, with reasonable promptness after a tender to such trustee of the material to be mailed and of payment, or provision for the payment, of the reasonable expenses of such mailing, unless within five days after such tender, such trustee shall mail to such applicants, and file with the Commission together with a copy of the material to be mailed, a written statement to the effect that, in the opinion of such trustee, such mailing would be contrary to the best interests of the indenture security holders or would be in violation of applicable law. Such written statement shall specify the basis of such opinion. After opportunity for hearing upon the objections specified in the written statement so filed, the Commission may, and if demanded by such trustee or by such applicants shall, enter an order either sustaining one or more of such objections or refusing to sustain any of them. If the Commission shall enter an order refusing to sustain any of such objections, or if, after the entry of an order sustaining one or more of such objections, the Commission shall find, after notice and opportunity for hearing, that all objections so sustained have been met, and shall enter an order so declaring, such trustee shall mail copies of such material to all such indenture security holders with reasonable promptness after the entry of such order and the renewal of such tender.

(c) The disclosure of any such information as to the names and addresses of the indenture security holders in accordance with the provisions of this section, regardless of the source from which such information was derived, shall not be deemed to be a violation of any existing law, or of any law hereafter enacted which does not specifically refer to this section, nor shall such trustee be held accountable by reason of mailing any material pursuant to a request made under subsection (b) of this section.

Sec. 313   Reports by Indenture Trustee

(a) The indenture trustee shall transmit to the indenture security holders as hereinafter provided, at stated intervals of not more than 12 months, a brief report with respect to any of the following events which may have occurred within the previous 12 months (but if no such event has occurred within such period no report need be transmitted):

>(1) any change to its eligibility and its qualifications under section 310;
>
>(2) the creation of or any material change to a relationship specified in paragraph (1) through (10) of section 310(b);
>
>(3) the character and amount of any advances made by it, as indenture trustee, which remain unpaid on the date of such report, and for the reimbursement of which it claims or may claim a lien or charge, prior to that of the indenture securities, on the trust estate or on property or funds held or collected by it as such trustee, if such advances so remaining unpaid aggregate more than one-half of 1 per centum of the principal amount of the indenture securities outstanding on such date;
>
>*(4) any change to the amount, interest rate, and maturity date of all other indebtedness owing to it in its individual capacity, on the date of such report, by the obligor upon the indenture securities, with a brief description of any property held as collateral security therefor, except an indebtedness based upon a

creditor relationship arising in any manner described in paragraphs (2), (3), (4), or (6) of subsection (b) of section 311;

(5) any change to the property and funds physically in its possession as indenture trustee on the date of such report;

(6) any release, or release and substitution, of property subject to the lien of the indenture (and the consideration therefor, if any) which it has not previously reported;

(7) any additional issue of indenture securities which it has not previously reported; and

(8) any action taken by it in the performance of its duties under the indenture which it has not previously reported and which in its opinion materially affects the indenture securities or the trust estate, except action in respect of a default, notice of which has been or is to be withheld by it in accordance with an indenture provision authorized by subsection (b) of section 315.

* See Footnote 4, Chapter 13, *supra*

(b) The indenture trustee shall transmit to the indenture security holders as hereinafter provided, within the times hereinafter specified, a brief report with respect to--

(1) the release, or release and substitution, of property subject to the lien of the indenture (and the consideration therefor, if any) unless the fair value of such property, as set forth in the certificate or opinion required by paragraph (1) of subsection (d) of section 314, is less than 10 per centum of the principal amount of indenture securities outstanding at the time of such release, or such release and substitution, such report to be so transmitted within 90 days after such time; and

(2) the character and amount of any advances made by it as such since the date of the last report transmitted pursuant to the provisions of subsection (a) of this section (or if no such report has yet been so transmitted, since the date of execution of the indenture), for the reimbursement of which it claims or may claim a lien or charge, prior to that of the indenture securities, on the trust estate or on property or funds held or collected by it as such trustee, and which it has not previously reported pursuant to this paragraph, if such advances remaining unpaid at any time aggregate more than 10 per centum of the principal amount of indenture securities outstanding at such time, such report to be so transmitted within 90 days after such time.

(c) Reports pursuant to this section shall be transmitted by mail--

> (1) to all registered holders of indenture securities, as the names and addresses of such holders appear upon the registration books of the obligor upon the indenture securities;
>
> (2) to such holders of indenture securities as have, within the two years preceding such transmission, filed their names and addresses with the indenture trustee for that purpose; and
>
> (3) except in the case of reports pursuant to subsection (b) of this section, to all holders of indenture securities whose names and addresses have been furnished to or received by the indenture trustee pursuant to section 312.

(d) A copy of each such report shall, at the time of such transmission to indenture security holders, be filed with each stock exchange upon which the indenture securities are listed, and also with the Commission.

Sec. 314 Reports by Obligor; Evidence of Compliance with Indenture Provisions

(a) Each person who, as set forth in the registration statement or application, is or is to be an obligor upon the indenture securities covered thereby shall--

> (1) file with the indenture trustee copies of the annual reports and of the information, documents, and other reports (or copies of such portions of any of the foregoing as the Commission may by rules and regulations prescribe) which such obligor is required to file with the Commission pursuant to section 13 or 15(d) of the Securities Exchange Act of 1934; or, if the obligor is not required to file information, documents, or reports pursuant to either of such sections, then to file with the indenture trustee and the Commission, in accordance with rules and regulations prescribed by the Commission, such of the supplementary and periodic information, documents, and reports which may be required pursuant to section 13 of the Securities Exchange Act of 1934, in respect of a security listed and registered on a national securities exchange as may be prescribed in such rules and regulations;

(2) file with the indenture trustee and the Commission, in accordance with rules and regulations prescribed by the Commission, such additional information, documents, and reports with respect to compliance by such obligor with the conditions and covenants provided for in the indenture, as may be required by such rules and regulations, including, in the case of annual reports, if required by such rules and regulations, certificates of opinions of independent public accountants, conforming to the requirements of subsection (e) of this section, as to compliance with conditions or covenants, compliance with which is subject to verification by accountants, but no such certificate or opinion shall be required as to any matter specified in clauses (A), (B), or (C) of paragraph (3) of subsection (c) of this section;

(3) transmit to the holders of the indenture securities upon which such person is an obligor, in the manner and to the extent provided in subsection (c) of section 313, such summaries of any information, documents, and reports required to be filed by such obligor pursuant to the provisions of paragraph (1) or (2) of this subsection as may be required by rules and regulations prescribed by the Commission; and

(4) furnish to the indenture trustee, not less often than annually, a brief certificate from the principal executive officer, principal financial officer or principal accounting officer as to his or her knowledge of such obligor's compliance with all conditions and covenants under the indenture. For purposes of this paragraph, such compliance shall be determined without regard to any period of grace or requirement of notice provided under the indenture.

The rules and regulations prescribed under this subsection shall be such as are necessary or appropriate in the public interest or for the protection of investors, having due regard to the types of indentures, and the nature of the business of the class of obligors affected thereby, and the amount of indenture securities outstanding under such indentures, and, in the case of any such rules and regulations prescribed after the indentures to which they apply have been qualified under this subchapter, the additional expense, if any, of complying with such rules and regulations. Such rules and regulations may be prescribed either before or after qualification becomes effective as to any such indenture.

(b) If the indenture to be qualified is or is to be secured by the mortgage or pledge of property, the obligor upon the indenture securities shall furnish to the indenture trustee--

> (1) promptly after the execution and delivery of the indenture, an opinion of counsel (who may be of counsel for such obligor) either stating that in the opinion of such counsel the indenture has been properly recorded and filed so as to make effective the lien intended to be created thereby, and reciting the details of such action, or stating that in the opinion of such counsel no such action is necessary to make such lien effective; and

> (2) at least annually after the execution and delivery of the indenture, an opinion of counsel (who may be of counsel for such obligor) either stating that in the opinion of such counsel such action has been taken with respect to the recording, filing, re-recording, and refiling of the indenture as is necessary to maintain the lien of such indenture, and reciting the details of such action, or stating that in the opinion of such counsel no such action is necessary to maintain such lien.

(c) The obligor upon the indenture securities shall furnish to the indenture trustee evidence of compliance with the conditions precedent, if any, provided for in the indenture (including any covenants compliance with which constitutes a condition precedent) which relate to the authentication and delivery of the indenture securities, to the release or the release and substitution of property subject to the lien of the indenture, to the satisfaction and discharge of the indenture, or to any other action to be taken by the indenture trustee at the request or upon the application of such obligor. Such evidence shall consist of the following:

> (1) certificates or opinions made by officers of such obligor who are specified in the indenture, stating that such conditions precedent have been complied with;

(2) an opinion of counsel (who may be of counsel for such obligor) stating that in his opinion such conditions precedent have been complied with; and

(3) in the case of conditions precedent compliance with which is subject to verification by accountants (such as conditions with respect to the preservation of specified ratios, the amount of net quick assets, negative-pledge clauses, and other similar specific conditions), a certificate or opinion of an accountant, who, in the case of any such conditions precedent to the authentication and delivery of indenture securities, and not otherwise, shall be an independent public accountant selected or approved by the indenture trustee in the exercise of reasonable care, if the aggregate principal amount of such indenture securities and of other indenture securities authenticated and delivered since the commencement of the then current calendar year (other than those with respect to which a certificate or opinion of an accountant is not required, or with respect to which a certificate or opinion of an independent public accountant has previously been furnished) is 10 per centum or more of the aggregate amount of the indenture securities at the time outstanding; but no certificate or opinion need be made by any person other than an officer or employee of such obligor who is specified in the indenture, as to (A) dates or periods not covered by annual reports required to be filed by the obligor, in the case of conditions precedent which depend upon a state of facts as of a date or dates or for a period or periods different from that required to be covered by such annual reports, or (B) the amount and value of property additions, except as provided in paragraph (3) of subsection (d) of this section, or (C) the adequacy of depreciation, maintenance, or repairs.

(d) If the indenture to be qualified is or is to be secured by the mortgage or pledge of property or securities, the obligor upon the indenture securities shall furnish to the indenture trustee a certificate or opinion of an engineer, appraiser, or other expert as to the fair value--

(1) of any property or securities to be released from the lien of the indenture, which certificate or opinion shall state that in the opinion of the person making the same the proposed release will not impair the security under such indenture in contravention of the provisions thereof, and requiring further that such certificate or opinion shall be made by an independent engineer, appraiser, or other expert, if the fair value of such property or securities

and of all other property or securities released since the commencement of the then current calendar year, as set forth in the certificates or opinions required by this paragraph, is 10 per centum or more of the aggregate principal amount of the indenture securities at the time outstanding; but such a certificate or opinion of an independent engineer, appraiser, or other expert shall not be required in the case of any release of property or securities, if the fair value thereof as set forth in the certificate or opinion required by this paragraph is less than $25,000 or less than 1 per centum of the aggregate principal amount of the indenture securities at the time outstanding;

(2) to such obligor of any securities (other than indenture securities and securities secured by a lien prior to the lien of the indenture upon property subject to the lien of the indenture), the deposit of which with the trustee is to be made the basis for the authentication and delivery of indenture securities, the withdrawal of cash constituting a part of the trust estate or the release of property or securities subject to the lien of the indenture, and requiring further that if the fair value to such obligor of such securities and of all other such securities made the basis of any such authentication and delivery, withdrawal, or release since the commencement of the then current calendar year, as set forth in the certificates or opinions required by this paragraph, is 10 per centum or more of the aggregate principal amount of the indenture securities at the time outstanding, such certificate or opinion shall be made by an independent engineer, appraiser, or other expert and, in the case of the authentication and delivery of indenture securities, shall cover the fair value to such obligor of all other such securities so deposited since the commencement of the current calendar year as to which a certificate or opinion of an independent engineer, appraiser, or other expert has not previously been furnished; but such a certificate of an independent engineer, appraiser, or other expert shall not be required with respect to any securities so deposited, if the fair value thereof to such obligor as set forth in the certificate or opinion required by this paragraph is less than $25,000 or less than 1 per centum of the aggregate principal amount of the indenture securities at the time outstanding; and

(3) to such obligor of any property the subjection of which to the lien of the indenture is to be made the basis for the authentication and delivery of indenture securities, the withdrawal of cash constituting a part of the trust estate, or the release of property or securities subject to the lien of the

indenture, and requiring further that if

(A) within six months prior to the date of acquisition thereof by such obligor, such property has been used or operated, by a person or persons other than such obligor, in a business similar to that in which it has been or is to be used or operate by such obligor, and

(B) the fair value to such obligor of such property as set forth in such certificate or opinion is not less than $25,000 and not less than 1 per centum of the aggregate principal amount of the indenture securities at the time outstanding, such certificate or opinion shall be made by an independent engineer, appraiser, or other expert and, in the case of the authentication and delivery of indenture securities, shall cover the fair value to the obligor of any property so used or operated which has been so subjected to the lien of the indenture since the commencement of the then current calendar year, and as to which a certificate or opinion of an independent engineer, appraiser, or other expert has not previously been furnished.

The indenture to be qualified shall automatically be deemed (unless it is expressly provided therein that any such provision is excluded) to provide that any such certificate or opinion may be made by an officer or employee of the obligor upon the indenture securities who is duly authorized to make such certificate or opinion by the obligor from time to time, except in cases in which this subsection requires that such certificate or opinion be made by an independent person. In such cases, such certificate or opinion shall be made by an independent engineer, appraiser, or other expert selected or approved by the indenture trustee in the exercise of reasonable care.

(e) Each certificate or opinion with respect to compliance with a condition or covenant provided for in the indenture (other than certificates provided pursuant to subsection (a)(4) of this section) shall include (1) a statement that the person making such certificate or opinion has read such covenant or condition; (2) a brief statement as to the nature and scope of the examination or investigation upon which the statements or opinions contained in such certificate or opinion are based; (3) a statement that, in the opinion of such person, he has made such examination or investigation as is necessary to enable him to express an informed opinion as to whether or not such covenant or condition has been complied with; and (4) a statement as to whether or not, in the opinion of such person, such condition or covenant has been complied with.

(f) Nothing in this section shall be construed either as requiring the inclusion in the indenture to be qualified of provisions that the obligor upon the indenture securities shall furnish to the indenture trustee any other evidence of compliance with the conditions and covenants provided for in the indenture than the evidence specified in this section, or as preventing the inclusion of such provision in such indenture, if the parties so agree.

Sec. 315   Duties and Responsibility of Trustee

(a) The indenture to be qualified shall automatically be deemed (unless it is expressly provided therein that any such provision is excluded) to provide that, prior to default (as such term is defined in such indenture)--

> (1) the indenture trustee shall not be liable except for the performance of such duties as are specifically set out in such indenture; and
>
> (2) the indenture trustee may conclusively rely, as to the truth of the statements and the correctness of the opinions expressed therein, in the absence of bad faith on the part of such trustee, upon certificates or opinions conforming to the requirements of the indenture;

but the indenture trustee shall examine the evidence furnished to it pursuant to section 314 to determine whether or not such evidence conforms to the requirements of the indenture.

(b) The indenture trustee shall give to the indenture security holders, in the manner and to the extent provided in subsection (c) of section 313, notice of all defaults known to the trustee, within ninety days after the occurrence thereof: *Provided,* That such indenture shall automatically be deemed (unless it is expressly provided therein that any such provision is excluded) to provide that, except in the case of default in the payment of the principal of or interest on any indenture security, or in the payment of any sinking or purchase fund installment, the trustee shall be protected in withholding such notice if and so long as the board of directors, the executive committee, or a trust committee of directors and/or responsible officers, of the trustee in good faith determine that the withholding of such notice is in the interests of the indenture security holders.

(c) The indenture trustee shall exercise in case of default (as such term is defined in such indenture) such of the rights and powers vested in it by such indenture, and to use the same degree of care and skill in their exercise, as a prudent man would exercise or use under the circumstances in the conduct of his own affairs.

(d) The indenture to be qualified shall not contain any provisions relieving the indenture trustee from liability for its own negligent action, its own negligent failure to act, or its own willful misconduct, except that--

> (1) such indenture shall automatically be deemed (unless it is expressly provided therein that any such provision is excluded) to contain the provisions authorized by paragraphs (1) and (2) of subsection (a) of this section;

> (2) such indenture shall automatically be deemed (unless it is expressly provided therein that any such provision is excluded) to contain provisions protecting the indenture trustee from liability for any error of judgment made in good faith by a responsible officer or officers of such trustee, unless it shall be proved that such trustee was negligent in ascertaining the pertinent facts; and

(3) such indenture shall automatically be deemed (unless it is expressly provided therein that any such provision is excluded) to contain provisions protecting the indenture trustee with respect to any action taken or omitted to be taken by it in good faith in accordance with the direction of the holders of not less than a majority in principal amount of the indenture securities at the time outstanding (determined as provided in subsection (a) of section 316) relating to the time, method, and place of conducting any proceeding for any remedy available to such trustee, or exercising any trust or power conferred upon such trustee, under such indenture.

(e) The indenture to be qualified shall automatically be deemed (unless it is expressly provided therein that any such provision is excluded) to contain provisions to the effect that all parties thereto, including the indenture security holders, agree that the court may in its discretion require, in any suit for the enforcement of any right or remedy under such indenture, or in any suit against the trustee for any action taken or omitted by it as trustee, the filing by any party litigant in such suit of an undertaking to pay the costs of such suit, and that such court may in its discretion assess reasonable costs, including reasonable attorney's fees, against any party litigant in such suit, having due regard to the merits and good faith of the claims or defenses made by such party litigant: *Provided,* That the provisions of this subsection shall not apply to any suit instituted by such trustee, to any suit instituted by any indenture security holder, or group of indenture security holders, holding in the aggregate more than 10 per centum in principal amount of the indenture securities outstanding, or to any suit instituted by any indenture security holder for the enforcement of the payment of the principal of or interest on any indenture security, on or after the respective due dates expressed in such indenture security.

Sec.316   Directions and Waivers by Bondholders; Prohibition of Impairment of Holder's Right to Payment

(a) The indenture to be qualified--

(1) shall automatically be deemed (unless it is expressly provided therein that any such provision is excluded) to contain provisions authorizing the holders of not less than a majority in principal amount of the indenture securities or if expressly specified in such indenture, of any series of securities at the time outstanding (A) to direct the time, method, and place of conducting any proceedings for any remedy available to such trustee, or exercising any trust or power conferred upon such trustee, under such indenture, or (B) on behalf of the holders of all such indenture securities, to consent to the waiver of any past default and its consequences; or

(2) may contain provisions authorizing the holders of not less than 75 per centum in principal amount of the indenture securities or if expressly specified in such indenture, of any series of securities at the time outstanding to consent on behalf of the holders of all such indenture securities to the postponement of any interest payment for a period not exceeding three years from its due date.

For the purposes of this subsection and paragraph (3) of subsection (d) of section 315, in determining whether the holders of the required principal amount of indenture securities have concurred in any such direction or consent, indenture securities owned by any obligor upon the indenture securities, or by any person directly or indirectly controlling or controlled by or under direct or indirect common control with any such obligor, shall be disregarded, except that for the purposes of determining whether the indenture trustee shall be protected in relying on any such direction or consent, only indenture securities which such trustee knows are so owned shall be so disregarded.

(b) Notwithstanding any other provision of the indenture to be qualified, the right of any holder of any indenture security to receive payment of the principal of and interest on such indenture security, on or after the respective due dates expressed in such indenture security, or to institute suit for the enforcement of any such payment on or after such respective dates, shall not be impaired or affected without the consent of such holder, except as to a postponement of an interest payment consented to as provided in paragraph (2) of subsection (a) of this section, and except that such indenture may contain provisions limiting or denying the right of any such holder to institute any such suit, if and to the extent that the institution or prosecution thereof or the entry of judgment therein would, under applicable law, result in the surrender, impairment, waiver, or loss of the lien of such indenture upon any property subject to such lien.

(c) The obligor upon any indenture qualified under this title may set a record date for purposes of determining the identity of indenture security holders entitled to vote or consent to any action by vote or consent authorized or permitted by subsection (a) of this section. Unless the indenture provides otherwise, such record date shall be the later of 30 days prior to the first solicitation of such consent or the date of the most recent list of holders furnished to the trustee pursuant to section 312 of this title prior to such solicitation.

Sec. 317 Special Powers of Trustee; Duties of Paying Agents

(a) The indenture trustee shall be authorized--

> (1) in the case of a default in payment of the principal of any indenture security, when and as the same shall become due and payable, or in the case of a default in payment of the interest on any such security, when and as the same shall become due and payable and the continuance of such default for such period as may be prescribed in such indenture, to recover judgment, in its own name and as trustee of an express trust, against the obligor upon the indenture securities for the whole amount of such principal and interest remaining unpaid; and
>
> (2) to file such proofs of claim and other papers or documents

as may be necessary or advisable in order to have the claims of such trustee and of the indenture security holders allowed in any judicial proceedings relative to the obligor upon the indenture securities, its creditors, or its property.

(b) Each paying agent shall hold in trust for the benefit of the indenture security holders or the indenture trustee all sums held by such paying agent for the payment of the principal of or interest on the indenture securities, and shall give to such trustee notice of any default by any obligor upon the indenture securities in the making of any such payment.

Sec. 318 Effect of Prescribed Indenture Provisions

(a) If any provision of the indenture to be qualified limits, qualifies, or conflicts with the duties imposed by operation of subsection (c) of this section, the imposed duties shall control.

(b) The indenture to be qualified may contain, in addition to provisions specifically authorized under this subchapter to be included therein, any other provisions the inclusion of which is not in contravention of any provisions of this subchapter.

(c) The provisions of sections 310 to and including 317 that impose duties on any person (including provisions automatically deemed included in an indenture unless the indenture provides that such provisions are excluded) are a part of and govern every qualified indenture, whether or not physically contained therein, shall be deemed retroactively to govern each indenture heretofore qualified, and prospectively to govern each indenture hereafter qualified under this title and shall be deemed retroactively to amend and supersede inconsistent provisions in each such indenture heretofore qualified. The foregoing provisions of this subsection shall not be deemed to effect the inclusion (by retroactive amendment or otherwise) in the text of any indenture heretofore qualified of any of the optional provisions contemplated by section 310(b)(1), 311(b), 314(d), 315(a), 315(b), 315(d), 315(e), or 316(a)(1).

Sec. 319 Rules, Regulations, and Orders

(a) The Commission shall have authority from time to time to make, issue, amend and rescind such rules and regulations and such orders as it may deem necessary or appropriate in the public interest or for the protection of investors to carry out the provisions of this subchapter, including rules and regulations defining accounting, technical, and trade terms used in this subchapter. Among other things, the Commission shall have authority, (1) by rules and regulations, to prescribe for the purposes of section 310(b) the method (to be fixed in indentures to be qualified under this subchapter) of calculating percentages of voting securities and other securities; (2) by rules and regulations, to prescribe the definitions of the terms ``cash transaction'' and ``self-liquidating paper'' which shall be included in indentures to be qualified under this subchapter, which definitions shall include such of the creditor relationships referred to in paragraphs (4) and (6) of subsection (b) of section 311 as to which the Commission determines that the application of subsection (a) of section 311 is not necessary in the public interest or for the protection of investors, having due regard for the purposes of such subsection; and (3) for the purposes of this subchapter, to prescribe the form or forms in which information required in any statement, application, report, or other document filed with the Commission shall be set forth. For the purpose of its rules or regulations the Commission may classify persons, securities, indentures, and other matters within its jurisdiction and prescribe different requirements for different classes of persons, securities, indentures, or matters.

(b) Subject to the provisions of chapter 15 of Title 44 and regulations prescribed under the authority thereof, the rules and regulations of the Commission under this subchapter shall be effective upon publication in the manner which the Commission shall prescribe, or upon such later date as may be provided in such rules and regulations.

(c) No provision of this subchapter imposing any liability shall apply to any act done or omitted in good faith in conformity with any rule, regulation, or order of the Commission, notwithstanding that such rule, regulation, or order may, after such act or omission, be amended or rescinded or be determined by judicial or other authority to be invalid for any reason.

Sec. 320   Hearings by Commission

Hearings may be public and may be held before the Commission, any member or members thereof, or any officer or officers of the Commission designated by it, and appropriate records thereof shall be kept.

Sec. 321   Special Powers of Commission

(a) For the purpose of any investigation or any other proceeding which, in the opinion of the Commission, is necessary and proper for the enforcement of this subchapter, any member of the Commission, or any officer thereof designated by it, is empowered to administer oaths and affirmations, subpoena witnesses, compel their attendance, take evidence, and require the production of any books, papers, correspondence, memoranda, contracts, agreements, or other records which the Commission deems relevant or material to the inquiry. Such attendance of witnesses and the production of any such books, papers, correspondence, memoranda, contracts, agreements, or other records may be required from any place in the United States or in any Territory at any designated place of investigation or hearing. In addition, the Commission shall have the powers with respect to investigations and hearings, and with respect to the enforcement of, and offenses and violations under, this subchapter and rules and regulations and orders prescribed under the authority thereof, provided in sections 20 and 22(b) and (c) of the Securities Act of 1933.

(b) The Treasury Department, the Comptroller of the Currency, the Board of Governors of the Federal Reserve System, the Federal Reserve Banks, and the Federal Deposit Insurance Corporation are authorized, under such conditions as they may prescribe, to make available to the Commission such reports, records, or other information as they may have available with respect to trustees or prospective trustees under indentures qualified or to be qualified under this subchapter, and to make through their examiners or other employees for the use of the Commission, examinations of such trustees or prospective trustees. Every such trustee or prospective trustee shall, as a condition precedent to qualification of such indenture, consent that reports of examinations by Federal, State, Territorial, or District authorities may be furnished by such authorities to the Commission upon request therefor.

Notwithstanding any provision of this subchapter, no report, record, or other information made available to the Commission under this subsection, no report of an examination made under this subsection for the use of the Commission, no report of an examination made of any trustee or prospective trustee by any Federal, State, Territorial, or District authority having jurisdiction to examine or supervise such trustee, no report made by any such trustee or prospective trustee to any such authority, and no correspondence between any such authority and any such trustee or prospective trustee, shall be divulged or made known or available by the Commission or any member, officer, agent, or employee thereof, to any person other than a member, officer, agent, or employee of the Commission: Provided, That the Commission may make available to the Attorney General of the United States, in confidence, any information obtained from such records, reports of examination, other reports, or correspondence, and deemed necessary by the Commission, or requested by him, for the purpose of enabling him to perform his duties under this subchapter.

(c) Any investigation of a prospective trustee, or any proceeding or requirement for the purpose of obtaining information regarding a prospective trustee, under any provision of this subchapter, shall be limited--

>(1) to determining whether such prospective trustee is qualified to act as trustee under the provisions of subsection (b) of section 310;

>(2) to requiring the inclusion in the registration statement or application of information with respect to the eligibility of such prospective trustee under paragraph (1) of subsection (a) of section 310; and

>(3) to requiring the inclusion in the registration statement or application of the most recent published report of condition of such prospective trustee, as described in paragraph (2) of subsection (a) of section 310, or, if the indenture does not contain the provision with respect to combined capital and surplus authorized by the last sentence of paragraph (2) of subsection (a) of section 310, to determining whether such prospective trustee is eligible to act as such under paragraph (2) of subsection (a) of section 310.

(d) The provisions of section 4(b) of the Securities Exchange Act of 1934 shall be applicable with respect to the power of the Commission to appoint and fix the compensation of such officers, attorneys, examiners and other experts, and such other officers and employees, as may be necessary for carrying out its functions under this subchapter.

Sec. 322   Court Review of Orders; Jurisdiction of Offenses and Suits

(a) Orders of the Commission under this subchapter (including orders pursuant to the provisions of sections 305(b) and 307(c)) shall be subject to review in the same manner, upon the same conditions, and to the same extent, as provided in section 9 of the Securities Act of 1933, with respect to orders of the Commission under such Act.

(b) Jurisdiction of offenses and violations under, and jurisdiction and venue of suits and actions brought to enforce any liability or duty created by, this subchapter, or any rules or regulations or orders prescribed under the authority thereof, shall be as provided in section 22(a) of the Securities Act of 1933.

Sec. 323 Liability for Misleading Statements

(a) Any person who shall make or cause to be made any statement in any application, report, or document filed with the Commission pursuant to any provisions of this subchapter, or any rule, regulation, or order thereunder, which statement was at the time and in the light of the circumstances under which it was made false or misleading with respect to any material fact, or who shall omit to state any material fact required to be stated therein or necessary to make the statements therein not misleading, shall be liable to any person (not knowing that such statement was false or misleading or of such omission) who, in reliance upon such statement or omission shall have purchased or sold a security issued under the indenture to which such application, report, or documents relates, for damages caused by such reliance, unless the person sued shall prove that he acted in good faith and had no knowledge that such statement was false or misleading or of such omission. A person seeking to enforce such liability may sue at law or in equity in any court of competent jurisdiction. In any such suit the court may, in its discretion, require an undertaking for the payment of the costs of such suit and assess reasonable costs, including reasonable attorneys' fees, against either party litigant, having due regard to the merits and good faith of the suit or defense. No action shall be maintained to enforce any liability created under this section unless brought within one year after the discovery of the facts constituting the cause of action and within three years after such cause of action accrued.

(b) The rights and remedies provided by this subchapter shall be in addition to any and all other rights and remedies that may exist under the Securities Act of 1933, or the Securities Exchange Act of 1934, or the Public Utility Holding Company Act of 1935, or otherwise at law or in equity; but no person permitted to maintain a suit for damages under the provisions of this subchapter shall recover, through satisfaction of judgment in one or more actions, a total amount in excess of his actual damages on account of the act complained of.

Sec. 324   Unlawful Representations

It shall be unlawful for any person in offering, selling or issuing any security to represent or imply in any manner whatsoever that any action or failure to act by the Commission in the administration of this subchapter means that the Commission has in any way passed upon the merits of, or given approval to, any trustee, indenture or security, or any transaction or transactions therein, or that any such action or failure to act with regard to any statement or report filed with or examined by the Commission pursuant to this subchapter or any rule, regulation, or order thereunder, has the effect of a finding by the Commission that such statement or report is true and accurate on its face or that it is not false or misleading.

Sec. 325   Penalties

Any person who willfully violates any provision of this subchapter or any rule, regulation, or order thereunder, or any person who willfully, in any application, report, or document filed or required to be filed under the provisions of this subchapter or any rule, regulation, or order thereunder, makes any untrue statement of a material fact or omits to state any material fact required to be stated therein or necessary to make the statements therein not misleading, shall upon conviction be fined not more than $10,000 or imprisoned not more than five years, or both.

Sec. 326   Effect on Existing Law

Except as otherwise expressly provided, nothing in this subchapter shall affect (1) the jurisdiction of the Commission under the Securities Act of 1933, or the Securities Exchange Act of 1934, or the Public Utility Holding Company Act of 1935, over any person, security, or contract, or (2) the rights, obligations, duties, or liabilities of any person under such Acts; nor shall anything in this subchapter affect the jurisdiction of any other commission, board, agency, or officer of the United States or of any State or political subdivision of any State, over any person or security, insofar as such jurisdiction does not conflict with any provision of this subchapter or any rule, regulation, or order thereunder.

Sec. 327   Contrary Stipulations Void

Any condition, stipulation, or provision binding any person to waive compliance with any provision of this subchapter or with any rule, regulation, or order thereunder shall be void.

Sec. 328   Separability of Provisions

If any provision of this subchapter or the application of such provision to any person or circumstance shall be held invalid, the remainder of the subchapter and the application of such provision to persons or circumstances other than those as to which it is held invalid shall not be affected thereby.

Glossary

Many of these definitions are from the *Corporate Trust Reference Manual and Securities Processing*, 3d ed. (American Bankers Association); *A Guide to Registered Municipal Securities* (Government Finance Officers Association) and a glossary prepared by The Cannon Financial Institute.

Ad Valorem Tax

> A direct tax based on the value of the property. Counties, school districts, and municipalities usually are--and special tax districts may be--authorized by law to levy such taxes on property other than tangible personal property.

Advance refunding

> A financing structure under which new bonds are issued to repay an outstanding issue prior to its first call date. Generally the proceeds of the new issue are invested in government securities that are held in escrow.

Agency Account

> An account in which the title to the property constituting the agency does not pass to the trust institution but remains with the owner of the property (who is called the principal and in which the agent is charged with certain duties with respect to the property.

American Depository Receipt (ADR)

> A security that represents shares of foreign stock or bonds; a negotiable receipt for foreign securities held by the foreign correspondent bank of an American depository bank.

Arbitrage
> The simultaneous buying and selling of separate but related currencies, securities, or goods in separate markets (often foreign) in order to profit from the difference in their prices.

Arbitrage bonds
> Any bonds the proceeds of which are reasonably expected (at the time of issuance of the bonds) to be used directly or indirectly:
>
> 1. to acquire higher yielding investments, or
>
> 2. to replace funds which were used directly or indirectly to acquire higher yielding investments.

Assessment bond
> A type of special-tax municipal bond. Repaid from related taxes, such as real estate or property tax.

Asset-backed security
> A security for which income and principal payments are secured by specific assets such as a pool of mortgages, car loans, etc.

Asset Conservation, Lender Liability, and Deposit Insurance Protection Act of 1996
> The liability of a trustee for any environmental contamination is limited to the assets of the trust for which it is a fiduciary. No longer is a trustee held personally liable for environmental contamination for simply serving in such a capacity.

Attorney-in-fact
> An agent acting for the security holder under a power of attorney to effect a transfer.

Auction rate securities
> Securities that use an auction, or bidding, mechanism to periodically reset the rate at which dividends or interest payments are to accrue. Although the auction mechanism

was first applied to corporate preferred stock issues, it is now used to structure debt offerings as well.

Authentication

A manual certification appearing on a bond or note executed by the trustee (or its agent) under an indenture, or by a fiscal agent under a fiscal agency agreement, under which the bond or note is issued, stating that it is one of the bonds or notes referred to in the relevant indenture or fiscal agency agreement.

Back-up withholding

Established by the Interest and Dividend Tax Compliance Act of 1983. Requires paying agents to withhold 28 percent of interest, dividend, and principal payments to investors who have not filed an exemption certificate, certified taxpayer identification number, or social security number with the paying agent.

Balloon payment

A scaled method of bond interest payment (or mortgage payment) that provides for a final payment that is proportionally higher than previous payments.

Banker's Acceptance (BA)

A corporate bank draft (usually for a future delivery of foreign goods) whose payment has been guaranteed and stamped ``accepted'' by the corporation's bank.

Bankruptcy Abuse Prevention and Consumer Protection Act of 2005

Act was passed and principally noted to address consumer debts. Under the Act personal bankruptcies fall under Chapter 13 where debtors formulate a plan of repayment. The Act created a new Chapter 15 for international or Cross-Border insolvency cases and amended several corporate bankruptcy provisions.

BANS (Bond Anticipation Notes)

    Municipal notes maturing in less than one year issued in advance of a new bond issue. Proceeds from bond issue will repay note with interest.

Basis point

    A term used in stating bond interest; 100 basis points equal 1 percent.

BDUG

    The Bank Depository User Group of Depository Trust Company (DTC), a user panel assembled to work with DTC on refining and enhancing DTC services on an ongoing basis.

Bearer security

    A negotiable security that is not registered in regard to interest or principal. It is presumed in law to be owned by its holder. Title to bearer securities is transferred by delivery.

Beneficial owner

    The true owner of securities that may be bearer or registered in the name of another, such as a nominee.

Best efforts

    An underwriting method whereby the investment banker sells as much of an issue as possible.

Bid Price

    The price at which the market maker will buy a security. Bid and asked prices are quoted by market makers on over-the-counter stocks.

Blue sky laws

    A popular name for various state laws enacted to protect the public against municipal securities fraud.

Bond certificate

    An interest-bearing debt obligation, under whose terms a

borrower contracts, inter alia, to pay the holder a fixed principal amount on a stated future date and normally a series of interest payments during its life. A long-term debt instrument. In this sense, it may also be referred to as a debenture or note.

Bond counsel

An attorney (or firm) retained by the issuer to give a legal opinion that a municipal issuer is authorized to issue proposed securities and has met all legal requirements necessary for issuance and that the interest on the securities will be exempt from federal income tax, and where applicable, from state and local tax.

Bondholders

Investors who lend money to an enterprise for a stated period of time and receive interest and repayment of principal. Their claims on a corporation's assets take precedence over the claims of preferred and common stockholders.

Bond opinion

Usually covers the following matters: (1) whether the bonds are valid and binding obligations of the bond issuer; (2) the source of payment or security for the bonds; (3) whether and to what extent interest on the bonds is exempt from federal income tax and from taxes imposed by the state in which the issuer is located.

Bond power

An assignment form separate from the one printed on the bond certificate.

Bond purchase agreement

An agreement between an issuer and the underwriter of the bonds, setting forth the terms of the sale, including price, premium or discount, interest rate, the closing conditions, restrictions on liability of the issuer, and any indemnity provisions.

Bond registrar

>A corporate agent responsible for effecting registrations of transfer and maintaining records of registered debt security holders.

Bond resolution

>The document(s) representing action of a municipal issuer authorizing the issuance and sale of securities. Such will also describe the nature of the obligation and the issuer's duties to the bondholders.

Book-Entry Settlement

>An accounting method for securities transactions and funds movements, whereby no physical movement of the certificates or funds is necessary. Instead, debits and offsetting credits (and vice versa) are posted to the accounts of the transaction's principals. These parties are usually members of the same securities depository, clearing house, Federal Reserve System, or they maintain special accounts with a common bank or broker.

Broker confirmation

>A receipt sent to a customer by a broker after trade execution. The "confirm" indicates customer name, broker account number, description of security, quantity, price, dollar amounts, delivery and receiving parties, etc. Also called Trade Confirmation, or Trade Confirm.

Broker/dealer

>A party who effects securities transactions on behalf of its customers, as well as for its own market position. A broker may not buy and sell from its own account; it charges fees for the services performed. A dealer may purchase and resell the securities to its customer, charging a markup for its services. A broker/dealer may serve the customer in either a broker or dealer capacity.

Bulldog bond

>A Sterling-denominated bond marketed in the United Kingdom by a non-British entity.

Bullet issue

> An issue of securities with no amortization feature in which the principal amount is repaid entirely at the maturity date.

Business day

> Always specifically defined in the Indenture or Fiscal Agency Agreement but usually means:
>
> 1. In the Euromarkets, when two related markets are open for banking business; in the Eurodollar market, a day when both London and New York banks are open for business
>
> 2. In the U.S. domestic market, any day, excluding Saturdays, Sundays, or legal or statutory holidays, on which business can be conducted.

Buy-in

> If the selling party to a securities trade fails to deliver, the buyer may buy the securities through other sources at the market price then prevailing. The defaulting seller is liable for the difference in price. (The buyer must notify the seller of its intentions to buy the securities elsewhere before resorting to the buy-in.)

Callable security

> A bond issue, all or part of which may be redeemed under definite conditions before maturity pursuant to indenture provisions.

Call option

> A short-term security that gives the owner the right to buy a security at a fixed price until a stated future date.

Call protection

> The period of time during which the issuer cannot call the security for redemption.

Call provision

> A feature of bonds or preferred stock that allows the issuer

to repurchase part or all of an issue before it matures.

Capitalization

Total amount of the various securities issued by a corporation. Capitalization may include preferred and common stock, bonds, debentures, and surplus.

Capitalized interest

A portion of the proceeds of an issue which will be used to pay interest on the bonds for a specific period of time, usually the period of construction of a project financed by the issue.

Cash settlement

Cash settlement usually takes place on trade date, avoiding the usual three-day settlement period.

Cede & Co.

Depository Trust Company's nominee name used on all registered securities DTC holds in storage on behalf of its participant banks and brokers.

Central Post Office (CPO)

The Central Post Office was created for filing of continuing disclosure information by municipal issuers. The CPO is located on the Internet at www.DisclosureUSA.org and is operated by the Municipal Advisory Council of Texas (TexasMAC). Filings are presently voluntary.

Clearstream and Euroclear

The European Clearing systems, which provide safe keeping, custody, and clearance services for holders of Eurobonds and Yankee bonds.

Certificates of Accrual on Treasury Securities (CATS)

CATS represent ownership in serially maturing interest payments or principal payments on specific underlying U.S. Treasury Notes and Bonds. Each CATS entitles the holder to receive a single payment at its maturity.

Certificate of deposit (CD)

> An interest bearing negotiable certificate representing a deposit with a fixed maturity issued by a commercial bank; being traded on a yield basis with interest computed for the actual number of days held on a 360-day year basis.

Chapter 11

> A chapter of the federal bankruptcy code. Among other provisions, directs the Securities and Exchange Commission (SEC) to aid the bankruptcy courts on corporate reorganizations. The SEC advises on plans submitted by the court and comments on fairness of the reorganization plan to the corporation's investors.

Charter, corporate

> The corporation's constitution granted by its state of incorporation, which specifies rules and limitations of ownership, operation, funding, security issuance, etc.

Chinese Wall

> A term used to separate the fiduciary function and the credit function of a bank so that, for a company for whom the bank also serves as trustee, information derived in the bank's fiduciary capacity will not form the basis for action on the lending side.

Classes of stock

> Common: Represents the principal ownership of the corporation, the first class to be issued and the last to be retired.

> Classified Common Stock: Division of the common stock usually into two classes, class A and class B, to differentiate controlling or voting power.

> Preferred: A cross between common stock and a bond. Holders receive dividends before profits are distributed to common stock holders.

> Cumulative Preferred: Dividends, if not paid to stockholders, are accumulated and paid at a future date.

Noncumulative Preferred: The stockholder is paid dividends if they are earned, without any cumulative provision.

Participating Preferred: The stockholder will receive a specified dividend and may also be entitled to additional earnings generally available to common stockholders.

Classified Preferred Stock: 4.25 PFD, Class A PFD, Class B PFD, etc. These distinctions usually relate to different rates or voting privileges.

Convertible Preferred: This class carries a provision giving a privilege to the stockholder to convert such stock into common stock.

Clearing house funds

1. Funds used in settlement of equity, corporate, and municipal bond settlement transactions. 2. A term to mean "next day availability'" of funds.

Close-end (mortgage) bonds

A type of security (usually first mortgage bonds) which prohibits any future sale of a junior issue with the same priority of lien on the corporate assets covered by the original indenture.

Closely held company

A corporation with a small number of owners, all living within one state at the time its stock is issued. The issue need not be registered with the SEC.

Closing date

The date on which a new issue's proceeds are paid to the borrower by the lead-manager against delivery of the securities in temporary or definitive form.

Collateral agent

A private financial institution, typically a bank and often the trustee, that serves as an agent for the credit enhancement provider. It holds and maintains the collateral which is pledged to the trustee to secure the obligations of the credit enhancer under the credit facility.

Collateral agreement

> The agreement under which a credit enhancement provider will pledge collateral (e.g., cash or readily marketable securities) to a collateral agent to hold as security for the bonds.

Collateralized mortgage obligation

> A bond with two or more classes of maturities secured by a pool of mortgages or mortgage instruments (e.g., ``Ginnie Mae's'').

Collateral trust bond

> Bonds secured by securities owned by the issuer that are deposited with an indenture trustee.

Commercial paper

> A negotiable, unsecured, short-term note issued in bearer form by a large and well-known corporation. Usually sold on a discount basis with a maximum maturity of nine months.

Competitive bidding

> A sealed envelope bidding process employed when various underwriter groups are interested in handling the distribution of a securities issue. The mandate or contract is awarded to one group by the issuer on the basis of the highest price paid, and lowest interest cost.

Compound interest

> Interest paid on original capital and on the interest that has been added to the capital. Interest can be compounded daily, weekly, monthly, quarterly, semiannually, or annually.

Comptroller of the Currency

> An official of the U.S. government, appointed by the president and confirmed by the Senate, who is responsible for the chartering, examining, supervising, and liquidating of all national banks.

Conduit financing

> Bonds issued by a governmental unit to finance a project to be used primarily by a third party, usually a corporation engaged in private enterprise. The security for such bonds is the credit of the private user rather than the governmental issuer. Generally, such bonds do not constitute obligations of the issuer because the corporate obligor is liable for generating the pledged revenues (e.g., industrial revenue bonds).

Construction fund

> A fund, usually held by the trustee under an indenture, into which proceeds of an issue are deposited for payment of authorized project costs.

Continuous net settlement (CNS)

> A securities trade settlement option which summarizes multiple transactions into a single net security settlement and a single net money affirmation, wherein the identity of the contra side is lost. The bank and broker settle all security and money transactions with the clearing corporation.

Conversion

> An indenture provision giving the holder of a bond or note the right to exchange it for other securities of the issuer (usually shares of common stock).

Conversion agent

> A bank designated by the issuer of convertible securities to convert, at the investor's request, debt or equity securities of the issuer into the number of shares of stock specified in the trust indenture or stock offering agreement. The Conversion Agent will requisition the shares of stock from the stock transfer agent and draw a check for any cash fraction thereof upon surrender of the convertible securities.

Convertible debentures
: Securities that may be exchanged for common stock of the same company at a set conversion price stated in the indenture.

Co-ops (Banks for Cooperatives)
: Banks that make loans to farmers' associations through issuance of bonds. These are not guaranteed by the U.S. government but are secured obligations of the banks that are under governmental supervision.

Corporate reorganization
: A major change in capital structure and financial operation of a corporation, often requiring new securities to be issued and/or exchanges of securities.

Corporate resolution
: A formal document issued by a corporation to make a statement, ratify actions, or grant authority to individuals to act for the corporation on specific matters.

Corpus
: The property within a trust account, the title to which vests in the person entitled to the future estate. See also principal.

Coupon bond
: A bearer bond with coupons attached. The interest on the bond is collected by detaching and presenting the coupons as they become due.

Covenant
: A provision in an indenture setting forth an undertaking or agreement of the issuer in regard to specific matters. Such may be either affirmative or negative in character.

Coverage
: The portion of pledged revenues available annually to pay debt service, as compared to the annual debt service requirement. The ratio is one indication of the margin of

safety for payment of debt service.

Credit enhancement

An external credit support of a debt obligation. Included are letters of credit, municipal bond insurance, and third-party guarantees.

Credit enhancement provider

Insurance companies, banks, S&Ls, municipal bond sureties, or other private financial institutions that provide additional security for tax-exempt bonds by guaranteeing or insuring the repayment of the bonds.

Current yield

Annual interest (or dividends) divided by current market price of a bond (or stock)

CUSIP

(Acronym for Committee on Uniform Securities Identification Procedures). A uniform numbering system administered by Standard & Poor's, under the auspices of the American Bankers Association, widely used to identify specific securities and their issuers. It includes corporate, municipal, state, federal, and some foreign issues. The CUSIP number appears on the certificates and in documents relating to securities processing.

Custodian

An agent, usually a bank, that safekeeps securities for its customers and performs dividend and interest collection services. It also buys, sells, receives, and delivers securities if so instructed by the customer.

Dated date

The date of a bond issue, printed on each bond, from which interest usually starts to accrue, even though the bonds may actually be delivered at some later date.

Dealer

An individual or firm in the securities business acting as principal rather than as agent. Typically a dealer buys for its own account and sells to a customer from its own inventory.

Debenture

An unsecured debt certificate backed by the general credit of the issuer.

Debt service

Payments of interest and principal on total borrowings that must be made by the obligor/issuer during the period in which its debt is outstanding.

Debt service reserve fund

The fund usually held by the trustee under an indenture established for the payment of debt service on bonds in the event pledged receipts are insufficient.

Deep discount bond

A bond sold at a substantial discount below its par value bearing interest at a rate significantly below the current interest rates or with no interest at all.

Default

The failure by the issuer of bonds or notes to comply with one or more of its obligations in the indenture under which the bonds are issued.

Defeasance

A general term reflecting the termination of the rights and interests of bondholders and extinguishment of their lien on any property or collateral pursuant to the terms of an indenture or bond resolution. May also refer to the termination of an issuer's obligations under such contracts upon the refunding of the issue or by provisions for the future payment of interest and repayment of principal.

Delayed delivery

A partial delivery of new issue securities to the lead manager subsequent to the closing date, pursuant to an agreement.

Delivery vs. payment (dvp)

> A physical delivery of securities against payment of the purchase price. Normally, payment is due on scheduled settlement date, even if securities are delayed.

Demand option

> A right, which may be evidenced by a certificate, given the holder of a debt security to sell it back to the issuer at any time prior to the security's maturity.

Depository agent

> An agent retained by the maker of a tender offer to receive securities forwarded to the agent by the owners, hold the securities, and make payment in cash and/or securities to the owners when so authorized by the maker of the tender offer.

Depository Trust Company (DTC)

> The New York and sole remaining depository serving institutional participants such as banks, brokers, insurance companies, and other high-volume securities traders. Through its nominee, Cede & Co., DTC acts as the sole registered holder of book-entry only new financings, makes interest, principal, and redemption payments to its participants, posts important notices of redemption and bankruptcy distributions, processes transfer positions among its participants, and holds the global certificates for trustee banks.

Derivatives

> Investment instruments that derive their value from the value of other securities. Options and futures are among the most basic.

Direct pay letter of credit

> A letter of credit that covers an amount equal to the principal of and interest on the bonds and that is drawn upon by the trustee on each bond payment date in an amount equal to the full amount of principal, interest, and premium, if any, due in respect of the bonds. Such letter

may also provide for reinstatement of the interest component after any drawing thereon in respect of interest unless the issuing bank notifies the trustee to the contrary within a certain period of time after such drawing.

Discount

The amount by which a security is selling below its par value. In the case of original issuance, this is referred to as the original issuance discount (OID).

Dividend

A proportion of net earnings paid periodically by a corporation to its stockholders as a return on investment.

Dividend, stock

Payment of additional shares of common stock by the corporation to the stockholders.

D.K. (Don't Know)

A D.K. results when the purchaser's clearing house or bank refuses to accept a security delivery simply because it ``doesn't know'' about it and is not expecting it.

Drop lock bond

A hybrid debt security issued as a floating rate instrument but that becomes a fixed-rate bond when its rate falls below a predetermined trigger rate.

Due bill

An assignment or similar instrument given by the seller in a trade to transfer title to dividends, interest, or other rights legally due to the buyer.

Due diligence

Investigation conducted by underwriters and their counsel and, in some cases, also by bond counsel and the issuer's counsel, to determine whether all material items in connection with the issuer, the issue, and the security for the issue have been accurately disclosed in the Official Statement, and that no material disclosure has been omitted.

Dutch auction

An auction technique used in selling securities in which progressively lower bids are accepted until the entire issue is sold. All bidders pay the lowest bid accepted.

Endorsement

The signature written on the back of a negotiable instrument (or in an accompanying power) that transfers the instrument to another party. The signer must have the legal right to transfer the instrument if the endorsement is to be valid.

Endorsement in blank

The signature of an authorized person on the back of a negotiable instrument, or on a separate power, which does not indicate the specific name of the party to whom the instrument is being transferred. Endorsement in blank makes the instrument as transferable if it were in bearer form.

Energy Policy Act of 2005

This Act repealed the Public Utility Holding Company Act of 1935 and transferred authority to the Federal Energy Regulatory Commission. A new Public Utility Holding Company Act of 2005 was enacted which had fewer restrictions that barred entities from ownership of public utilities.

Enterprise activity

A revenue-generating project or business which supplies funds necessary to pay debt service on bonds issued to finance the facility. The debt of such projects is self-liquidating when the projects earn sufficient monies to cover all debt service and other requirements imposed under the bond contract.

Equipment trust bonds

Bonds secured by machinery and equipment issued pursuant to an equipment trust.

Equity securities

Securities evidencing ownership of a corporation. Includes preferred and common stock of all types.

Erasure guarantee

Any irregularity in the assignment guaranteed by the broker or the commercial bank before the registration of transfer is effected.

Escheat

Revision of property to the state when there are no legal heirs or claimants.

Escrow

An agency providing for the physical holding of cash, securities, or documents until certain conditions called for in an agreement between two parties are met.

Escrow agent

An institution, usually a bank, designated by two or more parties to hold securities, funds, or documents that are to be delivered upon compliance with the conditions contained in the escrow agreement, usually within a specified period of time.

Euroclear

An international securities depository founded in 1968 and headquartered in Brussels, Belgium to hold cross-border securities for its members.

Eurocommercial paper

Commercial paper sold by foreign corporations.

Eurodollar certificates of deposit

> Negotiable, dollar-denominated, short-term bearer certificates that represent deposits in foreign banks or foreign branches of U. S. banks.

Eurodollars

> U. S. dollars deposited in any bank outside of the United States.

Eurodollar bond

> A U.S. dollar-denominated bond marketed wholly outside the United States (primarily in Europe). No registration statement is required under the Securities Act of 1933 to be filed with the SEC.

Euromarket

> General term for the European capital markets that comprise, inter alia, the markets for Eurobonds, Euro FRNs, Euro CDs/FR CDs, and Euro syndicated credits.

Eurosterling bond

> A sterling-denominated bond issued in bearer form only, marketed solely outside the United Kingdom and the United States.

Events of Default

> Specific defaults, whose occurrence and continuance permit the trustee (or a holder of bonds or notes) to exercise the remedies in the indenture under which the bonds or notes are issued.

Exchange agent

> A bank, usually the bond registrar, designated by an issuer of securities to process the exchange of bonds of an issue for other bonds of the same issue (e.g., registered bonds for bearer and interdenominational exchanges) or to process the exchange of bonds or stock for other securities of the same issuer or of a different company as a result of a merger or acquisition.

Exercise price
> The price set in an option. Also called the striking or strike price. The owner of the option has the right to buy or sell the security named in the option at the exercise price within a set period of time.

Extension letter of credit
> A letter of credit that provides for a single draw in the event of the acceleration of the bonds in an amount equal to all payments made on the bonds during the period of a specified number of days (usually ninety-one) prior to the occurrence of (1) an act of bankruptcy that triggers acceleration or (2) the drawing on the letter of credit if no act of bankruptcy has occurred.

Fail
> Failure of the seller to deliver securities to the buyer on settlement date and/or failure of the buyer to accept and pay for the securities. Also called a settlement fail.

Fannie Mae (Federal National Mortgage Association)
> A privately owned company that adds liquidity to the residential mortgage market by buying mortgages from the original lenders, such as savings and loans, banks, and insurance companies. Fannie Mae buys mortgages guaranteed or insured by government agencies, as well as conventional mortgages. To raise funds, it sells debentures, notes, and mortgage-backed certificates to the investing public and occasionally to the U.S. Treasury.

Farm Credit Administration
> An independent U.S. government agency that provides credit and financial services to farmers, ranchers, and allied businesses. For details, see: Co-Ops (Banks For Cooperatives): FICB (Federal Intermediate Credit Banks); FLB (Federal Land Banks).

FDIC (Federal Deposit Insurance Corporation)
> An agency of the U.S. government that insures depositors' accounts at most commercial banks and mutual savings banks.

Feasibility study

    A report of the financial practicality of a proposed project and financing thereof that may include estimates of revenue that will be generated and a review of the physical, operating, economic, or engineering aspects of the proposed project.

Federal funds

    1. Excess reserve balances of a member bank on deposit at a Federal Reserve Bank. This money may be made available to eligible borrowers on a short-term basis.

    2. Funds used for the settlement of money market instruments and U.S. government securities transactions.. A term used to mean ``same day availability" of funds. See also. Clearing House Funds.

Federal Reserve Requirements

    The dollar amount banks must deposit with a Federal Reserve Bank or hold in cash on their own premises. The purpose of the reserve requirement is to ensure that a bank remains liquid and does not lend out more money than it can afford. An individual bank may have more or less funds on reserve than its requirements dictate. A bank with a deficit borrows federal funds--or so called fed funds--from a bank that has an excess amount on reserve. The borrowing bank pays interest to the lending bank for the overnight use of the fed funds.

Federal Reserve System (FRS)

    Known as ``the Fed," it is the central banking system as established by the Federal Reserve Act of 1913. It regulates the nation's supply of money, determines the legal reserve requirement of member banks, oversees the mint, effects transfers of funds, promotes and facilitates the clearance and collection of checks, and examines member banks.

FHA (Federal Housing Administration)

> Responsible to HUD, the Department of Housing and Urban Development, it insures residential mortgages, settles claims for defaulted mortgages in cash, and issues registered, transferable debentures that have an unconditional U.S. government guarantee.

FHLB (Federal Home Loan Bank System)

> The federal system that supervises all nationally chartered savings and loan associations and mutual savings banks. State-chartered thrift organizations may also be eligible for membership. One purpose of the FHLB is to promote availability of funds for home loans and mortgages.

FICB (Federal Intermediate Credit Banks)

> Responsible to Farm Credit Administration, providing short- and medium-term financing to financial institutions that serve the farm credit market. See also Farm Credit Administration.

Financial adviser

> With respect to a new issue of municipal bonds, a consultant who advises the issue on matters pertinent to the issue, such as structure, timing, marketing, fairness of pricing, terms, and bond ratings.

FINS (Financial Industry Numbering System)

> A numerical code (similar in structure to the CUSIP numbering system) identifying financial institutions such as banks and brokerage firms. Used in security trade documents, depository accounting procedures, etc.

Fiscal agent

> A person, normally a bank or trust company, authorized to enter into a Fiscal Agency agreement with an issuer of bonds or notes (usually a government entity). The agreement provides for control of the issue and its servicing, but the Fiscal Agent does not have fiduciary responsibilities.

Float

>A colloquial term meaning the earnings on uninvested balances held by a bank.

Floater

>Common term used to describe a security with a variable interest rate.

Floating rate

>An interest rate that is not a fixed percentage of principal. The issuer typically ``pegs" the future rate it will pay to the future rate of a basic short-term financial instrument (such as a specific U.S. Treasury issue) and pays a small stated percentage above the rate.

FmHA (Farmers Home Administration)

>Agency of the Department of Agriculture that aids loan programs in rural areas. Its outstanding securities have a U.S. government guarantee.

Forwarding agent

>An institution, usually a bank, which receives securities during a tender offer and forwards them to the appropriate depository agent daily with an accounting record.

Fractional rights

>The residual portion of the total rights received by a stockholder in a rights offering that is too small to allow the purchase of a full share.

Freddie Mac (Federal Home Loan Mortgage Corporation)

>Supplies mortgage credit for residential housing, mostly through Federal Home Loan Banks. (The FHLB system serves thrift institutions much as the Federal Reserve System serves commercial banks.) Freddie Mac issues bonds, debentures, notes, and certificates.

Fully guaranteed obligations

>Obligations of some federal agencies that are fully guaranteed by the U.S. government for both principal and

interest.

Fully registered bonds

>Bonds that are registered for both principal and interest in a holder's name.

General obligation bond (GO)

>Municipal bond issues by any level of government below the U.S. government, which is backed by the full faith, credit, and taxing power of the issuer.

Ginnie Mae (Government National Mortgage Association)

>A corporation wholly owned by the U.S. government that buys mortgages from banks and other private lenders and resells them to investors. It issues and guarantees mortgage-backed bonds and pass-through certificates.

Global certificate

>A single certificate, in either bearer or registered form, representing an entire issue or maturity of an issue of securities. Such certificates are used in registered book-entry systems where issuers are obligated under state law to issue at least one certificate per maturity. For book-entry only bonds, the issuer will deliver the global certificate(s) to the securities depository where they are retained until maturity. Such certificates may also be used, especially in the Euro market, when definitive bonds are not available at the closing.

Good delivery

>A term referring to all conditions of a securities delivery that must be met by the seller. These include correct type of security and issuer, the right quantity and denomination, the presence of outstanding interest coupons, if any, proper endorsement and timeliness of delivery.

Gramm-Leach-Bliley Act of 1999

>Banks surrendered their blanket exception from having to register with the SEC as broker/dealers and agreed to thirteen specific activity focused exceptions from

registration in exchange for the right to engage in more activities, such as merchant banking.

Group of Thirty (G30)

An international group of senior financial managers that undertakes analyses of global financial issues. The Group issued a study in 1989 including nine recommendations for securities processing in global markets that are now unofficial guidelines for all markets to follow.

Granting clauses

The section of a trust indenture that sets forth the security for the obligations to be issued. It includes a recital of the consideration, a specific grant to the trustee, and a legal description of the real property if it is to be mortgaged.

Guaranteed investment contracts (GICs)

Investment offered by financial service institutions that pay investors a fixed rate of return, usually close to the current yield on high-grade bonds, for a stated term of generally not exceeding ten years.

Guaranteed mortgage certificates

Certificates backed by mortgages and also by a guarantee. FHLMC issues certificates of this type in registered form, backed by conventional residential mortgages.

Guaranty agreement

An agreement of a third party, for consideration, to pay debt service on an issue that is the primary obligation of another party or the promise of the primary obligor under a sale and leaseback by a separate agreement to pay debt service on the issue.

Holder of record

The person whose name appears in the records of the corporation.

Home office payment agreement

An agreement in connection with the private placement of debt securities, whereby in consideration of payments of principal being made to the holder without presentation of such security for notation of payment, the holder agrees that it will, before the disposition thereof, present such securities to the issuer (or its agent) for notation of payment or issuance of new security reflecting the unpaid balance thereof.

HUD (Department of Housing and Urban Development)

A U.S. department responsible for three groups that circulate funds for construction and major improvement of housing and urban renewal. (See Glossary entries under FHA, Ginnie Mae, and HUD Public Housing Notes and Bonds.)

Income Bond

Issued only to replace older bond issues on which a corporation has defaulted. Both principal amount and interest rate on the income bonds are greater than on the bonds they replace. Interest is paid only if earned, but unpaid interest accrues, to be paid when and if possible. Also called adjustment bonds.

Industrial revenue bonds

Issued to support the economic development of a community. Funds raised are used to construct facilities for lease to a corporation whose operations will bring jobs to the community. Repayment is based on the corporation's lease payments.

Investment Advisers Act of 1940

The Act provides that firms advising others about securities investment must register with the SEC.

Investment Company Act of 1940

The Act requires investment companies to file registration statements with the SEC disclosing to investors their financial condition and investment objectives and policies.

Interest coverage.

> Strictly speaking this is not actually a ratio, but it is an important consideration in the extension of credit--particularly long-term credit--to a corporation. The purpose of this measure is to determine the relationship between the company's earnings and its annual interest charges, and it is computed by taking net earnings before interest and income taxes paid. If extension of new credit is being contemplated, interest charges on the new debt should also be included. It is customary to take average earnings over a period of years and, if the industry is a cyclical one, to consider earnings during the poorest year. Of importance in connection with extension of long-term credit is the company's history of ample coverage of all fixed charges.

Investment banker

> A firm that deals with the long-term capital needs of corporations. When a company needs to raise new capital, the investment banker advises on whether to issue debt or equity securities. It further recommends the amount and terms of the financing and helps to sell the securities. Investment bankers are also called underwriters.

ISIN

> The International Security Identification Number, a 12-digit identifier used to uniquely designate securities that are traded across borders.

ISITC

> The Interface Standards for Institutional Trade Communication committee, formed by a group of U. S. banks and investment managers to develop and maintain standards used for securities message communication among participants in the U. S. securities industry.

ISO

> The International Organization for Standards, headquartered in Switzerland, which serves as the global

overseer of standards. Individual countries have their own internal groups, which are affiliated with the ISO.

ISO 6666

The published international standard for security numbers that affirms ISIN as the standard security identifier for cross-border securities.

ISO 7775

The published international standard for security message formats that generally conforms to the formats used on the Society for Worldwide Interbank Financial Telecommunications (SWIFT) network.

Issued and outstanding

The portion of debt and equity securities authorized for sale by a corporation's board of directors that has been sold by the corporation and is currently owned by the public. Excludes securities that have been repurchased from the public and are either held in the corporation's treasury or have been retired.

Issuer

A public or private entity that signs an evidence of obligation, such as a note, bond, or stock certificate, in return for which the issuer receives cash, goods, or services.

Jumbo

General term for a large-denomination certificate.

Junior lien

A security that represents a claim on the issuer's income or assets subordinate to the claim of another security.

Junk bonds

A generic description of high-yield debt securities typically issued by commercial borrowers to finance leveraged buyouts, generally subordinated to other indebtedness of the borrower.

Legal transfer

> Transfer of securities registered in the name of decedents, fiduciaries, trusts, corporations, partnerships, clubs, institutions, etc. Transfer of items that are not generally recognized as good delivery items

Letter of credit

> A financial instrument issued to a company (or individual) by a bank that substitutes the bank's credit for the company's (or individual's) credit. Frequently used by companies ordering goods from foreign suppliers with which they have no credit relationship.

Letter of erasure

> Letter signed by an authorized person indemnifying the transfer agent and the corporation against liability in effecting a transfer on an erased or altered assignment.

Letter of indemnity

> Letter signed by an authorized person indemnifying the transfer agent or indenture trustee and the issuer against liability in replacing a lost, stolen, or mutilated certificate.

Letter of transmittal

> A form used in transmitting securities to the depository agent in the case of a tender offer.

"Letter" stock

> Also called restricted stock. A special issue of common stock a corporation is legally permitted to sell without SEC registration to a small group of investors. The buyer must sign a letter of intent stating that the purchase is for investment purposes and will not be sold. "Letter Bonds" can also be issued.

Leverage lease

> A financing vehicle involving the acquisition of property by an equity investor (usually through a trustee) providing a minor portion of the cost thereof (with lenders providing the balance) and the leasing of such property to the lessee.

The lender's investment is usually represented by bonds under an indenture.

LIBOR (London Interbank Offered Rate)

Eurodollar deposits between banks. There is a different LIBOR rate for each deposit maturity.

Limited open-end indenture

A mortgage arrangement that sets a limit on the principal amount of bonds that may be issued in the future under the same indenture and with the same priority of lien on corporate assets.

Limited purpose trust company

Trust companies, state-chartered and regulated, that are permitted to perform specified trust functions.

Lost and Stolen Securities Program

A program, under the Securities and Exchange Commission's Rule 17f-1, dealing with the reporting of and inquiry about the loss, counterfeiting, and theft of securities. The Securities Information Center (SIC) is the central agency that handles reports and inquiries through its automated data base.

Lower floater

General term for a security with a variable interest rate and also having a tender feature.

Mark-to-market

The process of valuing a portfolio, a securities position, or a trade by multiplying the number of shares (or principal amount in the case of bonds) by the current market price per share (or per bond).

Market maker

A dealer that buys and sells specific issues in the over-the-counter market or on stock exchanges.

Market order
: An order for securities in which the buyer/seller does not specify an exact dollar price but agrees to trade immediately at the best price

Master servicer
: The entity specified in the prospectus supplement for a bond issue secured by mortgage loans that will administer and supervise the performance by servicers of their duties and responsibilities under serving agreements in respect of the collateral for the securities.

Mortgage-backed certificate
: A debt certificate secured by a pool of mortgages. Such certificates issued by Fannie Mae are secured by conventional mortgages and guaranteed for interest and principal.

Mortgage bond
: A debt security backed by a legal interest in specified real property of the issuer, pursuant to a deed of mortgage or indenture.

Multicurrency Accounting
: Used to describe accounting for international securities in both the currency of the local market in which the security is traded, as well as in the base currency of the investor.

Municipal bond
: Issued by a state or local government, or its agencies or authorities, or by a possession or territory of the United States. Such bonds are often called "tax-exempts," for interest paid on most of these issues is exempt from federal income taxes and also from state and local income taxes within the state of origin.

Municipal notes
: Debt securities issued by municipalities for a period of less than one year. (See also BANs, RANs, and TANs.)

Municipal Securities Rulemaking Board (MSRB)

> An independent, self-regulatory organization established by the Securities Act Amendments of 1975 that has rule-making authority through the SEC over dealers, dealer banks, and brokers in municipal securities.

Nationally Recognized Municipal Securities Information Repository (NRMSIR)

> Organizations authorized by the MSRB to receive from municipal securities underwriters, issuers, and dissemination agents disclosure materials pertaining to such securities and to retain those materials for public access.

Negative pledge agreement

> Agreement by an issuer or by the entity providing security for an issue not to create any new debt or to pledge or encumber its revenues and/or assets except under specified limitations or conditions.

Negotiable

> The condition of an instrument, the legal interest in which can be transferred by delivery, without need for endorsement. Bearer securities are inherently negotiable, whereas registered securities can be rendered negotiable by the completion of a power of assignment.

Net interest cost (NIC)

> A common method of computing the interest expense to the issuer of bonds, which usually serves as the basis of award in a competitive sale. The NIC allows for premium and discount and represents the dollar amount of interest payable over the life of an issue, without taking into account the time value of funds.

"No action" letter

> An SEC staff letter stating that the staff has determined not to recommend to the Commission that it take any enforcement or injunctive action against a particular issuer, or other party to a transaction, based on the facts

and circumstances set forth in the letter to the staff that requested such a Letter.

No call provision

An indenture provision prohibiting the optional redemption of a debt issue before a specified date or its maturity.

Nominee

A financial services entity that holds its customers' securities as custodian and/or as investment agent for trust portfolios; a mechanism for simplifying securities deliveries between banks, brokers, institutions, and individuals, as well as simplifying dividend and interest payments by issuers.

Nonrefundable provision

An indenture provision prohibiting the optional redemption of debt securities for a specified period by using funds borrowed at an interest rate less than that borne by such securities.

Notice of redemption

A publication and/or mailing of the issuer's intention to call outstanding bonds prior to their stated maturity date, in accordance with the bond contract.

Offering circular

A document usually prepared by the underwriters of an issue setting forth basic information on the issuer and the issue to be offered in the primary market.

Official statement

A document published by a municipal issuer disclosing material information on a new issue, including purpose of issue, how such will be repaid, and the financial, economic, and social characteristics of the issuing entity.

One-and-the-same guarantee

Certification used in the event that the signature of the security holder differs slightly from the name appearing on the face of the certificate.

Open-end mortgage bonds
: Issued under an indenture that allows additional series of bonds to be issued in the future under the same indenture.

Option
: A right to buy (call) or sell (put) a fixed amount of a given security (usually stock) at a specified price within a limited period of time.

Original issue discount (OID)
: The excess of the stated redemption price at maturity of a security over the issue price. Individual security holders are required by law to report as income a portion of the discount each year until maturity.

Par value
: The face value of a share of stock or debt certificate having no relation to its market value.

Pass-through certificates
: Securities that represent undivided interests in pools of mortgages. Principal and interest payments from the mortgagors are passed through to certificate holders as received. Because mortgagors may prepay mortgages, the pass-through payments to certificate holders fluctuate.

Payable date
: 1. The date established by a corporation's board of directors for payment of a dividend to the stockholders of record. Usually fifteen to twenty days after record date; or

  2. The date fixed in an indenture or bond resolution for the payment of interest or principal.

Paying agent
: An institution, normally a bank, authorized by the issuer to pay the principal of (premium, if any) or interest on debt securities on behalf of the issuer.

Point

One percent of par value. Because bond prices are quoted as a percentage of $1,000, a point is worth $10 regardless of the actual denomination of a bond.

Poison pill

Rights or warrants granted to stockholders that become exercisable if a raider obtains a specified percentage of the company's shares.

Pollution control bonds

A type of municipal bond, similar to industrial revenue bonds, whose proceeds are used to fund construction of air and water pollution control facilities.

Premium

The amount a security may sell above its par value. In the case of a new issue of stock or bonds, the premium is the amount the market price rises over the original selling price.

Private activity bonds

Bonds issued by a municipality that are not classified as governmental bonds. They are tax-exempt if they constitute qualified bonds as determined by the Tax Reform Act of 1986.

Private placement

The sale (to a limited number of institutional investors) of securities not involving a public offering and exempt from registration under the Securities Act of 1933.

Project notes

Municipal notes with maturities ranging from three to twelve months that provide short-term financing for federally assisted public housing and urban renewal projects. HUD may guarantee these notes as to principal and interest.

Prospectus
: Official document that must be given to buyers of new SEC-registered public issues. Describes the issuer's products and business and the industries in which it competes, physical facilities, management background, etc., and presents historical financial statements. Describes the issue and intended use of the funds to be received. The SEC neither approves nor disapproves the prospectus, which is an abstract of the lengthy registration statement filed with the SEC.

"Prudent man" rule also known as the Prudent Person Rule
: A common law standard of conduct, which requires a fiduciary or trustee to deal with the trust estate as if it were such fiduciary's or trustee's own property. In effect, a standard of due diligence and care.

Public housing bond
: Debt securities issued by state or local governments to provide funds for loans made to developers, home buyers, and lending institutions that service home buyers. HUD (Department of Housing and Urban Development) may guarantee some of these bonds.

Public utility revenue bonds
: Municipal bonds issued to raise funds to create or improve electric, gas, water, and sewer services.

Put option
: A right, which may be evidenced by a certificate, given to the holder of a debt security to sell it back to the issuer, at one or more fixed future dates prior to the security's maturity.

RANs (Revenue Anticipation Notes)

Municipal notes maturing in less than one year, issued in expectation of revenue from particular projects.

Rating agency

A private company that rates the creditworthiness of bonds; the three most well known are Moody's Investors Services, Standard & Poor's Corporation, and Fitch, Inc.

Rebate calculation

A mathematical calculation to determine if funds held in accounts for tax-free bond issues have earned more than permitted by law (an amount greater than interest paid on the outstanding tax-free bonds.) The calculation must be done annually and the excess segregated and remitted to the Internal Revenue Service every five years.

Record date

1. The date set by the directors of the corporation that determines eligibility to receive the current declared dividend.

2. In the case of bonds, the dates fixed in the indenture that determine eligibility to receive the current interest payment. The standard record dates are: the fifteenth day of the month preceding a payment on the first day of the following month; and the last business day of the month preceding payment on the fifteenth day of the following month.

Red herring

Short preliminary form of a prospectus available to potential investors in a new issue before the prospectus is published. Contains company and industry information, financial statements, etc., but does not indicate price per share, which is determined just before the issue is offered for sale. Called a red herring because the front cover bears a legend printed in red announcing that it is not the final official prospectus.

Refunding

    Issuance of new debt securities to replace an older issue.

Registrar

    A bank, normally the trustee or fiscal agent for a debt issue, maintaining the records of bearer certificates registered as to principal only and certificates in fully registered form. The Registrar processes registrations of transfer and exchanges of such securities.

Registration statement

    The statement (or document), including any amendment thereto filed with the SEC in connection with the proposed sale of securities to the public.

Reinvestment agent

    A bank, usually the paying agent, designated by the issuer of securities, to reinvest upon the written request of the security holders all or part of the dividends or interest to be paid to such security holders.

Regulation AB

    Regulation AB updates and clarifies the registration requirements for asset backed securities. Trustees, unless acting as a naked trustee, must file a compliance statement, annual assessment report, and an accountant's attestation report with the SEC.

Regulation 9

    The regulation of the Office of the Comptroller of the Currency, establishing standards and procedures for national banks acting in a fiduciary capacity and managing collective investment funds.

Regulation R

    Regulation of the SEC that governs bank securities broker activities under the Gramm-Leach-Bliley Act and addresses four areas: third-party brokerage (networking) arrangements, trust and fiduciary activities, sweep accounts, and safekeeping and custody activities.

Regulation S

> Regulation of the SEC that is available only for offers and sales of securities outside the United States. Securities acquired overseas may be resold in the United States only if they are registered under the Securities Act of 1933 or an exemption from registration is available.

Remarketing agent

> A bank or investment banking firm that agrees to remarket bonds tendered or "put" by their owners after the initial issuance.

REMICS (Real Estate Mortgage Investment Conduits)

> Tax-advantaged vehicles created by the Tax Reform Act of 1986 to hold real estate mortgages and issue securities representing interests in those mortgages.

Repurchase agreement (Repo)

> A contract between a seller and buyer of U.S. government and other securities under which the seller agrees to buy back the securities at a specified price after a stated period of time. In the interim, the seller has the use of the buyer's funds, for which the seller pays a fee.

Resolution Trust Corporation (RTC)

> Established by the Financial Institutions Reform, Recovery, and Enforcement Act of 1989, the RTC is responsible for the sale and disposition of assets of thrift institutions that were in receivership on November 1, 1989, or that fail after that date until August 9, 1992.

Revenue bond

> A state or local government bond on which the interest and principal payments are met from the revenues produced by the project financed by the bond issue. Water, sewer, gas and electrical facilities, roads, and bridges are typical projects.

Reverse Repo

> A repurchase agreement originated by a customer who

needs securities temporarily but does not want to buy them outright. The customer holds the securities for the duration of the reverse repo agreement or can place them in another repo agreement to yet another party. Also called a resell agreement.

Round lot

The usual unit of trading in a security or a multiple thereof. A round lot of stock is generally one hundred shares; for bonds, $1,000 par value is typical.

Rule 144 A

A regulation of the SEC, under the Securities Act of 1933, that exempts from registration the resale of privately placed securities to ``qualified" institutional investors, thus creating a viable secondary market for such securities.

Rule 10b-5

A regulation of the SEC, under the Securities Exchange Act of 1934, that makes it unlawful for any person to employ any devise, scheme, or artifice to defraud; to make any untrue statement of a material fact; or omit any true statement of a material fact or to omit a material fact necessary in order to make the statements made, in light of the circumstances under which they were made, not misleading; or to engage in any act, practice, or course of business that operates or would operate as a fraud or deceit upon any person, in connection with the purchase or sale of any security.

Rule 387

The New York Stock Exchange rule governing extension of delivery versus payment (DVP) privileges by its member brokers. Basically, brokers can extend DVP privileges to customers who participate in the institutional delivery system and provide for book-entry settlement if the issue is eligible for depository services.

Sallie Mae (Student Loan Marketing Association)

A privately owned, U.S. government-sponsored

corporation founded to help students repay educational loans. Under its warehousing program, Sallie Mae makes large loans to lending institutions that grant loans to students. Under its loan purchase program, it makes direct loans to students.

Samurai bond

A Japanese yen-denominated bond marketed in Japan by a non-Japanese entity.

Sarbanes-Oxley Act of 2002

The Act strives to provide investors with accurate and timely disclosure of financial data of issuers and to ensure that audits are performed by independent accounting firms and according to accepted auditing standards.

Secondary market

1. A term referring to the trading of securities not listed on an organized exchange.

2. A term used to describe the trading of securities other than a new issue.

Securities Act of 1933

Statute requiring, among other provisions, the filing of a registration statement before the public sale of new securities, disclosing through a prospectus substantial information on the issuer and the issue, and for furnishing the prospectus upon distribution of such security.

Securities Exchange Act of 1934

Statute providing for the regulation of securities exchanges and over-the-counter markets, as well as the establishment of the SEC.

Serial issue

Bonds that mature on a scheduled basis over several years, thereby allowing the issuer to amortize the loan over a period of years. Almost all municipal bonds are serial issues.

Settlement date

> The date on which a contract for the purchase or sale of securities is to be completed or settled.

Shelf registration

> A procedure allowed by the SEC permitting qualified issuers to file a single registration statement covering its long-term securities financing plans for a two-year period.

Signature guarantee

> A guarantee (normally obtained from a commercial bank or securities dealer) of the seller's endorsement, which appears on the stock or bond power accompanying the security being sold. Such guarantee affirms (1) that the person who signed the power is the person in whose name the securities are registered or is authorized to act on behalf of such person and (2) that the signature is genuine. The actual signature guarantee has been replaced by the medallion program.

Sinking fund

> The periodic retirement of portions of a debt issue before the stated maturity of the issue (by repayment or purchase), pursuant to the terms of an indenture.

SLGS (State and Local Government Series)

> U.S. government securities issued to municipalities at various interest rates to ensure that issues of tax-free bonds do not violate arbitrage rules. These bonds do not trade in the open market and are carried in book-entry form only at the Federal Reserve Bank.

Spread

> The difference between the bid and asked price (or yield) in the quotation of a security, or between two security issues of differing maturities; the difference between an underwriter's bid on a bond issue and its resale price to the public; or the difference between what funds cost a bank and the rate at which its lends such funds.

Standard & Poor's
: A financial services firm that rates bonds and offers financial publications and computerized information that provide pertinent facts about thousands of issues.

Standby letter of credit
: A letter of credit that covers an amount equal to the principal of and a portion of the interest on the bonds and that provides for a single draw in the event of the acceleration of the bonds.

Stop order
: A notification by a holder of a security requesting the obligor, the trustee, or its agent(s) not to effect registration or transfer of such security nor to pay it upon maturity or redemption.

Street name
: When a certificate is registered in the name of a bank, brokerage firm, or its nominee, it is said to be in street name. Securities are sometimes registered in this manner to facilitate delivery, collection of dividends and proxies, etc. All securities purchased on margin must be registered in street name.

Stripping
: Removing interest coupons from bonds, with the intent of selling the coupons separately from the certificates.

Subscription
: 1. The procedure of buying securities by exercising rights or warrants.

    2. The purchase of part of a bond issue on original issuance by members of the selling syndicate.

Surety bond
: A bond from a surety company by which the replacement of a lost or stolen security is made possible.

Syndicate

> A group of underwriters formed to purchase (i.e., underwrite) a new issue of securities from the issuer and offer it for resale to the general public. One member will be designated as lead manager to administer the syndicate's operations.

TANs (Tax Anticipation Notes)

> The most common type of municipal note, sold in anticipation of tax receipts.

Tax anticipation bill

> A special class of security, occasionally sold by the U.S. Treasury to corporations. Usually matures one week after a tax date but can be turned in at full value when taxes are paid, thus earning an extra week's interest.

Tax Increase, Prevention and Reconciliation Act of 2005

> The Act requires that all tax-exempt interest paid to bondholders on municipal bonds must be reported to the IRS in the same manner as interest paid on taxable obligations.

Tax tails

> A series of short-term taxable bonds added to a tax-exempt bond for the purpose of paying cost of issuance expenses not allowed under federal regulation by reason of exceeding 2 percent of bond proceeds.

Tender agent

> Private financial institution, usually a bank, that will serve as agent for the trustee or the remarketing agent to accept bonds that are tendered or ``put'' under the provisions allowing the bondholders to require the bond issuer to repurchase the bonds at certain times or intervals.

Tender offer

> 1. Offer to buy made to holders of a particular issue by a third party. Detailed offer is made by public announcement in newspapers and by personal letter to

each stockholder

2. Offer by a corporation to buy back a portion of its own shares. This is normally done when the corporation has excess cash and when it believes the market price of its stock is unreasonably low. The reduced share count may result in higher future dividends-per-share on the remaining shares.

Tombstone

An advertisement placed by underwriters in a newspaper or other publication announcing the sale of a new issue, reflecting the name of the issuer, description of the issue, interest rate, maturity, and names of the underwriting syndicate.

Tranche

A term used to designate a particular class or series of securities within a specific issue that is different from the other classes or series of that issue in some fundamental entitlement such as interest rate, maturity date, or some other inherent right.

Treasury Stock

Previously issued stock that a corporation has bought back from its stockholders. Not entitled to vote or receive dividends.

Turnaround rules

A set of rules imposed on registered transfer agents by the SEC pursuant to section 17A of the 34 Act.

USA PATRIOT Act of 2001, as amended

The Act was passed to deter and punish terrorism in the United States and around the world. Foreign money laundering policies and procedures were tightened.

Underwriter

An entity that purchases a large block of securities at the initial offering. The underwriter acts as a wholesaler between the issuing entity and a syndicate or between the issuing entity and the general investing public.

Underwriting agreement

The contract between the investment banker and the corporation, containing the final terms, conditions, and prices of the issue.

Uniform Acts

A series of model acts promulgated by the Commissioners on Uniform State Laws designed to standardize state laws governing a particular activity. State legislatures may modify their existing laws or conform new laws to the proposed Uniform Act.

Unit investment trust (municipal)

A fixed portfolio of municipal bonds sold to investors in fractional, undivided interests, usually in denominations of $1,000. The same bonds are held in the portfolio until they mature or are redeemed.

Unsecured debt

An obligation not backed by the pledge of an issuer's assets. Unsecured bonds are called debentures or notes.

Variable rate securities

Floating or variable interest rates on either short- or long-term securities whose interest rates are adjusted as often as weekly, monthly, or quarterly. The rate is a function of a market indicator, such as the prime rate, the U.S. Treasury Bill or Bond rate, or a combination of both.

Warrant

A certificate, either attached to a debt security or issued separately, that gives the holder the right to purchase a specified amount of another security (either a debt security or common stock) issued by the borrower, for a limited period of time, which may lapse before, on, or after the maturity of the debt security.

Withdrawal by transfer

> A method by which a depository participant can obtain physical securities from the depository to forward to a buyer. The depository takes securities from inventory, has them registered in the name of the new owner, and sends the new certificates to the participant or buyer.

Yankee bond

> A U.S. dollar-denominated bond marketed publicly in the United States by a non-U.S. corporation or governmental entity. A registration statement for such issue is required to be filed with the SEC.

Yield to maturity

> The discount rate that makes the present value of a bond's cash flow until maturity equal to the bond's market price. Yield to maturity takes into account the total interest payments to be received until maturity, plus the difference between current market price and the par value the investor will receive at maturity; it expresses this total return on capital on an annual basis.

Zero coupon

> A term applied to debt securities that are offered initially by the issuer without provision for periodic payments of interest, the final payment at maturity covering principal and all interest due for the life of the security.

INDEX

Abandoned property, *see* Escheat
Acceleration, right of, 249, 359
Account review, 429
Accounting:
  agent, 391
  balance sheet, 15-20, 192
  canceled certificates, 392
  covenant, 192
  final, 234
  interest, 392
  principal, 394
Administrator:
  accountabilities, 462-468
  appraisal, 474 et seq.
  competencies, 465-468
  handbook for, 469
  performance review, 476
  position profile, 462
  training guidelines, 469-471
Advance Funding Program Notes, 108
Advances by trustee, 82, 92, 258, 283, 411
Adverse claims, 415
Affirmative covenants, 185
After-acquired property, 47, 121, 187, 306, 417
Agent, appointing documents as, 365; *see also particular agency appointments*
Allowed claim, 312
American Bar Foundation, model indentures, 54
American Law Institute, project of, *see* Federal Securities Code
Annual report, by trustee, 281, 525
Anticipation notes, 106
Appraisal, employee, 475-480
  performance review, 476
Asset-backed securities, 28, 327
  REMIC reporting, 337
Assets:
  current, 16
  definition, 16
  fixed, 17
  net current, 21, 200
Authenticating agent, 367, 369, 384
Authenticating trustee, 415

Authentication, certificate of, 132, 367

"Backup withholding", 402n
Balance sheet, 15
Bankruptcy:
  "clawback", 412
  compensation of trustee, 321-324
  "cramdown", 305
  as Event of Default, 247
  "impairment", 305
  municipality, 302
  proof of claim, 312
  reorganization, 91, 307
Bankruptcy Code (1978), 301-308, 419
Bearer interest, 372, 376-380
  accounting for, 392
Board of Directors:
  authority of, 14, 97, 99n
  resolution of, 141, 146, 172, 365
  of the trustee, 260
Bona fide purchaser, 395
Bonds, *see* Indenture securities
Bond fund trusts, 339
Bond registrar, 136, 366-371
Bondholder, *see* Security holder
Book-entry-only, 373, 399
Borrowing, forms of, 16, 21-23, 103
  Covenants, 200
  Municipal 104, 106
Business plan:
  annual, 445
  needs analysis, 439
  strategic, 441

Capital:
  methods of supplying, 20-24
  requirements, as trustee, 68, 99n
  working capital, covenant, 200
CERCLA, 264
Certificate immobilization, 399
Certified Corporate Trust Specialist, 472n
"Chinese Wall", 77
Co-agent, 364, 380
Collateral security:
  conflict, as to, 73, 512, 514

custody of, 334
dealing with, 127, 179, 335
provisions for, 179
release of, 167, 181
significance of, 73
Collateral trust agreement, 37
Collateralized mortgage obligations, 327
Commercial paper mode bonds, 110
Compensation, as trustee, 41, 82,232
in bankruptcy, 301, 306, 322
Competencies:
interpersonal, 467
knowledge, 465
managerial, 466
skill, 465
Conclusive reliance, 98
Conflict of interest, 75, 89, 295
eligibility requirements, 68, 282
report as to, 281
Commentaries on Indentures (1972), American Bar Foundation, 59n
Construction fund, 339
Conversion agent, 385
Convertible debentures, 3854
Corporate mortgage, *see* Trust Indenture
Corporate officers, 14
The Corporate Trust Indenture Project (1956), Rogers, 59n
Corporate trustee, *see* Indenture Trustee
Corporation:
board of directors, 14
by-laws, 13
financial statements, 14-20
powers of, 12
status in other states, 78
Co-trustee, 81, 121
Counsel:
fees, 98
protection to trustee, 85, 88, 117, 128
recovery of expenses for, 98
for security purchasers, 66
for trustee, 80, 97
Counsel, opinions:
as to conditions precedent, 146, 172, 237, 529
as to filing-recording, 187

Coupons:
  accounting for, 392
  demise of, 376
  payment of, 376
  as separate obligations, 376
Covenants:
  as to dividends, 204
  enforcement of, 184, 273
  as to "event risk", 197
  evidence as to compliance with, 122, 194
  as to financial accounts, 192
  of further assurances, 187
  insurance, 190
  maintenance, 150, 190
  as to merger, 52, 207
  negative pledge, 203
  as to "no-default", 186, 207
  payment of indenture obligations, 188
  payment of taxes, 189
  as to pledged collateral, 50
  as to "poison puts", 197
  as to prior lien bonds, 188, 200
  protecting collateral lien, 186
  as to recording, 187
  as to releases, 52
  as to sale and leaseback, 201
  as to sinking fund, 151
  as to subsidiaries, 206
  United Kingdom trusts, 359
  working capital, 200
Creditors' committee, 306, 309, 314
Critical issues analysis, 439
Critical needs analysis, 441
Current assets, 15, 200
Current liabilities, 16, 200
CUSIP number, 220, 382
Custody, 341

Debenture, *see* Indenture securities
Debt ratio, 23, 145, 160
Declaratory Judgment Act, 270n
Default:
  administration, 251-263
  Event of, 246

notice of, 256
waiver of, 294,
resignation of trustee required, 410
Defeasance, 53, 227
"in substance", 238
Depository Trust Company, 135, 138, 222, 354, 363
Depreciation, 18, 160
Direct placement contracts, 26, 66, 114, 158
Discovery, 95
Discretionary powers, 40
Dividends, 13
  on conversion, 387
  covenant restricting, 204
Due diligence, 332,

Earned surplus, 205
Eminent domain, 177
Energy Policy Act of 2005, 424
Entry, trustee's right of, 249, 262
Environmental liability, 264
Equipment trusts, 338
Escheat, 240
Escrow agent, 239, 341
Eurobonds, 134, 352
Euromarket, 352
  common depository, 353
Evaluation:
  for critical issues analysis, 439
  of staff, 473
Events of Default, 241, 278, 285
Exchange agent, 383
  under Bankruptcy Code, 317
Exculpatory clauses, 62, 84, 88, 251

Facsimile signatures, 48, 366
Federal Reserve Act, sec. 25(a), 93
Federal Securities Code, 413
Filing:
  Bankruptcy petition, 300
  covenant, 160, 192
  disclosure, 280
  financing statement, 243n
  responsibility of trustee for, 124 -129
  registration statement, 124, 147

see also Uniform Commercial Code
Financial ratios, 15, 142
Financial statements:
  balance sheet, 15
  covenants with respect to, 192
  Financing:
    international, 351
    methods of, 20-24
    municipal, 104
    trends, 27-32
Foreclosure, 262, 290, 294
Foreign issuers, 352
Forms:
  1099B, 225
  T-1, 124, 130n
  T-2, 130n
  T-6, 130n
Franchises, 121, 189
Funded debt:
  amortization of, 200
  covenant, as to, 200
  definition, 16
Funded property, 161, 175
Further assurances, covenant of, 187

Going concern, as measure of value, 38, 121, 166, 190, 266
Governing law, 126, 357
Gramm-Leach-Bliley Act of 1999, 421
Granting clauses, 47, 120
Grantor trust, 330
Group of Thirty, 57, 139, 224, 372

Home office payment, 26, 219

Immobilization, 399
Impairment, 305
Income and retained earnings statements, 17
Incumbency, certificate of, 365
Indemnity:
  for replacement securities, 395
  by security holders, 290
Indenture, model, 54
Indenture securities:
  accounting for, 391

   asset-backed, 327
   authentication of, 367
   convertible, 229, 385
   denominations, 135
   Eurobonds, 134
   exchange of, 383
   immobilization of, 364
   issuance, 22, 131
   lost, reporting of, 395
   registration of, 366
   uncertificated, 57, 138
   variable rate, 103, 108
Indenture trustee:
   compensation, 81
   conflicting interests, 69
     ownership of securities, 71
      affiliations, 74
   development of concept of, 60
   discretionary powers, 247
   distinguished from other trustees, 61
   eligibility, 67
   essential function, 40, 60-64
   exculpatory provisions, 83
   fees, 41
   litigation and discovery, 94
   master trustee, 104
   qualification in foreign states, 77
   removal of, 55, 56, 63, 206
   reports of, 277
   resignation of, 68, 79, 81, 90, 401, 508
   standards of conduct, 85
   successor, 67, 81, 338, 402
Indenture trustee, responsibilities of:
   accounting for indenture obligations, 391
   for acts beyond authority, 12
   conflicting interests, 70
   on default, 251
   eligibility requirements, 68
   as to escheatment, 123, 240, 486
   as to governing law, 125, 357
   inherent obligations, 86, 308, 310, 360
   in reorganization proceedings, 308
   standards of conduct, 40, 86

Independent expert:
  accountant, 14, 147, 192
  engineer, 65
Individual trustee, 61, 80, 125
Industrial development bonds, 29
Institutional investors:
  amendment of agreement by, 66
  importance of, 25
  purchase of securities by, 65
Insurance:
  certificate of, 190
  covenant, 190
Interest:
  accounting for, 233
  on bearer bonds, 376
  covenant as to, 188
  defaulted payment of, 246
  record date for, 374
  on registered bonds, 374
  variable rate, 108
Interest and Dividend Tax Compliance Act of 1983, 226, 373
Interstate Commerce Commission, 167
Inventory, 16, 417
Investment Advisors Act of 1940, 420
Investment bankers, 24, 55, 114, 329, 345, 352
Investment Company Act of 1940, 419

Job description, administrator, 462
Junk bonds, 196

Leasehold estate, 121
Leases, 121, 201
  see also Equipment trusts
Letter of Credit, 33n, 109
Liquidation, judicial, 249, 269, 300, 318
Liquidity facility, 109
Litigation, 95, 359
Lost, stolen and destroyed securities:
  adverse claim, 395
  replacement of, 395
  stop order, filing of, 379

Maintenance:
  covenants, as to:
    insurance, 190
    property, 186, 190
    working capital, 200
Management:
  annual business plan, 445
  critical issues analysis, 439
  critical needs analysis, 439
  divestiture planning, 491
  marketing, 452
  performance reviews, 480
  strategic planning, 441
Manpower audit, 460
Master trustee, 106
Medallion program, 369
Medium term notes, 21, 28, 103
Merger, 52, 207
Model debenture indenture, *see* Indentures, model
Mortgage:
  Maintenance covenant, 150
  property, dealing with, 126, 171
  refunding, 37
  satisfaction, 238
  trust as, 36-38
  see also Trust Indenture
Municipal bonds:
  advance funding program notes, 108
  anticipation notes, 106
  pool financing, 104
  secondary market disclosure, 276
  variable rate, 108
  see also Accounting
Municipal pool financing, 104
Municipal Securities Rulemaking Board, 275, 403n, 427

Needs analysis, 439
Negative covenants, 195, 359
Negative pledge, 204
Net current assets, 16, 200
New York Stock Exchange requirements:
  form of securities, 136
  good delivery, 136
Newspaper, authorized, 223
No default certificate, 122, 147, 175, 411

Notes, *see* Indenture securities

Objectives:
  financial, 445
  guidelines, 462-467
Obligor:
  affiliations between trustee and, 75
  appointment of successor trustee by, 83
  covenants, 50
  dealing with mortgaged property, 166, 171-178
  definition of, 72
  insolvency of, 247, 267, 299
  permitted relations between trustee and, 89
  removal of trustee by, 83
  reports of, 126, 160, 174, 281, 411
  right of possession, 53, 239
  trustee as creditor of, 75
  trustee ownership of securities of, 72
Owner trust, 330

Partnership, 11
Pass-throughs, 330
Pay-throughs, 330
Paying agent:
  appointing documents, 365
  for interest, 372
  notification by if Event of Default occurs, 258
  other than trustee, 235
  for principal, 381
  tax reporting, 225
Pennsylvania Corporate Loans Tax, 373
Performance review, 476
Planning process, 437
  flow chart, 448
Poison put, 197, 214
Pooling and servicing agreement, 328
Position profile, administrator, 461, 474
Prior liens:
  covenant as to, 187, 203
  default under, 246
  retirement of, 143
Private placement agreements, *see* direct placement contracts
Product divisionalization, 450
Project financing, 29, 345

Property additions, 142
Prospectus, 118, 124, 274, 406
Prudent man standard, 88, 199, 251, 309, 534
Public Utility Holding Company Act, 179
Put/demand options, 27, 210

Qualification, of indentures, 408
Quarterly performance review, 479

Recent Developments in Debt Financing and Corp. Trust Administration
  (1967), Kennedy and Landau, 59n
Recitals:
  as estoppel, 120
  in indenture contract, 46
  responsibility of trustee for, 120
Recommended Certificate Standards for Registered Bond Issues
  (1974), American Bankers Association, 148n
Record date:
  for consents, 537
  convertible debentures, 388
  purpose of, 375
  regular, 374
  special, 389
Recording:
  covenant as to, 187
  filing of financing statement, 127
  purpose of, 125
  responsibility of trustee for, 126
  as to supplemental indentures, 129
Redemption:
  affidavit as to, 212
  of convertible securities, 229
  deposit of funds for, 233
  notice of, 219
  partial, 158
  premiums on, 218
  procedure for, full, 157, 217
  procedure for, partial, 157, 226
  pro rata, 159
  provisions for, 49
  sinking fund, 155
Registered interest:
  accounting for, 233
  disbursement of, 374

Registrar, *see* Bond registrar; Transfer agent
Registration statement:
   requirement for, 124, 275, 406
   eligibility and qualification of trustee, 408
Regulation:
   OCC regulation, 79, 97, 428, 541
   SEC Rule 144, 26
   SEC Rule 144A, 67, 296n, 354
   SEC Rule 415, 28, 116, 124
   see also Trust Indenture Act; Uniform Commercial Code

Release of property:
   general provisions governing, 52, 171, 526
   protection of purchaser, 164
Remarketing agent, 109
Remedial provisions, 65, 123, 248
REMIC reporting, 337
Reorganization:
   under chapter 11, 304-308
   role of indenture trustee in, 266, 308-320
Reorganization trustee, 304, 307
Resignation, of trustee:
   effective date of, 410, 517
   provision for, 68-74
   required by Trust Indenture Act, 68, 410
Revenue bonds, *see* Municipal Bonds
Risk management, 215, 427

Sale and leaseback, covenants, 201
Sarbanes-Oxley Act of 2002, 334, 423
Satisfaction of indenture, 231-233
SEC Release:
   33-6242 (Sept. 1980), 430n
   33-6499 (Nov. 1983), 34n
   33-6862 (Apr. 1990), 33n
   33-6892 (May 1991), 130n, 297n
   34-23856 (Dec. 1986), 230n
   34-27928 (Apr. 1990) 33n
   39-2263 (May 1991), 130n
SEC Rules:
   144A, 26, 67, 296n
   415, 28, 116, 124
   17Ad-1(g), 402n
   17f-1, 403n

Secondary market disclosure, 276
Securities Act of 1933, 25, 52, 67, 118, 275, 328, 354, 406
Securities Acts Amendments of 1975, 426
Securities Exchange Act of 1934, 193, 275, 406, 494
Securities and Exchange Commission, 406, 485, 494
Securities Information Center, 395
Securities processing regulations, 425
Security holders:
  collective action by, 34, 44, 293
  consent of, 67, 287, 293
  default, waiver of, 294
  limitation on rights of, 44, 290
  lists of, 283
  modification of indenture by, 287
  party to indenture, 42-44
  proof of claim for, 312
  removal of trustee by, 83
  reports to, 281
  suit for principal and interest by, 292
Security interest, under UCC, 65, 120, 127, 416
Security registrar, *see* Bond Registrar
Serial maturities, 152
Shelf registration, 28, 124, 412
Signature guarantee, 368
Sinking fund:
  application of, 151
  computation of, 152
  covenant as to, 48, 150
  default in, 246
  market purchases, 155, 213
  purpose of, 150
  tender of bonds for, 212
  tickler for, 129
Stockholders:
  immunity of, 51
  preemptive rights, 388
  subscription rights of, 390
Stop payments, 228, 379, 395
Strip call, 217, 227
Subordination, 44, 93
Subscription agent, 390
Successor trustee, 69, 83, 410
Supplemental indentures, 54, 129

Tangible assets, 16, 201
Tax anticipation notes, *see* Anticipation notes
Tax Equity and Fiscal Responsibility Act of 1982, 59n
Tax Reform Act of 1984, 148n
Tax Reform Act of 1986, 103, 350n
Temporary bonds, 48
Tender of securities, 157
   offer, 213
Tender agent, 111, 391
Testamentary trust, 40
Tickler record, 122, 129
Training program, 460

Transfer agent, 363, 366, 426
   see also, Bond registrar
Transfer pricing, 445
Trust Indenture:
   amendments to, 54, 287
   as a contract, 42-46
   covenants, 50
   growth and development of, 35
   issuance of bonds, 49
   granting clauses, 47
   "mechanical" provisions, 48
   models, 543-58
   as a mortgage, 38
   pledged collateral, 50
   recitals, 46
   recording of, 126
   redemption of bonds, 49
   releases, 52
   remedies, 51
   satisfaction of, 231
   simplified, 33n, 57
   supplemental, 54, 129, 141, 2971n
   as a trust, 39-41
Trust Indenture Act of 1939:
   history of, 405-409
   purposes of, 405
   reports required by, 53, 192, 281
Trust Indenture Reform Act of 1990, 410-413
Trust Indenture Act, sections:
   303, 99n
   304(a), 350n
   304(d), 430n

305(b), 420n, 429n, 430n
310(a), 99n, 125, 430n
310(b), 70-72, 75n, 101n, 411, 430n
311, 90-93, 430n
312(b), 297n
313(a), 271n, 276, 291n, 411, 420n
313(b), 271n, 291n
313(c), 291n
314(a), 122, 193, 208n, 430n
314(b), 130n, 187
314(c), 59n
314(d), 59n, 173
314(e), 59n
314(f), 59n
315(a), 100n, 182n, 270n
315(b), 270n
315(c), 100n, 252
315(d), 100n, 271n
315(e), 291n
316(a), 204n
316(b), 297n
316(c), 297n, 430n
317(a), 270n
318(c), 130
326, 101n

Trustee, *see* Indenture trustee
Trustee, co, *see* Co-trustee
Trustee, individual, *see* Individual trustee
Trustee, reorganization, *see* Reorganization trustee
Trustee, U.S., *see* United States Trustee

UK trusts, 351
Ultra vires acts, 12, 177
Uncertificated securities, 57, 138, 399
  see also Indenture securities
Unclaimed funds, 240
Underwriters:
  affiliations between trustee and, 75
  compensation of, 114
  report, as to, 77
Underwriting, 32, 114
Unfunded property, 141, 171

Uniform Commercial Code:
  application of article 8, 403n, 415, 135
  application of article 9, 128, 416
  filing under, 65
  financing statements, 65, 129, 416
  lost, stolen or destroyed securities, processing of, 395
  obligations under, 414
  perfection of security interest, 127
  termination statement, 243n
Uniform Unclaimed Property Act, 240
Unit Investment Trusts, 344
United States Trustee, 326n
USA Patriot Act of 2001, 423

Variable Rate Demand Bonds, 107
Variable rate securities, 108
Voting trusts, 343

Working capital, 17, 190
  covenants as to, 190